DALITS IN 21ST CENTURY

DALITS IN 21ST CENTURY
Ambedkarite Perspective

Dr. K. Jamanadas

KALPAZ

ISBN : 978-81-7835-980-9

Price: ₹ 950

First Published 2014

Published by

Kalpaz Publications
C-30, Satyawati Nagar,
Delhi-110052
Ph. : 9212142040
E-mail: kalpaz@hotmail.com

Laser Typesetting : Shah Computer Graphics, Delhi
Printed at : G. Print Process, Delhi

Cataloging in Publication Data--DK
Courtesy: D.K. Agencies (P) Ltd. <docinfo@dkagencies.com>

Jamanadas, K.
Dalits in 21st century : Ambedkarite perspective / K. Jamanadas.
p. cm.
Includes bibliographical references (p.).
ISBN 9788178359809

1. Dalits--India--History. 2. Dalits--India--Social conditions--21st century. . 3. Caste--India--History--21st century. 4. Ambedkar, B. R. (Bhimrao Ramji), . 1891-1956. I. Title.

DDC 305.56880954 23

Dedication

American Slogan was
"Rosa sat so Martin could walk;
Martin walked so Obama could run,
Obama ran so your children can fly"
Such a Rosa would also arise in India
I dedicate this tract
To
That future ROSA
and wish
She comes from the
Community of Scavengers

Contents

Preface

I. Preliminary

Historically

A new book, again, on Dalits! Why?

Hindus have *Chaturvarnya* system of four-fold watertight divisions of Brahmins, Kshatriyas, Vaishyas, and Shudras. The masters of Hindus are the Brahmins. Untouchables are outside this division. Nearly twenty per cent of India was untouchable. The untouchables formed the lowest strata of Hindu society and were condemned as Untouchables, Unapproachable and Unseeables by the caste Hindus. They had different names in different parts of the country, being called Outcastes, Untouchables, Pariahs, Panchamas, Atishudras, Avarnas, Antyajas, Namoshudras etc. and were divided into hundreds of exogamous castes.

Their social disabilities were horrible. Their touch, shadow and even voice were deemed by the caste Hindus to be polluting. So they had to clear the way at the approach of a caste Hindu. In Peshava rule, they had to hang a small earthen pot in neck as spittoon and a broom to waist to clear footmarks.

They were forbidden to wear gold and silver ornaments, or use metal utensils and new clothes, to eat ghee or sweets, to wear footwear and were forced to dwell in the dirty, dingy and unhygienic outskirts of villages and towns, and forced to live in dark, unsanitary and miserable smoky shanties or huts.

They were denied the use of public wells, ponds and other water resources and were condemned to drink any filthy water they could find. Their children were not admitted to schools attended by the caste Hindu children. Barbers and washermen refused to render them service.

Their occupations were mean, they were forced to be illiterate, forbidden from all public services civil, police and military and were forced to follow hereditary occupations of street-sweepers, scavengers and shoemakers. Some skinned carcasses, tanned hides and skins and worked with leather, some worked in bamboos and cane and mowed grass. More fortunate ones tilled the land as tenants, worked as labourers in fields, a great number of them subsisted on food or grain given to them as village servants and also ate carrion. They worked as bonded farm labours, they were born in debt and perished in debt. They were born Untouchables, they lived as Untouchables and they died as Untouchables.

They were called 'Hindus' and though they worshipped the gods of Hindus, observed the same festivals, the Hindu temples were closed to them. They were treated as worse than beasts. This picture is still true of villages and small towns, and to some extent even in the cities.

Revolution and Counter-revolution

That untouchability started as a religious persecution against the Buddhists, is now well established. Ambedkar has proved that Untouchables originally were broken men and then the followers of Buddhism. They fought against the Vedic Hindus, and did not give up beef-eating, and so they were degraded as Untouchables. This is now accepted by all. [W&S Vol. 7 - Untouchables]

It is now well realised that is the history of India is the history of conflict between the Buddhist and the Brahmins for centuries. In this conflict, with periodic ups and downs, the Buddhists lost and were reduced to the stage of the untouchables. Buddhist temples were usurped and converted to the Brahmin temples. The nuns in the Buddhist temples were converted to temple prostitutes at Devadasis. The Buddhist monks were killed, and some had to run for of their lives out of the country. Society was divided into numerous castes and untouchability started.

Human Rights

It was only during the Buddhists times that the human rights were well preserved and justice, equality and fraternity have prevailed. During other times, the rights were confined to the rights to Brahmins and the right of the cows. There were only two periods when the human rights prevailed, one - from Buddha to Patanjali, in the historical times and two - Phule to Ambedkar in modern times.

Buddha caused revolution and opposed the Vedic *Chaturvarnya* and *yajnyas*. Patanjali effected counter-revolution after Pushyamitra Shunga murdered last Buddhist king Bahidratha (c.185 BCE), and brought back *Chaturvarnya* and *yajnyas*, and got Manu Smriti and Bhagwat Gita written. This Brahminic counter-revolution prevailed till Nathas-Siddhas brought back Buddhism under the leadership of Gorakhnath. This transformed through various stages in Bhakti religion, which in reality a form of Buddhism.

Counter-revolution Brought Ruin to Indian Masses

As long as Buddhism was a living force in India, the alien aggressors were assimilated. Swami Dharma Teertha has argued that same would have happened to Muslim if Buddhism were in force. It must be realised that India became slave country because of castes, and because the Dalits were not allowed to use the weapons and bear the arms.

The great persecution of Buddhists in East India under the Brahminist rulers-the Sena-s, pioneers of Kulin system – is notorious. Islam did not spread by the sword everywhere. When Muslims attacked Bengal, the Buddhists there welcomed the aggressor soldiers as *Bodhisattvas* and the result was that Bengal became Muslim. Similarly, Kashmir became Muslim because of Brahminic arrogance.

When the British came, it were the Dalits who won India for the British. And not only the Dalits won India for the British, but they also saved it back in 1857, when Brahminic forces wished to drive them away.

Before the advent of Tilak, the main contradiction in India was between Brahmins and non-Brahmins since work of Mahatma Phule. Tilak converted this contradiction into conflict of Hindus versus Muslims. It was taught by Brahminical Social Order (BSO) that the main enemies of the Hindus in India were Muslims and Christians, (who were converted mostly from the Dalits).

At the time of transfer of power in 1947, by creation of Pakistan, they solved their problems. They got rid of Christians by dispatching the British back. And they got rid of Muslims, by putting them in Pakistan. Now the main cause of worry that remained in India, for the Brahmins, were the Dalits, living in India, their leader Ambedkar and their religion Buddhism.

Let us prevent counter-revolution succeeding

Ambedkar had given India the Constitution of India, and their religion as Buddhism, is true. But both these things are unwanted for the BSO. Let us be pretty sure that what the BSO would do is try their level best to remove both these things from their lives. Babari Masjid was demolished on sixth of December, the day of mourning for Dalits. When Pokhran was done, it was said the 'Buddha smiled'. All these show that they are very anxious about Dalits, Ambedkar and Buddhism.

Brahminic scholars today, like Shrinivas Dixit, accept that present day Hinduism has more of Buddhism in it than Brahmanism, as discussed by us in '*Materialism in Ancient India.*'

But the caste system is prevailing with brutal force. Ambedkar declared revolution through '*Annihilation of Caste*' in 1936. He brought back liberty, equality, justice, and fraternity by giving the Constitution and brought back original Buddhism, so that Constitution is preserved and properly implemented. But this is only in theory. The real ground reality is the BSO is in full force. All measures are being taken to enforce system of castes with all its ugliness. They are even trying to bring back those who have discarded Hinduism and converted to Islam and Christianity.

Shudra-s, i.e. the OBCs are the backbone of Brahmanism. When they get fully awakened, then real revolution would start. Who would lead the revolution? Ambedkar said the Dalits would have to lead the revolution. That is the reason, the world is looking at the activities of the Dalits. That is why a new book!

II. Plan of This Tract

1. Dalits - Victims of Caste System

In this chapter, we try to project how the world hardly knows much about Untouchability, as is also the experience of Prof. Kancha Ilaiah. The Story of Untouchability in India explains how untouchability started as religious persecution of the Buddhists around seventh century CE. How Slavery is different from Untouchability and how slavery is less cruel than untouchability, is explained, and how untouchability was practiced in historical time, before and after transfer of power, is traced. The rules of caste are so perverse that even the rich and ruling Brahmin family like that of Tagore-s had to suffer caste discrimination. The perverted sexuality of the BSO wanted to see the open breasts of women of lower castes in South India and the lower castes had to struggle even for decent dress to cover the breasts of their women.

BSO wants to kill the women of lower castes who are achievers, so these women are branded as witches and killed. Dalit kids cannot use school loo but have to clean them and Dalit women more humiliated when raped according to a study is narrated. Even the dignitaries like Dalit MP and Chairman of SC/ST Commission is denied entry to the temple in Orissa. Even now the Dalit grooms cannot ride a mare, and even there are caste-wise separate kitchens in medical colleges and police. Mark Tully, BBC Reporter reported rampant practice of untouchability and was disenchanted with activities of Gandhi. Inter-caste marriages are taking place in spite of danger by violence by panchayats suggesting a silent revolution. How UPA failed to use Rs. 72,500 crore for Dalits and how welfare of Dalits is mere lip service is explained and that even Nehru was not free from Caste feelings is explained.

2. Dalits and Dalits

In this chapter, we explain how contradictions developed among various Dalit sub-castes, after Dalits, in Poona Pact, were cheated by Gandhi, who coined a derogatory name *Harijan*, which was name of children of temple prostitutes, dividing untouchables into Dalits and Harijans. The *Chamchas* created by Poona Pact opposed Ambedkar and divided the community into two warring groups. Dissatisfaction among them was because of uneven developments caused by not following advice of Ambedkar but of Gandhi. The BSO instigated and caused rift among these sub-castes on the issue of reservations. The need for unity and Ambedkar's advice discussed. Problems of reservations discussed. Kanshiram's work '*Jati todo samaj jodo*' is discussed and speech of Dr. Ambedkar on sub-caste contradiction narrated. It is stressed Dalit Unity is not enough and SC/ST/OBC unity required. Ambedkar always wanted a broad based political party, but had to form a caste based party SCF under compulsion by deceit by Cripps Mission, who conspired with *Savarna*-s. A time would come when we would have to destroy our caste identity.

3. Dalits and Atrocities

In this chapter, we described in short some gory cases of Dalit atrocities, like Khairlanji massacres, Dharmpuri incidence, and a glorious case of Tsunduru Trial. Also the recent cases of 'Khap Terror' are discussed in detail.

4. Dalits and Adivasis

In this chapter, we discussed the creation of Adivasis is post-Buddhistic, contrary to traditional view and is because of their religious persecution against their original Buddhist religion. Problems of VJNT are discussed, and some information of Criminal Tribes given. Attempts of BSO to convert Adivasis to Hinduism through the '*Kumbh-Mela* for *Shabri*' is discussed. Lastly, it is stressed that Ambedkarism is the only solution for Adivasis.

5. Dalits and Muslims

In this chapter, we discuss how in historical times, Brahmins were benefited by Muslim Conquest. We discuss the Kashmir problem historically how a Buddhist Kashmir became a Muslim country because of Brahminic arrogance. How Aggression by tribal forces of Pak was repelled and Kashmir saved for India by Dalit soldiers. Now solution from Ambedkarite perspective is suggested: 'Chinab Formula' – the solution is partition of Jammu and Kashmir. The question of 'Confederation – India, Pak and Bangladesh' is discussed, explaining how both Hindus and Muslims ignored Ambedkar's advice during partition of India leading to tremendous human tragedy. Nature of 'Dalit-Muslim-Unity' is discussed and how SC/ST/OBC/Muslim Unity was broken by Tilak is explained. Lastly it is explained why Ambedkar did not accept Islam.

6. Dalits and Christians

In this chapter, we discussed why Christians failed in India, the unchristian side of Christian churches where they educate the children of BSO, who are going to kick them out. '*Jesus lived in India*' describes the Revolutionary side of Jesus, which the present day Indians Christians do not discuss. Ambedkar's Advice to Christians is narrated and Phule-Ambedkar *Sahityik Melawa* September 2000 is described where the Christian leaders were afraid of even denouncing murder of Graham Stains. Lastly is discussed the problem of discrimination against Dalits in churches, and graveyards.

7. Dalits and OBCs

In this chapter, we discussed the backwardness, pride and vanity of the 'Other backward classes' – the Bahujans and how Manu degraded them. How the Buddhist kings were given status of Kshatriya by rite of *Hiranya garbha* etc. How the OBCs lost their identity under the illusion of Kshatriya-hood, how they are present day tormentors of Dalits, is explained. Problems of Maratha Race and *Gotra*-s are discussed. History of conflict on *'Riddles in Hinduism'*, created for awakening of OBCs, is traced and how the OBCs remain cultural slaves of BSO is explained. It is lamented that there was no healthy discussion on the remaining Riddles. A neglected message of Ambedkar to OBCs of 1947 is narrated. The attempts to awaken OBCs are discussed, and it is suggested that the OBCs – the real owners of this country – must reclaim Temple Treasures. The 'Shiva Dharma' Movement, on which I have written a monograph, is discussed in brief.

8. Dalits and Brahmins

In this chapter, we discussed 'Who Are the Real Enemies of Dalits Today?', elaborating activities of *Samajik Samarasata Manch* of RSS, and various techniques of BSO to rule over the masses. Brahminic strategy to govern Hindus and the RSS attempts to reverse the ideology of Phule-Ambedkar is elaborated. How the 'Non-Brahmin priests' in Brahminic temples are not tolerated is discussed. How the Land grants to Brahmins made them landlords is explained.

9. Dalits in Foreign Lands

In this chapter, we explain how Ambedkar had warned a century ago that if not checked in time, the caste problem would become a world problem. The problem of caste in UK today is discussed with the 'Equality-Bill' in Britain, banning caste-based discrimination in UK. How Dalit Intelligentsia considered caste worse than Race at the time of Durban Conference. Justice Verma, Chairman of NHRC, taking a view contrary to the government's on caste, said, 'Caste discrimination can be raised at international fora'. Geneva's 'World Conference on Racism' – 2009, 'Durban II' is described, where it was stressed that **Caste is Racism in all but name.** The work of Ms. Pillay praised, who suggested creating an "observatory on discrimination". Indian National Bureau of Crime Report (2006) gives the statistics of Crimes against Dalits; it is quoted in U.N. Human Rights Council, 2008, Geneva, and atrocities against Christians and Muslims narrated.

Ms. Navi Pillay, high commissioner for human rights, said, "Caste is now on notice" and believed, "Slavery and apartheid could be removed, so now caste can be removed through an international expression of outrage." Lastly, views of CPI on Durban Conference are expressed.

10. Dalits and Communism

In this chapter, we discussed that contrary to opinion by some, Ambedkar had no love for Communism. How he preferred Buddhism to Communism is explained in detail. Story of woes of Dalits of Bengal under Communist regime is detailed and Marichjhapi and the Revenge of Bengali Bhadralok is explained. views of Raja D., the CPI Leader on OBC reservation in higher education are praiseworthy, but not implemented by Central Govt. Views of Com. Sharad Patil of '*Satyashodhak Communist Party*' based on ideology of 'Marxism–Phule–Ambedkarism' and Caste and Communists discussed with Land Reforms and Abolition of Castes in Communist regimes.

11. Dalits in British Army

In this chapter, we discussed Ambedkar's arguments at Round Table Conference. It were the Dalits who not only conquered India for the British, but also saved it during the 'Sepoy Mutiny' – '*bhat pandya che band*', as M. Phule described it. Battles of Wadgaon and Koregaon described. The history of '*The Great Maratha*' – Mahadji Shinde, who was free from caste and religious bias, is narrated. Nana Phadnavis had caused problems for Mahadji, otherwise, the course of Indian History would have been different. Lastly, story of Matadin Valmiki, a forgotten hero of 1857 Sepoy Mutiny is narrated. Mangal Pande did not fight for country; he fought for preserving his caste.

12. Dalits and Reservations

In this chapter, we traced the History of Reservations starting from Phule through Shahu to Ambedkar. We discussed Poona Pact in detail and provided replies to the objections raised by elites, especially after the Mandal Commission. The problem of reservations in so-called 'Private' Sector is discussed. We argue that the Corporates are in no sense 'private'; they are public and must behave like public bodies. We discussed various techniques of business castes to rob the masses, who must prepare to fight back. The question of reservations in centres of high learning is discussed. Disgusted Dr. Kancha observed: "We should close down the IITs and the IIMs as they pander to the upper-caste economy'. Lastly, the opinions of many dignitaries, including men in power, are mentioned.

13. Dalits and Saints

In this chapter, we discuss the role of Saints stressing importance of Gorakhnath. History of Bhakti movement is traced through the Nathas and Siddhas, who were precursors of Bhakti. Ambedkar's view on Role of Saints from the view of point of 'annihilation of caste' was that the struggle for the saints did not have any effect on society.

14. Dalits and Sikhism

In this chapter, we discussed *Dera*-s, their emergence, number and role. Caste conflicts and recent violence in Punjab are discussed, and so is the Dalits assertion in Punjab. Why Sikhism is facing an urgent and violent sectarian crisis is discussed. The feudal attitude and honour killings are discussed. Lastly, the formation of New '*Ravidassia Religion*' is discussed.

15. Dalits and Periyar

In this chapter, we discuss activities of E V Ramasami Periyar in south, about which BSO denigrates him without refuting his points and some Dalits also join with BSO in blaming him. All charges against him are discussed and how his activities are pro lower castes. Viacom struggle is discussed, and compared with Mahad and Nashik. Ideals and acts of Self Respect Movement for Dalit upliftment discussed. The Self-Respecters even organised seminars on Buddhism in early thirties. And Periyar was the first for burning of Manusmriti, even before Ambedkar. Periyar supported Ambedkar and had criticised Gandhi. Periyarists also supported 'Devadasi Abolition Bill' and 'Sarada Act'.

16. Dalits and Buddhism

In this chapter, we discuss Buddhism: Is it a Caste, A Sect or a Religion? Ambedkar had said unless one severs the links harshly with old traditions, one cannot progress. Have we given up our caste after conversion? BSO depicts Buddhism as '*Panth*' of Hinduism. Buddhism is the national religion of India. We discussed how India would become once again Buddhist, stressing Ambedkar's religion is not same as traditional Buddhism. Sawarkar's view that *ahimsa* of

Buddha is responsible for defeat of Hindus, is refuted. Those Eventful Days Of The Great Mass Conversions are my personal experiences. RSS leader Dattopant Thengdi was present as boy serving snacks in private party meeting of Ambedkar in Shyam Hotel, he says. Was he spying on Ambedkar? Sawarkar criticised Babasaheb's Conversion, his writings narrated. Lastly, the tendency BSO to depict Buddha as Hindu is well known, our lament is even Dalai Lama and Goenka also participate in such RSS meetings.

17. Dalits and Planning Commission

In this chapter, my own letter to a Member of Planning Commission is narrated, highlighting my own ideas about various subjects like oil crisis, bullet trains, smaller states, land reforms, education, health care, military services etc.

18. Dalits Tomorrow

In this most important chapter, are discussed all those items, which seem to have remained unfulfilled from the Ambedkar Agenda.

Let us bring in **Dayabhag** – most crucial part of Hindu Code that is not passed. It would weaken Caste system. Let us kill **Village** Republics – Ambedkar remarked village as 'a sink of localism, a den of ignorance, narrow-mindedness and communalism'. Let us stop **Bonded** Labour – which denotes feudal tendency among the village upper castes. Let us become **Governing** Class – Political power is Master key. Rule of Kanshiram Mayavati described. Let us protect our **Constitution –** It is an eyesore to BSO and they want to destroy it, and bring in dictatorship. Let us enforce the **Atrocity Act** – it is a good deterrent badly implemented. Let us remove **Manual scavenging** – Ruling BSO is not serious about this. Let us stop Discrimination of Dalits in Calamities **Relief** works – which is seen practically in all natural or man-made calamities. Let us stop Caste Discrimination in **higher centers** of learning – which has become a usual practice these days in IITs, IIMs etc. Let us create **human capital –** unemployment is cause of all ills. Let us bring in **rule of lower castes** – how rule of Lalu Prasad, Mayavati, Nitish Kumar was beneficial is explained by Meghnad Desai.

Acknowledgements

A lot of my writing was done during previous years because of various Dalit, Bahujan and Buddhist Fora on Internet. I got valuable guidance from these sources. I might mention a few names: Ms. Gail Omvedt, Dr. Wasnik, Er. Priyadarshi, Prof. Shiva Shankar, Vidya Bhushan etc.

Most of my writings were published on '*Dalit Voice*'. V.T. Rajsheker, the editor of 'Dalit Voice' – sorry it is stopped – was a constant companion and guide. I am glad that I received valuable guidance and help from him, for which I am extremely grateful. The present book contains some material that was published on these fora in prototype, which is now revised and updated.

I am extremely sorry about the sudden and sad demise of a great young friend and well-wisher Prof. Dr. Ajay Kamble, Ph.D., Head of Department of History Ambedkar College, whose ideas were always of immense help. I like to offer my sincere condolences.

Mr. L.K. Madavi, the Adivasi Leader, who attended the Durban Conference had been a great help on matters of Conference and provided literature. Mr. Vijay Mankar of AIMBSCS and his organisers too provided with a lot of literature on Dalit issues.

I received many ideas and guidance from a great number of friends. I am indebted to many of my friends and colleagues who helped me with discussion, guidance and suggestions. There are many friends who helped; I like to name a few. I would specially mention Mr. M.M. Sao, Principal of Buddhist College, Dr. Mrs. Sarita Jambule, Ph.D., an expert on Marathi Saint literature; Dr. Anil Surya, Ph.D., an expert on Dalit Literature. Dr. Esadas Bhadke, Ph.D., an expert in Marathi Literature; History Researcher Acharya T.T. Julme, Poet Loknath Yashwant, Ph.D scholar Ms. Ranjana and her husband Sunil Jambhule, all helped. Thanks are due to Mr. Amar Khade, our young friend, who discussed many issues, provided with many books and also helped with proof reading. Dr. Chothve, Principal of FES College and Dr. Sheikh, Principal of Sardar Patel College helped me with providing access to their libraries.

I express my sincere gratitude to all of them.

Acknowledgements

1

Dalits-Victims of Caste System

World Knows Nothing about Untouchability

Kancha Ilaiah Avers

In a signed article by Kancha Ilaiah, titled '*Untouchability In A Flat World*' in '*Deccan Chronicle*' of October 2005, author observes that even the students of the famous prestigious elite and expensive Wheaton College in Chicago, where he had delivered lecture celebrating 'Dalit Freedom Week' have remained ignorant of the world around them even in a globalised world.

Thomas Friedman's book '*The World is Flat*', having a chapter on India's untouchability, is creating waves in US campuses. Friedman argues that, unlike China, India as a country will not be unified and homogenised because of caste and untouchability. Friedman, however, sees a slight ray of hope in the English medium schools. The guest speaker Prof. Ilaiah found that only about half a dozen students had read Friedman's book, and even these select few were not familiar with the practice of untouchability in India.

Prof. Ilaiah remarks about future of Dalits of India:

> "The English educated upper castes of the country can compete with American students as they too are establishing their Wheatons and Harvards in India. But the Dalits and other lower castes will be left out of the "flat world" and will be consigned to menial tasks such as sweeping roads, scavenging and traditional cultivation...."

In the Hollywood seminar at Los Angeles, where Prof. spoke to an audience of producers, directors, actors, scriptwriters, TV anchors and documentary filmmakers, he surprisingly found even these opinion makers, like the students, did not understand the caste system and untouchability.

Prof. Ilaiah explains the reasons for such attitude:

> "Maybe this lack of awareness is also due to the conscious decision by upper caste intellectuals, filmmakers, artists, and writers not to present the true picture of India to the world, since it would not be "nationalistic" to do so. In this flat world, we should honestly tell people about the evils in our country. Silence is a sin."

Prof. Ilaiah explained to the students that Caste, untouchability and poverty are not going to be problems for India alone. It will inevitably become a problem for the US and other countries too, and they too would from the hunger, poverty, ignorance and untouchability. He stressed that the efforts to end discrimination, poverty, caste and ignorance have to be speeded up if the benefits of the 'flat world' have to be provided to all sections of people.

The Story of Untouchability in India

Dr. Ambedkar Explains

Dr. Ambedkar explains why and when Untouchability started in India. Let us see it in his own words. In the Preface to his book, '*The Untouchables, who were they and why they became Untouchables*' he observes:

"The thesis on the origin of Untouchability advanced in the book is an altogether novel thesis. It comprises the following propositions:

(1) There is no racial difference between the Hindus and the Untouchables;

(2) The distinction between the Hindus and Untouchables in its original form, before the advent of Untouchability, was the distinction between Tribesmen and Broken Men from alien Tribes. It is the Broken Men who subsequently came to be treated as Untouchables;

(3) Just as Untouchability has no racial basis so also has it no occupational basis;

(4) There are two roots from which Untouchability has sprung:

(a) Contempt and hatred of the Broken Men as of Buddhists by the Brahmins:

(b) Continuation of beef-eating by the Broken Men after it had been given up by others.

(5) In searching for the origin of Untouchability care must be taken to distinguish the Untouchables from the Impure. All orthodox Hindu writers have identified the Impure with the Untouchables. This is an error. Untouchables are distinct from the Impure.

(6) While the Impure as a class came into existence at the time of the Dharma Sutras the Untouchables came into being much later than 400 A.D.

These conclusions are the result of such historical research as I have been able to make." [W&S Vol. 7, p. 242]

What is meant by Broken men

Dr. Ambedkar has thus very clearly established the origin of Untouchability being due to contempt of Buddhists. Those Buddhists who being "broken men" were living outside the villages, did not give up beef eating, unlike Brahmins who did, were condemned to be untouchables. His theory remains till date unchallenged.

The "broken men", are defined as "strangers or fugitives from other territories, men in fact, who have broken the original tribal bond which gave them a place in the community and who had to obtain and thus get on as best as they might in a new tribe and new place. Broken men were thus created at times of the disordering of society." [Nair: 1959: 29]

Servitude in other Countries

It was my experience that it was difficult to explain to my Irish and British friends what the caste system is or what the Untouchability is. These friends brought up under egalitarian Christianity could not apprehend that there could be human beings, who are not allowed to touch others, people whose touch pollutes. They were more surprised that there are some humans whose even sight or approach also pollutes, the 'unseeables' and 'unapproachables'. There are some Tribals – Adivasis – who live in forests and hills and most have not even seen a Railway train. And some were called "Criminal Tribes", who were enjoined to earn their living by crime only. All these today come under general term of Dalit and together form about a quarter of population of more than 1,000 millions of Indians.

But my foreign friends knew about slavery, both in ancient Rome and of American Negroes. Millions of slaves in ancient Rome were treated with the greatest cruelty, beaten up and sent to a prison, had to work with fetters and were branded. English society also had its servile classes. In America, a Negro suffered great miseries during his capture in Africa, his travel by ships and during his toil in America. What is of importance is that these unfree, unprivileged classes have disappeared as a separate class and have become part and parcel of the great society. The question is, why Untouchability did not disappear in India?

Slavery in India

Contrary to claims by some, Slavery, as distinct from Untouchability, is a very ancient institution of the Hindus. Manu, and the other Smriti writers recognise it. It was applied to both the touchables as well as the untouchables, continued throughout all history down to the year 1843 CE, when it was abolished by the British Government by law. **But Slavery is different from Untouchability and slavery is less cruel**. Untouchables hiding their caste to become slaves, were punished during the Peshava Brahmin rule. For details see Ambedkar [W&S vol. 12: 741 ff]

Which is Worse Slavery or Untouchability?

Legally defined either as a piece of property or as one who is not a person, *de jure*, it might appear that the slave was worse off than the untouchable. But, *de facto*, condition of the slaves was better than that of the untouchables. Roman Slave was educated, participated in trade, banking and industry and earned money. Many were shopkeepers selling every variety of food, bread, meat etc., others dealt in clothing, sandals, shoes, gowns. They were in civil services and Municipal Corporations, working both with head and hands. They worked in the Treasury and Mint, as clerks and financial officers with freedmen and slaves. Though they were not allowed to fight in the Army, they were employed as non-fighting servants. In the fleet, slaves were common enough.

Negro Slaves in the United States

The *de facto* position of the Negro in the United States, during the period of legal slavery, shows that there was no segregation and slaves were allowed education, worked in military and could become judges, artisans and could purchase their freedom, and were getting same wages as whites. The white and black seamen and soldiers had fought and messed together in the Revolution. A Negro was conducting a private school for white students.

Dalits v/s *Slaves Compared*

Dr. Ambedkar compared the condition of the slaves in ancient Roman Empire and Negroes with the condition of the Untouchables of present times, and remarked that no Untouchables are engaged, in professions such as those of Librarians, Amanuenses, Shorthand writers etc. None are in such intellectual occupations as those of rhetoricians, grammarians, philosophers, tutors, doctors and artists. None are engaged in trade, commerce or industry. The condition of the Untouchable was worse than that of a Negro slave. There are no untouchables as artisans, and no instance of an untouchable maintaining a school where Brahmin children come in search of learning. Such a thing is unthinkable in caste-ridden Hindu India, but it has happened in the United States of America.

Unlike a Dalit, there was no stigma attached to the person of a slave, and no gulf, social or religious, which separated the slave at any rate in Rome from the rest of the society. In outward appearance, colour or clothing he did not differ from the free man, he witnessed the same games as the freemen, he shared in the life of the municipal towns, and employed in state service, engaged himself in trade and commerce as all free men did. Marriage between slave and freed slave was very common. Slave was touchable and even respectable.

Slave did not have to worry about availability of work. Slave gets his bread, his clothes and his shelter whether it is boom or depression. The slave was property and being valuable, the master took great care of the health of the slave. In Rome, the slaves were never employed on marshy and malarial land.

The slavery was never obligatory, but Untouchability is. A person was "permitted" to hold another as his slave. There is no compulsion on him if he does not want to. A Hindu on the other hand is 'enjoined' by his religion to hold another as an untouchable. There is compulsion on the Hindu, which he cannot escape whatever his personal wishes in the matter may be.

Lastly, slavery was personal, but Untouchability was for the whole group of caste and there was no freedom from it and no way to buy back the freedom.

Untouchability has none of the advantages of the unfree social order unlike slave. The Untouchable has no entry in the higher arts of civilisation and no way open to a life of culture. He must only sweep. He must do nothing else. Untouchability carries no security as to livelihood. None of the Hindus is responsible for the feeding, housing, clothing and health of a Dalit.

Why Slave Upgraded and Dalit Degraded

But suppose Roman society had practiced Untouchability, and had an objection to buy vegetables, milk, butter, water or wine from the hands of the slave. Suppose Roman society had an objection to allow slaves to touch them, to enter their houses, travel with them in cars, it would have been impossible for the master to train his slave and to raise him from semi-barbarism to a cultured state.

Roman religion was never hostile to the slave. It did not close the temple doors against him; it did not banish him from its festivals. The slave informally formed a part of the family, and considered under the protection of the same gods. The law insisted that a slave's grave should be regarded as sacred. Roman mythology provided no different heaven or hell for slaves.

The cruelties and atrocities practiced by the Hindus against the Untouchables were more cruel than those practiced by the Americans upon the Blacks. They are not known to world, unlike latter's plight, because there is no Hindu, who will not do his best to conceal truth in order to hide his shame. These are not matters of ancient past. That is why we have seen in 2002, how hard the Upper Caste Indian Rulers tried to keep the Discriminations of Caste away from the Durban Conference (WCAR – World Conference Against Racial and other Discrimination– at Durban).

The Sanction of Religion

Inequality, no doubt, exists everywhere in the world. But it never has had the support of religion. With the Hindus inequality is the official doctrine of the Hindu religion. Caste and Untouchability are not mere dogmas, unlike other dogmas relating to the condition of the soul after death. Every Hindu must observe Caste, and Untouchability, throughout his daily life, as long as he lives. This is not mere tradition or custom, but it is **religion**. That is why it will be seen that the conditions have not improved a bit after more than half a century of self rule, if anything, they are worsened.

Atrocities on Dalits

If one wishes to make a list of only the reported and documented atrocities, as the majority of them are not reported to authorities and all those reported are not registered, the list would run into volumes bigger than the Encyclopedia Britannica. Hence, it is futile to make such an attempt. Neither it is necessary nor feasible to list all the gory instances to understand the plight of these hapless people. Suffice it to mention a few representative instances from different times, different regions, and their different immediate reasons, and different forms such atrocities can take.

Historical Times

Recently, Brahminic scholars tried to blame Muslims for start of Untouchability. This is false and mischievous. As a matter of fact, it existed before Islam came to India. The real cause of Untouchability, as proved by Dr. Ambedkar, lies in the hatred and contempt of Buddhists by the Brahmins, the leaders of the Hindus. Therefore, we have to peep through the pages of history to find out instances of persecutions of Buddhists. The subject is dealt with in detail by us elsewhere [Jamanadas: 2004]

The persecution really started with the start of counter-revolution against Buddhism by Pushyamitra Shunga, around 185 BCE, under guidance of his *purohit* Patanjali. Pushyamitra had ordered mass genocide of Buddhists and offered hundred *dinars* for a head of a Bhikku. There was religious persecution by Nara, a Kashmir ruler of first century BCE and by Hun ruler, Mihirkula (510-530 CE). The persecution by Gauda King Sashanka (7th century CE) is well known. He uprooted Bodhi tree, destroyed footprints of the Buddha and killed thousands of Bhikkus.

After Harshavardhana, in seventh century CE, the situation became very harassing for the Buddhists. The **Rajput Age was the darkest period in the history of India** for the Buddhist persecution was on peak. Untouchability had started as a religious persecution.

When the Muslims came, they annihilated the Buddhist external symbols like idols and monasteries, and gave a final blow to Buddhism, causing its fall. But the Buddhist population, which by this time had become untouchables completely, found great relief from Brahminic hostility by converting to Islam. Untouchables like Malik Kafoor became high officers under Khilji and Khusrukhan even became the Sultan.

There remained a large population among the "untouchable" Buddhists, who did not get converted to Islam, had now to face double persecution. On one hand they were already under Brahminic oppression, on the other the Muslims considered all the non-Muslims as "Hindus" and tortured these Dalits considering them as "Hindus".

Movement of Medieval Saints

During 800 years of Muslim rule, till the British came, there was hardly any relief to those Dalits, who did not convert to Islam. The relief started only after the British came. Even the movement of non-Brahmin saints did not remove their disabilities during the medieval period, because these saints preached equality 'in the eyes of god', not necessarily in the eyes of man and remained indifferent to practice of Untouchability. On the contrary, the movement of saints prevented the possible revolt by the Depressed Classes.

Kind hearted Brahmin saint Eknatha touched untouchable children, not because he disliked Untouchability, but because he believed, bath could wash away the sin of touch of an untouchable. Even then Eknatha's sons severed all relations from his father, and performed a '*ghat shraadha*', a Brahminic religious rite to declare a living person dead. Brahmin saint Ramdas has averred that even a corrupt Brahmin is greatest among three worlds and an untouchable though learned and wise is of no use. Same was preached by Tulsidas in *Ramcharit Manas* (Tulsi Ramayana).

Rule of Shivaji a Bahujan King

Shivaji's (1630-1680) rule was egalitarian, treating all on equal footing, neither it was an anti-Muslim Rule nor the Brahmins had any special privileges over other castes. The untouchables were given place in his army. He was not a '*go brahmin pratipalak*' (protector of cows and Brahmins) contrary to Brahminic propaganda.

One of the wives of Shivaji was also an untouchable, and this untouchable wife was given due respect at the time of his coronation, says Keluskar in his "*Shiv Charitra*". Sharad Patil has mentioned this. Sharad Patil, in his recent book says that, this untouchable wife, whose name is unknown to the history, was killed by pushing her down the fort by the Brahmin ministers after they poisoned Shivaji to death, and he dedicates this book to her. [Sharad Patil: 2004: 80]

Condition of Dalits during the Peshava Rule

Peshava Rule was a Brahminic Rule, the Dalits could not enter the town when the shadows were long, i.e. in morning and evening, as shadow of a Dalit was polluting. A Dalit had to tie a small earthen pot in his neck as a spittoon and a branch of a thorny tree or a broom to waist, so that the spit or foot marks of Dalit do not pollute others walking on the streets. Brahmins always ensured that every one followed his or her Caste Rules, and any transgression was severely punished. Peshava Rule was no exception to this, rather they were more strict in following this rule than others, as is well documented.

The practice of slavery was different during Peshava rule. Usually the Untouchables were not allowed even to become slaves. Those who were wrongly appointed as slaves, if detected later, were severely punished. Female slaves, called '*kunbin*' or '*batkin*' were more in number than males. In 1795, when an untouchable *Chambhar* woman tried to become a slave as domestic maidservant, the whole family had to be purified by '*prayaschita*' (punishment). Similar examples are found about Mahar batkins also. S.R. Tikkekar explains why: "The slaves were clothed and fed, sometimes much better than the free man of their standing and were allowed to possess property." [Gawai: 1990: 112]

When a Mahar tried to buy and sell fish, he was prohibited by royal order admonished and threatened with death penalty if the offense was repeated, says a note in '*Peshava Rojnishi*' (Diary of Peshava) [Gawai: 1990: 113].

Unpaid bonded forced labour

This was practiced in great numbers and various types of works were involved including construction of government and private building works of houses, temples and forts. For these twenty-four hour duties, they were paid some cash or kind, some '*maan-paan*' or '*hakal-jama*' and a small piece of land called '*inaam*'. Dalits were buried alive in foundations of forts and public buildings and sacrificed during digging of wells, during medieval times, to bring good omen to completion of work.

During Sepoy Mutiny 1857

"Sepoy Mutiny" of 1857, which the Brahmin scholars even now, arrogantly glorify as 'the first war of Independence', was in fact for liberation of Brahmins. All the leaders like, Tatya Tope, Laxmibai, Nanasaheb, were Brahmins, and even the soldier, Mangal Pande, who fired the first shot, was a Brahmin. The cause was also the caste, in British army, the soldiers from high and low caste had to intermingle and inter-dine causing degradation of Brahmins. Mahatma Phule, who aptly called this Mutiny as mutiny of "Bhats and Pandes" (*bhat pandya che band*), expressed happiness that the mutiny failed. [*Infra*]

Mahatma Jotirao Phule

He was the first to struggle for upliftment of Untouchables, by starting the first school for Dalit girls in 1848. Rajashri Shahu of Kolhapur, later, implemented Phule's teachings in his own small state, for which he had to suffer at the hands of Brahmins like Bal Gangadhar Tilak.

Periyar Ramasami Naikkar

He started Self-Respect Movement in South India for upliftment of non-Brahmins, and also led the "*Viacom satyagraha*", which was for allowing the Dalits to walk over a particular street, near a Brahminic temple.

Gandhi and Dalits

It is a wrong propaganda that Gandhi was friend of Dalits. The fact is Dalits consider him as their enemy number one. He deprived Dalits of the political rights given by 'Communal Award' by the British. For that he started 'fast till death' and to save his life, the real savior of Dalits **Dr. Ambedkar had to sign Poona Pact under duress** in 1932.

After Transfer of Power in 1947

Some important Caste wars have taken place since 'independence'. Atrocities are a regular feature and not isolated incidents. They also indicate the causes, mechanisms and the forms of atrocities. As Dale Carnegie has said, 'Nobody kicks a dead dog', only those Dalits who struggle for their rights are targeted. The murders, rape and arson are matters of everyday life. There is still a 'two glass' system in town restaurants - a separate glass being kept for Dalits, still Dalits are not allowed in temples, still Dalit students are not allowed to sit with others, still the Dalits cannot use coloured head dress in Rajasthan, still they have to get down from bicycle after seeing a Upper Caste (UC) person, still they have to remove footwear while walking through streets in the colonies of so called Upper Caste. It is only recently that the Dalit women in South India started using clothes to cover their breasts if UC person was approaching. Even now there are killings, if Dalit bridegroom uses a mare to ride. Even now, there are bonded labours. Even now Dalit girls are forced into religious temple prostitution. Even now there are starvation deaths. Even now Dalits in South India are made to eat human excreta and urine.

The atrocities take place in every province for various different reasons. Just a few names could be mentioned. There was a **Kambalapalli** Carnage in Karnataka, where seven Dalits were burnt alive. Male students are murdered and girls are raped for passing examinations. There are arsons and killings for contesting elections. There was such a notorious **Billandla Halli** Incident.

There was a great Caste war in Gujarat. This was one of the most serious Caste riots against the Dalits in post-Independent India, lasting for months in 1981, in non-violent Gandhi's own Gujarat. Innumerable Dalits were killed, their property looted and burnt, women raped and molested.

There was The Marathwada Caste War after Maharashtra Government passed a resolution to rename Marathwada University after name of Dr. Ambedkar. The attacks are always well planned, and well organised, and there was tremendous loss of property and life and loot arson rape and killings. Madhukar Taksande wrote that, only Buddhists were victims of attack, because only they are conscious and living with self-confidence and dignity, because of inspiration of Ambedkar's teachings.

There was a Ghatkopar-Carnage in July 1997 in Bombay following the desecration of statues of Buddha and Ambedkar, where ten people died and 32 injured in police firing. There were repercussions all over Maharashtra, where several Dalits were killed, there was rape and molestation and arson all over the state.

Caste wars in Bihar have their own peculiarities and are fought on regular basis in rural Bihar. Their struggle mostly related with rural life, bonded labour and agriculture. The oppressors are the organised gangs called 'Sena' (army) of upper castes heavily armed with firearms, and their attacks are a regular feature done with military precision.

There were incidents in Punjab and Haryana. In Jhajjar upper caste Hindus killed five Dalits allegedly for skinning a dead cow. Atrocities on students are very frequent in University campus, as was seen recently in Aurangabad and Hyderabad.

Maharashtra saw most brutal rape murder episode in Khairlanji recently, when mother and daughter were raped and stakes put in their private parts; and two young sons murdered.

Such were and are the atrocious conditions under which the Untouchables did live and are still living their lives. We have discussed the details elsewhere. [Jamanadas: 2002: 206 ff. See also *infra*]

This is what the Untouchability is all about. It started around 400 to 600 CE. During those times, the Buddhist temples, mutts and viharas, all over the country were taken over by the Brahmins, during the Rajput period – the 'Dark Age' of India. The practice of Untouchability under the religious rules of *Smritis* like that of Manu and others, was in full swing under the supervision and guidance of Shankaracharya and his disciples and rulers – of the newly created caste – the Rajputs.

It is not properly realised that the so-called crusade of Kumaril and Shankara against Buddhism meant nothing but killing of the unwilling Bhikkus and the conversion of lay Buddhists into slave Dalit Bahujan castes and make them untouchables. *Prabodhankar* Thakre holds Shankaracharya responsible for start of Untouchability. [*Devala cha dharma aani dharma chi devale* – Thakre : 1928 : 6-8]

Numerous Buddhist temples and viharas-s, had a number of Buddhist nuns, That was the time that the Buddhist nuns were degraded to the status of Devadasis, subject discussed by us in '*Devadasis Ancient to Modern*', Kalpaz, 2007.

Tagore-s Suffered Caste Discrimination

[http://www.mainstreamweekly.net/article2003.html] (Accessed Nov. 14, 2012), An article in '*Mainstream*', Vol. XLVIII, No. 20. May 8, 2010, titled '*Two Events in Tagore's Life*' by A.K. Biswas, former Vice-Chancellor, B.R. Ambedkar University, Muzaffarpur (Bihar), describes how the family of great First Nobel Laureate of India had to suffer in Caste India, how he attended a Namashudra Conference, and how he was banned from entering Jaganath Temple of Puri, and how he prayed not to be reborn in Bengal.

Poet in Namashudra Caste Conference

Twelve years after he was awarded the Nobel Prize in 1913, Rabindranath Tagore had participated in a caste conference organised by the Namashudra-s, held in East Bengal (now Bangladesh), though the venue was not specified.

A.K. Biswas observes:

> "Though the Calcutta Municipal Corporation's official mouthpiece discloses that the poet went to East Bengal in 1925 and participated in a conference organised by the *Namashudra-s*, it did not say anything about the venue of the conference even if this marks a striking turning point in the poet's career."

The entry in the '*The Calcutta Municipal Gazette Tagore Memorial Special Supplement*', Saturday, September 3, 1941, editor Amal Home, p. 90, reads as: "attends the Namashudra (Depressed Classes) conference".

The Namashudra-s, who were called Chandal Till 1911, though a second largest caste in Bengal, were untouchables and occupied (or even today do occupy) the lowest rung in the ladder of social hierarchy. Biswas observes:

> "No ancient scriptures, of which the Hindus are proud, ever uttered a word or ordinance free from abuse, hatred, contempt or invective against the caste. 'Tagore, nevertheless, was in their midst to attend a conference. Why? What prompted him to do so? There is golden silence in academic circles. No light appears to have ever been thrown on it though Tagore attended that conference of socially degraded people over eight decades ago. The event might have been even erased from the community memories of the *Namashudra*. The poet, I guess, did not participate in any other caste conference."

A vast mass of literature is produced on the Tagore, but his participation in a Namashudra conference is not a piece of information worthy of elite curiosity, excitement and probe, observes Biswas.

Biswas wonders:

> "What really inspired the poet to go to the Namashudra-s, and what did he speak to them in the conference? Did he have a message of social and political or ethical import for them? What did, on the contrary, the Namashudra-s tell their honourable guest in their address presented to the Nobel Laureate? Did the contemporary media cover the event as breaking news? Or did the media or intelligentsia altogether cold-shoulder the poet's role for the socially despised and deprived people?"

Biswas wishes someone would research the role that Tagore played for the untouchables in Bengal and bring out 'the inclusive kaleidoscopic worldview of one of the unrivalled humanists India has ever seen'.

How an uphill task for the Namashudra was it to reach Rabindranath Tagore and secure an appointment for attending an untouchable conference, wonders Biswas, and comments:

> "It is only natural to assume that the elite society of Calcutta and country denounced Tagore for the misadventure! Bengalis took pleasure in insinuating that there was Portuguese blood running in the veins and arteries of Rabindranath Tagore. He did not visit East Bengal ever again thereafter." [Nirod C. Chaudhuri, 'Tagore Nobel Prize' in *Illustrated Weekly*, Bombay, Vol. XCV, 10, Sunday, March 11, 1973]

Tagores' Entry Banned in Jagannath Temple, Puri

It may not be news to many that the entry of the Tagore-s of Calcutta was banned in the Jagannath temple of Puri. At least many might have heard in whispers but disbelieved and dismissed it as slanderous gossip.

The Tagore-s of Calcutta were the richest in the metropolis, they were nevertheless banned entry into the sacred Jagannath temple at Puri, Orissa. They were Pirali Brahmans, a degraded class in the Bengali priestly hierarchy.

The people of Bengal by and large know their story of degradation.

In September 1803, forces of East India Co. conquered Orissa and camped near Puri. A delegation of priests of Lord Jagannath of Puri called on the commanding officer.

> " ... the **oracle** of the Puri Jagannath Temple proclaimed that it was the desire of the deity that the temple too be controlled by the (East India) Company and the latter undertook to maintain the temple buildings, pay the Brahmans and do everything for the service of the deity as was customary." [Swami Dharam Teerth, *History of Hindu Imperialism*, 1935, p. 151. W.W. Hunter recorded: "A deputation of Brahmans accordingly came into the camp, and placed the temple under his (Lt. Colonel Campbell) protection without a blow being struck." [*A Statistical Account of Bengal*, Cuttack and Puri, Vol. XIX, 1877, London]

Regulation IV was enacted in 1806 and the East India Company imposed a pilgrim tax for entry into Puri. [Between 1806 to 1831, the pilgrims tax, grossed to a sum of Rs 1,24,37,570; expenditures on the temple management and rituals on average, amounted to Rs 54,973 per annum. Meeting all expenses on account of the Jagannath temple, the Company earned a balance of Rs. 12,83,130. [Col. Laurie, "Puri and the Temple of Jagannath", article in *The Calcutta Review,* Vol. X, September, 1848, pp. 251 and 261] The tax was ultimately was revoked on vocal criticism of the Christian Missionaries and Englishmen who were aghast at the role played by the Government of East India Company in promoting, preserving and protecting idolatry. Indians could not be expected to be vocal against the British control, management of the Jagannath and his temple as blind faith in His oracle was blindly obeyed by them. Further similar tax by Mughal Emperor Aurangzeb in the medieval era has received harsh criticism. But the pilgrim tax imposed long later has been spared from focus in the same vein. This myopia is calculative. The historians do not want to expose the advisers of the takeover of the shrine and consequent tax regime under the legal frame.]

Regulation IV, which received assent of the Governor General on April 28, 1809, debarred castes, for example, Lolee or Kusbee, Cullal or Soonree Machoowa, Nomosooder or Chandal, Gazoor, Baugdee, Joogee or Noorbauf, Kahar Bawrey or Doolia, Raujbunsee, Peerally, Chaumar, Dome, Paun, Teor, Bhooimalee and Hadee from entry in the temple. The Tagores were Peerally [now spelt as Pirali] Brahmans, who were degraded in the Bengali hierarchical pretension and orthodoxy. However, Regulation XI of 1810 exempted the Peerally from the scope of the ban.

None other than Bengali Brahman advisers could have suggested for banning the entry in the Puri temple of castes, for example, Rajbanshi, Jogi, Peerali, Sunri, Buimali and Dulia in the Regulation

Any Bengali Hindu, whose caste has been tainted by willful or inadvertent intercourse with people of other religions, mainly Islam, was called Pirali. The Tagores' misfortune on this score owes its origin to an episode during the Mughal era. An ancestor of the Tagore dynasty, it is said, had a land dispute in the district of Jessore [now in Bangladesh] with a relation. A revenue official, Amin, had called both the parties to his camp for mediation. The Tagore in dispute went and smelt beef, which was being cooked in the Amin's kitchen. **Smelling in Bengal is considered equivalent to half-eating.** So the Tagore lost his caste for half-eating the beef. The stigmatized Tagores came to be identified as Pirali Brahman after the Amin, named Pir Ali Khan, and suffered social stigma for generations not excluding Rabindranath. Their glowing achievements and accomplishments in education, scholarship, art and culture, trade and commerce remained unsurpassed. But they were more like social lepers in the orthodox scale in Bengal. So much so that they never married their daughters into kulin (superior) Brahman families. Nor did they allow and welcome kulin brides into the Tagore family. The marriage of Rabindranath's youngest daughter, Mira, is a case in point. She was married to a kulin, Nagendra Nath Ganguly (Gangopadhyay), and it was a disaster. She had a miserable, stormy life as it floundered *ab initio*. Letters exchanged between Tagore and his daughter as well as son-in-law speak eloquently about the unfortunate state of their marriage. It caused deep agony and excruciating pain and helplessness for the sensitive and affectionate father who could not intervene in it anyway.

The Poet abhorred Rebirth as a Bengali

The great poet, says Biswas, 'at the end of the day became extremely wary of the Bengali people', because his detractors drove him up the wall. They hurt him mercilessly where he was most vulnerable. And he bled profusely: they savagely targeted his literary works, which were the edifice of his creativity and glory. When the Nobel Prize was conferred on Tagore the detractors in a mad rush scrambled for demonstrating their admiration by offering memorials to him on behalf of his countrymen. This offered him the opportunity for some plain talk.

Rabindranath wrote:

"The calumny and insults from the hands of my countrymen which have fallen to my lot have not been very small in amount. Till now I have borne all this in silence. In such circumstances, I am yet unable to understand fully how I have come to receive the honour, which I have got from abroad?"

He adds further:

"How can I shamelessly appropriate to myself the honour, which you are making to me as representatives of the country? This day of mine will not last forever. The ebb-tide will set in again. Then all the squalor will expose of the muddy bottom itself bank after bank."

Finally he delivered the shot with perfect equanimity of mind:

"So I submit this to you with folded hands that I would place my head on whatever is true, however harsh that might be; but I am unable to that which is a delusion created by momentary excitement. In certain countries friends and guests are welcomed with wine. You have placed before me a goblet of wine of your honour. I shall raise it to my lips, but I cannot gulp down this heady draught to take into my heart. I want to keep my mind free from this intoxication."

When the Nobel Prize was announced the poet was in England; he was very much hesitant to return to India for fear of torture and mudslinging at him by his gifted Bengali detractors, who could not get over the shock and awe of Tagore being crowned with such a glory.

Biswas avers that the Bengali intelligentsia had harassed, humiliated and persecuted Tagore all his life, though he was the first Indian Nobel Prize winner. His literary abilities were questioned and ridiculed with insinuations and innuendos no end. They even asked him if he had engaged paid agents to spread his fame and campaign for him. Biswas quotes from Tagore's letters in support of this.

Tagore wrote in disgust:

"I have almost brought to its end the span of life in my Bengali birth. And the last prayer of my tired life is that **if there be rebirth may I not be born in Bengal again.** … I am an outcast, let my lot be cast among those whose conduct does not conform to the *Shastras* (scriptures), but whose judgment is consistent with Dharma (righteousness).

Macauley had observed:

"What the horns are to the buffalo, what the paw is to the tiger, what the sting to the bee, what beauty … is to woman, deceit is to the Bengalee. Large promises, smooth promises, elaborate tissues of circumstantial falsehood, chicanery, perjury, forgery, are the weapons of the Lower Ganges."

Biswas comments:

"Indians hate Macauley. They worship Tagore. But what Tagore said was materially little different from Macauley. Imagine Tagore's prayer, stunning as it were mere seven years before his death: "If there be rebirth may I not be born in Bengal again."

A Struggle for Decent Dress

The Upper Cloth Mutiny

[http://www.expressbuzz.com/edition/story.aspx? Title=The+struggle+of+the+downtrodden+for+a+decent+dre&artid=ftilhLjFHDo=& SectionID=1ZkFjmWuSA=&MainSectionID=1ZkFjmWuSA= &SEO=Channar+Lahala,+-Joy+Balan+Vlaathangara,+Brahmins, & SectionName= X7s7i%7CxOZ5Y=] (Accessed Thursday, April 26, 2012)

Dalits had to struggle even for decent dress and to cover upper part of chest covered in certain parts of India. Even today, the tradition demands that the Dalit women should not use blouses. A story from Kerala as reported by R. Ayyapan on 27 July 2009, in expressbuzz.com

Thiruvananthapuram: Exactly 150 years ago, on July 26 of 1859, Travancore Maharaja officially declared and granted lower caste Nadar/ Channar women the right to cover their breasts after half-a-century of violent struggle called 'Upper Cloth Mutiny'.

Beginning of all Revolutions

"Cries for equality began to rise not just from various parts of Kerala, but from the whole of South India after the Channar Mutiny. The agitation to end '*oozhiyam vela*' or work without pay, the agitation to secure entry into temples, the agitation to secure the right to walk on public roads, all these struggles that went on to change the face of Kerala were inspired by the success of the Upper Cloth Mutiny,"

So writes historian Joy Balan Vlaathangara in his book '*Vaikuntaswamiyum Samoohika Navothanavum*'.

Brahmin Women Too

"*Namboodiri* ladies could not wear upper body cloth while at home. Though they were allowed to cover their breasts while venturing out, they had to remove it in the temple, in front of the idol. In the case of Nair women, they could not cover their breasts in front of Brahmins," Joy writes in his book. Ezhava women secured the right to cover their breasts in 1865. Nair women stopped exposing their breasts in front of Brahmins even later. Further late, the Brahmin community too did away with the demeaning condition they had imposed on their women.

Work of Christian Missionaries

It was western influence and the work of Christian missionaries that motivated labourers who had migrated to Sri Lanka to work in colonial tea plantations returning with enough money to lead European lifestyles. Converted Nadars, too, started wearing upper clothes and saw it as a sign of social progress.

The Violent Opposition

The upper castes, including the royalty, did not take kindly to these progressive thoughts. An account says that a lower caste lady who went to the palace of the Attingal Rani wearing an upper cloth had her breasts chopped off by royal decree. Out on the streets, the upper castes unleashed violence on Christian Nadar women who had their breasts covered.

The British order covering breasts

In 1814, Travancore Resident and Diwan Colonel Munro issued an order to the effect that Christian Nadars could wear upper clothes. Unmindful, the upper castes continued with their attacks. Eight years later, in 1822, Munro issued yet another order which once again gave Nadar Christian women the right to cover their breasts.

Upper caste backlash

The order sparked a mighty backlash. D. Daniel, in his book '*Travancore Tamils Struggle for Identity*', notes:

> "Covered Christian Nadar women were attacked in markets and other public places and their jackets torn by upper caste men in places."

Court Verdict has no effect

The missionaries intervened and got a favourable verdict from the Padmanabhapuram court in 1823. Still, nothing changed. Samuel Mateer in his '*Land of Charity*' relates an incident, in 1828, in which a group of Nadar Christian women who went to depose before a lower court were forced, in the presence of the Diwan, to remove their upper clothes and leave it at the outside entrance before entering.

A Turning Point

The year 1829 marked a turning point. That year, a royal decree was issued asking Christian Nadars to bow to the existing codes of the caste system.

> "This united the Christian and Hindu Nadar communities. They began to appear in public places and in temples with their upper bodies covered", Joy writes.

Work of Vaikunta Swami

Vaikunta Swami, who had set up the '*Samathwa Samajam*', acted as the unifying force. "While the missionaries worked only for the converted, Vaikunta Swami ignored the barriers of caste and strove for the uplift of all the backward classes", Joy writes.

Again Violence by Upper Castes

The upper castes reacted violently. But once the Nadars responded with ferocity, violence abated. It was in 1858 that violence once again reared its head.

> "Nair men, with machetes tied at the end of long poles, used to stand far way from lower caste women and tear their jackets,"

Samuel Mateer's 'Land of Charity' describes how an official dealt with two 'covered' Nadar ladies who were walking to the Neyyattinkara market.

> "He tore their jackets, tied them with a rope and hung them from a tree in full public view."

The Nadars Retaliated and Succeeded

The Nadar response was more severe. They looted upper caste shops and terrorized upper caste areas. The Government was forced to act to restore at least a semblance of peace. Madras Governor, through the Travancore Resident, told the Travancore King that the condition of women in Travancore does not put the Travancore rulers in good light. Aayilyam Thirunal, then made the decisive move to grant Nadar women the right to cover their breasts.

Brand as Witch and Kill

Upper Caste Men Brand Dalit Sarpanch's Daughter-in-law "Witch"

An article in *The Hindu* on

[http://www.thehindu.com/news/states/other-states/article2869614.ece] (Accessed Feb. 11, 2012), by Smriti Kak Ramachandran depicts another way of atrocity by branding important elected Dalit women to get rid of them. The Gist:

When Norti Bai, sarpanch of Harmara in Rajasthan, refused to give in to the demands of upper caste men in her village, her daughter-in-law Ram Peari was branded a "witch." The villagers called for Peari's "social boycott" and excommunication.

In Alwar district in the State, Sunita Bairwa of Bahedakhah was assaulted because the upper castes were unhappy about a Dalit being elevated to *sarpanch*.

These and similar testimonies were shared at a day-long public hearing on caste bias and atrocities faced by Dalit elected representatives, held here on Tuesday. Organised by the All-India Dalit Mahila Adhikar Manch, the event highlighted the stories of discrimination and violence against Dalit women elected representatives from in Bihar, Uttar Pradesh and Rajasthan.

> "It took us days to get the police to file a complaint. I was victimised because we are from the lower caste and my mother-in-law was doing some good work for the village. The upper caste men could not tolerate it, they wanted her to toe their line and when she refused to, they accused me of being a witch and of performing black magic on another woman," said Ram Peari.

Most elected representatives facing harassment complained that the police and the administration were also not supporting them. "As chairperson of the district council of Aurangabad, I am not even kept informed of the day-to-day functioning. When I raise important issues, I am told that because of my caste, I will not even be heard," complained Ranju Devi from Bihar.

In her village, she alleged, her husband was beaten up by upper caste men who objected to her candidature.

No Change in Status

Syeda Hameed, Member, Planning Commission, who addressed the hearing, said the status of the Dalit women representative was same as it was years ago. The Centre and State governments would have to work collectively for the empowerment of Dalit women and there was need for a multisectoral approach to development and proper implementation of policies, she said.

The Recommendations

Following the testimonies, a jury put forth certain recommendations. They called for establishing a special office in each district to act as a support mechanism for Dalit, Adivasi and women panchayat presidents. The office should provide advice, training and information as well as monitor the performance of duties and interventions by others such as panchayat members and government officials.

The special office should mediate and resolve problems encountered by panchayat representatives.

In another recommendation, the jury said the State Election Commissions should set up a fund to provide basic financial support towards election cost to Dalits, Adivasis and women in general falling within a stipulated low household income bracket.

It called for setting up an autonomous statutory directorate for all reserved panchayats at the State level, headed by a Dalit, Adivasi woman IAS officer, and assistant directorates at the district level, headed by a Dalit/Adivasi woman officer below the rank of IAS, to function under the directorate. These two institutions should fall under the jurisdiction of the Legislative Assembly through the Governor. They should monitor and review the pre and post-election performance of the reserved panchayats, and submit annual reports to the Assembly.

The jury called for mandating the National and State Scheduled Caste, Scheduled Tribe and Women's Commissions with sufficient powers, funds and staff to specifically inquire into political obstruction or violence committed against Dalit women and men, Adivasis and other women elected representatives.

A resolution to strengthen the legal framework such as the SC/ST (POA) Act, 1989, and enforcement agencies particularly those focussing on Dalit women was passed.

Dalit Kids cannot Use School Loo but have to Clean Them

[http://timesofindia.indiatimes.com/India/Dalit-kids-cannot-use-school-loo-but-have-to-clean-them/articleshow/4699387.cms] (Accessed Saturday, February 04, 2012)

Dalit kids cannot use school loo but have to clean them

25 Jun 2009, 0330 hrs IST, Akshaya Mukul, TNN

"In Bihar, teachers complain to the Dalit parents that their children wear dirty clothes and they smell in the classrooms"

"During a school visit in Rajasthan, while asking who gets beaten up regularly and why, children immediately pointed out to a student. He was a Dalit"

"Teachers don't give proper attention to us. We have to sit on the ground. It's very difficult...The quality of food (mid-day meal) is also very poor. We also get very little food in lunch as we are served the last, our stomach does not fill" – a Dalit girl student in Bihar.

In UP, Dalit Girls are Seldom Allowed to Use the Toilets in Schools

The study conducted by the National Campaign on Dalit Human Rights - Dalit Arthik Adhikar Andolan and supported by UNICEF shows that discrimination of various kinds plays a big role in the high dropout of Dalit children from schools. The report was submitted to UNICEF.

Discrimination of Dalit Students

The study conducted in 41 primary schools, 36 middle schools and 17 secondary schools in Nalanda district of Bihar, Hardoi in Uttar Pradesh, Jodhpur in Rajasthan and Beed in Maharashtra examined various facets of discrimination, right from going to school, in the classroom and in the mid-day meal.

The report says physical access to schools is the biggest problem for Dalit children. In Bihar, UP and Rajasthan, most of the schools are situated in the dominant caste localities and Dalit children have to travel on an average half-an-hour to reach school. In the case of middle and high schools, Dalit children have to travel almost 3-4 kilometers in all the states. It is only in Maharashtra that Dalit children do not have to travel that far. But here too, the schools are located in dominant caste areas.

Asked why they came late to school, Dalit children gave various reasons including household chores, school distance, inability to keep track of school time and also the fact that they had to wait for other friends to go in a group due to fear from dominant caste children. In the school, it was found that participation of Dalit children was minimal. The morning assembly was invariably always conducted by upper caste children. In the class, Dalit children were made to sit at the back and in some schools of Bihar on the barren floor while mats were given to upper caste children. Even the notebooks and homework of the Dalit children were not checked by teachers.

Menial jobs Enforced

As per the report, Dalit children in UP were also assigned menial caste-based tasks like cleaning the yard, filling up water buckets and cleaning the toilets. This led to other children treating them badly and considering them inferior. And what was shocking was that Dalit girl children were seldom allowed to use toilets. Dalit children are kept out of even functions like Independence Day.

Dalit Women More Humiliated when Raped: Study

Studied for the First Time

[http://articles.timesofindia.indiatimes.com/2009-12-15/india/28110136_1_dalit-women-sexual-assault-upper-castes] (Accessed on Saturday, February 11, 2012)

Dalit women more humiliated when raped: This is the result of Study by Nandita Sengupta, TNN Dec 15, 2009, 05.21pm IST. The excerpts:

NEW DELHI: Dalit women who have suffered caste rapes were subjected to more humiliation than other women similarly assaulted, says a first of its kind research study detailing the psychological trauma of women raped.

Foul words used

When Dalit women are assaulted, offenders use foul language vilifying the woman verbally, says the survey, invariably calling them prostitutes. "The feeling of being dehumanised, of having been demeaned is far greater for Dalit women", says clinical psychologist Rajat Mitra, who led the study conducted by NGO Swanchetan that works with victims of sexual assault. Mitra notes that in any other rape, the victim is not called a 'prostitute'.

Titled 'A research study on sexual assault', it was done through detailed interviews of victims identified by state-level NGOs and government homes as well as by inviting victims to take part in the survey via posters and radio announcements. Of the 122 identified, 66 women agreed to the interview. The questionnaire's themes were identified and built on basis of data collected over the last 10 years and conducted in the last two.

Studies across 12 states

Studies were conducted across Delhi, Meghalaya, Assam, Karnataka, Tripura, Maharashtra, UP, West Bengal, Andhra Pradesh, Jammu & Kashmir, Bihar and Gujarat. "Whenever a Dalit woman is raped, it gets connected to all other sufferings and discriminations. Dalits being in a disadvantaged position and there's no resilience, no bouncing back," says Mitra.

Rape as Tradition

"The women shared that during the attack, the men seemed to have more pleasure in humiliating their origins and background", adds Mitra. The report details their almost-ritualistic ostracism after the rape where older Dalit women also attempt to explain rape as 'tradition'. It is extremely important, says Mitra, for a different rehabilitation policy for Dalit women with special training for mental health professionals, judiciary and police sensitizing them to the caste angle. The Dalit women notched higher trauma levels on every factor studied except for 'despair' and feeling betrayed. This, concludes Mitra, also demonstrates how rape for Dalits, is an inter-generational trauma and not restricted to a one-time event.

International condemnation may be useful

UN Human Rights Council in Geneva is considering that caste-based discrimination be recognised as a human rights violation. Shyam Babu, fellow, Rajiv Gandhi Foundation hopes that the international condemnation will have an impact in forcing the redressal machinery to work on caste crimes as a priority area.

Dalit MP in Orissa Denied to Enter the Temple

[http://news.oneindia.in/2011/06/25/dalit-MP-in-orissa-denied-to-enter-the-temple-aid0156.html] (Accessed December 21, 2012) Dalit MP in Orissa denied to enter the temple, Saturday, June 25, 2011. Some excerpts.

Puri, Jun 25: Caste discrimination that still prevails across the country has reached its height when the chairman of the National Commission for Schedule Castes was denied entry at a temple in Puri.

PL Punia, a Dalit himself is considered as 'untouchable' who was allowed just till the compound, but found the main temple doors shut. The MP said that he would take up the matter. "I will summon the Chief Secretary of Orissa within 15 days and seek explanation from him over the matter. After that I will take action against this illegal practice which is very much within the jurisdiction of my commission," Punia said.

The Kali temple has restricted the entries of the dalits since 80 years. But, the controversy, 2010 when three schoolgirls dared to cross the boundary to offer prayers raised protests regarding this issue. They were dragged out by higher caste villagers and insulted, which led to a series of violent clashes.

Dalit Grooms Ride into Trouble

[http://daily.bhaskar.com/article/MP-IND-dalit-grooms-ride-into-trouble-2426014.html] (Accessed 8:05 PM 3/7/2012)

Dalit grooms ride into trouble, a news item from Indore says. In the 64th year of India's independence, at least seven examples of Dalit groom being violently obstructed disrupted and harassed for riding ceremonial horse are on record in MP last year, as recorded by a voluntary organisation, Jan Sahas.

> "These are the cases where we are providing legal and other assistance to the victims. All of the cases are under trial. Actual numbers could be many times more," said Asif Sheikh of Jan Sahas.

They quote an example of the Police station officer advising to 'better adhere to the custom prevalent in his village'.

Caste-wise Separate Kitchens in Medical Colleges and Police

In a signed article by Nalin Verma, titled '*Yadav chapati, Brahmin kachauri on medico menu*', dated Tuesday, September 15, 2009, a new aspect of practice of Untouchability and caste discrimination is seen.

[http://www.telegraphindia.com/1090915/jsp/nation/story_11493999.jsp (Accessed on 1/1/2012)]

The author states that the dictum *jaati ki roti jati mein; jaati ki beti jati mein* (dining and marrying within the caste), has entered also kitchens of premier medical colleges, as seen by names of dishes served to medical students of Shri Krishna Medical College and Hospital in Muzaffarpur, North Bihar, such as '*Yadav chapatis*', '*Rajput paranthas*', '*Bhumihar puris*' and '*Brahmin kachauris*' etc.

While the Bihar health minister Nandkishore Yadav seemed surprised by the practice, which has been going on for decades, health secretary C.K. Mishra was aware and said that the primordial practice should be discarded.

The virus of caste consciousness is not confined to medical colleges alone and has entered the kitchen of the Bihar Military Police School. State police constabulary comprises jawans from almost all castes and religions. Yadav, Dalit and Brahmin jawans have their own kitchens and the Brahmins don't touch the food from a Dalit kitchen.

K.K. Jha, the general secretary of Bihar Police Association pointed out that even Chief Minister Nitish Kumar and police top brass was aware of the practice. "But no one has done anything to address the issue," he added.

Mark Tully on Untouchability Gandhi and Ambedkar

Mark Tully, toured many villages and came to conclusion that untouchability prevailed all over, with some cosmetic changes and also the system of bonded labour locally called '*halawaha*'. There was poverty, illiteracy and great anger among the Dalits. The veteran journalist representative of BBC for many decades was a great admirer of Gandhi, as he said, 'Gandhi has always been little short of God to me'. Now at the retirement stage, he observes:

> "... I have seen countless similar statues of Ambedkar in different parts of India but for the first time a statue made me wonder whether in my admiration for Gandhi I had paid insufficient attention to Ambedkar. I had often written of Gandhi's movement to eradicate untouchability and ensure the Dalits were honoured, of his calling them *Harijans*, or Children of God. But that was perhaps **romantic** or at least **unrealistic**, whereas Ambedkar had been

thoroughly realistic in calling those who belonged to his and other untouchable castes Dalits, or the oppressed."

At last Mr. Tully realised the work of Gandhi was just eyewash, whereas Ambedkar wanted real fundamental changes, as he says:

"In the late thirties the Mahatma devoted himself to dealing with the problems of villages and villagers. The problems he addressed were lack of sanitation, deficient diet, and inertia. Ambedkar on the other hand saw the problem as cultural. He once asked, 'What is a village but a sink of localism, a den of ignorance, narrow mindedness and communalism?' Although Ambedkar's words are very harsh I can now understand why he passed that judgment on village India."

[http://www.bangaloremirror.com/article/81/20111029201110291952317 4cb0804e2/%E2%80%98Gandhi-has-always-been-little-short-of-God-to-me%E2%80%99.html]

Silent Revolution: Rise in Inter-caste Marriages

According to Subodh Ghildiyal and Swati Mathur, reporting from New Delhi in TOI, TNN, 31 January 2010, there is going on a 'Silent revolution: Rise in marriages of others to Dalits'. Inter-caste marriages, which are documented, involving Dalits seem to be on rising trend. In 2006-07, 3,945, in 2007-08, 4,205, in 2008-09, 4,750 and estimated 2010, 5,862

Dr. Ambedkar had advocated 'inter-caste marriages' as a way to annihilation of caste. Vivek Kumar, sociologist in JNU, however, is not happy and he points out there is nothing to be glad about the documented figures in spite of Govt. incentive of Rs. 50,000 to each couple. He said:

"The numbers are impressive for sure. But you have to scratch the surface to see how many such ties are between OBCs and SCs. Also, in SC-upper caste marriages, how many are women from upper castes?"

Regional figures show Andhra Pradesh and Maharashtra lead the chart, Kerala and Karnataka being next, all nearing four figures each. Remarkable are figures in Haryana, in spite of all its '*khap panchayats*' and honour killings, around a hundred every year. In sharp contrast, Gujarat, Uttarakhand, Punjab and West Bengal seem unaffected by the winds of change, Bengal reporting zero inter-caste marriages. People in power seem to be afraid to support such marriages. Real 'caste-less-ness' is still a long way off, say the experts as only *Anuloma* marriages, i.e. male from Dwija castes, predominate.

[http://timesofindia.indiatimes.com/india/Silent-revolution-Rise-in-marriages-of-others-to-dalits/articleshow/5518307.cms]

UPA failed to use Rs. 72,500 Crore for Dalits

[http://timesofindia.indiatimes.com/India/UPA-failed-to-use-Rs-72500-crore-for-Dalits-Study-/articleshow/4740334.cms]

UPA Failed to Use Rs. 72,500 Crore for Dalits: Study

5 July 2009, 1310 hrs IST, IANS

A news item from New Delhi, in *Times of India* shows that a voluntary organisation National Campaign on Dalit Human Rights (NCDHR), after a study of India's budget documents, underlines that a sum as great as Rs.72,500 crore ($15.16 billion) that should have been earmarked for the Scheduled Castes (SCs) under a special scheme, has been denied to them during the last five years by the United Progressive Alliance (UPA) government.

The "special component plan" (SCP) was the scheme, wherein a strategy was evolved way back in April 1975, that every central ministry must allocate funds from its annual plan for Dalits according to the population. SCs population today being 16.2 per cent of India's 1.1 billion population, Rs.129,000 crore should have been earmarked, but as much as Rs.72,500 crore was not earmarked during 2005 and 2009, the NCDHR has pointed out. About this, NCDHR remarks:

> "The figures of allocation are a mute witness to the history of denial of exclusion. It is not only for the last five years; this trend is observed for the last 28 years since the inception of the special component plan in 1979-80,"
>
> About the interim budget of the UPA government in February, it observes: "Out of 75 ministries and their departments, only 16 have allocated funds under the SCP. Out of these, nine ministries have allocated token amounts below five per cent. Labour and Employment, Science and Technology, Bio-Technology, Panchayat Raj and Textiles are some of the examples," says the study.

Departments Following Guidelines

NCDHR, however, concedes that human resource development, social justice and empowerment, rural development, women and child development and health ministries did make allocations according to the Dalit population.

What is SCP

It came into being in 1979-80. Before that only Rs. 433 crore had been spent on SCs and Scheduled Tribes (STs) together in the 30 years. According to the Planning Commission guidelines, these funds cannot be diverted for any other purpose.

The ruling Congress and its UPA allies allocated Rs.15,280 crore for SCs in its interim budget in February while it should have set aside Rs. 34,413 crore for this fiscal, says NCDHR. "This is even lower than last year's allocation," points out the study.

> "While the total increase in the plan outlay is 15.74 per cent, it is unacceptable that at this critical time of financial crisis, the amount for the socially and economically vulnerable sections is drastically reduced. The amount denied is 55 per cent this year!"

Objectives of SCP

As envisaged by the Planning Commission of India, the major objectives of the SCP are:

1. Substantial reduction in poverty;

2. Creation of productive assets in favour of SCs to sustain the growth likely to accrue through development efforts;

3. Human resource development of the SCs by providing adequate educational and health service; and

4. Provision of physical and financial security against all types of exploitation and oppression.

Welfare of Dalits is Mere Lip Service

[http://www.hindustantimes.com/ StoryPage/ StoryPage. aspx?sectionName =RSSFeed- India&id= 0fd2ca1c- 1227-481d- b8bd-8544690f892 6&Headline= Welfare+of+ Dalits+is+ mere+lip+ service] An article by Vikas Pathak, *Hindustan Times,* New Delhi, July 26, 2009, 'Welfare of Dalits is mere lip service'

- 21 Dalit women are raped and 11 Dalits murdered in the country every week.
- Just 30 per cent scheduled caste households have electricity; just nine per cent get access to sanitation.
- In many hostels built by the government for the community, children don't know how milk tastes as food supplies meant for students never reach them.
- More than half of Dalit students drop out before class 8, the highest proportion in Bihar, Assam and West Bengal.
- 40 per cent of the nation's scheduled caste citizens are agricultural labourers, have no land and work for others.
- Untouchability — banned under the Constitution — is "rampant", 45 per cent of all cases coming from Andhra Pradesh alone.
- The Congress and the Bahujan Samaj Party may be wrangling over their votes in Uttar Pradesh, but the miseries of a majority of the nation's 16 crore Dalits are still not heard.
- A classified report of the Scheduled Caste Commission for 2004-05, in possession of HT, confirms this. State of Affairs
- The Scheduled Caste Commission, mandated by the Constitution to highlight Dalits' suffering, hasn't bothered to file its annual report for four years.
- The reports are a single-point source of information on the living conditions of Dalits and become public only when they are tabled in Parliament.
- In the past seven years, it has filed two reports. The last report was submitted in 2004-05.
- The 2001-02 report hasn't been tabled in Parliament, violating Article 338(6) of Constitution. To make matters worse, the Commission

mandated by the Constitution to highlight the Dalits' suffering, hasn't bothered to file its annual report for four years. In the past seven years, it has filed reports only twice.

- Before 2004-05, the last annual report submitted by the Commission was in 2001-02. This, too, is yet to be tabled in the Parliament.
- The reports are a single-point source of information on the living conditions of Dalits in the country. These become public only after they are presented before Parliament. Still, no report has been placed before the House since 2001, violating Article 338(6) of the Constitution that states:

"The President shall cause all such reports to be laid before each House of Parliament along with a memorandum explaining the action taken or proposed..."

Scheduled Castes Commission Chairman Buta Singh refused to comment on the issue without consulting relevant records.

"This shows the level of concern that governments have for Dalits. All talk of social inclusion is just that, talk," said sociologist Vivek Kumar, associate professor, Jawaharlal Nehru University, who specialises in Dalit issues.

"Ensuring that Dalits get their rights is the responsibility of the state, including the SC Commission. State governments, too, have to forward a report to the Centre under SC/ST Rules 1995. All these agencies are shirking responsibility," said Sirivella Prasad, general-secretary of National Dalit Movement for Justice.

Minister of State for Social Justice D. Napoleon told the Rajya Sabha on July 9: "The (2004-05) report of the Commission is yet to be laid in Parliament. Action taken reports from the ministries concerned on (it) have been obtained and are under compilation."

Social Justice Minister Mukul Wasnik could not be reached for comments despite several attempts made by HT.

The central bureaucracy, as was expected, has passed the buck to the states.

"The problem lies with state governments," said a senior official of the Ministry of Social Justice and Empowerment requesting anonymity, as he is not authorised to speak to the media.

"The Commission's recommendations are sent to them for responses, and they delay the process."

The last report tabled before the Parliament, recommends the creation of a Scheduled Caste Human Development Index; spending part of expenditure on the welfare of scheduled castes depending on the proportion of their population in the state and sensitising the police on laws related to Dalits.

Nehru and Caste

Secular Nehru had no Time for Caste Politics

[http://ibnlive.in.com/news/secular-nehru-had-not-time-for-caste-politics/93541-37.html] (Accessed on Saturday, February 11, 2012)

On 45th death anniversary of Jawaharlal Nehru, on May 27, 2009, Lord Meghnad Desai and Inder Malhotra participated and Kancha Ilaiah joined them later in debate on CNN-IBN.

Nehru was praised for starting in public domain heavy industries, steel mills, large dams and nuclear reactors, and his foreign policy of non-alignment. Lord Meghnad Desai lamented that Nehru brought state control over businesses.

Nehru missed Caste problem

At this point Kancha Ilaiah joined the debate. He said, "Nehru has missed out the major issue of abolishing caste and equalizing democracy on the basis of complete democratic principal of equality and liberation." He argued how caste still plays the trouble maker in Indian society today and pointed to the Punjab issue of caste wars creating strife. Nehru tried to define secularism in terms of religion without realising that secularism and democracy cannot be established unless caste is abolished in this country, as warned by Dr Ambedkar repeatedly, said Ilaiah.

Inder Malhotra, blaming partition, observed that Nehru ignored problem of caste because of refugee's problem. Whereas, Desai observed that Nehru was socially conservative his socialism was very elitist creating well paid and protected educated working class ignoring the rural poor, who suffered because of unemployment, low growth and increasing poverty. So Nehru did establish democracy but left the caste system intact.

Nehru missed Language Problem

Kancha Ilaiah also blamed Nehru for not having made English the national language of India. Malhotra lauded Nehru for making Hindi the national language in 1965. Ilaiah pointed out that Nehru scuttled E V Ramasami Periyar's efforts to make English the national language with Ambedkar joining the chorus. Malhotra, however, felt that the proposal to make English a national language was not all a practical one.

Desai pointed out that the democrat was so busy with nation building in terms of infrastructure that **he completely forgot the social reforms** side of the story. "Except for the fact that he was a democrat, there is not much we can say about him", said Desai.

Non-alignment, a Big Mistake? Foreign Policy

He did not take sides with anybody in a world frozen virtually into two hostile, fully armed, power blocks, which was a stroke of genius, Malhotra lauded. Malhotra disagreed with Desai that Nehru neglected defense but argued that his China policy was a complete failure.

Bottom line

Thus, we see Nehru ignored the good advice of Periyar and Ambedkar in matters of language and caste and only succeeded in creating a state capitalism with heavy bureaucracy with upper caste hegemony in bureaucracy and legislature, judiciary and armed forces.

• • •

2

Dalits and Dalits

Dalits are not a Single Homogeneous Caste

Dalits are a conglomeration of castes, with different names in various language regions. Their struggles for upliftment, which stated only during times of Mahatma Jotirao Phule, had not much of direct relationship between different provinces during the pre-Ambedkarite days. The different Dalit castes even within same language area had their own contradictions among themselves. It was only during Ambedkarite era that there developed good interrelationship between the Dalits of different provinces.

Cheated by Gandhi in Poona Pact

Ambedkar had to sacrifice the welfare of Depressed Classes to save life of Gandhi in his coercive fast. That is the reason why Dalits consider Gandhi as enemy number one. They say the cruelty of Hitler destroyed half a generation of Jews, but violence and cruelty of Gandhi destroyed hundreds of future generations of Dalits.

Dalits were cheated by Gandhi and his followers in Poona Pact. Osho Rajnish said about the glass of orange juice given by Rabindranath Tagore to break the coercive 'fast unto death' of M.K. Gandhi at the conclusion of Poona Pact, "**But this orange juice, this one glass of orange juice, contains millions of people's blood!**" (See Hindi book) [Bhakkar : 1994 : 43]

Inhuman Qualities of Hinduism

Graded inequality, ban on inter dining, forced endogamy, polluting touch, and restriction on occupation are enumerated as evils of Hindu caste system. These features are seen also in *avarna* castes. *Avarna* castes are no less dangerous to society than *savarna* castes. And Ambedkar's Annihilation of Castes applies equally to both.

Dalit and Harijan

It was a medieval Gujarati Brahmin saint poet, Narsi Mehta, who "invented" the name *'Harijan'* for fatherless children of *Devadasis* – the temple prostitutes. But Gandhi applied this name to SCs, knowing well the obscene meaning of the word. If it was somebody else not knowing Gujarati language, and life and literature of Narsi Mehta, there might have been some excuse. But Gandhi was well conversant with Gujarati language also knew well that Devadasis were temple prostitutes. [V. T. Rajshekhar: *Gandhi and Ambedkar*, p. 24, DSA, 1989]

Those untouchables, who understood and follow ideology of Phule, Shahu, Ambedkar and Periyar, are the **Dalits**, and those following ideology of Tilak, Gandhi and Golwalkar are **Harijans.** Dalit is one who revolts against oppression. A Dalit is not merely a SC. More one tries to depress him, more he bounces back like a football, Harijan is one who meekly surrenders and follows the BSO (Brahminic Social Order). This is how the Ambedkarites see the situation.

Recent History of Harijans

What does the history of last century prove? Were there no Harijans who submitted memoranda against Ambedkar to Simon Commission? Were there no Harijans who claimed that they did not want separate electorates? Were there no Harijans who foiled the political progress after Poona Pact in whatever little was obtained for all by Ambedkar? Were there no Harijans who opposed Ambedkar and defeated him in elections, siding with BSO? Were there no Harijans who deserted Ambedkar and opposed him on the issue of religious conversion calling it a 'political stunt'?

Poona Pact Created Chamcha Age

Our people have become subservient dummy stooges of others, popularly termed *'chamchas'*, who rush to the feet of men in power, get kicked out with complete loss of their self-respect. They can only beg for self prosperity, and do not understand that power is something that cannot be obtained by begging, begging only begets petty alms.

Even at this stage, infighting among the sub-castes is counter-productive and injurious to the interest of their own caste. It is the leaders of BSO, who make them fight by showing a carrot to the stooges. It is a post-Poona-Pact-phenomenon of proliferating *Chamchas*, big and small. The Ambedkarites have by now acquired enough knowledge and experience to identify these stooges and keep away from them. If some one likes to remind the people of this situation, let him not be labeled as selfish.

Sad Controversy

The news items of rivalry between the two different groups of Dalits, time and again, are published, especially in Andhra Pradesh. It makes one wonder whether we are dealing with an Inter-Dalit controversy, or Harijan - Dalit controversy. Even if it is the latter, it is our duty to convert the Harijans to Dalits. It should be our intention to patch up the differences and not increase the rift.

Madiga-s and Mala-s

There are contradictions among the sub-castes of Dalits in all regions. The rivalry of sub-castes Madiga-s and Mala-s among the SCs of Andhra was the worst one, even resulting in sub-caste violence. As a result they asked for separate quota within SC quota and was granted by the Governments and judiciary, but is not yet clearly marked. Some people supported and opposed this categorisation. I was among those who opposed and had rightly averred that only the enemies of SCs would rejoice the division and fragmentation of SCs.

Ambedkar's Annihilation of Castes

Dr. Ambedkar's '*Annihilation of Castes*' is as important a document as Marx's 'Communist Manifesto'. Therein Ambedkar stressed that the sanction behind the Brahminic *shastras* must end and the Bahujans must stop considering themselves as Hindus, and shall not follow the tenets of Brahminic *shastras*. He had given special emphasis on the 'Manu', and considered it to be a political book, rather than a law book, or you may call it the Constitution of Ancient and Medieval slave India. Only in Ambedkar's India a new Constitution is provided to this country.

He had specifically advocated that the process of abolition of castes must NOT start with abolition of sub-castes. He averred that if the process stops at that level, we would end up by strengthening the caste system. What applies to sub-castes equally applies to castes within the SC/ST group. Annihilation of castes was what Dr. Ambedkar wanted. It could only be achieved through social amalgamation by inter-caste marriages, and to promote that the sanction behind the Brahmin *shastras* must end. This was what was intended.

Why Uneven Development?

Why some castes among the SC/ST could not progress? This is the question one must answer with some clear vision and self-introspection. It must be agreed that, in spite of equal opportunity given by the reservations, which started at the same time for all SC/STs, the progress made by different castes among the SC/ST is not uniform. There are many reasons, which must be understood before we devise ways and means to bridge the gap of disparity among the SC/ST castes. The main point is that, Dr. Ambedkar had given a call to:

(1) Renounce traditional caste professions,

(2) Send children to school,

(3) Leave the villages and shift to cities.

Gandhi advised 'stick to ancestral works', 'scavenging is noble profession' and 'educated scavenger should scavenge better, he must earn his living by scavenging and not by learning', 'build self-sufficient villages'.

Some people followed Ambedkar and were called Dalits. Some followed Gandhi's ways and were called '*Harijan-s*'. They did not change. Those people who abandoned their ancestral callings and gave up the dirty means of livelihood, which they were ordained to follow by the Brahminical scriptures for centuries, progressed faster and those who stuck to their old professions lingered behind.

Why There is Dissatisfaction?

The main reason is that there is supposed to be a restriction imposed by judiciary to limit reservations in services and education to 50 per cent. If every one gets ones proper share in national assets and governance according to ones population, there would not have been any dissatisfaction among any groups. Artificial scarcity is created by limiting quota of reservation to fifty per cent avarna-s leaving 50 per cent for the *savarna-s*.

Under what circumstances judiciary has given this ruling and what are legal ways to counter it, must be debated by the legal luminaries from among the Bahujan-s and people should take steps legal or legislative to amend the constitution, if needed, to ensure that every caste must get their rightful share in running of government, i.e. in legislature and executive, including judiciary, as Kanshiram says "*jisaki jitani sankhyaa bhaari, usaki utani bhaagidaari*". I consider this is the **only method**, by which dissatisfaction among the various castes can be reduced. When there is enough for everybody, nobody should grumble. There is now grumbling because share of 85 per cent people is appropriated by 15 per cent.

OBCs are Misled by Savarna Forces

Reservations must be on economical grounds, say the Manuvadi-s. As everybody knows, they are the people against caste-based reservations. Unfortunate part of this is that, even the OBC people, who are co-sufferers, are brain washed to support this argument. They are made to believe that the OBCs can't get jobs and education because of SC/ST reservations. They should be explained that:

1. Even after more than sixty-five years, SC/ST strength is not complete as per their quota, and SC/ST are not the ones responsible for grabbing share of OBCs.
2. OBC's share is grabbed by those from 15 per cent, who rightfully deserve only 15 per cent and are now holding about 70 per cent of seats of power, prestige and payment.
3. It is not very difficult, even today, for *savarna-s*, to obtain a false certificate of being SC/ST by corrupt means, how much easier it would be to obtain a fake income certificate of low income for these people.

The question of enlightenment of OBCs is rather crucial. They have been brain washed by upper castes for centuries to be against Dalits. Their ignorance is phenomenal and their prejudice is outstanding. In spite of countrywide movement by BSP (Bahujan Samaj Party) for Mandal Commission, there are many among

OBCs who believe that it is something, which is meant for upliftment of Dalits alone and not of OBCs. If we succeed in convincing the OBCs that caste based reservations are good for them, most of Bahujan's problems will end and a strong Bahujan Samaj will emerge.

What is the Meaning of Unity?

There are people fighting for Dalit-Muslim-BC unity for a long time. This is same thing what Kanshiram calls 'Bahujan Samaj' taking this word from old Buddhist literature. It is simple formula of 85 per cent Bahujans versus 15 per cent *Alpjans*.

But what is the meaning of unity. When different groups live in physical proximity, and have desire in them to come closer and unite, the ultimate step is social unity where whole society becomes one and there is full harmony and rapport with matrimonial relationships between groups which were differing to each other and may even be antagonistic. This is the ideal state and should be the ultimate aim. That is 'annihilation of castes', as Dr. Ambedkar envisaged. But it could take centuries to achieve and has to pass through various stages.

Religious harmony is an earlier stage, and that also takes tremendous will power to unite and strong urge for it and is also a lengthy process.

The first stage is, of course, **political** unity, which must be achieved before there is any kind of dialogue possible within the groups. When we talk of unity, **we only mean political unity at this early stage of understanding**. If we can develop among all these groups, goodwill and friendship even on only political lines, it will be a great achievement. At the movement these groups are warring groups, there is not even a dialogue, let alone sense of common belonging.

Shyam Hotel Party Meeting

In meeting of selected workers in Hotel Shyam in Nagpur, during the days of Conversion, Ambedkar had expressed his anguish for infighting among the workers and expressed his desire to launch a party, which will have people from all castes. He asked the workers to develop readiness to work in association with other castes. Also he was in touch with Socialist leaders for a new broad based party to come. Unfortunately, the party of his vision, (RPI) could not go beyond its scope of one single caste. Even that got shattered into pieces in due course.

It was Kanshiram, who paved the way of political unity among the various groups and also started a campaign of *jati todo samaj jodo* and tried to assimilate people of different castes, an aim that was very dear to Dr. Ambedkar. He is also gone. Mayavati is trying to tread the path, paved by him. Let us wish her success.

Sub-Caste Rivalry is a Creation of BSO

It is true that inter-caste rivalry is pushing SCs to Manuvadi parties in most of the provinces. This phenomenon of dummies, i.e. *chamacha*-s is not new. It started after the Poona Pact. As a result, we find, even hundreds of MPs are insulted by refusing an interview by the President, and strange it may seem, none had guts even to protest. These dummy seats are lost to the Dalit cause. It is necessary to motivate various castes for **Separate Electorates** for SCs, rather than their fragmentation.

Problems of Reservations

The problem of political reservations, is to be considered as an integral part of Constitution making of free India. It has many problems, but not the problem of categorisation. Mr. Naik, a member of Mandal Commission had asked for dividing OBCs into two categories. But this was not agreed upon by the Commission. If it is not suitable for OBCs, there is all the more reason to discard it for SCs and STs. In the question of Reservations in the services and education, the problems, according to me, are:

1. Remove 50 per cent limit, arbitrarily fixed by judiciary.
2. Extend to all Central and State Govt. departments and semi-Govt. organisations and Public Sector Units.
3. Extend to promotions.
4. Extend to private industries.

These problems can be solved only through political power. When these problems will be solved, we, the 85 per cent people, will be in a position of being givers of reservations rather than beggars.

Reservations

The question of reservation is linked with participation in the governance of the country. Two types of reservations are in vogue. Political reservations are as per Constitution are time bound. They are being renewed every ten years. These are being demanded by the Dalit leaders to be scrapped out, but BSO is bent upon continuing them. Why? Because it gives them an opportunity to recruit the stooges who can raise their hands in support of their resolutions in Parliament and Assemblies. These seats are total loss to the Ambedkarite cause as there are no separate electorates.

The reservations in services and educational institutions are according to different Article of the Constitution, and have no time limit. There is heartache among the *savarna-s* about these, and repeated attacks made on these some times openly and many times in guise of some pretext or the other.

Schedules Made in Hurry

What is to be done? One must accept that when schedules of castes and tribes were made, to be incorporated in the constitution, there was a tremendous hurry. Many were left out and many were superfluous. This was known to the founding fathers of constitution, so an arrangement was made to review the schedule periodically. This should be taken in spirit of adjustment and not of antagonism. But at the same time we should prevent categorisation within SC/ST. This will weaken the masses and perhaps that is what the BSO wants. Dalits must not play in their hands.

Reservations Pleasing BSO

Dalits get only those reservations, which are pleasing to BSO. For decades RPI was demanding abolition of political reservations of SC/STs. But they are forced on us. Whereas nobody demanded reservations for women, but they are granted in a hurry and when some people wished to link caste based questions with it, the bill is shifted to select committee. We, thus get what is good for them, without any consideration for what we want.

Cause of Anguish

All said and done the question remains, why should some castes rely on the others for their upliftment. Visibly they see that the competitor for them in jobs etc. is a person from other sub-caste whose caste fellows are already in service. He is the only fellow from his caste but cannot be selected as he is weaker than the other competitor. Then he likes to have a reservation for his own caste. This is the scenario at the present time.

Kanshiram's Work '*Jati Todo Samaj Jodo*'

Whatever little is achieved politically in UP by Kanshiram and Mayavati is not because of strengthening of *chamar* jati, but due to cooperation of all the various small castes. They have asked to strengthen all Bahujans to come together and work for common good of all Bahujans including Dalits.

Kanshiram in post Ambedkar era gave a slogan of '*Jati Todo Samaj Jodo*'. This is happening gradually as many caste groups are talking freely of Ambedkarism and are turning gradually away from Brahminical Social Order and forming new religions like '*Shiva Dharma*' in Maharashtra and '*Ravidasia*' religion in North India. And some are actually converting to Buddhism, like Laxman Mane and his vast group of castes in Maharashtra.

Hostility of media is proof of their success. The *savarna* media – print as well as electronic – has been always opposed to the progress of Depressed Classes. Its propaganda should, therefore, be considered as mischievous and instigation for the *savanna*-s against SCs / STs.

It should be welcome that the MLAs of BSP have shown courage to append their *jati* names to their names. It is an effect of political power achieved by unity of all small castes. The very fact that Bahujans under Mayavati can organise inter-caste hockey matches shows the affinity created by Mayavati among those castes and not the rivalry. All this indicates that Kanshiram and Mayavati have asked to strengthen all Bahujans to come together and work for common good of all Bahujans including Dalits.

Mayavati and Kanshiram never worked for "separate but equal" castes. Neither Dr. Ambedkar, nor Shahu, nor Phule worked on these lines. They always worked to bring all together, demolishing walls among the castes, never ever, they advocated salvation of any individual caste or that of an individual person within a caste. A letter by Dr. Ambedkar to a Mang youth is proof thereof. (DV. June 1-15,1997)

In addition to that, I give here a direct evidence of speech of Dr. Ambedkar.

Speech of Dr. Ambedkar on inter Sub-caste Contradiction

On his way to Matang Conference, Dr. Ambedkar delivered a speech at Karkam dist. Sholapur on 31.12.1937 (published in "Janata" 8.1.38) [Ed. M.F. Ganjare, Vol. III, p. 130 ff.]

As it is in Marathi, is not well known outside Maharashtra. I translate an extract from it:

> "... First, it is a misfortune of all of us that there is no unity among the various castes such as *Mahar*, *Chambhar*, *Bhangi* etc. prevailing among the untouchables. The real reason for absence of this unity is the existence of caste distinction (*jatibhed*) in the Hindu society. *Mahar-s, Mang-s*, *Chambhar-s* or *Bhangi*-s are not responsible for this caste discrimination. Caste discrimination is the gutter of dirty water (*gataar gangaa*) coming flowing to us from above. This is the shit (*narak*) flowing towards us. And because of this, we have to face the bitter fruits and its consequences.
>
> "The painful part of it is that, Hindus, not only do not remove the caste discrimination among themselves, but on the contrary, they strive for strengthening the differences among the untouchables, taking undue advantage of their ignorance. They support *Mang-s* and raise them against *Mahar-s*; They support *Chambhar-s* and raise them against *Mahar-s* and *Mang-s*. They spread their policy of discrimination among us and thus prevent our unity. But though the original responsibility of the caste distinction is on Hindu society, for us, to forget our responsibility would be suicidal.
>
> "It is our foremost duty to remove the caste distinctions among ourselves and prevent the entry of policy of discrimination among us. Unless we achieve this, we would never prosper. We must completely abolish the ban on inter-dining and inter-marriage among the *Mahar-s* and *Mang-s* etc. If every caste sticks to its own caste for its pride, if *Mahar-s* remain *Mahar* and *Mang*-s remain *Mang*, we would not be able to fight the injustice against us.
>
> "What is there so great about the names *Mahar* and *Mang*, that you should feel proud of it? What bright history comes in front of your eyes by uttering these names, so that you should strive for preserving old traditions? All society is considering these names contemptible. Today you have no value even equal to that of garbage in the rubbish junk. So you must not have any pride for these names. You should understand that both our societies are getting crushed under one common grinding stone, and work united. Talking about *Mahar*-s, about this, they are not willing to follow any caste distinction. They are ready to have inter-dinning and intermarrying with *Mang-s, Chambhar-s* or *Bhangi-s.* And if they are hesitant, I undertake that I will compel them for it." [Ganjare, Vol. III, p. 130]

Guiding Principle for Sub-caste Unity

What should be the Governing principal? This is the main question. Without any hesitation it must be understood that the guiding principle is Ambedkarism. The leadership crisis should not crop up. Usual tendency in this country is that people follow only the leader of their own caste. We have to create a culture where person should not be important. It should be the principle. The people should be willing to vote for candidates of other castes, higher or lower, and people should be willing to follow the leadership of other caste person if he is preaching the principle of Ambedkarism. This is an essential feature of avoiding caste rivalries in the mission. All must be willing to accept *Bahujan-Vaad.* That is the need of the day. Then only you can become givers of Reservation instead of beggars of Reservations.

We can find this kind of situation in modern Uttar Pradesh. The workers of BSP, of all the different castes follow their Dalit leader and voters of BSP, vote for candidates of any caste as per orders, and the top leaders follow the principle of '*jiski jitni sankhya bhari uski utni bhagidari*' during the distribution of seats. This balance is not easy to achieve and it shows the adeptness of the leaders.

Dalit Unity is not Enough

Without in any way denigrating the efforts of those who are striving for Dalit Unity, I feel, even if all the Dalits of India, of all castes, shades and colours, unite, they cannot achieve any power without the help of other oppressed castes, as they are only about 16 per cent or so. And in the absence of power, caravan of Ambedkar will be on retrograde journey.

Cripps Mission Conspires with Savarna-s

The participation of the backward classes, the OBCs, is the backbone of the Bahujan movement. Dr. Ambedkar always had in mind such a unity. That is the reason, why he formed 'Independent Labour Party', which involved all Bahujans. But he was forced to form a caste-based party – SCF – due to BSO conspiracy.

Sir Stafford Cripps, the former Labour leader in Britain, was appointed as the leader of the house in National Government by Winston Churchill. He had earlier visited India before, in 1939, and was guest of Gandhi in Sevagram Ashram, and had good relations with Gandhi, Nehru and Jinnah. The Cripps Mission reached India 23rd of March 1942 and declared his plan on 29 March 1942. The Mission met Dr Ambedkar on 30th March 1942.

All the established leaders of the upper castes, both in Congress and Communist Party were worried that the reigns of power might go to the lower caste, led by Dr. Ambedkar, as his power was growing through the Labour movement. That is the reason why Sir Stafford having connived with the Congress and Communist leaders, during those five days, refused to recognise Dr. Ambedkar, the leader 'Independent Labour Party' as representative of the depressed classes. This was the result of conspiracy between the Congress and Communist leaders, and Sir Stafford Cripps, that took place within five days from 23rd to 29th of

March 1942. That was how Dr Ambedkar was forced to start the 'Scheduled Castes Federation' in 1942, the first resolution of the new party being of condemnation of Cripps Commission. As a result, the upper caste Leaders like Parulekar etc., left the newly formed SCF. [Chimankar : 1993 : 63 ff.]

Dominant Castes Blamed in Vain

Some people criticize those who talk of 'Unity' saying that they belong to a 'dominant caste' within SCS, and so have an unfair vested interest in 'unity'. This is rather an injustice to their efforts. The dominance, within the Dalit castes, they achieved, is not the cause of their 'Unity talks', but it is the result of it. It was because these castes followed the ideology of Phule, Shahu and Ambedkar, they got just some marginal dominance. Before that, the condition of all Dalit castes was more or less same, none was dominant and all were subservient to Brahminic Social Order.

Should we not destroy our identity?

Are various leaders ready to give up their identity on argument that Dalit liberation must get priority over all other demands? One does not have to give up ones identity, if we are talking at this stage of only political unity. But if we unite only politically at this stage, a time will come, when we have to unite religiously and socially also. At that time, I would like to ask these leaders, "Can they afford not to dissolve their identities?" If they did, their castes would be wiped out by the BSO. One has only to see the way these sub-castes are fighting among themselves just for crumbs; they have forgotten that their real enemy, BSO, is safe and secure in its own citadel.

• • •

3

Dalits and Atrocities

Khairlanji Massacres

[http://en.wikipedia.org/wiki/Kherlanji_massacre] (Accessed Feb. 11, 2012 From Wikipedia.

Khairlanji massacre refers to the 2006 lynching-style murders of a Dalit family by members of the politically dominant, but backward *Kunbi* caste in a small village Khairlanji, Bhandara district of Maharashtra, where on 29 September 2006, four members of the Dalit Bhotmange family were slaughtered.

The women of the family, mother Surekha and daughter Priyanka, were paraded naked in public, before being murdered.

Protests against the killings in the Khairlanji took place in various parts of Maharashtra, including Mumbai. The Indian media did not cover this incident until the Nagpur protests. Later it was discovered that the culprits were from the politically powerful *Kunbi* OBC caste. Initial reports suggested that the women were allegedly gang-raped before being murdered. Though CBI investigations revealed that the women were not raped. There are allegations of bribery of doctors who performed the post-mortem, and of corruption.

There were allegations that the local police shielded the alleged perpetrators in the ongoing investigation. A government report on the killings, prepared by the social justice department and YASHADA – the state academy of developmental administration, has implicated top police officers, doctors and even a BJP MLA Madhukar Kukade in an alleged cover up and hindering the investigations.

In December 2006, CBI filed a charge sheet against 11 persons under charges of murder, criminal conspiracy, unlawful assembly with deadly weapons and outraging the modesty of women.

In September 2008, six people were awarded the death sentence for the crime. However, on 14 July 2010, the Nagpur bench of the High Court commuted the death penalty awarded to the six convicted to a 25-year rigorous imprisonment jail sentence.

HC Verdict on Khairlanji: Diluting the Design Justice

[http://www.countercurrents.org/teltumbde090810.htm] (Accessed on Dec. 20, 2012) Article 'HC Verdict On Khairlanji: Diluting The Design Justice' By Anand Teltumbde, 09 August, 2010 on Countercurrents.org. The Gist:

On 14 July 2010, the justices A.P. Lavande and R.C. Chavan of the Nagpur bench of Bombay High Court commuted the death sentence of six convicts in the Khairlanji Dalit killings case to 25 years imprisonment.

The High Court did not think there was a caste angle or any planning or outraging modesty of women was involved in the crime. The whole episode reveals, in a microcosm, the character of the state vis-à-vis Dalits.

High Court did not think it was the "rarest of the rare" case and confirmed that there was neither caste angle nor any planning involved in the crime. Expectedly, it caused flutters among Dalits.

Design Justice and Stupid Us

Khairlanji, in which a Dalit mother and her daughter and two sons were lynched by the upper caste village mob to death as the culmination of a long caste conflict was initially sought to be suppressed but it burst out into a spontaneous statewide agitation. While the government came down heavily against this agitation, labeling it as *Naxal* induced, it had to invite CBI to investigate it and designate the session court at Bhandara as the 'fast track' court.

The state, however, managed not to lose its control over the outcome and appointed its prosecutor ignoring the nomination of advocate Shashi Bhushan Wahane as proposed by one organisation that played a big role in exposing the incident.

As it was churned out in legal proceedings, the fast track court, which was constituted with the premise of application of the Atrocity Act (Scheduled Caste and Scheduled Tribe (Prevention of Atrocities) Act, 1989), came to the conclusion that there was no caste angle to the crime (and hence this Act did not apply), there was no outrage of women's modesty and it was not a premeditated crime. Thus, it painted this gory atrocity as a simple crime that gets committed in a feat of rage.

The judgment was hailed as the landmark because it was for the first time that deaths were awarded in the case of caste atrocity.

Khairlanji had a heavy context of a decade long caste conflict, for anyone to see but unfortunately the prosecution failed to present it to the court. Rapes as reported by fact finding teams was out of bounds because of the lacuna in post mortem, but the women's naked corpses cried aloud that their modesty was outraged. The prosecution failed to establish what was so obvious. It also failed to show that it was planned when the villagers knew that Surekha and Priyanka had identified the assaulters of Siddharth Gajbhiye to the police. Having taken out all winds of its sails, the court still punished as many as six persons with death sentence.

Victim of the Caste of Mind

The major lacuna in the Khairlanji case is the denial that the atrocity was a caste atrocity. The argument that it was a result of revenge for being implicated in a case can be extended to virtually any and everything reducing the Atrocity Act to nonsense. How can anyone prove that a crime is committed because of caste? The Atrocity Act therefore had a simple definition of an atrocity as a crime committed by a non-SC/ST on an SC/ST person. Considered as the 'only act with teeth', it gets completely neutralised by courts getting into a question of its applicability. It becomes a cast of mind of the judges to see or not see a crime as a caste crime. If Khairlanji, a veritable text book case of a caste atrocity, could be rejected as a caste crime, it would be better if they scrap the Atrocity Act altogether and save Dalits from the false consciousness that the state is concerned for them.

Atrocity Act

Much acclaimed by the Dalits and equally hated by the non-Dalits, the Atrocity Act has been controversial right from the day it became applicable. While there is so much clamor about it completing 20 years, it is forgotten that it became applicable only after its rules were framed full six years after (in 1995) it was promulgated. Immediately, Shiv-Sena in Maharashtra, Samajwadi Party in UP and such others elsewhere raised hue and cry against it and demanded its scrapping. The rules specify an elaborate infrastructure comprising special courts, panels of advocates to be prosecutors, monitoring machinery, etc. But as it stands, nowhere its rules are fully complied with. As a result, even the prime minister had to express concern over the low conviction rate in atrocity cases, over a much-constricted base because of the reluctance to register crime under it by the police. As a matter of fact, in a factual analysis it would turn out as another ploy of the state to fool Dalits. It just seeks to see crime against SC/ST little more stringently than the IPC. One of the appeals of the CBI challenged acquittal of all the accused from various sections of the Atrocity Act, which notwithstanding the absence of serious efforts on its part, could be considered inconsequential in the face of extreme punishment of death and life imprisonment.

Khairlanji is the crime of not only the civil society but also the state. Rather one can see major role of the state actors in its making and thereafter in denying justice to the victims. The Atrocity Act significantly provides for trial and punishment of these actors. Although, all the fact finding reports highlighted the crime of the state officials in Khairlanji, this aspect remained inexplicably untouched in the prosecution case. Also, there is no attempt to challenge the acquittal of the three persons in the appeal, one of whom is said to be the close relation of a local NCP MLA.

Death as Deterrent

The death penalty appears to be the sole focus yesterday of the cause of celebration and today of despair of Dalits. Besides, the primitive notion of sadistic revenge, death penalty is mistakenly taken as deterrent. It has been an established fact that death penalty does not deter crime.

Almost all the developed countries have abolished it and have far lesser crime rates than those, which still have death penalty. The United States is one of only three industrialised democracies that still have it; the others being Japan and South Korea. However, many states in the USA do not have death penalty. It could be revealing to see the impact of the death penalty as a deterrent by comparing the crime rates in the states practicing death penalty and those who do not within the US. The data on crime rate from 1990 to 2007 show that the states without the death penalty have had consistently lower murder rates; the percentage difference being as high as 46 per cent. Morally the death penalty is just not sustainable. Death penalty in modern jurisprudence remains as an anomaly. The state just does not have authority to destroy life. If at all, only the victims of atrocity could have the moral claim to avenge the crime in a mode of war.

As an aside, it is distressing to see Dalits demanding death punishment, which empirically appears to be almost reserved for the lower castes. Some years back, a Gaya-based human rights activist and PUCL member Prabhat Kumar Shandilya had pointed out that people belonging to only Dalit and lower castes, Tribals and minorities were awarded death sentence and **no culprit of upper caste ever went to the gallows after the Independence**; with the only exception of Nathuram Godse and Narayan Apte, the killers of Mahatma Gandhi, and lastly Dhananjoy Chatterjee, who had raped and killed a 14-year-old schoolgirl in Calcutta. A veritable cent per cent reservation for the lower castes and minorities to the gallows!

State Rewards Khairlanji

The caste atrocities are no ordinary crime; they are backed by the caste ideology and culture. The committers of these crimes are charged with self-righteousness. It does need force to shake them out of their belief system. And that force could verily be the state force. It can be the real deterrent, only if the state has the will. The track record of the state, however, reassures the committers of caste crimes that could go on. Khairlanji murderers were well aware of the crime they were committing. But they were reasonably sure that they would manage to escape through the labyrinthine process of law. In fact they had almost managed the cover up at local levels which could only crack under pressure of public outrage. It is still rumoured locally that the kingpins are already out. It reveals in microcosm the character of the state vis-à-vis Dalits.

Khairlanji had history of caste conflicts. Having eliminated the only assertive family of Bhotmanges, the balance two Dalit families were further subdued. The village had become a virtual police camp. Even before the disgust of the world over the brutal murders had waned, the state government this year rewarded Khairlanji with rupee one lakh under the states's tanta-mukta abhiyan (dispute-free campaign). The meaning is clear: the state gives a damn to Dalits!

Dr. Anand Teltumbde is a writer, political analyst and civil rights activist with the Committee for the Protection of Democratic Rights, Mumbai.

YASHADA Report on Khairlanji Dalit Atrocities

[https://groups.google.com/forum/#!msg/wnta/gi0csYV08/VdVMhXCNH1kJ] (Accessed on Dec. 20, 2012), date 12/5/06

'Conspiracy of Silence'

In the report prepared by a government agency Yashwantrao Chavan Academy of Development Administration (YASHADA) that provides administrative training and also sensitises the administration on atrocity-related issues, has severely indicted senior police officials and doctors for their attempt to cover up the rape of Surekha and Priyanka Bhotmange, two of the four victims and recommended stringent action against them, including making them co-accused in the state, booking them under the Prevention of Atrocities Act and treating them on par with terrorist. Four officials have been so far suspended in the matter.

The report also points out at the lapses in the conduct of the following key officials:

1. **Pankaj Gupta.** Special Inspector General of Police, Nagpur. He accepted a bribe from interested elements for making a statement that the incident did not involve rape.

2. **Dr. Shende.** Who did the post-mortem. He did not check the possibility of a sexual attack on women victims though their bodies were found naked and did not perform the necessary tests. Blood samples were not taken in spite of a written requisition from police.

3. **Madhukar Kukade.** Local MLA. He was present during the postmortem of Priyanka Bhotmange's body. (by mentioning this the report hints at pressure from higher ups to fabricate post-mortem's findings).

4. **Dr. P. S. Pasricha.** Director General of Police. He did not visit Khairlanji even after Chief Minister Vilasrao Deshmukh and Deputy Chief Minister R.R. Patil had been there. The report says this reflects insensitivity at the top levels of the police department towards communal atrocities and sends totally wrong signals to the police machinery in the state.

The report has been prepared after interviewing 28 persons and examining the documents. The report says the medical authorities committed 'extremely serious neglect, perhaps of deliberate nature, during post-mortem of Priyanka Bhotmange's family'. The report also states that 'the district authorities such as district magistrate, superintendent of police, and civil surgeon remained aloof and indifferent throughout the sequence of events, hence allowing the crime and subsequent manipulation of evidence'.

Who Conducted the Probe?

The investigation was conducted by Ratnakar Gaikwad – Director-General of YASHADA and nodal officer, SC/ST (Prevention of Atrocities) Act 1989. The report was prepared by Dr. Babasaheb Ambedkar Research and Training Institute, Department of Social Justice (GOM) and Centre for Equity and Social Justice (CESJ) all of which are part of government.

What the Report Recommends?

1. Negligent officers, instead of being transferred/ suspended should be made co-accused. Inquiry under Prevention of Atrocities Act, 1989 should be initiated against them. They should be denied service benefits like pension and gratuity.
2. Atrocities on Dalits be viewed on par with terrorism and the accused be dealt sternly under provisions of a stringent act to control organised crime.
3. The government should conduct a survey of all the villages to find out whether untouchability is prevalent anywhere.
4. In case of reports against discrimination or atrocities in a village local level functionaries such as *talathi*, *anganwadi* worker, *gramsevak*, *police patil* etc. be suspended immediately.
5. A section on atrocities be included in the school curriculum and teachers be given special training on equity and social justice.

[Joshi Parikshit, 'Conspiracy of Silence' *Mumbai Mirror,* December 4, 2006. pp. 1 and 4.]

Dharmpuri

[http://www.indianexpress.com/news/love-and-violence-in-dharmapuri/1035856/0] (Accessed December 17, 2012), article titled '*Love and violence in Dharmapuri*', by V Shoba: dated Sun Nov 25 2012. The salient points:

When N Divya, a Vanniyar from Sellankottai village, and E Ilavarasan, from the neighbouring Dalit colony of Natham, fled due to parental opposition to get married, a caste panchayat held on the morning of November 7 by leaders from both communities ruled that the girl be returned to her family.

Distraught at her decision to stay with her husband, Divya's father, G Nagaraj, who worked at a cooperative bank, allegedly committed suicide by hanging himself.

This is said to have provoked a 1,500-strong mob to rampage through Natham and two smaller Dalit settlements, Kondampatti and Anna Nagar, where it set ablaze over 200 houses, damaged at least 50 others, and allegedly looted valuables and cash worth lakhs of rupees.

Surrounded by lush turmeric and sugarcane fields, Natham looks as if it was struck by lightning. Roofs have caved in, revealing blackened rooms with furniture and books burnt to a crisp and walls broken by long cracks. Twisted ceiling fans hang by wires, switchboards have melted and TV sets stand gutted. Broken tiles litter porches and no livestock remain in the colony. Millets, saved for next year's crop, have begun germinating in the midst of the clutter.

Police guard the road branching off the Tirupattur highway towards Natham and escort Dalit children to school in vans. With their houses gone and no land to call their own, observers estimate that it will take the people of Natham at least 20 years to regain their economic standing.

On that ruinous day, more than a thousand caste Hindus had taken to the streets, bearing Nagaraj's body, shouting war cries and felling trees to block access to the Tirupattur highway. The women and children of Natham were left to scamper across to the sugarcane plantations and the woods beyond.

Villagers say they have known about the love affair for at least a year. Ilavarasan's parents, anticipating trouble, reportedly fled the village soon after the couple eloped. "The girl's family knew too. In January, the Vanniyars beat him up and warned him to stay away. But you see, they eloped over a month before the violence. Why the sudden rage now," asks Indira, 23.

The population of Vanniyars, an intermediate caste inhabiting parts of northern Tamil Nadu, is estimated at 11-12 per cent, while the Parayars constitute about six per cent. "The Vanniyars here live in about the same economic conditions as the Dalits".

The people of Anna Nagar, a colony of about 50 houses built on government-allotted land, say the mob laid siege not just to Dalit villages, but also to their progress in society. "The men who stormed into the village shouted obscenities. One said, 'We are burning the books of your children. This should set you back by a generation'," says Santosh Kumar, whose house was among the 36 that were set ablaze. "'Today is our Deepavali,' shouted another," says Shanthi, who lost her house worth Rs. 25 lakh and 480 gm of gold.

This is the first time someone from this village of 40 houses has married outside his or her caste and the consequences have been disastrous.

Police say the couple, whose marriage seemingly angered a caste mob into vicious retaliation, is safe at an undisclosed location. As the caste war continues to rage in the minds of people, the Dalits of Natham cradle a fragile hope that one day, they won't be refugees in their own village.

Tsunduru Trial: A Glorious Chapter

[http://archive.insightyv.com/?p=517] (Accessed on Monday, January 09, 2012)

Tsunduru Trial: A Glorious Chapter in the Struggle for Dalit Empowerment and Justice.

Struggle for Dalit Empowerment and Justice

On 31st July 2007, a history was created. In a country where the conviction rate against the culprits of caste atrocities is less than two per cent, 21 caste-Hindus were sentenced to life imprisonment and 35 others given one-year rigorous imprisonment for killing Dalits in Andhra Pradesh. The sentence was delivered by the country's first ever Special Court set up under the SC/ST Prevention of Atrocities Act, 1989.

On August 6, 1991, eight Dalits were hacked to death in broad daylight, with over 400 caste-Hindus chasing them along the bund of an irrigation canal in Tsunduru village of Guntur District, Andhra Pradesh.

Unable to tolerate the spread of education and rise in the living standards among the local Dalit community, the caste-Hindus hoped to terrorize and break the growing self-confidence of the Dalit community.

The Dalit community started its historic battle to seek justice, fighting against the dominance of caste-Hindus, active connivance of the police and apathy of the local administration.

The Struggle and its Impact

Swathy Margaret and S. Jaya describe below the importance of this struggle and its impact:

Karamchedu (1985) and Tsunduru (1991) are not mere incidents of atrocities against Dalits but are significant landmarks in the history of Dalit movement in Andhra Pradesh. Both led to the articulation of a new sense of self-respect.

Dalit Mahasabha, the harbinger of Dalit movement, which was formed in the wake of Karamchedu, took up the Tsunduru incident in an exemplary manner. Under their consummate leadership, the massacred Dalits were cremated right in the middle of the village Tsunduru and the place was named Raktakshetram (The Land of Blood), a live reminder of the atrocity.

They brought together the shattered community, scattered all over the district, and sheltered them in well maintained camps for nine months, with meager resources and without any help from the state agencies.

Over the next two years, the Sabha saw to it that 450 families were given help. The Sabha ensured that the traumatised community settled back in their own village and stood on its feet again - psychologically, economically, socially and politically - to be able to continue their lives and struggle for justice, on their own. It got pucca houses, cash compensation of rupees one lakh each, some got government jobs and some got agricultural land of half acre each. Some of the young Dalit activists abandoned their education, refused marriage and dedicated themselves to the cause of Tsunduru.

Anil Kumar, a key witness to the incident, was killed in police firing when they were staging a dharna to set the law in motion. The emergence of a strong Dalit movement also led to an important change in the left politics of Andhra Pradesh.

All these developments had a bearing on the trial. The first witness was unable to give her account due to distress.

Testimony was given on 1st December, 2004, by Merukonda Subbarao, the first President of the Tsunduru Victims Association, a 56-year old daily wage-worker, identified and named 40 of the accused standing in the courtroom, from among the 183 accused and did not falter despite the judges' requests to repeat the identification. He also withstood the cross-examination by the defense counsel.

That the Tsunduru Dalits are no longer afraid to give witness, offers a just cause for celebration. They understand that it is the positioning of the court in the Dalitwada, and all that it symbolises that has made this moment possible.

Terror Khap Panchayats

Honouring Dalits with Blood

[http://www.countercurrents.org/attri110110.htm] (Accessed Feb. 05, 2012), an article by Pardeep Singh Attri, "*Honouring Dalits with Blood*", on 11 January, 2010 on www.Countercurrents.org, some details of Khap Panchayats and honour killing are seen. The gist:

'Khap' (group of 84 villages) is a system of social administration and organisation in northern India, highly influencing in Haryana, Rajasthan and western Uttar Pradesh, with sole purpose of maintaining clan / caste system alive and they have done it with perfection. They have always worked as anti-Dalit, anti-women, and anti-modernisation.

Why Dominated Landlords Are Furious

After the green revolution, in 1970s, *Jajmani* system was broken up and Dalits got liberated from bonded labours, and also prospered economically to some extent. In 1992, '73rd amendment of Indian constitution' reserved seats for Dalits in *Gram Panchayat-s*, *Panchayat Samiti-s*, *Zilla Parishad-s*, and Dalits were ready to sit beside them. The upper caste people could not tolerate this when they have been forcing Dalits to drink their urine in shoes and sleepers for years. The rise in global level education and economic opportunities for everyone, including Dalits, in Haryana, also made possible love/inter-caste/inter-community marriages.

Kangaroo Courts

'Khap Panchayats', sometimes equated with 'Kangaroo Courts', are generally against modernisation as they had temporarily banned playing cricket at many places, and the usage of DJ's in marriages giving the reason that it 'disturbs animals'. These bans were effective for few days only, but the ban on expelling Dalits from village and boycotting Dalits remains effective for life long.

They value animals more than humans. In Rajasthan, state government has established special shelters for six Lac cows under "Rajasthan GAO (cow) Seva Commission", spending Rs. 5.2485 billion.

Righteous Kill: Stark Realities

The author explains the working of these Khap Panchayats as under:

"It is estimated that every year hundreds of married couples are murdered, are asked to leave the village, are asked to break their marriages and accept each other as brother-sister, are paraded naked, and blackened their faces by their families in order to regain/retain 'family honour', on the ill-fated instructions of 'Khap Panchayat'. And mostly those suffer in these crimes are Dalits. The decisions about killing, burning homes, raping Dalit women etc. are taken by these "Khap Panchayats" collectively at the open places without any fear. It's not always the family of boy or girl (as promoted by these 'Khap Panchayat') who kills or orders to kill but the 'Khap Panchayat' members plays an active role in executing rapes, murders. If they (boy/girl) escape, their family members are being murdered/killed, gang-raped or fined heavily."

Author narrates some gory tales of their activities.

1. Jhajjar (Haryana), which is developing fast (coming NTPC thermal power plant and AIIMS-like hospital), the condition of Dalits is as miserable as was 100s years ago in the area. Social boycott of Dalits in this area is a common thing.
2. Number of cases of caste killing/honour killing are being reported from this area.
3. Recently, an upper caste girl tried to marry lower-caste boy, girl's sister was helping in this. But both the girls were found dead in next day.
4. In Dadri, district Bhiwani of Haryana caste panchayat ordered boycott the newlywed couple, ordered them to 'escape from village' and their families were fined heavily.
5. Two years back in district Kaithal (Haryana) a couple was killed and their bodies were thrown in river on the orders of these 'Caste Panchayats', in another case, a couple was killed and their dead bodies were kept in front of everyone in village so as 'everyone can learn a lesson from this'.
6. All these acts of 'Khap Panchayats' are not limited to Haryana only; you can see the impact of 'Khap Panchayats' in Uttar Pradesh, Madhya Pradesh and Punjab also.
7. Recent days in district Muzaffarpur of Uttar Pradesh a women was raped by her 'father-in-law' and 'Khap Panchayat' ordered she should accept his 'husband as a son.'
8. In another district Saharanpur, 40 years old women was paraded naked in village and 'Khap Panchayat' ordered to rape her 17 years old daughter and people acted on the same lines. Police didn't even register the case.
9. In Meerut district, almost same happened when inter-caste marriage happened.

Judicial verdicts

After two days of 'International Human Rights Day', on 12th December, 2009 while commuting death sentences of two persons involved in honour killings 'Supreme Court' accepted 'caste' as a 'stark reality' in honour killings said:

> "The 'caste' is such a concept that grips a person even before his birth and does not leave him even after his death the vicious grip of the caste, community, religion, though totally unjustified, is a stark reality."

On the same day (12th December, 2009) another landmark judgment came from Judicial Magistrate, (though after 11 years of case proceedings!) which imposed fine on 'Khap Panchayat' for issuing a '*fatwa*' excommunicating a person from the 'Khap' and calling for his social boycott. This is the first time that any court in Haryana has penalised a 'Khap Panchayat'.

In another news on 25th November, 2009 'The International Jat Intellectual Meet' calls for drive against honour killings. The author says,

> "I seriously doubt the goodwill intensions of these decisions as this can be just to show the 'world' that we are concerned about humanity, mankind while celebrating 'International Human Rights Day'."

Author laments that,

> "Nothing happens to people like Mahendra Singh Tikait, farmer leader in western Uttar Pradesh when speaking on behalf of 'Khap Panchayats' he comments like 'only whores chose their own partners.' Why no action was taken against him, who degraded the whole women society?"

Denying 'Constitution', Implementing 'Manusmriti'

Author quotes Articles 13(1), 13(2) and 13 (3a) from the Indian Constitution and comments:

> "Though everything is written so plainly in the Constitution of India about the equal rights for everyone, irrespective of religion, caste, colour, creed, etc; even today after 60 years of Independence, 'Khap Panchayat' are greatly influencing and are capable of petrifying people in the northern region. By keeping 'Khap Panchayats' alive aren't Government's trying to make Manu smile?"

On the Part of Governments and Dalits

Author laments that,

> "Much has been written and said about the issue of 'Khap Panchayats' by intellectuals and academician but there has always been a lack of any initiative to dissolve 'Khap Panchayats' or call these illegal on the part of Government. Not even a single leader has ever stood against (forget about the standing against this system, many local leaders of Congress and other parties have glorified acts of 'Khap Panchayat') this cruel system, which may be because of Government's own petty political reasons. Another thing, why all these killings are clubbed together in the list of 'murders', **if we can have separate laws for 'Sati' and 'Dowry' then why can't we have separate special laws to handle these 'Khap Panchayats'?**

Author recommends correcting the lack of representation of Dalits in police and print media, creation of strong Dalit leadership and concludes:

> "There is a strong need of active participation of everyone including NGOs, police, Panchayat bodies and serious/strong laws, (not merely paper tigers!), against the crimes of Khap Panchayat".

Author acknowledges Advocate Dr. S L Virdi, whose article on the same subject published in Punjabi magazine "*Begampura Saher*", as his source of inspiration.

Protest against Caste Discrimination in Educational Institutions

On 19th October 2012, protest meeting was organised at Jantar Mantar, New Delhi to protest against educational crimes by high ups, under Progressive Medicos Forum, and Insight Foundation. They claimed that the educational institutions have been discriminating the reserved category students. The recent example was from Vardhman Mahavir Medical College where many reserved category students were repeatedly failing for last six to seven years in the same subject but when the exam was conducted under close supervision of Delhi High Court, surprisingly, all passed!

They demanded the National Commission of Scheduled Caste and the Indian government to immediately initiate legal actions and lodge criminal case against the names listed in the report and provide justice to the students.

> "The Commission [NCSC] should initiate Legal action, including the suspension from job, permissible under the law, including the prevention of Atrocities Against the Scheduled Castes and Scheduled Tribes, 1989, against Dr. V. K. Sharma, former Principal; Dr. Shobha Das, HoD of Physiology; Dr. Jayashree Bhattachrjee, the present principal; and Dr. Raj Kapoor, Professor of Physiology and a Liaison Officer for resorting to caste based discrimination and neglecting of the duties assigned to them, not by omission, but by commission."

[Prof Mungekar Committee Report on caste discrimination in Vardhman Mahavir Medical College, Delhi, Page 18]

Honour killing: Engineering student killed by girlfriend's mother

[http://www.indianexpress.com/news/honour-killing-engineering-student-killed-by-girlfriends-mother/845939/] (Accessed March 7, 2012) A news item 'Honour killing: Engineering student killed by girlfriend's mother' from Agencies: Faridkot (Punjab), Tue Sep. 13, 2011:

In a case of honour killing, an engineering student, who was missing since last month, was allegedly killed by the mother of a girl with whom he had an affair, police said on Tuesday. Amandeep Kaur, who was arrested on Monday, during interrogation confessed to pushing Gurtej Singh into a canal as she was against her daughter's relationship with the youth, they said.

Gurtej, a student of Adesh Engineering College, had gone missing from his house on the night of August 26. His family had received ransom calls demanding rupees one crore.

The victim's father Sherjhang Singh had filed a police complaint against the girl's family, alleging that he was abducted by them as they were against the affair.

Khap Programme of Amir Khan

[http://www.indianexpress.com/news/man-who-appeared-on-aamir-khan-s-khap-show-shot-wife-says-it-s-honour-killing/1036804/0] (Accessed Nov. 27, 2012), Man who appeared on Aamir Khan's khap show shot, wife says it's honour killing.

Apurva : Bulandshahr, Tue Nov 27 2012, 02:36 hrs

It was a death foretold. Before he was gunned down in broad daylight on November 24, Abdul Hakim, 29, who had appeared on Aamir Khan's Satyamev Jayate to speak out against khap panchayats, knew of a possible plot to eliminate him. An hour after he complained to the police about it, he was shot dead.

He is survived by his pregnant wife, Mahwish, 24, and 18-month-old daughter.

> "My family did this. They have been threatening to do this since 2010, when we eloped. They said he was from a lower section of society and I could not marry him. What society orders someone's death?" said Mahwish.

After eloping in October 2010, the couple fled from their village of Adholi to Delhi, where they were provided shelter by an organisation called Love Commandos.

Sanjoy Sachdev, chairperson of Love Commandos, said he helped them appear on Satyamev Jayate. "They were a testament to the work we do, and so we forwarded their names to the show," he said.

About four months back, the couple returned from Delhi to settle down in Badhgarhi, about three kilometres from Adholi.

> "We knew something was wrong, because there were some people from Mahwish's family who were waiting by the road in front of our village. We did not want trouble so we went to the police," said Hakim's brother, Yusuf, 36.

Acting on their plea, the police detained one Haroon for questioning and summoned Hakim and his brother to the police station.

> "He and Yusuf identified Haroon and returned home. My husband had to go and get some medicines for me since I am due to give birth any day now. Five minutes after he left, a boy came running to the village and screamed that five men had grabbed Hakim," said Mahwish.

According to Yusuf, when he reached the main road, Hakim was lying in a pool of blood. "We saw men running away but could not chase them since we had to help Hakim. We rushed him to a hospital, but it was too late," said Yusuf.

In his FIR, Yusuf has named Salman Iqbal, Gullu, Malik, Asif and Sarvar. The latter two are Mahwish's relatives. "Mahwish's family, the landlords of our village of Adholi, were always against the marriage. They had even issued a fatwa for their deaths," alleged Yusuf.

But the police have denied charges of an honour killing. "So far, we believe it was a personal enmity between Hakim and Salman Iqbal. Investigations show that Hakim had misbehaved with Salman's mother on Saturday, after which Salman shot Hakim," said SSP Gulab Singh.

"This was an issue between two people from the same village, between Salman and Hakim. The couple have been living here for four months without any such incident," he said, adding that while Asif has been arrested, the others would soon be nabbed.

"Salman Iqbal and two others had threatened my husband's cousin last year, seeking our whereabouts. We had filed a case against him. On November 24, Salman warned my husband to take back the case or face death," alleged Mahwish.

Since Sunday night, Mahwish has been on TV shows, speaking to the media. "She has collapsed from exhaustion a few times but refuses to quit. She wants justice and will not stop for anything," said Yusuf.

Mahwish said the police had promised them protection. "That is why we decided to come back to the village. We had even applied for police protection but none was given. They have given us guards now, but it is too late," she said. Mahwish, wife of Abdul Hakim, who killed in an alledged honour killing at village Badhgarhi in Bulandshahr.

Amendments to Honour Killings Act 1860

[http://www.indianexpress.com/news/upa-govt-eyes-constitutional-amendment-sword-to-slay-the-honour-killings-monster/1037002/0] (Accessed Nov. 27, 2012), News item informs that 'UPA govt eyes Constitutional amendment sword to slay the 'honour killings' monster', Agencies: New Delhi/Meerut, Tue Nov 27 2012 on 'Honour killing':

The Centre today said it was seriously considering a Constitution amendment to deal with honour killings, as it sought a report from the Uttar Pradesh government on the murder of a man featured in Aamir Khan's show on the problem.

Minister of State for Home R.P.N. Singh described as "unfortunate" the suspected honour killing of 29-year-old Abdul Hakim, who was shot dead in Bulandshahr last Thursday.

Hakim (29) and his wife Mahwish had participated in the honour killing episode of Khan's show 'Satyamev Jayate' to speak against the problem. Mahwish has alleged that her family members were behind the death of her husband.

Mahwish eloped with Hakim in October 2010 after which the couple got married and were staying in Delhi following opposition from the man's family, according to police.

BSP chief Mayavati accused the Samajwadi government of mishandling the case while BJP leader Smriti Irani spoke of the deteriorating law and order situation in the state.

> "We have already asked the state government to send us details of the killing that has taken place. This is something that the Government has taken seriously. What has happened in UP is unfortunate. We are still waiting for details from the UP government," R.P.N. Singh told reporters in New Delhi.

Singh said the Government is "very seriously trying" to amend the Constitution to deal with the incidents of honour killings in the country.

"The matter is already pending with the EGoM," the Minister said, adding the panel headed by the Finance Minister is deliberating on how to bring about the amendments to the Honour Killings Act which dates back to 1860.

The police have claimed that the murder was not a case of honour killing as none of the accused named in the FIR by the deceased's brother was from Mahwish's side.

Aamir Khan termed the killing as a sad incident.

"Law alone is not sufficient to curb honour killings. What is needed is a change in the mindset of the people," the actor said in Meerut.

Recalling their interview taken at the time of the TV show, Khan said the couple had expressed apprehensions about their murder. The actor also offered to provide the tapes of the couple's interview for the show to the police for investigation.

Can Love Conquer Caste?

Violence Faced by Those Supporting Inter Caste Marriages

[http://www.washingtonpost.com/wp-dyn/content/article/2008/11/21/AR2008112103971.html?hpid=topnews] (Accessed Sunday, February 05, 2012), 'Can Love Conquer Caste?' Indian Government Supports Mixed Unions, But Couples Who Defy System Face Violence, By Emily Wax, *Washington Post Foreign Service*, Saturday, November 22, 2008.

The following is the gist of an article by Emily Wax in Washington Post Foreign Service, Saturday, November 22, 2008.

New Delhi —— She was a Anita Pharti, now 41, a gutsy Dalit student leader known for hunger strikes and provocative street theater at universities across the country, exposing the plight of India's beleaguered lower castes, fell in love in Iraq nearly 18 years ago with a Rajput youth Rajeev Singh, now 45, who He was a worldly gadfly with a passion for ending nuclear proliferation and exposing environmental crimes.

They fell in love in Iraq nearly 18 years ago while campaigning for peace before the Persian Gulf War. Their romance bloomed, and within three months they were engaged, and married a year later.

But their marriage a year later ushered in another war. In tying the knot, they openly defied India's deeply entrenched taboos against inter-caste marriage. Anita Pharti, now 42, came from the Dalit caste, still known as untouchables, the lowest in India's social order. Her husband, Rajeev Singh, 45, is a Rajput, traditionally a landholding caste that had for centuries ruled over Pharti's peasant community.

Emily Wax narrates their woes after a warry marriage:

"My family was completely aghast," Singh recalled, sitting with Pharti in their cozy living room, where they have helped clandestine inter-caste couples elope. "My father said he wouldn't let it happen. But I felt so sure about Anita. We were able to fight back. **But we were the lucky ones. Many still get murdered for this.**" [Emphasis added]

Even though Indian Constitution, by Dr. Ambedkar legalised inter-caste marriage more than 50 sixty years ago, newlyweds are still threatened by violence, most often from their families. As more young urban and small-town Indians Hindus start to rebel and choose mates outside of arranged marriages and the caste commandments, killings of inter-caste couples have increased, according to a recent study by the All India Democratic Women's Association.

The Honour Killings

In the past month, seven so-called honour killings have targeting inter-caste couples have been reported. In the latest incident, a Hindu youth in Bihar was beaten by villagers this week and thrown under an oncoming train because he sent a love letter to a girl of a different caste. The attacks continue despite decades of government decrees intended to dismantle the bulwark of caste, which is widely seen as the glue of traditional Indian society but is considered among the most corrosive features of the emerging new India.

Emily Wax narrates a statement from Shashi Kiran, a lawyer in India's Supreme Court, who married outside her caste and is handling several honour-killing cases.

> "The recent rise in violence actually shows that the younger generation – especially women – are slowly gaining individual freedom in marriage. But the older generation still clings to the old ways where marriage is still a symbol of status, not emotional love," said Shashi Kiran, a lawyer in India's Supreme Court who married outside her caste and is handling several honour-killing cases. "It shows a society still in transition and wrestling with deep change."

A controversial incentive for inter-caste couples to marry, the government recently began offering $1,000 bonuses, which is nearly a year's salary for the vast majority of Indians. Smaller cash payments first started in 2006 after a Supreme Court ruling in which judges described several high-profile honour killings as acts of "barbarism" and labeled the caste system "a curse on the nation."

The unfortunate part is that such murders and atrocities are not properly punished. This is evident from the statement of a Dalit leader Ms. Meira Kumar, the then minister for social justice and empowerment, and now the Speaker of Lok Sabha, who observed:

> "The government is again deeply concerned over the low rate of conviction and high rate of acquittal of those people involved in incidents of atrocities on people belonging to lower castes", said Meira Kumar, the minister for social justice and empowerment, who is from a lower caste. "This is not the only way to end the caste discrimination, but one has to start somewhere.""

Emily Wax praises the work of Dr. B.R. Ambedkar, the country's most famous Dalit leader and chief architect of the Indian Constitution, who called for an end to caste consciousness more than 60 years ago, and he promoted inter-caste marriage as the most practical way to blur caste lines and render them irrelevant. She describes the Indian situation in these words:

> "Despite India's egalitarian veneer, there remains an invisible separation between the country's upper and lower castes that lasts from birth to death. Meals are rarely shared between Brahmins and Dalits, the top and bottom brackets of the caste system, which also includes a constellation of in-between castes. Restaurants are often self-segregated along caste lines. Some Hindu temples are off-limits to certain lower castes. Even among minority Christians – presumably a casteless religion — some graveyards are stratified by caste.
>
> "For most Indians, opportunities in education, employment and marriage are still determined by the ancient social hierarchy of caste. Despite economic growth that has helped create a burgeoning middle class, sociologists say the caste system still represents the highest barrier to social mobility. Fewer than five per cent of India's 1.1 billion people are Brahmins, while more than 70 per cent come from lower-level castes.
>
> "Some of the most recent honour killings are being investigated in small towns outside New Delhi. Several involve runaways from different castes who were slain for eloping. This summer, a father turned himself in to police after using a knife to kill his 19-year-old daughter for marrying a Dalit factory worker.

Overseas Cases

Emily Wax describes some cases from overseas too. There have even been cases overseas. In January, Subhash Chander, 57, an Indian immigrant living in Chicago, set a fire that killed his pregnant daughter, his son-in-law and his three-year-old grandson. He told investigators that his daughter had married a man from a lower caste without permission. Similar cases have been reported in England and Australia.

Emily Wax quotes Prem Chowdhry, author of the book '*Contentious Marriages, Eloping Couples*' saying that Encouraging inter-caste marriages would break down discrimination and weave together millions of caste-segregated families, creating a new generation of "India's version of Obama", said Prem Chowdhry. A very valuable suggestion has been put forward by Ms. Chowdhry:

> "But rather than pay inter-caste couples, she believes the government should help organise a countrywide discussion on inter-caste marriages. Popular culture should be the venue, she said, with soap opera plots, Bollywood actors and famous cricket stars used to start a dialogue. Caste has to be discussed more openly in modern India. We shouldn't be so arrogant as to deny one of our main weaknesses."

"Helping inter-caste marriage take off in India would be a major attack on the caste system," Chowdhry said. "For the future of India, it could mean much more time and energy to focus on lifting the majority of the country out of poverty."

Internet matchmaking sites in India allow those searching for love to list their caste, along with skin colour and educational background. Most women still prefer to marry within their caste, according to a survey by popular online matrimony site Shaadi.com.

Emily Wax tries to find out the cause of caste rules and comes to correct conclusion, why caste rules of marriage are so rigid:

> "Some interpretations of Hindu scripture appear to support the caste system, which dovetails with the idea of *karma*, in which one's birth is either high or low as a reward or punishment for behaviour in a previous life.

She seems to be optimistic that things would improve:

> "But sociologists say ideas about ambition and social mobility in India's new economy are slowly crumbling support for the caste system. The system has also taken hits from a programme of preferences for lower-caste Indians that has started to bring members of different castes together on college campuses and at work. In addition, there is a tiny but steadily growing number of young, urban Indians who are rejecting caste-based marriages arranged by parents, opting instead to find a person they are attracted to, regardless of caste. Pharti and Singh say they worry about young couples going through the same struggles they faced. They counsel skeptical parents about their children's inter-caste unions, and they help those in hiding get married and start a home."

She further narrates:

> "When Pharti told her parents she would marry a Rajput, her Dalit family was terrified. "My family worried that I would spend a lifetime of being abused for being Dalit," she said. "And because I was educated, I wouldn't be able to bear it. Even my Dalit activist friends said, 'You are marrying a Rajput? Are your fellow Dalits not good enough for you?'"

Caste is Hindu Terrorism

There were other tensions. At their wedding, Singh's father refused to participate in the ceremony, a slight against the bride's family that still makes them bristle with anger.

"To me, caste is Hindu terrorism," said Singh, looking over at the couple's two young sons playing nearby. "We just wish for a better future for India. And that can't include such obvious discrimination."

• • •

4

Dalits and Adivasis

Condition of Adivasis is Religious Persecution

Prehistoric Period

It is held by scholars like Sankhalia, that the people of Neolithic Age understood the use of fire, made pottery, cultivated grain and domesticated animals. The potter's wheel and the art of spinning and weaving are also traced from the Neolithic period. [Mahajan, in *Ancient* India, p. 28 ff.]

Some scholars believe that present day Adivasis are the survivals of this Neolithic Age; some of the Neolithic people were driven into hills and forests by later invaders and they are at present represented by the Gonds, Bhils, Santhals, etc. and a number of superstitious along with the worship of manes and spirits and Phallus images of stone and wood and the use of amulets, beads, sacred threads, shells, stones, etc., for curing diseases and keeping away the evil spirits can be traced to the Neolithic period. [Mahajan, *Ancient India*, [p. 28 ff.]

This could possibly be true only about the Adivasis in Andaman Nicobar, but the Adivasis in schedule V and VI areas, definitely are pushed to forests by the *Dwija* Rulers during the period, which historians called 'feudalism from below' as compared to earlier period of 'feudalism from above'. After the death of Harsha in mid-seventh century, small feudal states emerged. They gave grants to Brahmins, formed *brahmadeya* villages, *agraharas* and *deva-danas*. Brahmins thus became landlords and pushed away original residents to periphery, which was big forest or river or mountain, beyond which was '*pardesh*' – the other country. [See chapter on Brahmins]

Adivasis are Post Buddhistic

The idea that present day Adivasis are the "Original inhabitants" or *Mul-Nivasi-s* and are remnants of the Neolithic Age is a popular theory of many activists. But it is far from the truth. Sociologists do not believe that the present STs are that ancient, as mentioned by Nadgonde, who avers that sociologists do not think them to be the most ancient society or the most original residents. [Nadgonde, p. 2]

At the time of rise of Buddhism, the society was so much intermixed that no trace of pure Aryans, or pure Dravidians for that matter, was left. Rhys Davids has observed:

> "It is generally admitted that there are now no pure Aryans left in India. Had the actual custom been as strict as the Brahmin theory this would not be so. ... in Northern India the ancient distinction, Aryan, Kolarian, and Dravidian, cannot, at the time of the rise of Buddhism, any longer be recognised. Long before the priestly theory of caste had been brought into any sort of working order, a fusion, sufficient at least to obliterate completely the old landmarks, was an accomplished fact; and the modern division (on caste), though race has also its share in them, use different names, and are based on different ideas. [Rhys Davids, *Buddhist India*, p. 59]

Dr. Ambedkar also has expressed the similar opinion. It follows, therefore, that the creation of STs is a post-Buddhistic phenomenon, and the present day Adivasis are descendants of population, who were called Nagas and were Buddhist by faith, and after the fall of Buddhism were degraded to the present status by the ruling priestly class because Nagas had the enmity with the Aryans, did not worship Aryan Gods, did not perform *yajnya-s* but were devotees of Arhants, and Chaityas.

Thus the condition of Adivasis is the result of religious persecution against the Buddhists. We have discussed the subject in detail elsewhere. [Jamanadas: 2004. '*Decline and Fall of Buddhism*', Bluemoon Books]

Dalits and VJNT

Woes of VJNT

The Congress and the British believed that the Tribals are too uneducated, and too uncivilised and therefore should not have the right to vote. It was Dr. Ambedkar who said, let person be uncivilised, uncultured or uneducated, he is always able to understand what is good for him and therefore the Adivasis should also be given the right to vote. This was in 1928.

Motilal Nehru Report did not even mention the Adivasis 1928 in front of Simon Commission.

In 1928 in front of Simon Commission and 1933 in front of J.H. Hutton, the Census Commissioner, it was Dr. Ambedkar who said that Adivasis should get the constitutional rights right now in this constitution only.

The condition of VJNT is much more pitiable than those of the Dalits. Their population is estimated at 120 to 150 million people. They have no house to live in. There is no school for their children. There are police after them trying to catch them labeling them as criminals. Their identity is still as the criminal caste. Many of these VJNT people are denied the rights of citizenship, because their names are not in the voters list. There are no ration cards. There are no bank accounts. Therefore, what is required is their constitutional re-settlement.

Mass Conversion to Buddhism

[http://www.hindu.com/2007/05/28/stories/2007052806851200.htm] (Accessed 8:19 AM 2/4/2012)

Online edition of India's National Newspaper, *Hindu* of Monday, May 28, 2007, narrates how One lakh Tribals and followers of Dalit writer and VJNT leader Padmashree Laxman Mane converted to Buddhism at Mahalaxmi Race Course in Mumbai, in an article by Prachi Pinglay, who describes it as "A step taken to protest against Government's apathy towards basic needs of tribal people."

Around four lakh people attended the rally organised by the Republican Party of India to declare their support for this conversion on the golden jubilee year of Babasaheb Ambedkar's conversion to Buddhism.

A majority of the people who took the "*Deeksha*" were Tribals and followers of Sahitya Akademi winner and Dalit writer Laxman Mane, who has been touring the State after himself converting to Buddhism in October 2006.

Laxman Mane said: "Thousands of people from 42 different nomadic tribes have embraced Buddhism." He said Tribals did not follow Hinduism before also. However, he said it was a step taken to protest against the apathy of the Government towards the basic needs of these people.

The Population of the VJNT

Definition of democracy given by Dr. Ambedkar are as follows: Democracy is not merely a form of government, it is primarily mode of associated living conjoined communicated experience. It is essentially on the attitude of respect and reverence towards the fellowmen. Democracy is a form of method of government, whereby revolutionary changes in the economic and social life are brought about without bloodshed.

And Adivasis nine per cent, VJNT are 12 per cent, Dalits are about 17 per cent, and OBCs are about 32 to 35 per cent. [Mankar: 2011: 76]

Banjara-s, *Pardhi-s*, *Kaikadi-s* etc. there are many communities like these among the VJNT - about 12 per cent - which are really Tribals but are not declared as such. If they are declared as Tribals, and they get the status of Scheduled Tribes, the population of the Scheduled Tribes in India will become 21 per cent as the other Adivasis are already nine per cent. These VJNT people are mostly the Tribals, but they are not so declared like that because of two reasons.

First, in the Census of 1931 done by Mr. Hutton, these people declared themselves as the Hindu. And because of this, Mr. Hutton reported these people as of 'doubtful classification'.

Second, there was one leader among the *Banjara-s* named Ramji Bhanawat. Under his leadership VJNT people came to see Dr. Ambedkar, who told him that he was going Second Round Table Conferences and demand rights for Depressed Castes. You are Tribals; if you would put forward your constitutional demands, I would get special rights for you. But these VJNT people did not agree to be classified as Adivasis. [Mankar: 2011: 65]

Some Information of Criminal Tribes

Dr. Ambedkar had condemned the Brahminic culture for creating three groups of people, SCs, STs and Criminal tribes. We know a great deal about SCs and something about STs. Here is some information of Criminal Tribes.

Social Science Center at St. Xavier College, 5, Nagarpalika Marg Mumbai, under the leadership of Father Rudy Herediya, believes in the principles of Democracy and Socialism embedded in the Constitution of India. They are working on adventurous research projects in the field of Social Sciences for Change, for the benefit of Nomadic Tribes and ex-Criminal Tribes. Working under them is Centre for Learning Resources 8, Deccan College Road, Yerwada, Pune, which prepared bilingual text books for about 60 *balvadis* – run by their sister organisation 'Lokparishad' – in the language of Adivasis - *Lamani*, *Dhangari*, *Paradhi* etc. with Marathi. They claim that teaching in mother tongue is better.

They have established a "Sonthaymar Cultural Association" and propose to set up a Museum at Jejuri to preserve the folk traditions in Maharashtra. Following history is condensed from these books, which give some historical points about the tribes like Ramoshis and Paradhis.

History of Paradhis

The Paradhi community is labeled as ex-criminal tribes on one side and is struggling to stand on its own feet on the other. The Paradhis have many sub-castes like *Fase*-Paradhi, *Gav*-Paradhi, *Berad*-Paradhi, *Gay*-Paradhi, *Chita*-Paradhi etc.

All of them were declared criminal Tribes except the *Gav*-Paradhis, who had taken to farming and settled well during British rule having a good population in Amravati District. They have given up hunting and very few have now guns. Fairly well educated, they are in Government employment in good numbers.

Their culture and civilisation is changing fast with the changing times. Their traditional apparel used to be a '*pheta'* (head dress) and '*langoti'* (loin cloth) only. But things are now changing.

They worship nature and the goddesses more than the gods. They worship '*dhani'* and '*jarane'* by sacrificing goats.

There are only three surnames among them – Chauhan, Pawar and Solanke. There is no inter-marriage within a surname. Marriage system resembles that of other castes.

Their language is akin to Hindi that is spoken in rural Gujarat and Rajasthan. They claim descent from Rana Pratap and Prithwiraj Chauhan and original home in Gujarat and Rajasthan. Their colonies are on the outskirts of towns.

The term "Adivasi" denotes their 'political and social' identity. The terms indigenous and aboriginal are used by the Imperial States to enslave whole of Africa. In India, what the British could not do, was done by Independence. In the name of 'development', Adivasis are uprooted, exploited and again 'rehabilitated'; and this is called story of success in modern India. The strong edifice of modern India has lives of millions of Adivasis trenched under its foundation.

In the definition of modern India, an Adivasi means backward, having queer traditions, illiterate and devoid of history. Some of those who made this definition take refuge by calling them '*girijan*' (dwellers of hills) or '*vanvasi*' (dwellers of forests). They are already removed from the fields of arts and literature.

Because of these misunderstandings, Adivasis are faced with the problem of Identity Crisis. The reply to this question will be given by the now awakening Adivasi through the medium language in the modern terms, but still all traditions and customs would be its inseparable part.

History of Ramoshis

In 1871 the British Government declared some tribes as "Criminal". The established society did not oppose this, contrarily they seem to have liked it. Some clauses were:

1. Permission should be obtained from police while shifting from one location to other.
2. Govt. could send the group of people outside the bounds of a certain area.
3. Govt. got the right to form a 'settlement' and keep the groups of people there.

Before the British came, what was their history? Today's Ramoshi was called Boya, Berad and Vedan. In Andhra it was called Boya and in Karnataka and Tamil Nadu it was called Berad and Bedar. Ramoshis of Maharashtra have come from mostly Karnataka and their surnames are same as Berad-Ramoshi of Karnataka. Their original language is sothern. They first got settled in Karnataka and later migrated to Maharashtra. Word 'Bhuyal' in Berad's language seems to have originated from Boya though it is known in Maharashtra as Ramoshi-Berad, the name 'Ramoshi' is not older than 100-200 years.

1. Maharashtra. Ramoshis are Berads or Boyas. Ramoshi did not originate from '*Ram-vamshi*'. It is in use only for hundred to hundred and fifty years. Before that, they were called Berad or Bedar, as mentioned during rule of Peshavas.

Nar-veer Umaji Naik, in a letter of 1828, mentions as **'Ranvasi'** addressed to Ramoshis. Those days they were staying in hills and doing the job of protection of villages and crops in fields.

2. Andhra Pradesh. Boya, Dorabiddu and Valmiki are the names in vogue. Dorabiddu means sons of *Sardars*. Boya consider themselves as sons of *Sardars* and descendents of Valmiki.

3. Tamil Nadu. Name in vogue is 'Vedan'.

4. Karnataka. Names Berad and Bedar are in vogue. Bedar was word used by Muslims either to show the dauntless quality or may be inability to pronounce properly. Muslim books use word Bedar.

Meanings of Names

The names are Berad, Bedar, Nayak, Talwar, Nayavadi, Naykar, Valmiki, Palegar etc. each having distinctive meaning.

1. Nayak and Nayakar – During Kakatiya and Vijayanagar rules in Andhra a head of a region was called Nayak, and traditional 'vatandars' were called Naykar. Akin to Deshmukh and Desais in Maharashtra, were Palegar and Naykars. Many Berads became Palegar on their own bravery. Nayak in Telgu means Owner or Head. May be this is origin of word.

2. Naykvadi – was the title of Killedar. Those protecting outer walls of forts were called Nayakvadi.

3. Talwar – was name one doing work of village watchman or revenue work. For villege policing, carrying the land revenue to treasury headquarters, the workers had to bear arms, so called Talwar meaning sword.

Religious Customs of Berad-Ramoshis

1. *Devata* and *kulswami* – Ramoshis of Maharashtra worship *Khandoba* as 'kulswami'. Also worship *Mariaai, Kalubai, Janaai, Firanjaai, Tukaai, Bhairoba* etc., and also *Yellamma.*

Berads of Karnataka worship *Mallikarjuna, Mauti, Vekatesh* as main deities and also worship *Yellamma.*

Boyas worship Tirupati Venkat Ramana, *Mariamma, Kanathrathan* etc. Most of Berads are Shaivaites. They worship Shiva and engage Jangam or Lingayat Swami for religious functions.

2. Devak (Totems) – Every *kula* has separate totem. No marriages take place within same totem though surnames may be different. They include *pan-kanis, vasan-vel, surya-ful, umbar, jambhul* etc.

3. Caste Panchayat of Berad Ramoshis – The head is called Naik in Maharashtra and well respected. Previously they dealt with all disputes. In Karnataka he is called Nayak or Kahimani and Head of Boyas is called Naidu, Doraa or Sinhasan Boya. Their word is final and punishments differed, fine, feast to excommunication.

4. Wedding / *Barase* / *Marmik* – Lingayat or Jangam is required. Sometimes Brahmin does it. Remarriages and widow marriages are allowed. Groom pays to bride's father some *teej/dej/tyaj*. There was no dowry system.

5. *Barase* and *pachavi* – Child is named on 13th day. '*ghugarya*' are distributed. On fifth day '*pachava chi puja*' is performed. This time '*satwai*' is worshiped. Child is named on twelth or twentyfirst day.

6. Funeral rites – Burial was in vogue. Somewhere they cremate. On third or seventh or 12th day they do '*mati-lotne*'. '*uttar karya vidhi*' is performed that time.

At the burial place, the stones are arranged, *gulal* is sprinkled. On third day flowers and '*naivadya*' is offered.

History of Berads

There is no written history. Scanty writings are available by others. It has to be corelated with oral traditions.

The original man was Guh. According to Rajguru of Shorapur princely state, Berads come from Tamil Nadu migrating to Karnataka during Vijaynagar rule. Names of 14 ancestors are known to him but not whereabouts. The last was '*goshti pid nayaka*', a contemporary of Shivaji Maharaj. This means the history dates back to 800 years from Shivaji's known date of 1630. Epigraphs of eighth to Eleventh century mention 'Bed-Beda'; are they for the community?

During Vijaynagar rule, these Nayak kings were assigned duty of protecting province of Tungabhadra. After the fall of Vijaynagar, the kings of Shorpur became independant. They only came under Bijapur court for name sake. But the Bijapur court was always afraid of Berad Nayak Kings.

Later, during Maratha-Moghul conflict, Nayak kings played important role. After fall of Sambhaji and migration of Rajaram to Jinji, Moghul-Maratha conflict spread from Narmada to Tamil Nadu and from east to west coast. Moghul Emperors realised they were fighting with a hurt identity in 1695. But it was not possible to turn back. During this conflict, Berad Nayaks played a delicate and important role. The families of all important Maratha sardars and their treasury was in Vagana-gera (or Wakin-kheda), the capital of these Nayak kings. Therefore, Aurangzeb had to fight his last battle of his life against Berad Nayaks of Vagana-gera during 1705-06.

Struggle against the British

Inumerable Berads sacrificed their lives in uprisings against the British. History knows very few names. The important are:

1. 1820-1831 – Umaji Naik, Bhulaji, Pandu Naik – they rovolted in Pune, Nagar, Nasik, Satara, Solapur, Kokan. Most of participants in these rebelions were Ramoshis.
2. 1817 – Gokak, Pachapur regions in Karnataka, Nayaks organised and rebelled. They were mostly Berads.
3. Revolt of Kittur Channamma and Sangoli Rayanna in Karnataka had mostly Berads.
4. 1817 – Trimbak Dengale's revolt in Pune by sardars in Peshaai - mostly had Ramoshi, Bhil, Koli etc.
5. 1857 – Uprising of Rango Bapuji in Satara, rebelled in name of Chatrapati of Satara. Centres established for recruitment where Ramoshi Koli and Mangs were in majority. Two Madane Brothers of Ramoshi-wadi (Koregaon Satara) and Nana Ramoshi of Kundal were blown by cannon. Many Ramoshis from Tasgaon in Bijapur Taluka participated.
6. 1844-50 – Tukaram and Mahankal, two sons of Umaji Naik revolted.
7. 1857 – Berads of Village Halgali Dist. Bijapur Karnataka revolted against disarming act. 19 Berads were hanged at Mudhol.
8. 1857 – Raja Venkappa Nayak of Shurpur Dist Gulbarga rebelled. He died in struggle.

9. 1870 – 1880 Rebellion of Vasudev Balwant Phadake was participated by most of Ramoshis. Head was Daulati Naik, who died in fight against Capt. Daniel in Tisubai Hills. Hari Ramoshi was hanged at Jejuri and Berads at Mudhol.
10. 1910 – Veer Sindhur Laxman rebelled against Sansthanik at Jat and British, was killed by treachery.
11. Vajya - Baijya – fought against Saranjamdar at Kukudwad Dist. Satara.
12. 1942 – 'Quit India' movement and formed '*Prati-Sarkar*' – parallel Government. Most Ramoshis of Satara, Sangli, Pune Districts participated.

This account, taken from the writings of scholars of St. Xavier's College should be enough to establish that the Adivasis, the criminal Tribes – now known as VJ-NT, i.e. '*Vimukta Jati-Nomadic Tribes*' – have nothing in common with the Hindus, were not Hindus and are not Hindus. Their leaders like Laxman Mane have realised this and converted themselves to Buddhism.

A Kumbh for Shabri

Ram Puniyani Describes First Adivasi Kumbh

Ram Puniyani, in an article in HT Mumbai, Dec.15 2005, titled '*A Kumbh for Shabri*' gives details about a new Kumbh Mela organised for Adivasis, as follows:

He describes 'a new phenomenon' is started as a social engineering to Hindutvise the Adivasis, preparing for '*Shabri Kumbh*' on Feb. 11-3, 2006.

33 km. from Dist HQ, a huge Shabri Temple has come up on the hillock, which earlier was called *Chamak Dongar*.

New bogus Mythology and archeology created

Three stones, which were earlier worshipped as *Shivar deo* (the protector of the crops), have been renamed as those where Lord Ram sat while eating the bers (wild berries) given to him by Shabri.

A small lake/pond has been spotted and has been called as being the bathing place of Shabri's guru Matang rishi.

In Tribal version of Ramayana, there is no Shabri. In New mythology Dangs is supposed to be the derivative of Dandkaranya, of the Ramayana. Nearby a place of hot springs is projected as the creation of Lord Ram, for the benefit of sage Matang.

The whole lineage has been exactly located, where was Hanuman taking bath, what was the place of his mother, Anjani Devi etc.

To shame the scientific archeology, even the marks of a place where Ram's brother Laxman sharpened his arrow has been identified and has been brought up as one of the holy places.

Puniyani observes:

'One can see clearly the manipulation of legends and distortion of local beliefs to feed in to the politics of Hindutva in the region.'

Tribal property used

The rich teak wood trees from reserved and protected forests have been cut for temple and Kumbh, and the property and thus land of the Tribals is appropriated.

Pogrom of Adivasis

Dangs had come to lime light in 1998 for the attacks on Churches and burning of Bibles beating up of the Christians on Christmas Day.

This was just two years after BJP coming to power at the centre in 1996, and one year after Swami Aseemanand began his activities for 'protection' of Hindu faith.

Total population of Christians in Dangs is just about eight thousand forming less than half per cent of the total population of Gujarat. Serious threats, however, were falsely presented of area becoming Christian.

RSS volunteers spread message that missionaries are converting by force and fraud, and the violence started, under the umbrella of BJP Government in the state as well as at the Centre.

Real Problems of Dangs

Extreme poverty and illiteracy are their urgent problems. The awareness towards the problems of land rights and traditional forest rights of tribal have created a discomfort in the section of a population of elites.

The literacy being spread by Christian missionaries is a big obstacle to the suppression of their rights by the affluent sections who are big supporters of VHP and *Hindu Jagran Manch* (HJM).

Puniyani describes the bone of contention:

"As such the basic problem has nothing to do with whether Tribals are called *Adivasis* or *Vanvasis*, whether they believe in Christianity or Hinduism, the problem comes when they want to stick to their traditional rights, when they get empowered through education, the problem comes when they are organised to get their due. And here the role of Christian missions in empowering tribal cannot be excused by RSS affiliates, and so the '*Trishul Diksha*', and so the spread of hatred against Christians as the foreigners, '*Hindu Jago Christi Bhago*' (Awake Hindus, Exit Christians).

Puniyani explains that RSS does not want to convert Adivasis to Hinduism to educate and give them better life:

"The RSS affiliates with vast human and monetary resources in their hands have no interest in going beyond cultural indoctrination and cooption of Adivasis, they essentially want to aid in the process of **suppression of Adivasi rights** by cultural manipulation."

"The spread of anti-Christian sentiments, which form the base of violence now and then, are a cover to keep the Adivasis in a state of illiteracy and destitution. While they need the basic necessities, they are getting a Kumbh."

Puniyani concludes:

"Nothing could express the agenda of Sangh better than the sight of naked, half clad emaciated Adivasi children folding their hands in greeting and shouting Jai Shri Ram to our car returning after visiting the site of the proposed Kumbh!"

Next Shabri Kumbh in 2012

[http://articles.timesofindia.indiatimes.com/2010-11-23/surat/28228508_1_shabri-kumbh-dangs-kumbh-mela] (Accessed on April 6, 2012) Yagnesh Mehta reported in TNN Nov. 23, 2010, from SUBIR (DANG) that, soon after the arrest of Swami Aseemanand in connection with a series of blasts in minority dominated areas in the country, another Kumbh Mela at Shabridham on January 13, 14 and 15, 2012 was announced, and the fund raising started, the banners announcing the fair were circulated across the Dangs, and gathering of fifty thousands was expected.

Investigating agencies probing these blasts have gathered evidences indicating that the initial discussions to trigger the explosions had taken place at Shabridham during Shabri Kumbh held from February 11 to 13, 2006, and there was alleged involvement of one of its organisers Swami Aseemanand in the blasts.

The main focus of the previous fair was so called re-conversion of the Tribals **to Hinduism**, which helped BJP to win the Dangs Assembly seat for the first time in 2007, Vijay Patel being the MLA, who got nominated as a trustee of 'Shabrimata Seva Samiti'. He told that it was decided to organise the Kumbh every six years. Patel said, "The only aim of the fair was to create awareness about development among the Tribals."

Adivasis Demand ban on Shabri Kumbh Mela

[http://www.thehindu.com/news/states/other-states/article2929496.ece Accessed on 4/6/2012]

Special Correspondent of '*The Hindu*' from Mumbai on 25th February 2012, reports that, a delegation of Adivasis from Nandurbar met President Pratibha Patil while she was on a visit there and demanded a ban on the Shabri Kumbh Mela organised in the Dangs, stating that it had no sanction in any religious text.

Kishore Dhamale of the '*Satyashodhak Grameen Kashtakari Sabha*' said the Mela was organised in 2006 by Vishwa Hindu Parishad (VHP) leader Swami Aseemanand, who was later arrested for allegedly masterminding the Malegaon blasts. It also had the backing of Gujarat Chief Minister Narendra Modi.

The Sabha organised a large gathering of Adivasis near the Gujarat border and a resolution was passed calling for a ban on the Mela since there was no historical antecedent to this kind of a religious gathering on the lines of the Kumbh Mela.

The demand for banning the Mela was also made in 2006 by the People's Union for Civil Liberties, on the ground that it could pose a threat to the environment in the forest reserves of Dangs, but the Supreme Court did not entertain the application.

This year with Aseemanand in jail, reports said the Shabri Seva Samiti, decided not to go ahead with its plans to organise the Mela in January but planned smaller meetings, and decided to host Mela in 2018.

Mr. Dhamale said the Sabha has been opposing the Shabri Kumbh Mela on the grounds that a twisted story of Shabri was being used as communal propaganda to 'Hinduize or Brahminize' Adivasis. In a memorandum submitted to the President, the Sabha also demanded that Adivasis registered as Hindus in the Census must be changed to "adi-dharma." It also demanded the implementation of the forest rights act among other things.

Next Shabri Kumbh Only in 2018

[http://www.dnaindia.com/india/report_next-shabri-kumbh-only-in-2018_1623096 Accessed 6:20 PM 10/10/2012]

DNA Correspondent from Ahmedabad, on Dec. 8, 2011, reported that the much-hyped Shabri Kumbh Mela in the Dangs is extended to 2018, and it has been toned down, apparently because of Gujarat Chief Minister Narendra Modi's image makeover exercise known as '*Sadbhavna Mission*.' Samiti members, however, claimed that as per Hindu traditions a Kumbh Mela could be organised only after 12 years.

However, the change in the plans comes when the Samiti had been preparing for the Mela for nearly two years. The report further says:

"The move is a political decision. If Kumbh Mela happens the way it did in 2006, it will definitely attract similar attention from world over. The sole purpose behind organising the event was to keep Christian Missionaries away. If the Mela happens again, it is bound to become a political issue," said a source in Dangs, who wished not to be identified.

He added that if Mela is organised in such a grand scale as it was done in 2006, Modi's image makeover campaign 'Sadbhavna Mission' will go for a toss.

Recent News

[http://www.financialexpress.com/news/tribals-being-instigated-in-the-dangs-cop/1038891/0] (Accessed Dec. 14, 2012)

A Story, '*Tribals being instigated in the Dangs*', by Satish Jha from The Dangs, Dec. 01 2012, 04:01 IST, reads:

The Dangs: The police observer of tribal dominated the Dangs district has sent a report to the Election Commission claiming that Tribals are being instigated by Hindu fanatics in the region. Amitabh Kumar Das, the Bihar cadre IPS officer, has named Gujarat Chief Minister Narendra Modi in the report while saying that "constant vigil is required, though the region is peaceful".

In his November 26 report, Das has said, "The Dangs is a district heavily dominated by Tribals. These poor Tribals are instigated by the Hindu fanatics. They are encouraged by Gujarat Chief Minister Narendra Modi."

The letter has been marked to Vinod Zutshi, Deputy Election Commission in-charge of the Gujarat polls. It has also been marked to Chief Election Officer, Gujarat, Anita Karwal.

"During Modi's regime, the Sabri Kumbh was started to misguide local Tribals. The brain behind the Sabri Kumbh, Swami Aseemanand, is at present in jail in connection with the Malegaon bomb blast. At present, the situation is completely peaceful. But constant vigil is called for," Das says in the report.

Phone calls and SMSes to Karwal remained unanswered. But sources said Das's report has already created a stir and officials are tightlipped about it as it poses serious ramifications.

Das's report is largely based on the exercise of Sabri Kumbh organised in 2006, that was said to be a re-conversion exercise of Tribals from Christianity that became a major controversy.

The second edition of Sabri Kumbh was supposed to be held this January, which was called off. The reason is attributed to Modi's "*Sadbhavna*" fast here where religious leaders of all community had descended.

Das on Friday also accused Bihar's ruling alliance partner BJP of "pressurizing" him by slashing his increment for two years for "not supervising a 2001 postal securities theft case and being indifferent towards his discharge of his duties as Patna railway SP".

Das, who is posted at railways superintendent of police at Jamalpur, told *The Indian Express* from the Dangs: "One can see the very timing of action against me in the old postal securities theft case. I am not getting cowed down by the Bihar government. ... I am going to complain to the EC and seek justice."

He, however, said it would not be proper for him to discuss his report from the Dangs to EC in public domain.

Das had also stirred a controversy in 2007 Gujarat Assembly polls as a police observer. He had sent a similar report claiming, "There was fear among the minority because of communal agenda of Modi".

Earlier this year, Das won a major fight with the Bihar government after CAT directed the state government to promote him to the DIG rank. Das had approached the tribunal seeking promotion since all his batch-mates were promoted in 2009. — With ENS, Patna

Ambedkarism only Solution for Adivasis

Population of Adivasis of India

Right from Dangs from Gujarat to 24 Parganas of Bengal, going through Maharashtra, Madhya Pradesh, Chattisgarh, Andhra Pradesh, and Orissa is a belt of indigenous people of India. In this belt, live the 70 per cent of the population of Adivasis.

This is the great belt of Adivasis, who are sitting on the 70 per cent mineral wealth of India. It is not properly realised that there is no country in the world with so much population of Adivasis. According to 2001 census, 8.08 per cent was the percentage of Adivasis in India. There might be more Adivasis in Africa as the continent, but as a country India has got the greatest number of Adivasis.

Adivasi is an International Problem

It must be realised that the problem of Adivasi-s is not only the national problem, but it is the international problem. In 1957 International Labour Organisation of the United Nations, in 107th Convention, the Govt. of India had accepted that the Adivasis of India are the Indigenous people. In spite of this, in 1987, in the 169th convention of the International Labour Organisation, Govt. of India refused to accept that there are any indigenous people in the country. It was in 1989, under the Prime Ministership of Rajeev Gandhi that the Govt. of India denied the fact, in the United Nations, that India has got any population of 'Indigenous People'. And in 2001 the issue was raised by the Dalits in the United Nations Conference at Durban that the Dalits, OBCs, and the Adivasis are facing discrimination on caste lines in India.

Adivasis in Durban Conference

[http://www.ambedkar.org/bamcef/journal/march02/madavispeech.html] (Accessed Oct. 10, 2012) describes '**Awakening session no. 2**'

Mr. L.K. Madavi, a social Tribal activist from Chandrapur District of Maharashtra thanked 'Dr. Ambedkar Centre, Justice and Peace' and its head, Mr. Warhade, for his sponsorship to Durban Conference. His critical analysis was:

> **The discrimination based on Casteism was replaced with discrimination on the basis of work and decent is the failure of our people who represented at the Durban Conference.**

In India, Madavi observes, the Aryan-Brahmins are dominating as the whites are dominating in foreign countries. This is also a sort of racial discrimination. Both Dalits and Blacks suffer discrimination in employment, services and justice.

Explaining attitude of Indian rulers towards the problem of caste discrimination against SC/ST people, Madavi said that right from 1965 to 1999, the Indian Govt. was accepting in various International conferences the fact that the caste discrimination does exist in India. However, they also make false claim that due to the inter-caste marriages in 1997 the racial groups were demolished. He lamented that the 1993-year was celebrated in India as cultural year, though the entire world celebrated it as world indigenous year. Also now these people are saying at United States that there are no indigenous people residing here.

Almost 250 million Tribals are struggling in India for their existence and are facing the slavery under caste system, Madavi said. In the name of god, the girls of Indigenous people are sexually exploited by calling them as *Devadasis*. Crores of people are facing the problem of starvation and malnutrition.

Madavi stressed that there are 41 ST MPs in the Parliament out of total 119 SC/ST, and many MLAs but none raise any question of atrocities on SC/STs and non-implementation of Reservations either in Parliament or in Assemblies. That the common man's representatives could not speak out in the Durban conference is the failure of the representatives who attended the conference, he said.

He lamented that the Durban conference ended without any decision. On seventh Dec. America walked out of the Hall. In the Para 73 the discrimination on the basis of casteism was replaced with discrimination on the basis of work and decent is the failure of our people.

Role of Jaipal Singh in Constitution Making

It was the view of Ambedkar, as is well known, that the Constitution, how so ever good, does not work by itself; it needs people to work it. If the people who work the Constitution failed to do their job, it is not defect of the Constitution.

In spite of the various constitutional provisions for the Adivasis, it is unfortunate that these provisions are not properly implemented. And all the rights of Adivasis are taken away during the implementation of the programmes for their welfare.

The great leader of Adivasi-s in the Constitution Assembly was one Jaipal Singh. Also there was a Gandhi disciple Thakkar Bappa.

It was Jaipal Singh, a Munda leader from Jharkhand area, who said in the Constitution Assembly, that:

(i) We are the first inhabitants people of India.

(ii) We are not Hindus.

(iii) Adivasi has got its own culture, a different culture, and a different religion. If somebody like Hindu Mahasabha tries to make us Hindus, it means they are destroying our culture, and are conspiring to decrease our population.

The masses are led to be confused, that Ambedkar gave more facilities to only the Dalits, as Scheduled Castes, but not to the others. This is utterly untrue. Dr. Ambedkar has actually given more rights to the Scheduled Tribes than the Scheduled Castes, who got only reservations in education and services. This reservation has no time limit, only the political reservation has got the limit of ten years. OBCs also have got the similar reservations, but Scheduled Tribes, that is, Adivasis got more benefits than all the others. That is **the Right of Self-governance and Right of Ownership**. The land of Adivasis cannot be given to the non-Adivasis. This is the right of ownership of land. There is a lot of mineral wealth in this land, it cannot be given to others, without the permission of the Adivasi *Panchayats* and village councils of the Adivasis. The Rights of Self-governance are also given, and the expenditure from the budget allocation is to be controlled by the Adivasis themselves.

In the sixth schedule, the right of ownership goes even further and that is, **even the government cannot remove the mineral wealth without the permission of the village councils of the Adivasis, and it cannot be removed without paying the royalty**.

Dr. Ambedkar also made provision for the Adivasis that budgetary provision must be made providing a particular percentage for the benefit of Adivasi, and this money cannot be used for any other purpose.

Religion of Adivasis

We discussed, elsewhere, that Adivasis belonged to the religion of the Buddha. This is not only because the religion of the Buddha was basically a tribal religion of *Sakya-s* and *Koli-s,* but also in the later times the Adivasis prayed the Buddhist gods and goddesses. We have shown that Pandharpr, Shri Shailam, Jagannath Puri etc. are the old Buddhist shrines and the Adivasi people were devotees of the Buddhist deities. For example, original Devotees of Shri Pandharpur in Maharashtra were Adivasi *Dhangar-s*. Original Devotees of Shri Shailam in Andhra were Adivasi *Chenchu-s*. Original Devotees of Jagannath Puri were Adivasi *Savar-s*.

Nagendra Nath Basu has shown that there existed a form of Buddhism in tribal areas of Orissa during the Muslim rule and he found the remnants in 19th century. [See my books - '*Tirupati Balaji was a Buddhist Shrine*' and '*Decline and Fall of Buddhism*']

Eligible for Historical Compensation

Though the population of Adivasi's India is the greater than any other country in the world, there are indigenous people in other countries also. And there is the discrimination based on ethnicity in those countries. In India it is the problem of caste. In other countries, the problem is of ethnicity. In many countries, the movements of indigenous people, has borne success. In Mexico, Zapatista moment became successful. In Malaysia, moment of the sons of soil became successful. In America, Red Indians got the special rights. So we find that in many countries, the indigenous people of those countries got some kind of special rights.

This is clearly fit case for historical compensation; this theory says that to give economic compensation was the least that could be done for period of discrimination. This was given in Mexico and South Africa and Malaysia. In South Africa, under the constitution made by Mandela, the lands belonging to the Africans, which were captured by the whites were returned back to them or compensated by the market rates. In Malaysia, 30 per cent of land was reserved for the Indigenous people, and they got the right up 30 per cent of shares in the companys working on their lands. These rights they got under the international law. Some such similar thing also could happen in India. It is the contention of the present author that, the movement of the Adivasis if conducted properly by the leaders, there is no reason why the Adivasis of India will not get special privileges, like in other countries.

Destroying Adivasi Culture

They are destroying the Adivasi culture, and they are depriving the Adivasis from territorial position. An Adivasi becomes a non-Adivasi when he starts calling himself a Hindu. Many have fallen prey to Brahminic brain-washing and started inviting Brahmins in their marriages and many started worshiping the Hindu gods and goddesses. Gandhi never wanted to give any political rights to the Adivasis. It was Gandhi who had given the idea of changing the culture of Adivasis, and making them Hindus, through Thakkar Bappa. He knew that when they once become Hindus they couldn't claim separate rights. He started calling them as *Girijans*, meaning the residents of the mountains. The RSS developed the idea further and started calling them '*Vanavasi*', meaning residents of the forests. Example of Dangs is illuminating. [*Supra*]

But Dr. Ambedkar has given them not only the rights of culture of but also the rights of territory, in the Indian Constitution. That is the reason why the present rulers of the country are finding it very difficult to whisk them away from their lands, from their forests, from their waters, and from their possessions. And then the rulers now found a way of declaring them as Naxals and killing them, labelling them as terrorists. The Adivasi leaders like L.K. Madavi, in his *PATANA*, has rightly observed that those who were getting killed, as well as the police who kill them are both Adivasis. [www.ambedkar.org/jamanadas]

That is also the reason, they are bringing new laws in the form of SEZs. They even do not wish to give 26 per cent of the value of mineral wealth to the Adivasis. The day the Indian Constitution gets implemented fully, the Adivasis would be the richest people in the country.

Adivasis will also Join Hands with Ambedkarites

That the Adivasis were the Nagas and Buddhists is being realised these days by them and prominent Adivasi writers like Late Vyankatesh Atram have claimed that Buddha was an Adivasi. Another Adivasi scholar L.K. Madavi, who joined hands with Ambedkarites in WCAR, claims that "Gotam" which means a "bull" was the totem of Republic of Sakyas. All these people are in favour of Buddhism.

Nagendranath Basu has investigated the forest areas of Mayurbhanj in Orissa and discovered the people there, being Buddhists. Dr. Haraprasad Shastri, writing in 1911 in his Introduction to this book of Shri Nagendranath Basu, found out some groups in modern population, who were originally Buddhists. He mentions among them the followers of Goraksha Nath, Dharmaghadiya Yogis, many Guptas, Baidyas, Kars, Goldsmiths, Carpenters and Painters, Business class of Bengal, most of the Kayasthas, Sonar Baniyas, Vaishnava Sahajiyas. [Basu Nagendranath, *bhakti margi baudha dharma*, (hindi), Allahabad. p. 12]

These Adivasis were once civilised people and were Naga kings ["*Untouchables*" by Ambedkar], but are now deprived of education, status and condemned to the forests and hills for centuries, after fall of Buddhism. [See my "*Decline and Fall of Buddhism*"]

After Independence, they are deprived even of their forest lands, and they are displaced in the name of development, dams, projects and **even for housing of birds and animals**, never to be rehabilitated properly. Poor, destitute, uneducated, malnourished, they die in thousands each year of starvation. They are also now awakening and understanding Ambedkarism.

Ambedkar's efforts for Adivasis are being realised by them these days as they did participate in WCAR siding with the Dalit Organisations' demand of including Caste in Agenda, though many are still under the spell of RSS run *Vanvasi Kalyan* schemes. All these people are now realising that Dr. Ambedkar had strived for upliftment of BCs and Adivasis. The purpose of keeping Adivasis in sub-clause (2) of Hindu Code Bill was to make some provision for them and Hindu Law would "apply to them only if it is proved that Hindu customs and Hindu usages are prevalent in that class", and it will not apply to them unless "they have adopted the customs." [W&S, Vol. 14 part 2, pp. 886-7]

They are now realising that Ambedkar asked for right of Adult franchise for Adivasis, in 1928, Simon Commission Statement, commenting that Legislatures are the places where "social battles have to be fought, privileges have to be destroyed, and rights have to be won". He averred that their illiteracy should not come in way of giving them right to vote, as even an illiterate is intelligent and knows his welfare. [W&S, Vol. 2, p. 471]

Adivasis now know that disagreeing with the Britishers' idea of keeping the Adivasis segregated, during the evidence taken before the Joint Committee on Indian Constitutional Reforms in 1933, Ambedkar professed that these people should not remain primitive, should cease to be an isolated part of humanity and take part in the public affairs of this country like others. That they must not loose their lands and their lands be protected from money-lenders by suitable Laws. The education is more necessary for BCs and Adivasis, more than anybody else, he said, and wanted adequate representation for them in legislatures assuring the friendship of many BCs. [W&S, Vol. 2, p. 737 ff.]

• • •

5

Dalits and Muslims

Brahmins were Benefited by Muslim Conquest

Muslim Period–was it a Foreign Rule Over Indian Masses?

There is a lot of propaganda that Muslim period was a foreign rule over Indian masses, which were crushed under the foreign yoke. All this is a great and fake hate propaganda by the brahmanical scholars done with the intention of creation of hate towards the present day Muslims. Actually, it was this class who got the maximum benefits of Muslim Raj.

Here we have to remember that India has triple governance. Governance at the village and town level at the bottom, second is regional level and top most is national level. The local level governance is the actual governance. In India it makes no difference, who ruled at the top, at the local levels it was the Brahmins who always ruled. And their rule was as per the Laws of Caste. Swami Dharma Teertha observes:

> "The disappearance of Buddhism and the passing of political power into the hands of the Mohammedans, though they meant the extermination of national life, was a triumph for Brahmanism. ... in the period of national prostration and political chaos roughly from the eight to the twelfth century after Christ, there is a phenomenal revival, expansion and consolidation of the theocratic domination of the Brahmans. One prominent result of the invasion of India by the Mohammedans was that, so far as Hindu society was concerned, Brahmans became its undisputed leaders and lawgivers.
>
> "After the overthrow of the Hindu princes by the Mohammedans, the Hindu princes and chiefs lost a good deal of their prestige, but the leadership of the Hindus instead of passing into the new political authority, namely Mohammedan rulers, passed almost entirely to the Brahmans." [Kelkar S. V., '*An Essay on Hinduism*', p. 149]
>
> "There were no powerful Indian rulers to question their right to decide what should be or should not be the religion of the people, and by what principles their social life should be governed. When the Mohammedans had overcome

all opposition and settled down as rulers, unless some of them were fanatically inclined to make forcible conversions, they left the Hindus in the hands of their religious leaders and whenever they wanted to pacify them by quiet methods, they made use of Brahmans as their accredited representatives.

"Another great advantage was that, for the first time in history, all the peoples of India, of all sects and denominations, were brought under the supremacy of the Brahmans. Till then they had claimed to be priest of the three higher castes only and did not presume to speak for the Shudras and other Indian peoples except to keep them at a safe distance. The Mohammedans called all the non-Muslims inhabitants, without any discrimination, by the common name "Hindu", which practically meant non-Muslims and nothing more. This simple fact contributed to the unification of India more than any other single event, but also, at the same time, condemned the dumb millions of the country to perpetual subjection to their priestly exploiters. Indians became "Hindus," their religion became Hinduism and Brahmans their masters.

"The word Hindu itself is a foreign one. The Hindus never used it in any Sanskrit writing, that is those which were written before the Mohammedan invasion." [*An Essay on Hinduism,* p. 22, by Kelkar]

"When the Mohammedans came they called all people who were in India, but who did not belong to Mohammedan religion, Hindus.... All castes and creeds which did not acknowledge Mohammedan religion were Hindus." [*An Essay on Hinduism*, p. 29, by Kelkar.]

"Thus was the Indian people by an innocent accident of history, permanently subjected to a disastrous social and religious in the shaping of which they had no hand and could thereafter obtain no voice, but were entirely at the mercy of the Brahmans. Brahmanism became Hinduism, that is the religion of all who were not followers of the prophet of Mecca. Fortified thus in an unassailable position of sole religious authority, Brahmans commenced to establish their theocratic overlordship of all India." [Swami Dharma Teertha, pp. 123 ff.]

What did the Brahmins do first?

Swami Dharma Teertha explains the activities of Brahmins after they captured the power. It was creation of *shastras* to suit newer conditions. He observes:

"One of the first signs of Brahmanical revival, as in the past, was the promulgation of new *Shastras*, *Puranas* and other religious literature alleged to be the works of ancient sages. The priests must have been conscious of the untenability of their doctrines and their own unworthiness to lay down rules for the good of society, for **they wrote new works in the name of ancient authors and altered ancient works to suit their present contentions.** There is hardly any Sanskrit composition, which has not been tampered with, altered or added to by them. There is no famous Rishi or teacher in whose name they have not concocted scriptures. There is no sacred book into which fiction and legend and imaginary history have not been interpolated. The most ancient of scriptures, the Rig-Veda, has not escaped the profane hand of interpolators and its tenth book is wholly ascribed to gods as if to conceal their true origin and later authorship. Veracity as to facts was never a feature of Brahman authors, so much so that historical unreliability has become a universal literary characteristics of the Sanskrit language. The best critic would be unable to separate the grain from the chaff, to say where facts end and fiction begins. This is even more the case in regard to the so-called sacred literature. The period of brahmanical revival naturally abounds in such fraudulent Shastras and Puranas." [Dharma Teertha, p. 124 ff.]

Thus we see the Muslim Rule was also a Brahminic rule as far as the masses were concerned. Except for a small period of Akbar's rule, the masses suffered Brahmin tyranny in addition to Muslim fanaticism in between, till the British came to the rescue of common man. But even in British Raj, the masses could not escape tyranny of Brahmins, which continues till this date. All these are the ill effects of fall of Buddhism from ancient India.

Kashmir Problem from Ambedkarite Perspective

Region and the People

The state of Jammu and Kashmir has Muslim, Hindu and Buddhist population, mostly concentrated in valley, Jammu and Laddhak respectively. It is strategically situated with Tibet to east, China in northeast, Afghanistan to north-west, and Gilgit had become part of the State.

Most of the traffic was by land roads to the state and all the supplies were coming to state through the areas now gone to Pakistan, and the travel to state from Indian side was nonexistent. There was no communication by road from India to J & K till the declaration of Radcliff Award.

Maharaja Hari Singh was the ruler and Ramchandra Kak was the Prime Minister. Maj Gen Janak Singh replaced him before 15th August 1947. Later Mr. Justeice Meher Chand Mahajan replaced him. Hari Singh was considered to be a castiest ruler. He was not only against the Muslims but also against the Pundits. The Rajputs enjoyed 60 per cent seats in services, Muslims had no equal opportunity in trade and industry, outsider Hindus were welcome and out of 25 'jagirs' only two were of Muslims. [EPW 21.12.1991 q/b Dahat]

There was one political party under popular leader Sheikh Abdullah, the "National Conference", which was agitating for freedom and was more or less a counterpart of Indian National Congress. Maharaja thought majority Muslims will ruin his kingdom and Dogra Army could save that. Maharaja and Jinnah tried to curb the party.

After plan of leaving India was announced on June 3rd, 1947, Lord Mountbatten visited Kashmir and told Maharaja that British Government will not recognise J & K as a dominion state and he should better join any dominion -

India or Pakistan - before 15th August 1947. But J & K Government announced its decision to enter "Stand Still" Agreement with both India and Pakistan.

Even after signing the agreement, Pakistan cut of supplies of food, petrol and other essentials to J & K, and put pressure on J & K to accede to Pakistan.

Pak Aggression

The new Prime Minister (of Kashmir), on 15th October 47, complained to the British Prime Minister that Pakistan broke Stand Still Agreement and stopped supplies and stopped Railway service from Sialkot to Jammu, and requested him to advise Pakistan to deal fairly with J & K and stop raids on the border. There was also protest to Governor General Jinnah.

On 22nd October, all out invasion of J & K started, along Jehlam Valley road through N.W. Frontier Province, the raiders being tribesmen led by regular Pak officers. All Muslim forces in Muzafarabad deserted and joined the aggressors as advanced guard.

Brig. Rajender Singh could gather about 150 soldiers to fight against the raiders but he and all soldiers were killed. On 24th Oct., the raiders captured the Mahura powerhouse, supplying electricity to Shrinagar. Shrinagar was immersed in darkness. Raiders declared they would capture Shrinagar by 26th October 47.

How Kashmir was accessed

Government of J&K approached Government of India for military help on 24th October. New Prime Minister Mahajan reached Delhi on 25th October. GOI did nothing except sending V.P. Menon to Shrinagar. Both Mahajan and Menon went to Shrinagar. Maharaja was sent to Jammu for safety, and both came to aerodrome and in the morning reached Delhi.

Nehru was requested to send troops. Mahajan said, "Give army, take accession and give whatever powers you want to the popular party, but the army must fly to Shrinagar this evening, otherwise I will go and negotiate terms with Mr. Jinnah, as the city must be saved".

On this Nehru flew into rage and asked Mahajan to go away. Sheikh Abdullah, who was over hearing the conversation, sent a slip of paper to Nehru, which completely changed Nehru's attitude. Sheikh Abdullah wanted power in his hands and Maharaja to be only a constitutional head.

Accession agreed to

Indian Cabinet agreed to the accession and to send army. V.P. Menon and Mahajan again went to Jammu. Menon flew back with 'Instrument of Accession' signed by the Maharaja. After a long discussion in Defence Committee, it was decided to accept the Accession subject to proviso that "a plebiscite will be held in the State when the law and order situation allowed".

Dr. Ambedkar advised to send Mahar battalion, and also explained that guerrilla tactics to be applied. In early hours of 27th October, more than one hundred planes - civilian as well as RIAF - carried the soldiers with requirements.

Jinnah got furious and ordered General Gracy, the acting C in C of Pak Army to send Pak troops. But the General refused saying he required orders from Field Marshal Auchinleck, who flew next day to Lahore and explained to Jinnah that in the event of war breaking out, the British Officers in Pak Army would be withdrawn.

On 1st November 1947, Governor General Lord Mountbatten flew to Lahore, and suggested to Jinnah that the plebiscite should be under UN, but Jinnah pressed for it to be under joint control of Governor-Generals of both India and Pak.

On 4th November, Prime Minister of Pakistan, Liyakat Ali Khan announced the accession to India to be a Fraud.

Military Operations

Military operations were under Major General Kalwant Singh. The Mahar Battalions were employed as advised by Dr. Ambedkar. Their stay was for 18 months. Their work was highly appreciated. They stopped the aggression and repealed the enemy with great valor.

It was exclaimed that if they were allowed to fight fully, there would have been no POK.

Heroism in Kashmir

The *Times of India* 26.10.52 praised the valor of Mahar battalion in the following terms:

> "In Kashmir War in December, 1947, a battalion of the Mahar Regiment earned undying fame by its bravery and devotion to duty. The part, which this battalion played in the battle of Jhangar, will be written in the golden letters in the history of Indian Army.
>
> "On December 24th, 1947, enemy numbering between four to six thousand attacked our position near Jhangar, the attack being preceded by heavy mortar and small arms fire. It looked as if nothing could stop the onslaught of the tribesmen but the Mahars held their posts which matchless courage. In the hundreds of tribesmen were moved own by the devastating fire of the Mahar Machine gunners who when their ammunition was exhausted, fought the enemy in a hand to hand battle. The bravery of this battalion was recognised by the award of one Mahaveer Chakra and five Veer-Chakras to its men. Their matchless courage and devotion to duty played a most important part in turning the tide of the battle at a critical moment."

On the departure of these brave soldiers – without any break for 18 months – General Thimmaya, in his address to them, praised their work in high esteem saying, they "on all occasions behaved with highest sense of gallantry courage and endurance." And observed, "the name of your battalion will resound through the hills and the valleys for a long time to come."

United Nations and Cease Fire

The case was taken to United Nations on the persuasion of Lord Mountbatten, on 25th January 1948. This was against the advice given by Dr. Ambedkar to Nehru. Ambedkar desired that the aggressors must be evicted by force, but Nehru did not agree.

Pakistan denied any hand in the aggression. India maintained her position that legally Kashmir is part of India. Dr. Ambedkar had warned that this problem will not be solved by the United Nations, but it will become more complicated.

Ultimately, a Cease-Fire was ordered from 1st of January 1949.

Ambedkar's Solution to Kashmir Problem

Ambedkar talked on Kashmir problem on many occasions. On 10th October 1951, Ambedkar in a statement of Resignation from the Cabinet, showed his not merely dissatisfaction "but actual anxiety and even worry" about the foreign policy of India.

He said that, every country in the world was our friend in 1947 and today, after four years, all our friends have deserted us, and there is no one even to second our resolutions in the U.N.O. Reminding words of Bismark that, 'Politics is the game of the possible', and of Bernard Shaw that, 'good ideals are good but one must not forget that it is often dangerous to be too good', he criticized that India's foreign policy is in complete opposition to these words of wisdom uttered by two of the world's greatest men.

He termed it 'dangerous' and explained, the great drain on our resources made by our military expenditure, as **out of Rs. 350 crores of revenue we raise annually, we spend about Rs. 180 crores on the Army.** It is a colossal expenditure that has hardly any parallel. This colossal expenditure is the direct result of our foreign policy.

He said that our quarrel with Pakistan is on two grounds, one is Kashmir and the other is the condition of our people in East Bengal. We should be more deeply concerned with East Bengal.

Even about Kashmir, the issue on which we are fighting, who is in the right and who is in the wrong. The real issue to my mind, he said, is not who is in the right but what is right and he observed:

> "... my view has always been that **the right solution is to partition Kashmir**. Give the Hindu and Buddhist part to India and the Muslim part to Pakistan as we did in the case of India. We are really not concerned with the Muslim part of Kashmir. It is a matter between the Muslims of Kashmir and Pakistan. They may decide the issue, as they like. Or if you like, divide it into three parts; the Cease-fire zone, the Valley and the Jammu-Laddhak Region and have a plebiscite only in the Valley. What I am afraid of is that in the proposed plebiscite, which is to be an overall plebiscite, the Hindus and Buddhists of Kashmir are likely to be dragged into Pakistan against their wishes and we may have to face the same problems as we are facing today in East Bengal."

Ambedkar's views were praised by most of the national as well as international newspapers including the *Manchester Guardian*.

Tunnel to Kashmir

When the "Nehru Tunnel" was being contemplated, Ambedkar had opposed the very idea. He said:

> "... I find that Prime Minister had launched upon a project of digging a tunnel connecting Kashmir to India, Sir, I think it is one of the most dangerous things that Prime Minister could do. That might happen that the Prime Minister, in digging the tunnel, thinks that he alone would be able to use it. He does not realize that a conqueror who comes to the other side and captures Kashmir, can come away straight to Pathankot and probably come into the Prime Minister's House. I do not know".

He reminded that England was reluctant for Anglo-French Tunnel for fear of European Aggression in the event of occupation of France by enemy forces. He observed that someday, if China, Pakistan or Russia could occupy Kashmir and then this tunnel will bring the enemy in our courtyard. [Khaimode, Vol. 11, p. 100]

In this respect, we should give a thought to present day declaration by Atal Bihari Bajpayee of providing a Railway Link from Jammu to Kashmir.

Article 370 in the Indian Constitution

It seems Ambedkar was against Article 370 in the Constitution, which gives a special Status to the State of J&K, and it was put against his wishes. But I am not sure about this, as it is based only on statement of Balraj Madhok, who reportedly said, Dr. Ambedkar had clearly told SK. Abdullah: "You wish India should protect your borders, she should build roads in your area, she should supply you food grains, and Kashmir should get equal status as India. But Government of India should have only limited powers and Indian people should have no rights in Kashmir. To give consent to this proposal, would be a treacherous thing against the interests of India and I, as the Law Minister of India, will never do it."

Then SK. Abdullah went to Nehru, who directed him to Gopal Swami Ayyangar, who approached Sardar Patel asking him to do something as it was a matter of prestige of Nehru, who has promised SK. Abdullah accordingly. Patel got it passed when Nehru was on foreign tour. On the day this article came up for discussion, Dr. Ambedkar did not reply to questions on it though he did participate on other articles. All arguments were done by Krishna Swami Ayyangar. [Dahat:1997: 82]

Recent Discussion

During recent times, it was Ms. Tavleen Singh who in an article in *Sunday Express* of 20 April 2003, made a daring suggestion of third party international intervention by America in Kashmir dispute. She was correct in saying that India has already asked American help to tame down Pakistan and that we must realise to start with, that the problem cannot be solved domestically.

Now supposing with some good fortune, wisdom prevails on all sides and such talks do take place, what the Indian side hopes best to bargain for? What is not only just and reasonable but also possible under the circumstances for the Indian side?

The answer to this has been given long time back by Dr. Ambedkar, who had said, as mentioned previously, that, the Hindu area of Jammu and Buddhist area of Laddhak be separated from the Muslim area of the Valley. These non-Muslim areas should be the part of India and the valley be given independent status with every right to them to do what they want.

RSS Realises Bifurcation is Good

It is now after so many years that RSS has come to realise the sagacity of this formula and asked for bifurcation of J & K on such lines within Indian framework, but the pride and prejudice will not allow them to implement even that.

Rule by Force, How Long?

From Pakistan point of view, no matter which group of people rule over Kashmir, it is going to be a Muslim rule. What more does Pak want? Unlike Hindus with thousands of castes and groups, Muslim society is comparatively more monolithic. If the individuals do not matter, how does it matter to Pak, whether Kashmiri people feel more comfortable in India or not?

From Indian point of view, Indian spending in Kashmir directly and indirectly has been so great that lot of developmental works could have been possible in rest of India with that money. Now, further, it is contemplated to spend on Railways in Kashmir from the resources from rest of India, as if it is going to be with you till the sun and moon last.

The British could not rule India by the force of sword for long, will India or for that matter Pakistan rule Kashmir for long against their wishes? If the answer is negative, then why is the conflict?

Resources in Kashmir

After all, what are the resources available in Kashmir? Are they worth fighting for - for both India and Pakistan? It is not oil rich Iraq. Let us forget about border security, a point well discussed by Ambedkar in "*Thoughts on Pakistan*". Security of a country does not depend upon physical boundaries, these days. Otherwise, America would not have been able to attack Afghanistan or Iraq.

If the resources of Kashmir would have been plentiful, would the British have sold it to Gulab Singh Dogra, who not only surrendered himself but made Deelip Singh, the last heir of Ranjit Singh to surrender on 29th March 1849. As a reward of this, the British sold him the province of Jammu and Kashmir for 250,000 pounds sterling, and returned the treasury of Suchet Singh. Thus, the Punjab got slavery and the Dogras got the province of Jammu and Kashmir.

A Lost Case for India

The Hindus, as a matter of fact, lost Kashmir forever in thirteenth century, when a boy of tender age, Ratanju, of no fixed religion or nationality was refused entry to Hinduism, and was converted by a Muslim fakir Bulbulshah to Islam. His son Shahamir usurped the throne. Kashmir, a Buddhist and Hindu country till then, became Muslim very soon. It is said, those pundits, who refused to become Muslims, were put in gunny bags and drowned in river Jehlam by Ratanju and Shahamir. The place in Shrinagar where they were drowned, is famous even now by the name of '*watta mazaar*'. [Santram, *Sarita Mukta* Vol. 8, p.162.]

Chenab Formula

Muzamil Jaleel in *Indian Express* of 28 June 2003, wrote of Chenab Compromise. Though the official stance of both India and Pakistan says they want full control of Kashmir, they both are-may be under pressure from America - likely to come to accept the idea of compromise.

India would be happy if LOC becomes International boundary, which has been strongly refuted by Pak. Now and again India talks of POK, knowing well that there are no takers. What does Pak want to settle for-apart from full control of J & K - nobody knows. But Sardar Sikandar Hayat Khan Prime Minister of POK, last month, had called upon both Delhi and Islamabad to consider River Chenab as the Border-ostensibly a Pak motivation.

Australian Diplomat Sir Owen Dixon had expressed similar idea in 1950. Even in mid sixties, the Britain and US were urging both India and Pakistan for partition. In Pakistan media there seems to be support to Hayat proposal. Also the Kashmiri separatist leadership seems to favour the idea.

Will the caste-ridden India accept it? Those who were talking of '*Akhand Bharat*', had to accept the Partition of India, as predicted by Ambedkar. But India and Pakistan both had to suffer a lot during the process with loss of life, property and human suffering, as the **safeguards as advocated by Ambedkar were not followed**.

Now the talks are likely to start on the problem. Partition along the river Chenab, which runs north of Jammu is one of the proposals for long time. But the partition involves human angle and all those precautions advocated by Ambedkar during partition of India and Pakistan will have to be taken, if the human tragedy has to be averted.

[This was published on www.ambedkar.org on 1st July 2003]

Confederation – India, Pak and Bangladesh?

VTR Proposes Confederation

V T Rajseker, editor of Dalit Voice [Dalit Voice, May 16 – 31, 2007], in a speech in Pakistan, wherein he advocated formation of confederation of Pakistan, Bangladesh and India by retaining its existing boundaries and its rebuttal by Mr. N. Haq from Islamabad, who snubbed the editor for such an idea. Unfortunately, no debate took place, but I had expressed my views for whatever worth they are.

VTR had Always Maintained That View

It is not the new idea of VTR. When asked, whether he welcomed partition of India in 1947, he replied in 1991, in *Ready reference to Revolutionaries,* (p. 6)

> "The partition of India and Pakistan was a grave error. The upper caste leaders led by M.K. Gandhi, conspired to divide India. They feared if Muslims remained in undivided India, they would side with SC/ST/BCs, and the upper castes would be isolated and reduced to a minority. This was a conspiracy. We must undo the partition so that we may solve many of our problems ourselves. We are for '*Akhand Bharat'*, which is a Nazi slogan, now forgotten, meaning uniting Pakistan and Bangladesh back with India. Are the Nazis ready?" (The readers of DV know well that VTR uses word Nazi for RSS *Parivar*)

His Idea is Approved of by Ambedkarites

I do not think VTR's idea to be preposterous and if some cool heads work on it, may be the thought would appear that it is the only saner idea which would be agreed by all, if not today, tomorrow. Those who read Dr. Ambedkar's '*Thoughts on Pakistan*', I think, would agree with me.

Gandhi Knew about Partition

Though journalists like Jagan Fadnis maintain that M.K. Gandhi were kept in dark by Nehru and Patel about agreement between them and Lord Mountbatten regarding partition of India, it was not true. VTR has mentioned that when Babasaheb's book "*Partition of India Thoughts on Pakistan*" was seen by Rajaji Rajgopalchari, 'a Southern fox and extraordinary cunning Brahmin from Tamil Nadu', "he was one of the first persons to grasp the significance of partition and its advantages to Brahmins". He ran to Gandhi and explained him how giving Pakistan to Muslims is more beneficial for the Brahmins than to Muslims.

Though RSS were opposed to partition, Nehru and Rajaji thought that in undivided India, VTR says,

> "It would be difficult for the Brahmins to check the rising aspirations of the Shudras and the Dalits. And when the low caste (proletariat) unrest gets uncontrollable, they are certain to join with the Muslims and Christians, their co-sufferers, as both the sections are victims of common enemy. The socialist Brahmins…decided that unless the Muslims are driven out, they would prove to be greater danger to Brahmins inside. Brahmins forming less than five per cent of the total population of India will not be able to control much less thwart a revolution when it breaks out when the Dalits explode with the help of enemies of Hinduism, namely Muslims, Christians and Sikhs."

It was after Gandhi's consent, that all the wheels moved in accepting the proposal of Pakistan. VTR explains in detail in '*Why Godse killed Gandhi*' (1986), p. 38.

Can India ever become a Hindu Raj?

In the days of Hindu Mahasabha, in my childhood, there used to be a slogan, '*hindustan hinduo ka, nahi kisi ke baap ka*'. At least they should have said, '*nahi kisi* ***aur*** *ke baap ka*'. All think that India can be a Hindu nation. Is it possible? I think not. There is a trick in Hindutvawadis claiming population of Hindus to be 80 to 85 per cent. They include SCs and STs, whose population as a conservative estimate is not less than 25 per cent. If one adds 20 per cent Muslims, Sikhs, Buddhists and Christians, there remain only 55 per cent, about 35 per cent of whom are BCs and against the upper castes.

It is rather unfortunate that Muslim leaders also like to combine Dalits in Hindus. This, I feel, is their short-sightedness. This mistake was committed by the Muslim leaders of the past, and is committed by the present day leaders also.

Let us see what VTR had observed about this:

> "Godse accuses Gandhi of divide and rule, but how can anybody divide a people if they are not willing to be divided? Hindu caste system has divided the Hindus and that is why they are too willing to be divided. RSS leaders now and then express their fear that Hindus may be reduced to a minority in India. Their fear is genuine. When Dalits and Shudras realise their slavery under the Aryan invaders, the "Hindus" will be reduced to a minority. This is bound to happen soon. Already Dalits have declared they are not Hindus. So also the Sikhs. Many more will say so soon. Then the "Hindus" will become a minority." ['*Why Godse killed Gandhi?*' p. 32]

Ambedkar's views

Ambedkar's book, *Thoughts on Pakistan*, is a monumental book and deserves to be studied even now after partition by all Hindus as well as Muslims. It has maintained that though giving Pakistan to Muslims is beneficial to the Hindus, it is not beneficial to the Muslims to ask for and accept Pakistan.

Addressing the Hindus he said:

> "Once it becomes certain that the Muslims want Pakistan there can be no doubt that the wise course would be to concede the principle of it."

To Muslims, Ambedkar asked, "Must there be Pakistan?" and raised many questions like:

1. Because a good part of the Muslim population of India happens to be concentrated in certain defined areas, which can be easily severed from the rest of India.
2. Because there is communal antagonism between the Hindus and the Muslims?
3. Because the Muslims have lost faith in the Congress majority?

4. Because the Musalmans are a nation?
5. Because otherwise Swaraj will be a Hindu Raj?

He dealt with and answered all these questions. The last question was the most important one: "because otherwise Swaraj will be a Hindu Raj?" to which he himself answered:

> "If Hindu Raj does become a fact, it will, no doubt, be the greatest calamity for this country. No matter what the Hindus say, Hinduism is a menace to liberty, equality and fraternity. On that account it is incompatible with democracy. Hindu Raj must be prevented at any cost. But is Pakistan the true remedy against it?"

How to avoid Hindu Raj

He had also given the method to avoid the Hindu Raj. It was to put a ban on communal parties in politics. He said:

> "Not partition, but the abolition, of the Muslim League and the formation of a mixed party of Hindus and Muslims is the only effective way of burying the ghost of Hindu Raj."

Dalit Muslim unity

He stressed that the formation of a mixed party of Hindus and Muslims would not be difficult in India, because:

> "There are many lower orders in the Hindu society whose economic, political and social needs are the same as those of the majority of the Muslims and they would be far more ready to make a common cause with the Muslims for achieving common ends than they would with the high caste of Hindus who have denied and deprived them of ordinary human rights for centuries."

And he averred that such co-operation was seen when under the Montague-Chelmsford Reforms in most Provinces the Muslims, the Non-Brahmins and the Depressed Classes united together and worked the reforms as members of one team from 1920 to 1937, and observed that this was:

> "The most fruitful method of achieving communal harmony among Hindus and Muslims and of destroying the danger of a Hindu Raj."

As Mr. Jinnah, had the ability to organise and had the reputation of a nationalist,

> "Even many Hindus who were opposed to the Congress would have flocked to him if he had only sent out a call for a united party of like-minded Hindus and Muslims."

Initially, "Mr. Jinnah showed that he was for a common front between the Muslims and other non-Muslim minorities." But later he passed in 1939, a Resolution in favour of Pakistan. About this he observed that he has done disservice to Muslims. He explained what would happen if Pakistan came.

Pakistan is Worse than Useless

Ambedkar said:

"Take an all-India view. Can Pakistan prevent the establishment of Hindu Raj at the center over Muslim minorities that will remain in Hindustan? It is plain that it cannot. What good is Pakistan then? Only to prevent Hindu Raj in Provinces in which the Muslims are in a majority and in which there could never be Hindu Raj!! To put it differently Pakistan is unnecessary to Muslims where they are in a majority because there, there is no fear of Hindu Raj. It is worse than useless to Muslims where they are in a minority, because Pakistan or no Pakistan they will have to face a Hindu Raj. Can politics be more futile than the politics of the Muslim League? The Muslim League started to help minority Muslims (in India) and has ended by espousing the cause of majority Muslims (in Pakistan). What a perversion in the original aim of the Muslim League! What a fall from the sublime to the ridiculous! Partition as a remedy against Hindu Raj is worse than useless." [W & S 8 : 361 ff.]

A Question for Muslim Intelligentsia – What Muslims Achieved?

So what did the Muslims achieve by getting Pakistan? They achieved Muslim rule in Provinces, which in any case were to be ruled by the Muslims, even in Undivided India.

What did the Muslims loose by getting Pakistan? They put more Muslims under Hindu Raj – **more than the number escaping Hindu Raj** – by creating Pakistan. As is well known, the population of Muslims in India is more than in Pakistan.

Kashmir Problem

Present day conception is that Kashmir problem is the main bone of contention between two countries. I have expressed my views in 'Kashmir problem from Ambedkarite view point' first in www.ambedkar.org/jamanadas supporting partition of Kashmir. [See above]

Jagan Fadnis has said that Kashmir was an independent nation from 15th August 1947 till 27th October 1947. It was because Pakistan put their Armed Forces there, as infiltrators, that the Hindu ruler Hari Singh asked for help from India and Indian troops were sent to Kashmir after Hari Singh signed a pact of accession with India. Does the question occur to Muslim intelligentsia, what was the need of putting military in Kashmir? Was not Kashmir a predominantly a Muslim State? Why then the Action by military? Similarly was not East Pakistan a Muslim State? Why military action there? Views of Dr. Ambedkar on the **Linguistic Provinces** would be very useful to understand the problems.

Are we really fully sovereign?

Today both India and Pakistan pretend to rule their own countries. Are they really fully independent and sovereign? Can they really negotiate with, say for example, Iran for a pipeline without consent of USA? If we are willing to surrender to wishes of America, can we not ourselves solve our own problems by negotiations? If so, what is wrong in a Confederation?

Only Hindutvawadis oppose Confederation in India

Let us see who opposed to such an idea in India. Immediately after Independence, the Hindutvawadis used to clamour for '*akhand bharat*'. Later they stopped all such talk. When some junior members tried to speak of '*akhand bharat'*, the seniors in their group had admonished them. Since then only the non-Brahminical elements talk of it nowadays.

Ground Realities

If the principle of 'complete autonomy of Provinces' is accepted, the confederation of Pakistan, Bangladesh, India (and Muslim areas in Kashmir) can be a strong Confederation. Not only, it is feasible, but it is most desirable for both Muslims and non-Muslims of the sub-continent.

By this time people from both sides of border have realised that they cannot wish away the nation across the border. Why not try to learn to live with the realities? And the best way to do so is to have a confederation. Whether the ruling dignitaries like it or not, the masses should strive for it from both sides of border.

Nature of Dalit Muslim Unity

Ambedkar and Jinnah

This is in response to an article by Adv. Md. Karim (DV. June 1- 15, 97). It was a great misfortune that Dr. Ambedkar and Mr. Jinnah could not work together, Adv. Karim says. He says Azad was a stooge. He says the anti-Muslim activities are a symptoms and not a disease. He says Muslims are not a minority. He believes that population of Muslims could be more than presumed 15 per cent. He also quotes authorities to show that Islam is an egalitarian religion. All this need not be refuted and any Bahujan can agree with all these points. He avers that Muslim masses in India are in a need of allies to fight the existing system under the guidance of Islam. He advises his Muslim brothers to help the Dalits in all spheres, and keep good contacts for future interaction. This is quite correct. But the main point is, what kind of unity is sought for. He says:

> "The future of India lies in the unity of Dalits and Muslims - not under the banner of this party or that because no party is aiming at providing an alternative to the existing social, political and economic setup but under the **invigorating and revolutionary message of Islam** ..."

Why no political party is thought to be necessary? Is it an invitation for the Bahujans to adopt Islam? Is it a proletising work? If it is, well and good; nothing wrong in that; only that perhaps **DV is not a forum for it**.

Our experience of mixing religion with politics is always counter-productive. The combination does neither promote the religion nor the politics. The political meetings of RPI used to start with Buddhist prayers, the non-Buddhists in the party, gradually faded away. The religious sermons to Budhists used to end with request for support to RPI work, the non-RPI Buddhists stopped coming. I feel the two must not be combined, the religion and politics. I hope Adv. Karim does not wish to propagate religion from political platform.

What is the spirit of Islam?

Do the Muslims consider Dalits as non-hindus? I think, it is the first necessity that they must make a distinction between "Hindus" and Dalits. Dalit leaders - of all Dalit parties and groups, of all shades and colours - have time and again declared that. But Muslim leaders do not think about this. I think this is the main hurdle.

No doubt, Islam is a great religion. Also it can not be gainsaid that meeting of Ambedkar and Jinnah could not bear fruits. If the unity has to bear any fruits, today, it has got to be based **on secular points**. The basis has to be non-religious. It should be purely on political ideology. What is that ideology? I believe, that ideology could only be Ambedkarism. Our Muslim brothers have got to get themselves aquainted with **Spirit of Ambedkarism, which is different from Spirit of Buddhism.**

OBC Dalit Muslim Christian Relations

Present Situation–Failure of Ambedkarites

That, the participation of Dalits, Adivasis and OBCs in the Gujarat carnage has raised several questions with regard to the unity of SC/ST/OBC and Muslims in the present day, must be conceded.

It should also be conceded that there is a failure of Ambedkarites in preventing SC/ST/OBCs going into herd of RSS. They have forgotten their own carnage not very long ago in the name of Caste war for Reservations.

I have got my own doubts and reservations about the role of UN in Gujarat carnage. Whether it would have made much difference to ground realities, I doubt. Even then there might be a point there. We are seeing that even International Human Rights team is being refused permission to visit Gujarat.

Caste War in Gujarat

Sonia Gandhi said that in Gandhi's Gujarat, Godse's RSS is ruling and causing state violence against Muslims. Rhetoric apart, Gujarat had been violent in the past specially against the Dalits. We saw one of the most serious Caste riots against the Dalits in post-Independent India, lasting for months in 1981. We saw innumerable killings, loot, arson and molestation against the Dalits. The official figures of those affected in police firing alone were:- killed: 34, injured: 59. All areas of state were affected, but urban areas saw more violence than rural and tribal areas. The Caste war was fought against the SCs by police and UC together on the opposite side. Among the UC, most aggressive were Patidar Landlords in Kheda Ahmedabad and Mehsana Districts. [Desai I.P., *Caste, Caste Conflict and Reservation*, Surat, 1985, p.130 ff.]

Though it appeared to have started as an agitation by the medical students of UC demanding abolition of Reserved seats to SC/ST and OBCs, the mischief of such demands becomes obvious when we find that prescribed quota is not filled as yet, says Desai. [p.127] Students' demands were supported by Govt. and semi-govt. employees, LIC and Banks workers and lawyers, doctors, University teachers and other business and industry. Most fierce fighter force was land owning agricultural class from rural as well as urban areas. SCs had seven per cent, STs had 13 per cent and OBCs had five per cent reservations, but only SCs were targeted. Desai avers that caste prejudice prevailed: "Another thing that is barely concealed is the higher caste prejudice against the untouchables. How can these 'Dheds' demand equality with us? ..." [Desai: 136]

And Bose confirming the conflict is thus related to deep rooted caste prejudices among the upper castes on the one hand and the social mobility of the SC on the other. "In Gujarat SC constituting only 6.8 per cent of the total population has the highest literacy (27.74 per cent) among all the states except Kerala." [p.138]

In the background of this situation, how did the SCs join the RSS in riots against Muslims? As Sonvane says, in a STAR TV programme Rajdeep sought an explanation of this phenomenon from Udit Raj and C.B. Prasad, and it is true, as he adds that, both, however, avoided the true answer and dealt the issue in the way of politicians and not like intellectuals. Here lies the importance of ideology. I would like to comment that STs, (and probably SCs too) were lured with Gandhian thought and were not following the ideology of Ambedkar. This is the reason we want a society based on Ambedkar ideology. Here we, the Ambedkarites, must admit our own failure.

Uttar Pradesh Situation

I believe that Muslims are more mature politically than the Christians. In politics, many times, wrong decisions are taken by all. Muslims erred once - in siding with Mulayam Singh - but it may be corrected in future. If the Muslims in U.P., who can influence results of fifty per cent MP seats, had sided with Dalits under Mayavati instead of Yadava-s under Mulayam Singh, they would have been in a position to rule the state, or may be the country. After all, the kind of unity we are envisaging is only political and neither religious nor social.

At one time in mid nineties, Dalits under Mayavati and OBCs – Yadava-s – under Mulayam Singh combinedly ruled the State for some little time. They fell apart, due to an attempt on the life of Mayavati in what is known as 'Rest House Event' 1995.

Since then, both Dalits and OBCs seek the supports of Brahmins, and rule the state with Muslim support, but **Under Brahmin Influence** – Dalits and OBCs fight and die and the Brahmins rule, either way. That is the beauty of Brahmanism. Neither the Dalits, nor the OBCs learn any lesson.

Christians vis-a-vis Muslims

The main objection is against Muslims in Post Independence Era, when Kancha observes:

"... in the post-Independence period, no Muslim intellectual worth his name has worked among the Dalits, Adivasis and OBCs. No Muslim intellectual stood by Ambedkar when he started the liberative struggle of the Dalits. Following the Mandal movement no Muslim scholar wrote even one serious book formulating an Islamic understanding of caste and untouchability. How do bridges get built among communities? They get built only when one oppressed community gets the support of another and each relates to the other on a day-to-day basis. For that, a theoretical formulation is very essential."

SC/ST/OBC/Muslim Unity Broken by Tilak

In my childhood, Dalits participated in all Muslim festivals like *Muharam*. Our family was the "*kotwal-s*" to the "*sawari*" of *Gond* Raja, i.e. the patron was a Gond (ST), priests were Muslims and 'kotwals' were *Mahar-s* (SC), and the rest of the devotees were OBCs, mostly *Teli-s*, *Mali-s*, *Kunbi-s* etc.

My father - the richest Dalit in the District - used to consider it a honour to religiously escort the horse in front of *Tajiya* procession to *Rana* on ninth and tenth day of *Muharam*; my mother was religiously following the fifth and seventh of *Muharam* and 'beg' *jogava* from five houses to make *khichara*; and we children were made *fakirs* on that day, and all of us used to participate in ten day long celebrations during *Muharam*. After the death of my father, I myself escorted the horse, till I went to College in 1949. The *Durgah-s* of Baba Farid were visited by my family frequently and likewise by other Dalits and OBCs.

The various mohollas were having their own "*astana*" - place for *'sawari'*, with their own internal rivalries and quarrels, and the British Government had to make rules deciding the routes of processions and the precedence of each *sawari* and *Tajiya*. There used to be dancing of 'tigers' and 'Tantya Bhil'. All this used to be celebrated by the non-Muslims. Such was the unity among the SC/ST/OBC and Muslims.

The blame of breaking this unity and separating the lower castes from Muslims, must be placed, in my humble opinion, on the activities of B.G. Tilak, who started '*Ganesh Festivals*', and this gaiety and festivity gradually shifted from Muharam to Ganesh Festivals. Even the Tigers danced in Ganesh festivals in those in earlier days. Gradually all stopped and Ganesh festivals were "*brahmanised*", but even until ten years ago, there used to be *'quawali*-s' during Ganesh festivals.

It is well known that early '*satya shodhaks*' - the followers of Phule - had complained against Ganesh Festivals to British Governor without any effect. Thus Ganesh festivals were started not for creating awareness against the colonial rule-as claimed by Hindutwavadis - but against the movement of Phule and against the OBC - Dalit - Muslim unity that was being formed.

Dalits Benefited by Muslim Rule

When the Muslims came, they annihilated the Buddhist external symbols like idols and monasteries, and gave a final blow to Buddhism, causing its fall. But the Buddhist population, which by this time had become untouchables completely, found great relief from Brahminic hostility by converting to Islam. Untouchables like Malik Kafoor became high officer under Khilji and Khusrukhan became Sultan. Thus, there was empowerment of Dalits during Muslim rule. Hence Sonavane's view that the development of Shudras and Dalits during the Muslim and the British rule can be described best as 'providential' in the stochastical sense, cannot be termed as entirely true.

Why Ambedkar did not Accept Islam?

Book by Islamic Publication and our Response

Why Ambedkar did not accept Islam? This is the question raised by a scholar Prof. H. M. Z. Shams Tehran, in a book '*Dalit Agony and Islam*' – an anthology published (2003) by Board of Islamic Publications. The author is former Chairman, Dr. Ambedkar Chair Centre, Dr. Babasaheb Ambedkar National Institute of Social Sciences, MHOW, MP, and hence presumably conversant with views of Ambedkar.

The question is discussed, the author tells us, by A.K. Vail at some length. The points are:

1. Ambedkar had no access to original literature of Islam as his knowledge was based on English books, and

2. His knowledge of Islam was not wide, as observed by Sohanlal Shastri.

I think this is not true, and believe that Ambedkar knew Islam enough to know what is good and what is bad in it. But if this is true, it is shameful for Islamic scholars, that enough literature was not produced in English during 400 years of British presence in the subcontinent, and badly denotes the parochial attitudes of Islam.

3. Ambedkar loved Buddhism and did not like Bakhtiar Khilji destroying Buddhist centres. This action, the author says is contrary to tenets of Islam. Though Islam ordains destruction of Idols, it does not permit the destruction of 'places of idol worship'. He conveniently omits to mention that Nalanda was a place of Leaning and what he burned were the manuscripts on palm leaves. Also, let us not forget the recent destruction of Bamiyan Buddhas.

4. Ambedkar complained that brotherhood preached by Islam is restricted to Muslims only. Author says this is not true and intolerance, shown by some kings, was against the tenets of Islam, and quotes example of Caliph Omar respecting Christian sentiments in Jerusalem. This rhetoric is difficult to digest for me. More respect is shown by Muslims to Aurangzeb than to Akbar the great.

5. Ambedkar complains that Muslim Kings did nothing to remove untouchability. Author admits this fact but argues that it is the fault of Kings and not of Islam.

6. Ambedkar thought Islam was a rigid religion. The author feels it is fallacious and argues that improvements based on Qur'an are allowed. As a matter of fact, this fact alone is suggestive of parochial nature of Islam. This gives no chance to human mind to think beyond the scripture.

7. Author observes that Ambedkar did not favour Islam because of its fundamental nature, but argues, "even traditional Buddhism possesses more fundamental nature than Islam". Author forgets Ambedkar did NOT accept 'traditional' Buddhism. The tenets of Buddhism seen in '*Kalam Sutta*', where the Buddha says do not accept anything if it does not appeal to your mind even if the scriptures say so. This freedom of mind, giving no importance to scriptures is great thing in Buddhism.

8. Further the Author observes that while selecting Buddhism, Ambedkar accepted the advice of *Hindutwavadis* like Moonje and Sawarkar. This information, which is entirely based on Brahminic propaganda, is totally false. (See below)

9. Ambedkar could not gather enough courage against possible violent reaction from the Hindus, if he joins Islam. I see no reason to draw this conclusion. Does the author mean the old Muslims would not have helped new entrants to fight Hindu atrocities? After all, Ambedkar, in 1935, had announced, "We are fully conscious of the fact that to go anywhere we will, we would have to fight for our welfare if we took to Christianity, Islam or Sikhism...." [Keer: *Dr. Ambedkar* : 262]

10. Author, unfortunately, gives Brahminic arguments to say Buddhism is part of Brahmanism, without understanding the vital differences.

However, the author explains that Ambedkar thought highly of Islam and enumerates its good qualities – vitality, equality and fraternity. Ambedkar believes that invasions by Islam, caste system in Islam and unscientific attitude of Indian Muslims, in spite of rationality of the Prophet, are because of Hindu environment.

Ambedkar, champion for the cause of women, laments about position of Muslim women and criticizes *purdah* system in them. But the author argues that Qur'an does not ordain *purdah*. I have no knowledge about this.

The most important point in Ambedkar's writings is the brotherhood in Islam is restricted to Muslims only and that it is not universal brotherhood. Author puts forward strong arguments that Ambedkar misunderstood Islam in this respect. However, the concluding chapter of the book avers that Dalits must embrace Islam, so that they could be helped financially, and treated with equality and assimilated through matrimonial alliances. This proves equality in Islam is limited to Muslims.

Dr. Kancha Ilaiah's Estimate

'One of India's rare honest intellectuals', OBC scholar observes about why Islam is not attractive to Dalitbahujans.

> "...Islam is not attracting Dalit Bahujan masses because the people in Afghanistan, Pakistan and Bangladesh have not become modernist....Even in a spiritual democracy, people do not want to be poor, hungry and illiterate. I leave it to Islamic scholars to examine why Afghanistan, Pakistan and Bangladesh are unable to negotiate with democracy, capitalism and modernity...." [DV Sept. 1-15, 2008, p. 21]

He seems to exclude Indian Muslims; is this justifiable? I wonder.

Did Dr. Ambedkar Consult Moonje or Sawarkar While Deciding to Convert to Buddhism?

Above we have mentioned that it is Brahminic false propaganda. It can be seen in Wakipedia under Dr. Moonje as follows:

> "When Dr. Ambedkar announced his decision to join another religion by getting converted along with his followers, Dr. Moonje and Veer Sawarkar convinced him to join any religion of Indian origin. Initially, Dr. Ambedkar thought of joining Sikhism but later on joined Buddhism despite receiving tempting monetary offers from some religious leaders. Dr. Moonje thus succeeded in keeping all Dalit friends in a religion of Indian origin and soil, which otherwise could have been very disastrous for Hindus."

Dr. Moonje died on 4th March 1948 at Nasik about eight years before Conversion of Ambedkar. Sawarkar was very bitter about Ambedkar's conversion to Buddhism. He wrote articles in 'Kesari' condemning the conversion. He said Ambedkar's jump outside Hinduism fell within the courtyard of Hinduism, meaning Buddhism is offshoot of Hinduism. He also warned that the Buddhist might join with divisive forces in North East and strive for separate nation.

This episode mentioned by Wakepedia relates to events after his declaration at Yeola in 1935, and not before 1956.

Muslims were in touch with Ambedkar; they were on stage even during speech '*mukti kon pathe?*' (1936).

Ambedkar had concluded Poona Pact four years back and got some political privileges for the Dalits. He decided to convert to Sikhism. He did not wish to loose those by converting to Sikhism. So his colleagues asked him to consult Hindu leaders. It was not for which religion to take. It was to find out what would be Hindu leaders' stand about facilities. A statement was drawn at the end of talks. That contained:

1. Islam seemed to give the Depressed Classes what they needed politically, socially and economically.
2. Christianity had boundless resources available to it from America and England, and a Christian government behind it.
3. Sikhism had few attractions and was not so helpful to the Depressed Classes socially, financially and politically compared with Islam and Christianity; yet he preferred Sikhism in the interest of the Hindus. [Keer: 279]

Later Mr. Rajah, who had pact with Moonje, disclosed correspondence to Gandhi and Congressmen etc. This is the story of Dr. Moonje-Ambedkar talks. It was about selection of Sikhism. [See chapter on Sikhism] And it has nothing to do with selection of Buddhism. Twenty years passed from this time till the time of conversion. All these years the question of which religion to accept remained open.

When did this Question Get Closed?

Apparently, it seems, final decision came around 1950. **But to my mind**, the question remained open only till 1947. **Ambedkar hoped against hope that Muslim leaders would not opt for Pakistan.** In '*Thoughts on Pakistan*', he tried to convince Muslims that Pakistan is worse than useless.

I have discussed this problem in detail in an earlier article on Confederation. (See above)

Kashmir Problem

I have written an article 'Kashmir problem from Ambedkarite view point' in detail on the subject, some three to four years back. It was published in some magazines and also is available on www.ambedkar.org/jamanadas. I supported the view of Dr. Ambedkar, who had suggested partition of Kashmir. [See above]

Jagan Fadnis has said that Kashmir was an independent nation from 15th August 1947 till 27th October 1947. It was because Pakistan put their armed forces there, as infiltrators, that the Hindu ruler Hari Singh asked for help from India and Indian troops were sent to Kashmir after Hari Singh signed a pact of accession with India.

Does the question occur to Muslim intelligentsia, what was the need for Pakistan of putting military in Kashmir? Was not Kashmir a predominantly a Muslim State? Why then the Action by military?

Similarly was not East Pakistan a Muslim State? Why military action there?

Read Ambedkar on Linguistic states

Why Muslims of Pakistan wish to rule the Muslims of Kashmir? OR Why the Muslims of Pakistan tried to rule over the Muslims of Bangaladesh? These problems are not religious problems. These are ethenic, regional and mostly political problems. And the views of Dr. Ambedkar on the '*Linguistic Provinces*' would be very useful to understand the solution of these problems. No other Indian scholar seems to have devoted his thoughts, energy and efforts to solve these problems from the 'massical' way. But why blame the Muslims? Even Indian elites donot want to read and follow Ambedkar, whose advice still holds good after three quarters of a century.

Ground Realities

If the principles of complete autonomy of Provinces is accepted, the confederation is not only feasible, but it is most desirable for both Muslims and non-Muslims of the sub-continent. By this time people from both sides of border have realised that they cannot wish away the nation across the border. Why not try to learn to live with the realities? And the best way to do so is to have a confederation.

Ambedkar waited for Muslims to join Constituent Assembly

Constituent Assembly met on December 9, 1946, in spite of the fact the Muslim League had boycotted it, elected Rajendra Prasad as Chairman and on 13th December 1946, Nehru laid the foundation by Declaration of Objectives. On 15th December 46, M.R. Jaykar moved amendment, seeking postponement for Muslim League and States to join the Constituent Assembly. On 17th December 1946, Ambedkar was asked to speak and house was tense to hear him.

The Congress members were ready with their hands raised to oppose him. But at the end they praised him and the amendment was passed and Constituent Assembly postponed the consideration of the objective resolution till the next session.

That speech is worth considering by all. A few excerpts: [W&S 13:7 ff]

These paragraphs (5) to (7) set out the objectives of the future constitution of this country are non-controversial but very disappointing, coming from a socialist like Nehru. He criticized Nehru for that part of resolution, which "although it enunciates certain rights, does not speak of remedies". Even the usual formula that no man's life, liberty and property shall be taken without the due process of law, finds no place in the Resolution.

He felt that there should be **nationalisation of industry** and **nationalisation of land** would be necessary for doing justice socially, economically and politically.

The first four paragraphs are a matter of controversy. The controversy seems to be centred on the use of that word 'Republic'. As Dr. Jayakar pointed out in the absence of the Muslim League it would not be proper for this Assembly to proceed to deal with this Resolution.

> "I know today we are divided politically, socially and economically. We are a group of warring camps and I may go even to the extent of confessing that I am probably one of the leaders of such a camp. But, Sir, with all this, I am quite convinced that given time and circumstances nothing in the world will prevent this country from becoming one. (Applause): With all our castes and creeds, I have not the slightest hesitation that **we shall in some form be a united people** (Cheers). I have no hesitation in saying that notwithstanding the agitation of the Muslim League for the partition of India some day enough light would dawn upon the Muslims themselves and they too will begin to think that **a United India is better even for them.**" (Loud cheers and applause).

Whether it is legal or not to postpone the session, he observed:

> "Sir, I like to put the matter in a somewhat different way. The way I like to put it is this, I am not asking you to consider whether you have the right to pass this Resolution straightaway or not. It may be that you have the right to do so. The question I am asking is this. Is it prudent for you to do so? Is it

wise for you to do so? ... I suggest that another attempt may be made to bring about a solution of the dispute between the Congress and the Muslim League."

Solution of Muslim problem, according to Ambedkar was:

"Either there shall have to be surrender by the one party to the wishes of the other – that is one way. The other way would be what I call a negotiated peace and the third way would be open war."

Criticizing that many members talk of solving the political problems of this country by war, Ambedkar observed:

" ... That the war that they are thinking of, would be a war on the British. ... I probably may not have much objection to that sort of strategy. But will it be a war on the British only? I have no hesitation and I do want to place before this House in the clearest terms possible that if war comes in this country and if that war has any relation to the issue with which we are confronted to-day, it will not be a war on the British. It will be a war on the Muslims. It will be a war on the Muslims or which is probably worse, it will be a war on a combination of the British and the Muslims. ..."

Ambedkar quoted Burke, who, while repelling the idea of conquering the rebellious colonies under US subjugation, said:

"First, Sir permit me to observe, that the use of force alone is but temporary. It may subdue for a moment; but it does not remove the necessity of subduing again; and a nation is not governed which is perpetually to be conquered."

"My next objection is its uncertainty. Terror is not always the effect of force and an armament is not a victory. If you do not succeed, you are without resource for, conciliation failing, force remains: but, force failing, no further hope of reconciliation is left. ... A further objection to force is that you impair the object by your very endeavours to preserve it. The thing you fought for is not the thing which you recover; but depreciated, sunk, wasted and consumed in the contest".

Ambedkar further observed:

" ... If there is anybody who has in his mind the project of solving the Hindu-Muslim problem by force, which is another name of solving it by war, in order that the Muslims may be subjugated and made to surrender to the Constitution that might be prepared without their consent, this country would be involved in perpetually conquering them. The conquest would not be once and for ever. I do not wish to take more time than I have taken and I will conclude by again referring to Burke. Burke has said somewhere that it is easy to give power, it is difficult to give wisdom. Let us prove by our conduct that if this Assembly has arrogated to itself sovereign powers it is prepared to exercise them with wisdom. ..."

What Ambedkar observed sixty years ago regarding Hindu-Muslim problem, still holds true and **can form the guidelines for the Muslim population now living in India,** which is more than Muslim population in Pakistan.

Thus, my personal opinion is that, the final decision of Ambedkar to embrace Buddhism came after the Muslims effected the formation of Pakistan.

A Minority is Ruling India

Dalits, Bahujans and minorities do not realise that India is being ruled by an upper caste minority since 1947. Therefore, BSP had given a slogan '*vote hamara, raj tumhara, nahi chalega.*'

DV June 1, 2008, p. 21 says:

> "Mere three per cent Brahmins rule in the name of Marxism. Dalit-Muslim unity can destroy Bengal Brahminical hegemony", S.K. Biswas

DV Sept. 1, 2008 gives a table of Bengal statistics. It is a shocking statistics.

Editor observes that 6.2 per cent Brahmin, Kayastha and Baidyas (Bhadralok) are ruling Bengal because Dalits (29.2 per cent) and Muslims (23.6 per cent) are not united, and observes:

> "Instead of complaining against the Brahminical enemy, the Dalits and Muslims, the two principle victims of the enemy, must come together. That is the only solution."

How does Unity Take Place?

It is dictated by scholars that when different societies remain in close proximity and wish to unite among themselves, they have to pass through three stages. The first stage is political, where people live together under same rule, under same laws and under same political parties. Second is they adopt the religion and last stage is matrimonial alliances are established. In concluding sentence of the book 'Dalit Agony and Islam', Shamin A. Siddiqi seems to agree with this when he observes:

> " ... Thus future augers well provided both Dalits and Muslims work together, hand in hand, to develop the process of interpolitical actions and encourage their respective Muslim brothers and sisters to dine together and marry the girls of Dalits when they become Muslim and vice versa. ..."

The point to be noted is 'interpolitical' activities have got to be the starting point. The Muslims and Dalits have to be ready to work under one political party. But the picture we see today is that Muslims do not realize their own strength in political arena, are afraid of organising their own party, or joining one of the various Dalit parties in each state. Better still, would have been the state of affairs if they strengthen the hands of Mayavati instead of joining with Mulayam Singh. If they honestly join hands with Mayavati, they can become the rulers of India, not only of UP. But for that they first have to realize that Dalits are not Hindus.

Second point is that till the political unity is established, nobody should talk of proselytizing. That stage will come automatically, if the parties are honest. A time might come when both communities would unite and either become Muslims or Buddhists. Whatever happens, the first stage is political unity. Everyone should strive for that.

DV Sept. 1, 2008 also has an article, "If Dalits embrace Islam, together they become a mighty force". To this DV Editor has appended a long comment. He says the time is such that **Muslims should save themselves before trying to save Dalits.** He says during 61 years of independence Brahmins have reduced Muslims to slaves. I have been repeatedly saying that Muslims are being made 'untouchables'. But Muslims are not recognising their main enemy and not recognising the principal contradiction. They are living in the other world ignoring ground realities. So my only advice is: do not put horse before the cart.

• • •

6

Dalits and Christians

Let Us Remember Revolutionary Jesus

Dalit Struggle for a new identity

An article "Gospel and the Dalit Struggle for a new identity" by M. Deenabandhu, who teaches at Gurukul Theological College in Chennai, published in "International Review of Mission", Vol. LXXXIV No. 334, writing that the Dalits are the most exploited people in this "text book like" picture of social hierarchical society. He avers that the Indian Church comprises mostly of such people, and accuses the Church of "denying them participation", specially by the "wealthy and powerful institutional Church", and appeals the Indian Churches to stand behind them and the World Churches to have a new opportunity in Indian Churches for conversion of these dalits.

He tries to trace the origin of Untouchability in racial theory that those resisting aggression of Aryans became untouchables. He describes the dictates of "Manusmriti" as those imposed by "Aryans" against them. He made certain presuppositions such as: 1. They are different from main mass of "Hindus". 2. Their story is of saga of "service and self-sacrifice" as producers of food and servants of society. 3. Their struggle is for not only themselves but for establishment of new social order.

Dr. Ambedkar and Dalits

While agreeing with all three presuppositions put forward by him, and also thanking him for expressing the concerns about Dalits, we like to point out to the world community, that Dr. B.R. Ambedkar who struggled all his life for the Dalits, has brought in a huge amount of literature about Dalit History, their origin, their aspirations and their course of action to emancipate themselves. He had declared in 1935, that though born as a Hindu, he would not die as a Hindu, and in 1956, he denounced Hinduism along with millions of his followers and got converted to Buddhism and declared boldly, that he would bring whole of India to the path of Buddha. Unfortunately, within less than two months, he was found dead in the morning in his bed, by the lone occupant of the house - his second wife, who was Brahmin by birth.

This is not the proper place to narrate how Dr. Ambedkar explained the History of Untouchability, suffice it to say that his analysis of 'Broken Men' becoming Buddhists takes us farther into the past of Indian society through clearer paths than the work of any writer, Eastern or Western in this field. He started a struggle against the root cause of Caste. His followers, in trying to complete the mission started by him, are pursuing to such an extent that the enemy - the Brahmanical Social Order (BSO) - finds "Ambedkar Dead more formidable than Ambedkar Alive". It is a pity Mr. Deenbandhu seems to be ignorant about his work. Dr. Ambedkar quoted two causes for untouchability. One was general atmosphere of scorn and contempt for Buddhists, and other was habit of beef eating kept on by the broken men, while the Brahmins gave it up and became staunch vegetarians in order to regain their lost prestige and supremacy. It must be noted that, contrary to Deenabandhu's assertion, Manusmriti was not because of a struggle of Brahmins against Dalits but against Buddhists. Untouchability came much later than Manu. This should be enough to clear Deenabandhu's idea of origin of Untouchables.

Why Christianity Failed in India

In spite of spending millions and millions of rupees, there is appallingly low results, as explained by Dr. Ambedkar, who gives the main reason for it being that they approached Brahmins for disputations, and tried to woo them by opening hospitals and schools for them. The missionaries ignored the fact that *Chaturvarnya*, is the crucial matter for BSO, and to accept Christianity meant surrender of their power and prestige. Later missionaries realised this mistake and whatever now is seen is the result of this realisation and winning over the lower castes, as Dr. Ambedkar observes:

> "... The number of Christians we see in India today is due to the fact that some Christian missionaries saw the futility of this (wooing of Brahmins). If they had not realised this error and started to win over the lower classes, there would have been no Christians in India at all. ..." [W&S Vol. 5, p. 444]

Indian History

The study of Ancient Indian history reveals a struggle between the so called upper caste "*savarna-s*" on one side and the rest of population on the other. It had assumed different names, shapes and forms during the course of different periods of history, and the history of India is nothing but the history of conflict between these two ideologies. The present day protagonists of these are Phule, Shahu and Ambedkar on one side and Tilak, Gandhi and Golwalkar on the other. All the leaders of Christians and Muslims need to understand this point and explain it to the gullible ignorant and illiterate Christian and Muslim masses, that these are the only two ideologies in present day India, and sooner the people understand this, earlier they will be freed from their slavery.

Unchristian Side of the Indian Church

V. T. Rajshekhar, editor of "Dalit Voice", had commented that the missionaries are educating the children of oppressors, who tomorrow will come to power and see that these very schools, where they obtained first lessons of alphabets, be closed. It is like feeding milk to the serpents' offsprings. His prophecy seems to be coming true now. He had also suggested that at least 50 per cent of seats in all Christian convents must be given only to SCs and STs at no charge, and the deficit be made good by charging double fees from the children of oppressors. I do not think that article made any dent on missionaries; they are following their own ways.

What is the present status

The situation does not seem to be different even today. While the Dalits have understood that the cause of their misery is Brahmanical Social order, and they are struggling to fight against it, the Christians have found pleasure in appeasing the rulers. They are happy celebrating the birth of Jesus. They are not bothered why He was crucified, the question, they conveniently ignore. They ignore the revolutionary side of Jesus. Did you hear any missionary preaching that Jesus was such a revolutionary that His death was preferred by the rulers of those times, whose interests were threatened by His preaching, than that of a criminal? Do they teach you the revolutionary side of Jesus? On the occasion of Ester, let us remember Jesus as a revolutionary.

Revolutionary Side of Jesus

Whether one agrees or not, with his presumption that Jesus survived the Crucification and migrated to India, where he preached till his death in ripe old age, the revolutionary Jesus as depicted by Holger Kersten, in his "*Jesus Lived in India*", (Elements Books Ltd., 1994, Reprint 1997, USA), is worth remembering. He has explained the revolutionary side of Jesus's life. The political situation in Judea at the time of Jesus, was extremely turbulent, he says. Herod the Great (37-4 B.C.) had to deal with persistent civil unrest by guerrilla army of nationalist fanatics - men of strong religious convictions - trying to undermine Roman rule. Sadducees and Pharisees eventually compromised with Herod's successors and Rechabites continued to live in tents outside towns. Essenes and Nazarenes (to which Jesus belonged), returned from exile in Alexandria, perhaps after AD 6, when Herod's son was deposed, and started the struggle, which is described as:

> "Essenes and Nazarenes were actively and bravely taking on the full strength of the mighty Roman overlord even while the conformists Pharisees and Sadducees were becoming integrated into the overlord's political system." [p.131]

The local Jew population was lurching from crisis to crisis and hoping for the Messiah. The activities of Jesus continued only for two or three years. He used to cross borders from one province to another of Palestine. Why he should go to Jerusalem and by so doing give himself up, remains a mystery, Kerston feels. On his entry into Jerusalem he was jubilantly feted as king who would bring the promised "Kingdom of God". This concept of "Kingdom of God" appears to be a spiritual one for Christian tradition, but the masses of Jerusalem wanted something more worldly like a military commander and statesman like King David of the past, to free the land of Roman yoke. About a week before the festival of Passover, Jesus decided to leave his place of hiding in mountain of Ephraim (John 11:54) and along with his followers journeyed to the Capital. What happened next, is described as:

> "Five days before the great festival, they reached Jerusalem. Entering through the city gates, Jesus was noisily acclaimed by the crowds. But although Jesus was riding a donkey as a gesture of humility, meekness and peaceful intent, the acclamation was later to be tragically misunderstood, The whole city was in turmoil' (Matthew 21:10, Jerusalem Bible version). Jesus' strongly worded statements, and the equally forthright, not to say violent, methods he used in driving the traders out of the Temple, might perhaps in a different atmosphere have been understood as being allegorical to the people to rise up. Some of Jesus' words were the very opposite of conciliatory: 'Think not that I am come to send peace on earth: I came not to send peace, but a sword' (Matthew 10:34) And 'I am come to send fire on the earth; and what will I, if it be already kindled?' (Luke 12:49)."
>
> "The very first thing Jesus did in Jerusalem was to mount an attack against the authorities, an attack such as no one had dared to attempt before. With unmistakable directness Jesus remonstrated and barbed denunciations (Matthew 23) were a public settling of accounts with his antagonists in front of a great number of enthusiastic pilgrims. According to the Gospels, he even went so far as to drive the traders and money changers out to the place of worship. Of course, such an attack on the authority of the Temple officials could not be allowed to pass unchallenged - but care was required, for in such a tense situation any untoward action was liable to trigger a mass uprising. 'And the scribes and chief priests heard it, and sought how they might destroy him: for they feared him, because all the people was astonished at his doctrine' (Mark 11:18)
>
> "There was always the possibility of riots and other forms of civil unrest during the holy days of the festival, and Pilate (the Governor, as representative of the Emperor in Rome) hand marched in form Caesarea with his cohorts (each of 500 legionaries) to be ready to intervene if necessary. Such disturbances are only briefly alluded to in the Gospels. According to Mark, a certain Barabbas was taken prisoner together with 'them that had made insurrection with him, who had committed murder in the insurrection' (Mark 15:7). Mark also says that the chief priests and scribes 'sought how they might take [Jesus] by craft, and put him to death. But they said, Not on the feast day, lest there be an uproar of the people' (Mark 14: 1-2) If Jesus was to be liquidated, both great speed and great caution were called for.

> "The Pharisees first tried to get Jesus to incriminate himself in a public discussion. They asked him whether it was right to pay taxes to the Roman Emperor. If Jesus had replied in the negative, he would have been open to the charge of high treason, had he replied positively, he would have lost all the support and most of the interest of the people. Instead, he got out of the predicament by a stroke of genius (Mark 12:14-27). The Sadducees then attempted to ridicule his doctrine of reincarnation. "This attack too he parried skillfully (Mark 12:19-27)." [p.133]

Crucification and after effects

What happened next, and how He was crucified is a common knowledge. Such were the revolutionary actions of Jesus. Of course, the Jews had to pay the price as did Hindus for abandoning the Buddha. Swami Dharmatirtha has observed nearly sixty years ago:

> "The Jews of Palestine gave birth to a Jesus Christ; but they crucified him and rejected his religion; and their country passed into the hands of the Muslims where Britain now holds the balance between the Jews and the Muslims. India produced a Buddha, but when she rejected his religion of righteousness, she passed into the hands of the Muslims and Britain now holds the balance between the Hindus and the Muslims. The Jews became the kingless people of the world and the Hindus the only civilised nation that is not master of its own country. The two great religions, Buddhism and Christianity, rejected in the land of their birth, spread far and wide, and now sustain the religious life of the greatest nations of the East and the West, whereas the Hindus and the Jews rank as the orphans of humanity." [Swami Dharmatirtha, "*The Menace of Hindu Imperialism*", p. 110]

Present Christian Leadership

Present day Christian Leadership in India seems to have forgotten the Revolutionary Jesus. Not only that, they seem to have forgotten a compassionate Jesus, who worked for the poor and the destitute. Now they are no more egalitarian preachers. There is hardly any difference in a Brahmanic caste system and Christian priestly caste system. Even untouchability is practiced not only in the Churches but also in Christian graveyards. A Brahmin talks of Philosophy, a Christian talks of Theosophy, but a Dalitbahujan Ambedkarite talks of Sociology. Christians have never taken to agitational politics in the past, they always tried to favour the oppressors, and stand by them, except since last few years atrocities.

Christians and Muslims are Being Made "Untouchables"

For those, who forget history, history repeats itself. Remember how Buddhists were made "untouchables" by BSO through contempt and atrocities and denial of human rights. All those tricks and all those factors are in operation even today. They are not only directed against Dalits today, they are also directed against Muslims and Christians. They all are being gradually segregated and boycotted.

Those who cannot see the writing on the wall are doomed to perish. So let us all be awake and identify our enemy. The enemy of Christians and Muslims is not Communism or Buddhism; it is Brahmanical Social Order.

Social Service and Social Transformation

This is the important point, which one must understand. Medical ethics says, prevention is better than cure. Instead of curing a disease give more attention to its prevention. To mend a fracture is social service, to create environment so that fractures do not take place is social transformation. To give vitamin pills to malnourished Adivasi children is social service, to give their parents employment so that they can buy wholesome food for their children is social transformation. To give charity to a beggar is social service, to create social atmosphere so that nobody has to beg is social change. To give rice at Rs. two per kilo when market price is Rs. seven per cent is social service, to raise the income of the person so that he can buy the rice at market price is social change. To feed the hungry is social service, to create situation where nobody remains hungry is social change. To teach an illiterate is social service, to destroy the social structure which made him illiterate is social change. To open a new school in thee vicinity of an illiterate poor colony of *zopadpatti* could be social service, to motivate the poor hungry and illiterate man to send his child to school walking five kilometers away even on an empty stomach is social transformation. To protect a weak person by giving him weapons is social service, to make him strong enough to let him manufacture and use his own weapons is social change. To teach an egalitarian prayer to a school child may be social service, to dynamite the scriptures spreading inequality among human beings is a social change. To assure protection to scared minorities may be social justice, to give them power so that they can defend themselves is social transformation.

I have great respect for those missionaries who did a tremendous amount of good work in the past. If there were no such missionaries, there would have been no Phule, no Shahu and no Ambedkar, let alone Kanshiram and Mayavati. In my humble opinion, missionaries in India are doing social service, and are the very best at that, but still it is not social transformation. I think here lies the importance of Ambedkarism, which is not a political movement alone. It stands for not social service or social justice alone but for social transformation and economic emancipation.

The Remedy

While we remember Revolutionary Jesus, we may not forget that we cannot progress by merely "Dalit Unity", or by only "Dalit Muslim Unity", or by only "Dalit Christian Unity", we have to build a Bahujan Samaj, which is not an easy task. One has to understand the mechanics of Bahujan Samaj. Let us forget, for the time being at least, the international tensions between Christians and Muslims, between Christians and Buddhists and such similar tensions. Today in India, the dragon BSO is facing us and trying to devour us one by one. Under such circumstances, the Unity of all the Dalit Bahujans can be jeopardized if one talks of proselytizing. We are aiming at only a political unity of sufferers of the system. Let everybody stick to his or her own religion. There is no other choice - either unite or perish.

Ambedkar's Advice to Christians

The Speech Delivered to Indian Christians

Dr. Ambedkar, during the period of active consideration of choice of religion to adopt, delivered a speech to Indian Christians of Sholapur, (published in '*Janata*' of 5.2.1938), reproduced from '*Dnyanodaya*' :

> "From the available religions and personalities in the world, I consider only two Buddha and Christ for conversion. We want a religion for me and my followers which will teach equality, freedom among men, and how man must behave with men and God, how child should behave with father etc.
>
> "Missionaries feel they have done their duty when they convert an untouchable to Christianity. They do not look after their political rights. I find this is a big fault in Christians, because they have not entered into politics up till now. It is difficult for any institution to survive without political support. We, Untouchables, though are ignorant and illiterate, we are in movement. That is why we have 15 seats in the Legislative Assembly. Students are getting scholarships, there are government hostels. Such is not the case of Christian students. If an untouchable student getting scholarship get converted, his scholarship is stopped though his financial status remains same. If you were in politics, things would have been opposed.
>
> "Your society is educated. Hundreds of boys and girls are Matric. These people have not agitated against this injustice unlike the uneducated untouchables. If any girl becomes a nurse or any boy becomes a teacher they are involved in their own affairs, they do not get involved in public affairs. Even clerks and officers are busy in their work, he ignores the social injustice. Your society is so much educated, how many are District Judges or Magistrates? I tell you, this is because of your neglect towards politics, because there in nobody to talk of and fight for your rights. ..." [*Ganjare* Vol. III. p. 142 ff.]

Phule-Ambedkar Sahityik Melawa September 2000

In His Presidential Speech Prof. Mahendra Bhaware

Marathi literature is being discussed now, which is a welcome move. But this literature has not related itself with the core of Dalit literature. There is immense caste feeling among the Muslims. It is necessary that this reality should be brought out by Muslim authors. Even now they do not depict the Paigambar who denied *Chaturvarnya* system. On the contrary their ideals are Brahminic authors. Just one Javed Qureshi Pasha seems to be the lone figure writing with inspiration of

Phule-Ambedkar and relating to their ideology. Else there is none in Muslim Marathi Literature.

He further said:

After Babari demolition, the minorities are living under fear and loss of safety. Christians are facing horrible events. Murder of Graham Stains and his sons was gruesome. After this more atrocities are being committed all over India. Maharashtra is no exception. It has reached our Nasik also. How cruel the fundamentalists can become is seen from events in Nasik.

In this very city of Nasik, there was a Christian Marathi Sahitya Sammelan celebrated. But even simple voice of condemnation of these cruelties was not heard in the Conference. This gives rise to many questions. Whom these people wish to relate themselves with? They are a part of minorities. Are they even then a part of fundamentalist system? The Marathi Christian Literary people need to reply to this. Dalit compassion is related intimately with agony. Whatever is related with agony, Christ resides there. This is what Nirmal Anand says regarding Dalit compassion. If today's Christian Marathi Conference is limited its own religion, then what happened to the compassion of the Christ? This is the question that arises. If the literature is bringing forward the agonies of the minorities and the agonies of the women, such literature must stand on the side of transformation. Instead of speaking of past conferences, it is necessary to clarify the present stand of the movement.

Discrimination in Churches

[http://www.expressbuzz.com/edition/story.aspx?Title=Dalit+Christians+to+walk+out+of+Eraiyur+village&artid=dUMIflJeo/M=&SectionID=lifojHIWDUU=&MainSectionID=fyV9T2jIa4A=&SectionName=rSY%7C6QYp3kQ=&SEO=VCK]

An article titled 'Dalit Christians to walk out of Eraiyur village' by Yogesh Kabirdoss, published on 7th Oct. 2009 describes discrimination in Churches

04:25:00 AM IST Last Updated : 07 Oct 2009 06:58:52 AM IST

CHENNAI: Frustrated over the failure of the Roman Catholic Church to put an end to caste discrimination, Dalit Christians of Eraiyur in Villupuram district have decided to walk out of the village on Wednesday when the annual festival begins at the Our Lady of Rosary Church.

Eraiyur was under media spotlight last year when the Dalits of the parish were on a fast-unto-death in March. They alleged that Vanniyars were not allowing Dalits to use the pathway to the cemetery and not sharing with them the cemetery and the hearse. Vanniyars had their separate burial ground and own hearse to cart the dead there.

Besides, they had raised their voice against the sacred car with the idol of Our Lady of Rosary, taken out through the village streets during the main festival in May, not visiting Dalit colonies and the around 1,000 Dalit congregation not being allowed to contribute money for the conduct of the festival.

When the protest in March last year led to a police firing, killing two persons, a peace meeting was called and the archdiocese of Puducherry and Cuddalore gave an assurance to put an end to the discrimination.

But other than the common pathway issue, nothing else has been sorted out. A new hearse provided to the parish has not been touched by the Vanniyars, who have made one exclusively for themselves, G. Mathew, State Secretary of Viduthalai Chiruthaigal Katchi said.

With the VCK lending its support, the Dalits have resolved to boycott the church festival on Wednesday and vacate the village by moving to adjacent Elavarasankottai between 11 am and 8 pm.

The villagers claimed that representations to the archbishop had done nothing to put an end to the discrimination.

Reacting to the allegations, Vicar General of the diocese, Anthony Samy, said most of the issues had been settled and the one pertaining to the church car visiting Dalit colonies was in court.

• • •

7

Dalits and OBCs

The Other Backward Classes

OBC or 'other backward classes', as a matter of fact, are the real owners of the country. But all their paths to the progress are obstructed because they are entangled in what is known as '*bara baluterdar*' - the form of *jajmani* system, i.e. a kind of barter system to obtain free services from various craftsmen and pay them some grain at the time of harvesting. The head of the village is known in Maharashtra as Patil. He is the central point in this system. This system is going on for generations in the villages and, and is still going strong in most of the villages. It has got more importance in the northern India, in states like Rajasthan, Bihar and UP.

They pretend that they are not ignorant, but they have got no inkling of what are social justice, power and prestige. As a matter of fact, they do not understand what is the meaning of backwardness; they do not know what they are proud of. They do not know what exactly is meant by saying that the OBCs are the backward class. Till the formation of the Mandal Agitation, in 1978, they did not even know or rather they did not consider themselves as backwards. Their immense power is wasted because they are divided into hundreds and thousands of caste and sub-castes. Because of this, the wily political parties, headed by the *Dwija*-s, take undue advantage of these people and these OBCs, rather stupidly, consider it honourable to carry somebody else's flag on their shoulders. Thanks to Dr. Ambedkar, who considered their situation, and arranged article 340 in the Constitution of India.

OBCs have got a false vanity that they are superior to the SCs and STs, and this feeling is imbibed in their blood to a great extent. OBCs are a cursed community. The laws of Manu have already boycotted him and forbidden him from the sources of power, but he is proud that he is boycotted less than other castes below him.

Some of them are village heads, known as Patil in Maharashtra. When elected as '*Sarpanch*', he considers as if he had been elected to govern the whole world. Even an illiterate Patil usually gets elected as the '*Sarpanch*' of the village. The decisions of panchayats considered sacrosanct are implemented faithfully, even though illegal and antinational. Recently, a panchayat in Rajasthan, gave the decisions that the girls should be married in childhood. Not only that, they warned the Central government not to interfere in their customs and manners. They are in total darkness and still they do not want to get out of that darkness.

As a central point of the daily village economy system, he has got the first authority of worshipping the village gods. He is thus enslaved in gods, religion, customs, manners, rituals and traditions, which he cannot escape.

In the name of modernisation, the means of livelihood of OBCs are taken away by the capitalist system, putting them under great financial crunch. OBCs are already ill-educated and are under great influence of the religion and rituals and hegemony of the upper castes. He not only considers himself superior to the scheduled castes and tribes, but also to the other castes of the OBCs category itself.

All this needs to be corrected, and for this it is essential that the OBCs are awakened so that they come out of the influence of the religion, the rituals and unnecessary burden of expenses of gods and goddesses.

OBCs are known as the 'Bahujan Samaj', but are never in majority being divided into castes and sub-castes. Unless the OBCs come out of their caste prejudices and help forming the Bahujan Samaj community of all the non-Brahmin castes, there cannot be any progress of the OBCs. Dr. Ambedkar tried to awaken the OBCs in thousands of ways. Unfortunately, the desired results are not yet obtained.

It is not properly realised that whatever facilities OBCs got in India were not because of the OBC leaders, but because of Dr. Ambedkar. 'Backward classes of citizens', was the word that was used by Ambedkar for OBCs, in Article 16 (4). There was hue and cry in the Constituent Assembly then.

Problem of Kshatriya-Hood

Prof. Ashok Rana is a well-known OBC historian, orator, writer, thinker, and editor of '*Rationalist Teachers Association Bulletin*' (RATTA) from Amravati. Delivering the keynote address as the President of 'First Maratha History Conference' at Pune in May 2010, he talked on the '*Problem of Kshatriya-hood*'.

Who is Maratha?

Mahatma Jotirao Phule called Chatrapati Shivaji as '*Kulvadi Bhushan*', (glory of peasants) in his ballad on Shivaji. From his writings, it emerges that that the word '*Maratha*' was used by all castes in Maharashtra to identify themselves.

The day-to-day needs, manners and customs, gods and goddesses, and funeral rites are the same among all the castes among the peasants, like blacksmiths, masons, fishermen, carpenters, *kunbis*, etc. Opposite is the case of Brahmins; none of their customs are same as non-Brahmins. Therefore, Mahatma Phule concluded that, 'One who is not a Brahmin is a Maratha'.

Jadunath Sarkar observed that till the beginning of twentieth century, Maharashtrian Brahmin, if addressed as Maratha, used to feel insulted and would retort that, 'No, No, I am not Maratha; I am southern Brahmin'. I take this subject for discussion because, in history of Maharashtra, the recognition of Kshatriya-hood of Marathas had been a great problem, which was accentuated during times of Shahu Maharaj.

Hiranya-garbha-kings

Mostly the Buddhist kings were given status of Kshatriya by rite of *Hiranya garbha*, where he has to pass through a golden vessel under Brahminic *mantras*. In North India, four Rajput *kulas* were created by *yajnya* on mount Abu.

An arrogant verse is now-a-days found under the image of Parashuram. It says, *four Vedas on lips, a bow with arrows on back, this Brahmin-hood and Kshatriya-hood, is strong enough to* ***curse*** *and kill by* ***arrow***.

Such arrogance was expressed in the form of Parashuram time and again. Kartvirya Arjuna was killed by Parashuram. Kartavirya's son King Subhaum killed Parashuram. Jain History records this event, proving that the Jain kings had defeated Brahminic system.

Jains, who had rejected *Chaturvarnya*, authority of Vedas and system of *yajnyas*, later accepted these Brahminic systems. They were, therefore, rewarded with *Vaishya* status though not *Kshatriya-hood*. Because the Buddhists fought against all these three systems, they were made *Shudras*, and some of them were even degraded to be 'untouchables'.

One thing is certain from this that, the status of *Kshatriya-hood* depends on the whims and fancies of Brahmins. And it is restricted to an individual and does not automatically come to whole progeny. For this Brahmins declared that after Nanda Kings, there are no Kshatriyas; only Shudras and Brahmins exist.

Those who accepted to remain as subservient to Brahmins, now live under the illusion of their Kshatriya-hood and hypocritically deceive themselves. The castes in India like Maratha-s, Rajput-s, Yadav-s, Jat-s, Reddy-s etc. lost their identity under the illusion of Kshatriya-hood. And they helped the Brahmins in maintaining the hierarchy of castes by denigrating castes below them. This created many problems, which need to be understood to solve them.

Maratha Race and Gotra-*s*

After '*Vedokta*' episode during times of Shahu Maharaj in early 20th century, a lot of literature was created to prove Kshatriya status of Marathas and relationship with Aryan culture was claimed, forgetting that they were getting themselves enslaved under the Brahminic yoke. They claimed descent from Sun and Moon. If that is true, they become foreigners as Sun worship came from Iran. Some claim *Nag-Kula*, which came down from Harrapan culture.

Marathas also accept the concept of *Gotra*. This word means cattle shed and also body organs. Aryans came with cows. The owners had different names like Vashishtha, Yajnyavalka, Shandilya, Kashyap etc., which became *gotra* names.

If the second meaning is accepted, it means born from their organs. Those who are proud to declare themselves with *gotra* names, mean they are progeny of these ancient men. Thus, the Marathas become the progeny of Brahmins. These people forget that to have the *gotra* names means they are denying the existence of their own ancestors.

Satvahanas

They were first dynasty in Maharashtra, during 230 BCE. They promoted *Prakrit* language denying Sanskrit and belonged to *Nag-Kula*. Some kings were Jains and some were Buddhists. From them emerged today's Marathas, though some historians unsuccessfully tried, and even now try, to depict them as of Brahmin *kulas*.

Their history, thus, goes back to two thousand years and has been traced by historians through dynasties like Manavya, Haihay, Bhoj, Yadav, Nala, Kadamba, Maurya, Chalukya etc. All these names, today, have become the names of Kulas. Many surnames from *Nag-Kula* are found among all the castes of Bahujans, and hence whole Bahujan Samaj consists of Marathas, says Prof. Rana.

We have discussed *Vedokta* episode in '*Maratha Revolt against Brahmanism*' and *Hiranya-garbha*, in '*Tirupati Balaji was Buddhist Shrine*'.

Tormentors of Dalits

Real tormentors

Atrocities on Dalits are a regular feature for a long time. It has always been an OBC **hand** and the Brahmin **brain** that commits atrocities. Phule knew it, Shahu knew it, the Periyar knew it and Ambedkar knew it. But they did not blame OBCs; they blamed Brahmanism. Now the Sangh Parivar, for their own vested interests, tells us "because OBCs are immediate tormentors, they are the real enemies of Dalits and not the Brahmins". And their stooges are repeating their words.

Do not see caste of tormentor

Why should one see the caste of a tormentor? Any tormentor – of any caste - has to be fought against. Nobody has said that such tormentors should be spared. To derive conclusion of Dalit-OBC contradictions from such sentimental questions is not only stupidity but denotes tendencies of a traitor of the community by misguiding them on sentimental issues ignoring the real ones. It shows a tendency to purposefully instigate Dalits against OBCs and vice-versa, during the times when there is seen a tendency of OBCs awakening, however slight it may be. And for what reason? Just to please the RSS masters and prevent the formation of Bahujan Samaj?

An Ambedkarite friend asks: Why to be so parochial about OBCs? Instead of bowing before the Rationalist in Periyar, why should one search an OBC in him? What else except a parochial mind set it reveals? Do Ambedkarites search for a Kshatriya in the Buddha? Never!

As the press reports suggest, most of the actual tormentors of Muslims in 2002 Gujarat pogrom were SC/STs. Do the people hold them responsible? No! The press reports allegedly hold RSS rulers headed by Chief Minister Narendra Modi responsible. Why?

By the logic of RSS and their Dalit stooges, people should have blamed SC/STs. Somebody has rightly said, "it is not the gun that fights - it is the man behind the gun that fights, it is not the man that fights - it is the mind within the man that fights". What is the mindset of those who engineered the pogrom of Muslims? Is it of OBC or of RSS? If one searches this, one finds the answer whether to blame OBC mindset in oppressor or RSS mindset in oppressor – either of Muslims or of Dalits.

This should also decide whether the physical or the mental violence is worse from the victim's point of view. Let us remember Babasaheb has said that caste is a mental notion. People observe caste discriminations and untouchability not because they are cruel, but because they are mentally conditioned to act like that by the constant hammering by their religion.

Strategy of Dalits

Supposing we follow RSS ideology and consider OBCs as our enemy No.1, what next? OBCs will be your enemies with strong vigour. Are Brahmins going to accept Dalits as equals? We need to discuss the situation that is likely to arise. May be it becomes necessary to have strategic alliances with Brahmins, as Mayavati did in UP. But we have to consider seriously whether that be a permanent solution. The ideology of Ambedkar is the only ideology that can combat Brahmanism, provided we do not fall a prey to RSS techniques.

Those Dalits who advocate OBCs as number one enemy of Dalits must tell us the future strategy. Just saying Brahmins are not our enemies now, it is only half the strategy, what next, must be answered by them.

One has to observe the slow but sure change in OBC mindset, at least in a section of OBC.

The Attempts to Awaken OBCs

History of Conflict on 'Riddles in Hinduism'

The period from 1988 to 1993 was eventful for the Dalit Bahujan Muslim masses, especially of Maharashtra. Struggle of Ambedkarites was already going on for renaming Marathwada University after Dr. Ambedkar. Under such charged atmosphere, on 2nd October 1987, the '*Dhamma Chakra Pravartana*' Day, the Government of Maharashtra, published the volume IV of "Writings and Speeches of Dr. Ambedkar" – '*The Riddles in Hinduism*' at Diksha Bhoomi Nagpur.

On 30th October 87, '*Loksatta*' of Bombay published articles criticizing Government for this publication claiming that the '*Riddle of Rama and Krishna*' was derogatory to Hindu gods. Some people from Amravati filed petition in High Court against the publication. The '*Maratha Maha Sangha*' brought a '*morcha*' on winter session of Assembly at Nagpur. Education Minister declared that the Appendix would be deleted. *Morcha-s* and counter-*morcha-s* started. In Bombay Ambedkarites had a huge *morcha* and Government declared that they would reconsider the decision of deletion. On the day of decision, Shiva Sena brought a huge morcha of 250,000 and Government relented. Ambedkarites again organised a huge unprecedented *morcha* on 5th February 1988. The Government decided to add a remark that they do not agree with the contents of Appendix and retain the Appendix, with the consent of the opposition including BJP.

The newspapers carried articles in favour and against the 'Riddles'. Riots erupted. Many lives were lost, mostly of Dalits and OBCs. Not a single Brahmin suffered. *Loksatta*, Shiva Sena and Maratha Maha Sangha cannot be considered as orthodox, they call themselves followers of Shivaji, but kept on spewing venom. Many others participated, the fieriest attack being from Durgabai Bhagwat.

The lives of Dalit Bahujans were lost but there was a great awakening among the OBCs, specially the Kunbi-Marathas. The OBC leaders like Nagesh Chaudhari, the editor of '*Bahujan Sangharsh*', started appealing to the OBCs that the analysis and review of Hinduism by Dr. Ambedkar was for the benefit of Bahujans. He said, the 'Riddles' put forth by Ambedkar are to the Brahmins, but they pushed it on Bahujans. It was pity, he said, that some brainless OBC leaders are opposed to Ambedkar and Dalits. The real intelligent OBC cannot be a disciple of Rama and Krishna; he can be disciple of only Phule and Ambedkar, he averred.

They started serial "Ramayana" on TV channel. Kanshiram of BSP organised thousands of rallies to get implementation of Mandal Commission Report for benefit of OBCs. V.P. Singh Government had to implement it, albeit partly. RSS started '*Ram Ratha Yatra*'. Bajpayee said, "We had to start '*kamandal*' because they started Mandal".

Babari Masjid was demolished in 1992, on the Dalits' mourning Day, 6th December – day of demise of Ambedkar – converting it into a day of Victory for Sangh Parivar. Hindu Muslim riots erupted.

All these tragic events took place. But there was a silver lining to these dark clouds. The OBCs got awakened, at least partly. More and more people started thinking in lines of Nagesh Chaudhari. Many OBC leaders started awakening the OBC masses through their caste fora. The rise of "Maratha Seva Sangha" was one of such welcome events in 1990. It is this Maratha Seva Sangha, which brought in 'Shiva Dharma', and today it is trying to bring in changes among the Kunbis-Marathas.

Adv. Shashikant Pawar of 'Maratha Maha Sangha' was instigated by *Manuvadi*-s to start agitation against the 'Riddles'. But soon he realised his mistake and later apologized claiming that he was saved from the sin of burning the 'Riddles', as he burned only a bunch of newspapers. The media immediately stopped coverage to Shashikant Pawar as soon as he withdrew the agitation, says M.M. Deshmukh. ['*rashtra nirmate*', p. 20]

Conflict of Riddles Misrepresented

When Dr. Ambedkar wrote the '*Riddles of Rama and Krishna*', he utilised the symbolism of Rama and Krishna to represent the Brahminical social order of *Chaturvarnya* with 'Brahmin' supremacy and actually explained how the identity of Kshatriyas or OBCs was denigrated by the Brahmins. The movements of transformation, failed to bring forward this aspect of Ambedkar to the OBC 'Hindu' masses and therefore it became easy for RSS to project Ambedkar's writings as an attack on 'Hindu' gods and goddesses, and they succeeded in organising huge masses of 'Hindu' OBCs against the Dalit Buddhist organisations, with consequent aftermath.

Rest of the Riddles Remain Unsolved

The Riddles were divided into three groups:

PART I - RELIGIOUS

Riddle No. 1: The difficulty of knowing why one is a Hindu

Riddle No. 2: The Origin of the Vedas – The Brahminic Explanation or An Exercise In The Art Of Circumlocution

Riddle No. 3: The Testimony of Other Shastras on the Origin of the Vedas

Riddle No. 4: Why suddenly the Brahmins declare the Vedas to be infallible and not to be questioned?

Riddle No. 5: Why did the Brahmins go further and declare that the Vedas are neither made by man nor by god?

Riddle No. 6: The contents of the Vedas: have they any moral or spiritual value?

Riddle No. 7: The turn of the tide or how did the Brahmins declare the Vedas to be lower than the lowest of their Shastras?

Riddle No. 8: How the Upanishads declared war on the Vedas?

Riddle No. 9: How the Upanishads came to be made subordinate to the Vedas?

Riddle No. 10: Why did the Brahmins make the Hindu gods fight against one another?

Riddle No. 11: Why did the Brahmins make the Hindu gods suffer to rise and fall?

Riddle No. 12: Why did the Brahmins dethrone the gods and enthrone the goddesses?

Riddle No. 13: The riddle of the ahimsa

Riddle No. 14: From ahimsa back to himsa

Riddle No. 15: How did the Brahmins wed an ahimsak god to a bloodthirsty Goddess?

APPENDIX

Appendix I: The Riddle of the Vedas

Appendix II: The Riddle of the Vedanta

Appendix III: The Riddle of the Trimurti

Appendix IV: II Smarth Dharma

Appendix V: The Infallibility of the Vedas

PART II - SOCIAL

Riddle No. 16: The four Varnas - are the Brahmins sure of their origin?

Riddle No. 17: The four Ashramas – the why and how about them.

Riddle No.18: Manu's madness or the Brahminic explanation of the origin of the mixed castes.

Riddle No. 19: The change from paternity to maternity. What did the Brahmins wish to gain by it?

Riddle No. 20: Kali Varjya or the Brahminic art of suspending the operation of sin without calling it sin.

Appendix I: The riddle of the Varnashrama dharma.

Appendix II: Compulsory matrimony.

PART III - POLITICAL.

Riddle No. 21: The theory of Manvantara.

Riddle No. 22: Brahma is not dharma. What good is Brahma?

Riddle No. 23: Kali Yuga – Why have the brahmins made it unending?

Riddle No. 24: The riddle of the Kali Yuga.

Appendix I: The riddle of Rama and Krishna.

Thus there are 32 Riddles.

It was on the riddle of Rama and Krishna, the trouble started. But all other Riddles remained unsolved. It was natural that Brahminical elites would not discuss these topics. But what about the Dalits and other Bahujans? The OBCs? All these are silent, as if these topics are not important. I believe the OBCs must try and understand and come to the correct interpretations of these topics. Will they do it? Doubtful! Ambedkar has already mentioned there is a great dearth of wisdom among the OBC leaders. Let us hope the future generations do not forget the lives lost in the struggle of Riddles.

Why 'Riddles' were written?

Dr. Ambedkar wrote this volume for the purpose of future restructuring of the Indian nation. He believed that there is no future for a common Hindu unless he comes out of the quagmire of stupid ideas, rules and rites he is put in by the elites for thousands of years.

It could be argued that, in this age of scientific explosion, why explore the past subjects like Vedas, Upanishads, gods and goddesses, *Varna-ashram* system, castes, *Manvantara*, *Kali yuga* and *Kali-Varjya* etc. These are all dead subjects. But it must be realised that for a common man, these are not dead subjects. Common man is even today gripped and enveloped in stupid ideas spread by the Brahmins. Unless he is liberated from these ideas there is no future in Indian environment. The Brahminic propaganda that Hinduism is '*Sanatan*' meaning eternal and unchanging is the greatest hindrance in the way to progress. Ambedkar believes that this is false. He does not agree that Hindu society was always dynamic and at times even revolutionary.

Introduction to Riddles in Hinduism

'Riddles in Hinduism – An Exposition to Enlighten the Masses', is the full title of the book by Dr. B.R. Ambedkar, published posthumously by the Government of Maharashtra in 1987. In Introduction, Ambedkar says:

> "... It is intended for the common mass of Hindus who need to be awakened to know in what quagmire the Brahmins have placed them and to lead them on to the road of rational thinking." [Riddles: W&S 4: 1]

He states two purposes of this book:

(1) To 'make the mass of people to realize that Hindu religion is not *Sanatan'*,

(2) To 'draw attention of the Hindu masses to the devices of the Brahmins and to make them think for themselves how they have been deceived and misguided by the Brahmins.' [Riddles: W&S 4: 1]

He quotes Buckle, who observed in *history of civilisation*, that unless doubt begins there could be no progress, without doubt there would be no inquiry, and without inquiry there will be no knowledge; those who do not feel darkness will never look for light, and concludes:

> " ... If on any point we have attained to certainty, we make no further inquiry on the point; because inquiry would be useless, or perhaps dangerous. To doubt must intervene, before the investigation can begin. Here, then we have the act of doubting as the originator or, at all events, the necessary antecedent of all progress." [Riddles: W&S 4: 8]

OBCs Remain Cultural Slaves of BSO

As a matter of fact, the relationship of Dalit-Bahujans to 'upper' castes in all the political parties run by Brahmins, as various teams from A to E of Brahmanism in Kanshiram's terms, is like Rama and Hanuman, as put forward by Kancha Ilaiah, himself an OBC, whose observation about Congress applies to all parties under control of Brahminical Social Order (BSO). He laments that at such a time, when Ambedkarism was creating a small force of conscious people among Dalit-Bahujans, a large number of OBCs were, perhaps for the sake of fringe benefits - the fell down crumbs of spoils, willing to be trustworthy Hanumans. He describes the relationship as:

> "... The relationship between an 'upper' caste man and a Dalitbahujan caste man within Congress was like that between Rama and Hanuman. It is a common knowledge that Hanuman was a South Indian Dalit who joined the imperial army of Rama to fight against the South Indian Nationalist ruler - Ravana. Hanuman worked day in and day out in the interest of 'Ramrajya' (an anti-Dalitbahujan and anti-woman kingdom), yet his place in the administration was marginal and subservient. ..." [Kancha Ilaiah: 1998: 58]

Such Hanumans abound in plenty in all communities and are utilised in "proper way" by BSO in Many Forms.

Killing of Shambuka

Explaining how Rama killed the *Shudra* ascetic Shambuka to protect *Chaturvarnya*, Ambedkar had absolved Rama from blame. He had observed (in 1936):

> "Some people seem to blame Rama because he wantonly and without reason killed Shambuka. But to blame Rama for killing Shambuka is to misunderstand the whole situation. Ram Raj was a Raj based on *Chaturvarnya*. As a king, Rama was bound to maintain *Chaturvarnya*. It was his duty therefore to kill Shambuka, the Shudra, who had transgressed his class and wanted to be a Brahmin. This is the reason why Rama killed Shambuka. But this also shows that penal sanction is necessary for the maintenance of *Chaturvarnya*. Not only penal sanction is necessary, but penalty of death is necessary. That is why Rama did not inflict on Shambuka a lesser punishment." [Annihilation of Caste]

The story of birth of Rama

Ambedkarite scholar Dr. Vinod Anavrat explains how a story denigrating Kshatriyas was propagated through Ramayana:

> "Rama is an imaginary individual created through the imaginary union of a *rishi* with queen Kaushallya."
>
> "The very story of birth of Rama was created by the Brahmins by striking a hard blow at the identity of Kshatriyas, because, Rama was the progeny of sex with queen of Dashrath with royal consent. There was a great cunning intrigue in constructing such a legend in Ramayana. There was a struggle going on for supremacy between the Brahmins and Kshatriyas. Brahmins wanted to be supreme and give secondary place to Kshatriyas, and at the same time build the consent system among Kshatriyas to accept the second position. This was their prime object. This object, they achieved by sowing the idea in the birth story of Rama and hoisted the flag of Brahminic dominance."
>
> "In the guise of *Putra Kameshthi Yajnya*, one Brahmin *rishi* named Rishyashrung established sexual relations with the queens of Dashrath. As its result, Rama from Kaushallya, Laxman and Shatrughna from Sumitra, and Bharata from Kaikayi, were born. This means the Brahmins publicly propagated that the Kshatriyas though valorous in war, were impotent. At the same time, the idea was implanted that Brahmins not only are learned but also 'real men', and proved that the *Kshatriya-hood* (valor) of Kshatriyas is because of Brahmin seed. Under such circumstances, Kshatriyas would develop the feeling of keeping the secret of '*closed fist worth a lakh and a quarter*' and would automatically accept the domination of Brahmins; this was the Brahminic hidden strategy. All these points were carefully thought over and the story of birth of Rama was created and thus the pen achieved an easy victory over the sword." [Anavrat: 2011: 56]

To Create Casteless Society is the Aim

The struggle for destruction of Caste should have to precede the spread of Buddhism, but need not be a precondition. Equitable distribution of land and fast implementation of Land Reforms is the need of the day. The elite rulers know that this will dilute the hegemony of Brahmins, and so such reforms are not implemented by the present rulers for last half a century. Dalits feel and contrast the honesty of the British, who imparted education to lower castes knowing well that this will enable these people to drive them away.

Here comes the necessity of political power. None of your aims can be achieved without political power. The ground has to be prepared by the religious moral thought by the thinkers for a new rule to start, as explained by Dr. Ambedkar. Maurya Dynasty started after the Buddha and Mahavira, Christian states flourished after the teachings of Jesus, Islamic states flourished throughout the world after the Prophet, Shivaji established his kingdom after cultural revolution of Tukaram, and Ranjit Singh established his kingdom after the cultural revolution of the Sikh Gurus.

This is all true. But it is only a half-truth. The full truth is that, the religion to spread further, after initial planting of the seeds, requires the support of the State. Buddhism only spread after the efforts of Ashoka, Milinda and Kanishka. Brahmanism flourished after the counter-revolution by Pushyamitra Shunga and invasion and destruction of small republics of Nagas by Samudragupta. Islam spread in India not only by the efforts of Sufi saints but also the Sultanate at Delhi helped. Christianity spread in India not only by the Missionaries, who undeniably did a good job, but also by the rule of the Portuguese, the French and the British. Now that the British have left leaving the reigns of power to the Brahmanical Social Order (BSO), the religion of BSO is bound to flourish. But the flourishing of BSO means bringing back the slavery of the masses. That is the reason why RSS is trying to maintain power.

Unity of SC/ST is not Enough

The masses comprise of SC/ST/OBCs. The rule of democracy implies rule by majority, with safeguards to minorities. But in India it is other way round, the minority BSO rules and there are some trivial safeguards to the majority Dalit-Bahujans. If this has to change, there is a need of Unity of all "Natural allies". We all have to unite, dissolving our own identity if comes to that. I have written on this time and again. But the stages of unity start from political unity and end in social unity passing through the religious unity. Who are the "natural" allies of SC/STs, then? The OBCs, of course.

Atrocities on Dalits and OBCs

For a Dalit, atrocities are a part of daily life, as Raja Sekhar Vundru, mentions: "... Atrocities are part of their daily life. For Dalits persecution is as old as Shambuka, denial as old as Eklavya; revolution as old as Buddha; valor as old as Asura; slavery as old as *Dasyu* and untouchability as old as touch. Nevertheless, *Manu-dharma's* tentacles are widespread and all-compassing." ['*The Pioneer*, 30 Jan. 2000]

OBCs, except perhaps a few in "creamy layer", are also not immune from it. The fate of MBCs is not much different from that of Dalits. Phoolan Devi mentioned during one of her TV interviews shown recently after her murder, that every BC woman has to face possibility of rape, every day, when she goes to field to answer call of nature.

That was twenty years ago. It is happening even today. Let us see current news:

[http://www.countercurrents.org/george281212.htm] (accessed December 31, 2012), Goldy M. George writes under The *'Politics of Selective Protest'*:

"Narrating the experience of Dalit women in a villages in Tamilnadu, Cinthia Stephen quotes a girl in these words: 'there is no girl in our lane who has not been coerced or raped by the dominant caste men when they go to the fields to fetch water or for work'. Stephen's question is valid 'which upper-caste young woman, rural or urban, has ever had to brave repeated rape wthout to keep her family supplied with water?'"

Murder, rape, arson are events of every day life for Dalits and BCs. Dr. Tulsiram has observed:

> "... The religion based on caste system has annihilated millions of Dalits over the centuries. About three million Dalit women have been raped and around one million Dalits killed from the time of Independence. This is 25 times more than number of soldiers killed during the wars fought after independence. That is why Dalits do not need Aryan culture or Hindu Dharma based on caste any more...." [Dr. Tulsiram, *The Pioneer*, 30 Jan. 2000]

Caste Hatred towards Dr. Ambedkar

Many elites argue, these days, that all old scriptures are outdated and need not be criticized by opponents. But it must be remembered that the leaders of religion like Heads of *Pitha-s*, *Mahanta-s*, *Shankaracharya-s* or the leaders of organisations propagating the religion have done nothing to declare that these books are out of date and should not be followed. On the contrary, we find that even personalities like Ambedkar are denigrated on caste basis.

When Dr. Ambedkar was trying for "Hindu Code Bill", which was to remove the injustice on Hindu women, Jereshastri the then Shankaracharya of Sankeswara Pitha, wrote:

> "... Milk or Ganga water may be holy, but if it comes through a *nallah* or a gutter, it cannot be considered sacred. Similarly, the '*Dharmasastra*' howsoever it may be authentic, it cannot be considered authentic because it has come from a '*Mahar*' like Dr. Ambedkar. Ambedkar is a scholar, it is said that his study of scriptures is great, but he is an '*antyaja*'. How can the Ganga of Scriptures coming from the *nallah* of Ambedkar be holy? It must be

discardable like milk coming from the gutter..." ['*Nav Bharat*', daily, 21 Jan. 1950, q/b Yashwant Manohar 1999: p. 73]

What do OBCs have to say?

It has been repeatedly seen that the atrocities committed on SC/ST/Buddhists are always done by the OBCs, and never directly by the BSO. The hand that throws the burning torches over the huts of Dalits belongs to an OBC but his brain belongs to BSO. This is what all of us, the SCs, STs, and OBCs have to realize. Unless this happens, there can be no unity.

A Neglected Message from Dr. Ambedkar to OBCs

An article was published in Marathi local magazine by Suhas Sonwane based on daily *Loksatta*. The following is a gist of it, translated from Marathi. Mr. Gawande, a close friend of Dr. Ambedkar, who was then the Law Minister in Nehru Cabinet in 1947, asked for a message for the Maratha people to be published in the Souvenir of '*Maratha Mandir*' of Bombay. Ambedkar declined saying that he had no relation with the Organisation or the Marathas, but on persistent insistence, a message was given and it was published in the souvenir on 23rd March 1947. It was made available by Shri Vijay Survade and was undocumented till then. Dr. Ambedkar said:

> "This principle will apply not only to Marathas but to all Backward Castes. If they do not wish to be under the thumb of others they should concentrate on two things, one is **politics** and the other is **education**."
>
> "One thing I like to impress on you is that the community can live in peace only when it has enough moral but indirect pressure over the rulers. Even if a community is numerically weak, it can keep its pressure over the rulers and create its dominance as is seen by the example of status of present day Brahmins in India. It is essential that such a pressure is maintained, as without it, the aims and policies of the state cannot have proper direction, on which depends the development and progress of the state."
>
> "At the same time, it must not be forgotten that education is also important. Not only elementary education but higher education is most essential to keep ahead in competition of communities in their progress."
>
> "Higher education, in my opinion, means that education, which can enable you to occupy the strategically important places in State administration. Brahmins had to face a lot of opposition and obstacles, but they are overcoming these and progressing ahead."
>
> "I cannot forget, rather I am sad, that many people do not realize that the Caste system is existing in India for centuries because of inequality and a wide gulf of difference in education, and they have forgotten that it is likely to continue for some centuries to come. This gulf between the education of Brahmins and non-Brahmins will not end just by primary and secondary education. The difference in status between these can only be reduced by

higher education. Some non-Brahmins must get highly educated and occupy the strategically important places, which has remained the monopoly of Brahmins since long. I think this is the duty of the State. If the Govt. cannot do it, organisations like "*Maratha Mandir*" must undertake this task."

"I must emphasise one point here that middle class tries to compare itself with the highly educated and well placed and well to do community, whereas lower class all over the world has same fault. The middle class is not as liberal as upper one, and has no ideology as lower one, which makes it enemy of both the classes. The middle class Marathas of Maharashtra also have this fault. They have only two ways out, either to join hands with upper classes and prevent the lower classes from progress, and the other is to join hands with lower classes and both together destroy the upper class power coming against the progress of both. There was a time when they used to be with lower classes; now they seem to be with the upper class. It is for them to decide which way to go. The future of not only Indian masses but also their own future depends upon what decision the Maratha leaders take. As a matter of fact it all should be left to the skill and wisdom of the leaders of Marathas. But there seems to be a lack of such wise leadership among the Marathas."

What he said about Marathas, equally applies to all OBCs, and still holds true after more than half a century. Dr. Ambedkar wrote much to educate the OBCs. It is only now that OBCs are awakening gradually. It must not be forgotten that the future of this country depends on them.

Amartya Sen

Amartya Sen, when questioned by journalists about his preceptor and the father of his ideals on Welfare State, had acknowledged the Buddha as his '*guru*' and Ashoka as his ideal, a fact which never appeared in any BSO media. [*Prabuddha Bharat*, 30.4.2000]

Gold Treasure at India Temple

Temple Treasures Invited Foreign Invasion

It must be recognised that the wealth stashed in Brahminic temples have invited foreign invasions in the past. Describing Gaznavid invasion on Somnath temple, Ganguli explains the income of temple was from ten thousand villages and all this public moeny was for one thousand Brahmin *pujari-s,* who believed god would kill Muslims, and so did not stop merry making, during invasion. [*Struggle for Empire :* Ganguli: 1989 : 19 ff.]

Similarly Majumdar discussing general causes of Muslim victory, rightly observes:

"...The enormous wealth of the country was spent in building and enriching the temples, which they proved unable to protect, whereas the most appropriate use of these resources should have been to organize a common defence against the invaders, backed by a national effort. On the contrary, it was the very fabulous wealth of these defenseless temples and sacred towns which invited the foreigners and contributed greatly to consequent disaster." [*Struggle for Empire:* Majumdar : 1989 : 128]

Huge Treasure Found

[http://www.commodityonline.com/news/gold-treasure-at-india-temple-could-be-the-largest-in-the-world-40475-3-1.html (Accessed 6:45 PM 2/10/2012), NEW DELHI (Commodity Online) reports:

The treasure consisting of thousands of kilos of gold, diamonds, gems and silver ornaments, found concealed in different cellars at Sree Padmanabhaswamy temple, which was built in the 16th century by the kings of Travancore in Thiruvananthapuram, capital of Kerala. This could be the largest treasure of Gold found anywhere in India and possibly in the world. The vaults were opened on the orders of Supreme Court. Quick estimate was over a mind-blowing Rs. 1,00,000 crore ($22 billion), excluding its antique value of the rare articles. Two more cellars were yet to be opened. Analysts said the estimated amount is nearly three times the annual budget size of Kerala.

The priceless articles includes a gold sheaf weighing 500 kilos, an 18-foot gold chain weighing 10.5 kilos, a 36-kilo golden veil, quintals of gold granules and nuggets, crowns, numerous jewels and diamonds including those from Antwerp and rare coins from many countries including France.

This temple is thus the richest Hindu temple in India, bypassing the Balaji temple at Tirupati with gold worth Rs. 42,000 crore.

Security Needs

It has become a big headache for both Kerala and India governments because of security reasons. Security experts say that the Kerala Police do not have the means and expertise to provide security to such huge wealth. "You need laser-protected safes, digital surveillance and other such modern systems and programmes for providing security to things like this," a police official said.

Ownership Issues

The funds and the titles of Princely states in India were abolished in 1971. The descendants of the Travancore royal family, however, continued to control the Sri Padmanabhaswamy temple through the trust. The controversies have sparked off over who the real owners of this wealth are. Believers argue that the wealth belongs to the temple and should continue to be kept in the temple itself under foolproof security. However, some historians say that the treasure was actually public property hidden away by the erstwhile kings. Atheists and rationalists argue that the treasure could have been black wealth amassed by the kings and hidden in the temple for reasons of the peculiar security situation of those times. However, Uthradam Thirunnal Marthanda Varma, the present heir of the royalty, said he did not want to say anything about the treasure, describing it as the wealth of Lord Padmanabha. "I must not say anything about it. I am just seeing what is happening," he said.

The OBCs Must Claim Temple Treasures

Corruption Not Only in Politics

The problem of the corrupt religious mentality must be recognised. At present there are a lot of agitations going on against the corrupt practices. The leadership of this agitation, if one tries to fathom out, is with those people who are themselves beneficiary of these corrupt practices. Therefore, it is doubtful whether this agitation will be successful because those people whose interests are vested will not allow the agitation to succeed.

Along with the agitation for black money and the corrupt practices in the government it is also necessary that we must agitate against the black money that is stashed in the various religious institutions and the Hindu temples.

There is a question of the money that is stashed in the foreign banks. The amount that is stashed in the foreign banks is definitely less than the amount that is stashed in the temples within the country. It is also more difficult to bring back the money from foreign countries. In any case, enough noise was purposefully created in various media, that the concerned people must have taken precautions to shift it to safer places.

Money in Temples

Therefore, we must tackle this problem of the various temples first, which is comparatively easier and more rewarding. It must be realised that this amount belongs to the devotees who have donated to the temples. The custodians of the temples have already led a luxurious life on that money. It is the surplus amount present in temples after all the facilities to devotees, to the *pujari-s*, and renovation etc. of the structure etc. It is stored in the form of gold, ornaments, diamonds, land and bank deposits. The amount of such money, collected annually, as reported in a section of press, is more than yearly budget of the Government of India.

Unfortunately, those people who like to pretend to fight against the problems of corruption and black money are affected themselves by the pride of the caste and they believe that it is really justifiable to donate the money to the temples and they find nothing wrong in that money is uselessly lying in the temples at the command of custodians and is not useful to the devotees. It must also be understood that in majority of cases, the devotees are *Shudra-s* and *Ati-shudra-s* and the custodians are *dwija-s*. It must also be understood that there is nothing irreligious in claiming this amount for the benefit of common people for education and health purposes.

Whose Money is it Really?

It is argued by some that the feudal rulers mostly donated the money in the past, and so it should be under the government now. There could be no objection to this, provided it is be used for benefit of devotees, who are mostly *Shudra-s*, the OBCs, and not for making good the fiscal deficit, or paying salaries of government servants. The moneys donated by the feudal rulers also came from the *Shudra-s*, as Brahmins were exempted from all taxes. So the money must now be used for benefit of OBCs.

Illogical Arguments

At a prominent temple of Padmanabha in south India, a huge treasure was found. Some people objected to use of it for the people by the government arguing that it belongs to the 'deity'. The very same people wanted that the government should spend on the protection of the same treasure. Why should the money required for its protection be borne by state? When you keep your valuables in a locker of bank or safe deposit vault, they charge you the rent. Then, why should the state spend on expenses for protecting the valuables of the temple? It is the true that it is the duty of state to protect the property of citizens, but then state gets taxes from citizens. This property has not paid any taxes. So why should state spend on its protection?

The Principal Contradiction

The principal contradiction, in this country for last two thousand years, has always been between *Dwija-s* and *Shudra-s*. It was converted to that between Hindus and Muslims by the cunning of clever Brahmin Leader B.G. Tilak. And as result, the OBCs came under influence of Gandhi and the leaders of *Brahmanetar Paksha* (the non-brahmin party) dissolved their party in Congress around 1935, the original Brahminic party of India, which still maintains that quality. Unless the OBCs understand well that the fight is the really between the Brahminic and non-Brahminic forces, one cannot tackle the problem of black money. Unfortunately the right-wingers, left wingers or the followers of Gandhi do not seem to be concerned with these problems.

The great OBC leader Dr. Panjabrao Deshmukh had put in a bill in 1928 in the Central Provinces Assembly during British rule, known as the '*Devasthan Bill*'. Unfortunately, that bill could not be passed as the Hindu Sabha opposed it. Today the kith and kin of Panjabrao, the OBCs, are the ruling castes all over India. But times have changed; these OBCs have come under the influence of *Manuvadi* media and forgotten the teachings of Mahatma Phule, *Chatrapati* Shahu and *Prabodhankar* Thakre.

The effect of Manuvadi media is so strong that the OBCs could not understand that Mandal Commission was for their benefit. They did not understand the Hindu Code Bill was for their own benefit. Even today, they do not understand the recent awakening by Maratha Seva Sangh or by Purushottam Khedekar or their appeals for newer life style. They do not read journals of OBCs like *Maratha Marg* or *Bahujan Sangharsh*; they prefer Brahminic News papers and periodicals.

The time has come that along with the corruption and black money people should take up the problem of the money stashed in the Hindu temples. That is the need of the day.

Shiva Dharma Movement

Maratha Revolt Against Brahmanism

With the motivation by '*Dalit Voice*' Editor V.T. Rajshekhar, and with help from Maratha leaders and local workers of '*Maratha Seva Sangh*', I wrote a book, '*Maratha Revolt Against Brahmanism in 21st Century*', in 2004. VTR wrote the foreword.

I have discussed the *Dwija – Shudra* conflict and rise of Shiva Dharma, in detail.

Dalit Voice Editorial

V.T. Rajshekhar of *Dalit Voice* has supported the cause of Shiva Dharma. He advised them to take support of Dalits. He met all the top Maratha leaders of the Shiva Dharma movement at Pune, and found that the Maratha revolt against Brahmins has picked up high speed after the BORI incident of Jan. 5, 2004. He is satisfied with their argument:

> "The bogie of Marathas has to be first detached from the engine of Brahmanism or Hinduism. Once this bogie is detached from Brahmanism, the next step is easy. The Marathas will then understand that Buddhism is equally anti-Brahmin and is not far from Shiva Dharma".

He believes that Marathas regret anti-Dalit actions of *Namantar* and Riddles. He is convinced that both the anti-Dalit actions of the Marathas were done at the instigation of Brahmins. The Maratha leaders assured him that they would no more play into hands of Brahmins but henceforth would always stand by the Dalits. Whether it is Shiva Dharma or Buddhism, he thinks, the ultimate object is the same - fighting and finishing Brahmanism. Hence he appeals to Buddhists not to play into the hands of Brahminical forces but to support the Marathas in their sincere efforts to quit Hinduism. He feels this Maratha movement is the first revolt of a powerful upper caste landed gentry against Brahmins in the whole of post-independent India. He is sure of its success provided the leaders of the revolution properly guide the movement after preparing the mind of the masses of Marathas and also embrace the Dalits. He assures full support of *Dalit Voice.* [DV Editorial May 1, 2004]

Wishing success to them, I had also narrated the skepticism, doubts and criticisms by all including Dalits. One of the critics was Dr. Vanjari (now Anavrat), who had expressed his views as under.

Dr. Vanjari on Shiva Dharma

Dr. Vinod Vanjari from Nagpur, an active Ambedkarite scholar had criticized Shiva dharma movement. [DV, July 16-31, 2004] He feels that Maratha Seva

Sangha is keen on maintaining *status quo*. He wonders why they preferred god Shiva to Shivaji. He feels Shahu Maharaj would have been a better choice as their hero. Dalit Maratha unity would have had better chances then, he feels. He says that Marathas do not like Ashoka, though a Maratha, because he was anti-Brahmin. Buddha, Ashoka and Ambedkar all are untouchables for the Marathas. Labeling MSS as dishonest, he wonders how VTR is supporting them. He feels the Brahmins are exploiting Shivaji for their cause.

Present situation

Later, in 2011, he wrote a 180- page book [Anavrat: 2011] explaining his stand against their movement.

What is the present situation of Shiva Dharma now?

That way, they talk against Brahmanism even today. There was news item that Khedekar was even arrested for some of his writings. But the fact remains, they do not seem to have resolved differences between Marathas and Kunbis, they do not seem to have reduced the gap between Marathas and other OBCs, they do not seem to have come any nearer to Dalits either. One wonders whether they are against Brahmanism and *Chaturvarnya* system or they are just trying to achieve upward mobility of their own caste within the Brahminic social order without demolishing *Chaturvarnya*. Is this the real face of MSS? Let us hope not.

• • •

8

Dalits and Brahmins

Who Are the Real Enemies of Dalits Today?

Samajik Samarasata Manch

Some of Dalit intellectuals expressed view that OBCs, and not the Brahmins, are real enemies of Dalits. The idea that, the OBCs - and not Brahmins - were the real enemies of Dalits as they are the real tormentors, was spread by the RSS for last so many years through their '*Samarasata Manch*'.

So we have to learn how they do it. RSS is a multi-pronged octopus with many wings, *Samajik Samarasata Manch* (SSM) being one of its little known outfits, working to spread the RSS influence among the Dalits and Buddhists. (*Vanvasi Kalyan Ashram* is for Adivasis) Their usual strategy is 'five Cs' – 'Co-opt, Confuse, Collide, Consent and Conquest'. SSM was started on Ambedkar *Jayanti* of 1983, and was virtually under Dattopant Thengdi during his lifetime.

They started an Art Exhibition on life of Buddha just near the Nagpur Diksha Bhoomi, on *Gorakshan Sabha* grounds, on *Dasera* Day – *Dhamma Chakra Pravartan* day of Dalits – when nearly a million Ambedkarites assemble on *Diksha Bhoomi* every year. The whole crowd of Diksha Bhoomi saw the exhibition. There were some pictures of the Buddha, depicting traditional Buddha, against Ambedkar's ideas.

They organised meetings, published lots and lots of literature, arranged '*prachar-yatras*' in the name of Phule Ambedkar and other activities in cooperation with their student wing – ABVP – and started celebrating birthdays etc. of Ambedkar, Buddha and Phule and started converting Ambedkarites to Sangh ideology. Some Dalits were influenced and some joined them and became Ministers in their Government.

Some Ambedkarites opposed their ideas and others went to attend their functions. When their *yatra* came to my town, the RSS activists approached me to be chief guest in its reception. I politely declined saying that Ambedkarites had criticized Gangadhar Pantawne, a noted Dalit writer from Aurangabad who happened to attend their Manch.

Brahminisation of Phule Ambedkar

Why should the haters of Dalits and Buddha, Phule, Ambedkar should do their massive *'jay ghosha'* is a moot point. On Jayanti days, the first wreath on the Ambedkar statue is theirs in the wee hours of the morning. Their strategy is to praise Ambedkar but oppose his doctrines and cause confusion among the Dalits and thus finish the Ambedkarite movement, which over the years has eroded their power. It is neither necessary nor possible to review the massive *Samarasata* literature. It would be enough to mention a Marathi book, *"phule - ambedkara che brahmanikaran - sangh bhajapa che davpech"* ("Brahminisation of Phule Ambedkar - the Strategy of Sangh Parivar") by Ranjit Pardeshi, an activist of *Krantisimha* Nana Patil Academy, working for empowerment of women, and creation of classless casteless society, published on 6th December, 1996 from Yeole, Dist. Nasik. He has discussed the RSS strategy about Dalits, and is a good source for those who cannot read whole of massive Samarasata literature.

Phule and Ambedkar are considered as Social Revolutionaries because they opposed the Caste system, slavery of women, *'karmavaad'*, rebirth, *avatarvaad* etc., whereas the RSS had always been the supporter of these values. The Non-Brahmin political movement by *'brahmanetar paksha'*, started after death of Phule, had been the supporter of Phule Ambedkarite thought.

Sangh Parivar is expounding the idea that Phule Ambedkar were "Reformers of Hindu religion" to cause the confusion among the Dalits Ambedkarites. They are working among the Dalit colonies, (with a **temporary** substitution of blue flag on vehicle), the idea of "We are both Hindus, we are brothers of each other", in the name of Hindu Nationalism.

The fundamental contradiction in Indian society, culture, religion, literature and philosophy is between Brahmins and Non-Brahmins. Buddhist, Lokayat, Sankhya etc. are Non-Brahminic ideologies and the rest are Brahminic.

RSS removes the anti-Brahminic elements from Buddhism and adds the ideas of Vedantic philosophy, while presenting Buddhism. Many Hindu Buddhist Conferences, organised by them, have shown this. Guru Goenka ji, here, enters into treaty with the Shankaracharya, about which I have to condemn him in DV. The revolutionary side of Buddhism is concealed or kept secret and they project the Buddha as Reformer of Hindu religion and Buddhism as the reformed branch of Hinduism. We have recently discussed the subject in detail in *'Materialism in Ancient India'* (2012),

Pardeshi has explained in detail, under ten headings, how they are corrupting Ambedkarite thought. *Manuvadi-s* have deputed different people exclusively for each technique, but all of them work in tandem and never 'really' quarrel with each other. One must appreciate their hard work for nearly a century, though they are real enemies of Dalits. They studied Phule Shahu Ambedkar thoroughly, but Dalits do not study RSS. If they do, they would know how they are eroding "Ambedkar".

The gravest part is that, they are doing this with the hands of our own men – whom Ambedkar called stooges or Agents and Kanshiram called *'Chamchas'* –

and we do not even come to know this, and praise these '*Chamchas*' in ignorance. If one studies RSS techniques, one may be able to recognise these '*Chamchas*'.

What I am saying as "Phule Ambedkar", may be taken also to include all non-Brahmin ideals and idols of non-Brahmins modern and old, like Shahu, Periyar, Narayana Guru, Birsa Munda, Guru Ghasidas, Kabir, Raidas, Guru Nanak, Guru Gobind, Shivaji, Tukaram and many more, whose teachings are also corrupted and reversed to suit Brahmanism.

Technique 1. Struggle against Caste is Transformed into Caste Cooperation

Phule Ambedkar propagated that the country with multiple castes cannot become a nation and they ask for removal of castes, whereas Sangha Parivar claims that, there should be "*Samarasata*", and unity of "Hindu Rashtra" and that when these are achieved, the castes will 'automatically' disappear after progress of industry. "*Samarasata-vaad*" believes that there is no exploitation by the Brahmins and the Brahmin rule are the things of the past and that the traditionally exploited castes need not keep their arsenal ready against the Brahmins or Brahmanism, now renamed as *Hindutva* and declared 'different' from Hinduism.

As a result, Samarasata Manch of RSS opposes the Phule-Ambedkarite ideas of struggle against Caste exploitation on three counts:

1. They exclude Brahmin as an exploiter.
2. They oppose the unity of Shudras and Ati-shudras against the caste system, and
3. They oppose Revolutionary political struggle by the Dalits and Bahujans.

Technique 2. They Transform our Great Revolutionaries as mere "Reformers"

They say work of Hedgewar and Ambedkar was same and try to project Ambedkar as supporter of "Hindu *Rashtra*". Some of the statements of Ambedkar during his struggle against untouchability during early thirties are twisted and used for this purpose. What was Ambedkar's part of strategy in earlier years of struggle during Mahad-Kalaram *satyagraha*-s etc. is falsely projected as his policy. They never tell you what Ambedkar said about Vedas and Gita. We, as a rejoinder, ask them to follow 22 vows of Ambedkar.

Technique 3. Transformation of Phule's Materialism into Spiritualism

Phule propagated that the principal contradiction and main struggle in India for centuries has always been, as it is today, between Brahmins and Non-Brahmins. But the *Samarasata* Manch converts the "*Nirmik*" of Phule into god or "*Ishwar*" of Vedics and transforms his purely materialistic philosophy into spiritualistic.

Technique 4. Transformation of Casteless Nationalism into Supporter of Castes

While presenting Constitution to the Nation, Ambedkar averred that National integration would be achieved only by removing caste, and without this India will not become a nation. Sangh Parivar discovers a new formula that first there should be "*rashtra-ekatmata*" and then castes will disappear automatically.

Dattopant Thengdi, a very senior leader of RSS (See details in Chapter on Conversion) said:

> "If the '*samajik samarasata'* is created, the social equality comes 'automatically' and it becomes lasting. If there is no *samarasata*, equality will not come, and if somehow it is created, it will not last long. These '*samskaras'* are impressed on the minds of each and every '*swayamsevak'* in the '*shakhas'* of the R.S.S." ['*Samraste shivay samajik samta ashyakya*', p. 45, translated from Marathi]

A senior leader of BJP and former Deputy Chief Minister of Maharashtra, Mr. Gopinath Munde said:

> "Unfortunately, today some so called progressive group of people have started the march with a flag of revolt and rebellion are doing the politics of Caste struggle in the name of social reformation." [*Ajache Sandharbha* p. 3 q/b Pardeshi]

Pardeshi explains the policy of *Samarasata Manch* in these words:

> "In short, the policy of *Samarasata Manch* is to sell the Brahminic ideology **in the name of Ambedkar**. Ambedkar's statement that 'a nation emerges from caste destruction' is reversed to the new formula that 'end of caste will emerge from creation of the (Hindu) Nation'. Hedgewar and Golwalkar said, 'first Hindu '*sanghatan'* (organisation) and then '*rashtra nirmiti'* (creation of nation). Saying this they opposed the mass movement of M. Gandhi. This policy of RSS *Samarasata Manch* is the new version of the same ideology in the ninth decade of 20th century."
>
> "Ambedkar's ideal was of homogeneous society and integrated Nation. In its place they propagate cultural idea of supremacy of Brahmins and sell it to the masses in the name of Ambedkar. That is the policy of *Samarasata*" [Pardeshi: 1999: 7 – translated from Marathi]

Technique 5. Dalit OBC Problem

Ambedkarite idea of "Democratic Revolution with Dalits and Farmers friendship" is reversed to RSS propagated counter-revolutionary thought of "Dalits against Farmers struggle". Phule propagated that the '*Arya-Bhat*-s' captured the power by wily methods from the farmers' king Bali. All the *Mang*-s, *Mahar*-s, *Bhil*-s, *Koli*-s etc. should denounce their castes and unite. There should be end to moneylenders in agriculture.

Dr. Ambedkar even enumerates the castes that should participate in the Indian Democratic Revolution. He said the ex-untouchable castes, Tribals and Nomadic Tribes, would lead the movement and OBCs would be their friendly powers. They all together would fight against Brahminic forces.

RSS reverses this ideology of Phule Ambedkar. RSS through their *Samarasata* Meetings, time and again, says:

"Brahmins are no longer there in rural areas. The Sugar Factory barons and people in political power commit atrocities against Dalits in rural areas."

"Which castes are today in forefront in oppressing the Dalits? Today, you are not going to solve your problems by abusing the Brahmins or by burning the *Manusmruti*. So says Mr. Patange, the Provincial Secretary of *Samarasata Manch* in '*Ajche Sandharbha'*, p. 12" [q/b Pardeshi, p. 7]

Babasaheb had a strategy of reducing the gap in the OBC farmer community and Dalits. Communist and Socialist movements did not adopt the policy of opposing the caste system and did not support the Ambedkar movement.

Ambedkar helped the '*Samyukta Maharashtra Samitee*' in the struggle on Language problem. But the Leftists Non-Brahmin movement being under the influence of Brahmanism, the strategy of Dr. Ambedkar could not succeed.

For a long time, Maharashtra is being ruled by the powerful higher ups in Maratha community with higher ups in lower farmer castes and higher ups in Dalits as their subordinate participants with a lower status, in the multi-layered democracy. To bring this multi-layered democracy under the leadership of Upper Castes, the RSS has brought this concept of Dalits against farmer castes, avers Pardeshi. [Pardeshi, p. 7]

Post-Independent Maharashtra saw the rise of Maratha power, and Government was established under Higher ups in Marathas with second third level of castes in Backwards as their subordinates. It became necessary for the Brahmins to challenge this political set up, and there was the emergence of *Samarasata*. Thus Ranjeet Pardeshi proclaims that '**the Samarasata means the modernisation of the traditional *Brahmin-vaad*.**' [Pardeshi, p.13]

Technique 6. Dalit Muslim Problem

RSS transforms the 'Integrity based on secularism' to 'Diversity based on religious discrimination'.

Dr. Ambedkar analyses Hindu Muslim problem on two points. He avers that Muslim is not a homogeneous society but is divided in various caste groups. The higher castes among the Muslims and higher castes among the Hindus can come together to fight against the Dalits and the Non-Brahmin lower castes. As an example, Ambedkar quotes Muslim support to Hindu Upper Castes against the Dalit cause in Round Table Conference. And he suggests that we should have a united struggle of Dalits and lower caste Muslims against the rule of Upper Caste Hindus.

Ambedkar's incidental comments of Muslim rigidity in religious matters are being exploited by RSS to incite the lower caste Hindus against Muslims during riots. Ambedkar's ideal is the egalitarian society based on Dalit-Muslim-OBC unity. But RSS-BJP propagates multi-religious society under the thumb of Upper Castes. **This important contradiction is never highlighted by the RSS, and unfortunately is neither understood by Muslims nor by Dalits.**

Technique 7. Slavery of Women

Phule-Ambedkarism demands revolutionary changes in Male dominated Caste system. Phule criticizes old Brahminic texts for writings against women [*Satsar-*2]. Ambedkar fought against the Shankaracharya-s and upper caste conservative forces for reducing male dominance through Hindu Code.

Concepts of RSS about women are limited to glorification in **name only** without any real empowerment or reduction of gender inequality. They talk of all Brahminic ideals like '*stree-uddhar*', female education for support of Hindu '*rashtra*', '*matru-gaurav*', ideal mother for creation of ideal society, wife for protection preservation of Hindu Joint Family, as a worshipable deity, etc.

Yadav Rao Joshi, in '*vichar darshan*' mentions, "Women got more restrictions because they got glory". They reduce Phule Ambedkar to status merely of 'liberator' or 'educator' of women, thereby denying the revolutionary spirit of Phule Ambedkarism.

Technique 8. Denial of Forefront Position to Dalit Leadership

Ambedkar, time and again, stressed that Dalits will be in forefront of Democratic revolution. *Samarasata* tells Dalits to refrain from participating in all struggles against the system. Everybody from Dattopant Thengadi to M.G. Vaidya makes this appeal. M.G. Vaidya observes:

> "There is no need for a separate politics for Dalits. It is more necessary to have '*samarasata*' between Dalits and non-Dalits. To create '*samarasata*' is beyond the power of politics. Only those people who turn their backs towards the allurements of politics can do this work." [*Jivan Sandesh*, pp. 74-75 q/b Pardeshi, p.10]

RSS volunteers lament that followers of Ambedkar could not bring other castes under the 'pleasant shelter' of Buddhism apart from Mahars. Let us hope the Ambedkarites will give them no more chances to lament. Kanshiram's declaration that he would convert 30 million people to Buddhism could not come into effect due to his untimely demise, but VJNT leader Laxman Mane achieved success and various other groups are active.

RSS advises the middle castes and upper castes to take part in anti-Muslim riots. But for Dalits, they wish that Dalits should be busy in "cultural upliftment". They do not want that Dalits should take part in struggles against the caste. Pardeshi calls this as **a conspiracy to keep Dalits confined to Buddha Viharas** (doing *Vippasana* and *dhyana ONLY*), and labels it as a "*Samarasata Karasthan*" (intrigue). Thengdi advises that the 'uncultured' Dalit Castes should imitate the 'cultured' Brahmin caste, without which there would be no upliftment in *Varna* (*varnonnanti*). [Pardesi/14]

The present activities of Guru Goenka should be examined by Dalits with this perspective.

They are concealing the internal contradictions of Brahmin supremacy in Hinduism and highlighting only the external aspects of religion, and have succeeded in rearranging the construct to project Dalit and Muslims and Dalits and OBCs to be enemies of one another in the name of religion, and hierarchy of castes.

Technique 9. False Non-brahminisation of Brahminic Myths and Symbols

Ambedkar criticizes Adi-Shankara for organising a counter revolutionary crusade against the revolution effected by the Buddha. Whereas, RSS tells us that, "Shankaracharya was a hidden (*pracchanna*) Buddhist".

RSS now claims that removal of untouchability was the '*aadya-tam*' (most original) aim of RSS. The change in the meaning of RSS critique from Tilak era to Bhagwat-Gadkari era is interesting to note. These changes in Brahminic strategy have been well studied by Ms. Gail Omvedt. Taking anti-Muslim stand, Tilak gave Brahminic meaning to Ganesh and Shivaji Festivals. Shivaji was falsely projected as supporter of Brahmins and enemy of Muslims. Gail explains that though the Nationalism of Tilak was based on caste supremacy of Brahmins, the later era glorified Tilak as a leader of '*teli-tamboli*' (lower castes among the OBCs), and as 'Father of Indian unrest', and was falsely projected as leader of Non-Brahmins too.

Technique 10. From Racial Supremacy to Cultural Supremacy

Pre-Hedgewar days were the days of propagating supremacy of "Aryan Race", it is now replaced by "Supremacy of Hindu Culture" during Hedgewar era.

Before Tilak, the Muslims and Non-Brahmins were integrated, worshipping *Durghas* and observing *Muharrum* jointly. It was Ganesh festivals - which were opposed by the then '*satya-shodhak*-s' (followers of Phule) - that caused the gap. In eighties and nineties, when the elite among Non-Brahmins and Muslims were awakening and trying to come together, mostly due to the activities of Kanshiram and his fellow workers in BAMCEF and later DS4 and BSP, and were getting ready for a struggle for political power against Brahmins, the RSS felt a need to widen the gap between Muslims and non-Muslims. So the *Samarasata Manch*.

The *Samarasata*, on one hand was depicting supremacy of Brahmins as the creators of the Hindu culture, and on the other hand it was denoting separation of Non-Brahmins from Muslims. *Samarasata* then started wooing the OBCs on the pretext of 'same religion' and tried to keep away the "Buddhist-Dalits" and Muslims in the name of 'other religion'. Thus instead of Aryan Racial differences, they propagated the Brahmin supremacy - not as race as before - but now as caste.

Brahminic Strategy to Govern Hindus

Safronisation, Hinduisation or Brahminisation

These days everybody talks of "*Hindutva*", they say Hinduism is not a religion but a way of life. Why and what is the difference? All these acrobatics in phraseology are just to maintain supremacy of Brahmins, argues Prof. Ranjit Pardeshi.

Instead of Hinduisation, the other word some times used is *'Safronisation'*, perhaps due to color of RSS flag. But even this word conceals the concept of the Sangh, as saffron symbolises many other flags concepts. Therefore, neither Safronisation nor Hinduisation denotes the true concepts the R.S.S. The proper word must be Braminisation.

RSS Attempts to Reverse the Ideology of Phule Ambedkar

To combat inequality in Hinduism, Mahatma Phule suggested *'satya-dharma'* and Ambedkar accepted Buddhism. Phule and Ambedkar's alternative to Hinduism was based on anti-women-slavery, analysis of Brahmin religion, equality for all, anti-caste, anti-brahmin shastras and ignoring idea of god.

During early years of his struggle against Hinduism, Ambedkar DID say that Hindu religion needs reforms. On the basis of that RSS now claims that Ambedkar was also a 'Reformer of Hindu religion', bringing in Renaissance in Hindu religion, like Vivekananda and Aurobindo etc.

Ambedkar was not Reformer of Hinduism

As a matter of fact, Ramesh Patrange, in his Marathi booklet *'Dr. Hedgewar aani Dr. Ambedkar'*, equating Ambedkar with Hedgewar, gives an editorial in *'Bahishkrut Bharat'* dated 21st December, 1928 as a whole appendix. In that editorial Dr. Ambedkar had narrated the ill-effects of caste system and observed that if you have to avoid the destruction of Hindu religion, you must get rid of Caste System.

This perhaps in the eyes of RSS is 'Reformer of Hindu religion' and doing same work as Dr. Hedgewar. Thousand and one times Dr. Ambedkar had said, after 1935, that we - the Dalits - are not interested in reforming Hinduism, but the RSS has got selective amnesia about Ambedkar's teachings and they never project such quotes of Ambedkar. They do not quote from *'Annihilation of Caste'*, a declaration as important as *'Communist Manifesto'* of Marx.

This is one aspect of Hinduisation. It is noteworthy that RSS never refers to Ambedkar's criticism on Brahmanism. They always call it reform of 'Hindu' religion and not 'Brahmin' religion.

The other aspect of Hinduisation is whatever Ambedkar said about Islam to show the differences from Brahmanism is construed to wrongly project Ambedkar as having anti-Islamic convictions.

It must be remembered in both these examples it is the preservation of vested interest of privileged castes that is involved. But it is projected as interests of whole 'Hindu' religion and 'Hindu' people. What *Samarasata Manch* – an organisation of RSS – is doing is the glorification of 'Hindu' identity and propagation of hate of 'Muslim' identity, and their real interest is welfare of privileged castes. This internal aspect of *Samarasata* is always concealed. What they show is just an external aspect like religion, religious symbols, *mandir, masjid* etc.

Real Contradictions are Concealed

Because of the concealment of inner real aspects of so called Safronisation or Hinduisation, the criticism against it is limited to external symbolism and thus RSS succeeds in their politics. They can now take political advantages by limiting the discussion to 'Hindu *vs.* Buddhists' or 'Hindu *vs.* Secularists' or 'Hindu *vs.* Muslims', and never 'Hindu *vs.* Brahmins', which should be the real contradiction and which was brought forward by Phule, Shahu, Periyar and Ambedkar.

Because of the projection of only external aspects in contradiction, the RSS can depict religious minorities or secularists as enemies of the majority Hindu 'Nation'. For example, the upper castes, to safeguard their interests with the capitalists or feudal landlords, involve the lower class / caste 'Hindus' in conflict with the anti-Muslim politics. They declare the leftists both Dalit as well as non-Dalit as 'Appeasers of Muslims', and thus gain the sympathy of majority of 'Hindus' and the Dalits or Non-Dalit Lower Castes and even the Muslims do not realize the game-plan of RSS and remain divided against their real enemy.

Babari Masjid—Ram Janma Bhumi Contradictions

What is the real contradiction in Babari Masjid conflict? It appears externally as religious conflict for religious symbolism between the symbols of Hindus and those of Muslims. But is it really so? The real internal conflict is the caste conflict. How many lower caste non-Dalits (OBCs) realise this? When V.P. Singh tried to implement Mandal Commission recommendations for the benefit of OBCs, the RSS started the *Rathyatra* to scuttle this movement. Everybody will remember the words of Atal Bihari Vajpayee that time, 'because they started Mandal, we started *Kamandal'*, which he said in an open interview. (*Dharmayug*, 90, q/b Pardeshi p. 15)

Phule Denigrated

Second example can be cited of Gangal and Behre criticising Mahatma Phule as 'foul smelling dirt' about twenty years ago. This was the reaction of the conservative upper caste middle class elitists against the Bahujan castes. When protests were made against this by the people in movements against caste, a senior OBC leader of RSS, Gopinath Munde opposed this stand with the backing of second third level workers of lower castes like *Dhangar*, *Mali*, *Vanjari* and other OBCs, under the Brahminic leadership of the Sangh.

Conflict of Riddles Misrepresented

When Dr. Ambedkar wrote the Riddles of Rama and Krishna, he utilised the symbolism of Rama and Krishna to represent the Brahminical social order of *Chaturvarnya* with 'Brahmin' supremacy and not as the symbol caste of Kshatriyas. The movements of transformation, failed to bring forward this aspect of Ambedkar to the 'Hindu' masses and therefore it became easy for RSS to project Ambedkar's writings as an attack on 'Hindu' gods and goddesses, and they succeeded in organising huge masses of 'Hindu' OBCs against the Dalit Buddhist organisations, with consequent aftermath.

Examples of Brahminisation

All these are the examples of Brahminisation, but are purposefully and wrongly termed and projected as Hinduisation or Safronisation, thereby shifting the emphasis. The real concept that must be projected is that of Braminisation and not Hinduisation or Safronisation. It is absolutely necessary to bring forward the contradictions among the Bahujans and Upper Caste Hindus. Otherwise, it becomes easy for the Sangh forces to bring the common masses under the name of 'Hindu religion' and utilise them against those who want social transformation. The forces acting in Hinduisation are not the 'Hindu' *Bahujans*, but the Brahminic '*Alpajans*' (minority). This can be brought forward only by the concept of Braminisation. For that purpose it is necessary to preserve the ideals and idols of our great dignitaries like Phule, Shahu, Periyar and Ambedkar etc.

Polarisation of Society

It must be understood that it is always beneficial for the RSS and the makers of the caste to divide and achieve the polarisation of society in two warring groups- 'Hindu' and 'non-Hindu'. The elite Brahmins can then maintain their upper caste grip over the lower caste 'Hindus' – the Bahujans or OBCs – in the guise of expressing the glorification of Hindu identity as opposed to that of Christians, Buddhists and Muslims. This provides them good opportunity for the purpose.

Wrong Projection of Chatrapati *Shivaji*

Chatrapati Shivaji who was a *'kulvadi-bhushan'* (pride of lower caste *kulvaadis*), as described by Mahatma Phule, as he came from peasants *Shudra* caste, and rose to power by his own merit and valor. He is now wrongly projected by the Brahminic historians as *'go-brahmin-pratipalak'* (protector of cows and Brahmins), which he never was, as proved by Shejwalkar by examining the original letters of Shivaji. It was not Shivaji who called himself *'go-brahmin-pratipalak'*, but it were the Brahmins who called him so, when they approached him for favours. In the coronation seal also it is mentioned *'kshatriya kulvantas'* and not *'go-brahmin-pratipalak'*. The kingdom he established was egalitarian but the Brahmin historians call him founder of *'hindu paatshahi'*. They also project it was a kingdom of "*Shree*", sometimes they projected Ramdas as Shivaji's guru. Enough has been written to disprove these imaginary stories. Shivaji was never against the Muslims, but they project him as enemy of Muslims and use his name as a symbol for opposing the Muslim identity and instigate the lower caste Bahujans against the Muslims during riots.

Hindus did not exist before Muslim Rule

Before the SCs, STs and OBCs were included within the purview of 'Hindu' identity, there was a conflict and struggle between 'brahmins' and 'non-brahmins' in the religion, culture, philosophy, history and the society itself. When there were *'varnas'* and not castes, the thumb of Eklavya was cut by Dronachaya to preserve the *varna* supremacy of Arjuna, in the name of *'guru-daxina'* for the education NOT imparted by him. This grave injustice was glorified in the name of great *'guru-bhakti'* (devotion to guru). This shows the tendency of Braminisation during those days.

During the Satvahanas times in early centuries of Christian era in Maharashtra, there existed a process of Brahminisation by assimilating on lower status, of lower castes into same religious stream but it was always seen that the social grading among the various castes was maintained without any change. The author of *Dnyankosha* - the great Ketkar, explains this. It must be understood the concept Hinduisation is not historical. There were no 'Hindus' before the Muslims came and the concept of 'Hindu' came in existence during Turk Moghul era, and not before. Hence, the concept of Hindu cannot be used for guidance as a historical tool for transformation of society.

There was an ideological struggle between the Buddhists and the Vedantis, the basis of which was contradictions in *Varnas* - the Brahmins against the non-Brahmins. But the RSS Brahmin scholars can analyse this as "Hindu Vedantism" against "Non-Hindu Buddhism", and the defiant language of the today's Buddhists can be labeled as "anti-Hindu" and can lead to riots. This is because in the name of 'Hindutva'. the Bahujans can be appealed to and organised by causing confusion amongst them on the exploitation of caste - exploitation by the upper castes can be concealed.

Braminisation in Ancient Times

About the 'Social organisation and expansive acts done by Brahmins', Ketkar explains the activities of Brahmins during Vedic period. The aim behind these activities was to maintain the supremacy of Brahmins. It was nothing but Braminisation. The strategy applied during those days and techniques of cheating and deception used that time are still being used by RSS today in a refined manner. These techniques could be summarised as follows:

1. They relate the old stories with the ancestors of original inhabitants and pretend that their religion was same as that of Brahmins. This technique was used during Vedic times. Today, it is being used to show that the Ambedkar's Buddhism is same as old Brahminised Buddhism and aver that Ambedkar's Buddhism is just a part of Hinduism. This is done through various conferences, where even Dalai Lama and Guru Goenka participate.

2. During Vedic times, they performed *yajnyas* like *'vratya-stoma'* etc. to make the ineligible people eligible for *yajnyas*. Today, they admit ineligible Dalit Buddhists scholars in *Samarasta* movement and provide them – AND THEM ALONE – posts, property and prestige in social organisations, literary organisations, journalism, Universities, Governmental Institutions and the like and use them as propagators of RSS ideology.

3. It was necessary during Vedic times to create a false history and to label the various alien nationalities as prodigal sons and proclaim them to be the progeny of some Brahmin *'rishi'* on some non-Brahmin woman. Middle ages saw the corruption of history in formulating origins of great non-brahmin saints, like Raidas and Kabir Today the rebellious Phule is 'accommodated' as son of 'Hindu Ishwara', Phule's *'Nirmik'* is projected as god, and Dr. Ambedkar as 'a reformer of Hindu India'. These are the new strategies applied these days.

4. Ketkar explains that during the process of Braminisation, two principles were strictly adhered to.

One - it should be on mass scale, and **Two** - the relative status of various caste groups must be maintained in new caste situation and Brahmin supremacy not being jeopardized. Today this has been transformed making a vote bank in elections, to control the reservation policy for preservation of upper caste interests, to accommodate the awakened Bahujans' identity in the *'Hindutva'* at a lower status. While doing all these, to maintain the Brahmin supremacy, is the real challenge for the RSS.

New Idols of Brahmanism

Only the names of Hedgewar, Golwalkar, Deoras, Sawarkar etc. were in the scriptures of Sangh in the past. They had now to add M. Gandhi, Phule, Ambedkar etc. Some share in prestige, power, property has to be given to upwardly mobile individuals from among the lower castes, but the main principle of 'not disturbing the social order of status of caste' is still rigidly observed.

As they have to establish the relation of original inhabitants with their religion, now they started telling a false imaginary story that Ambedkar visited the *'shakha'* of RSS and found many untouchable volunteers there. Ketkar had said that in olden times such imaginary stories served a great cause of Brahminisation, as some castes like *'Andhra'* etc. were called *'Vishvamitra-putra'*. So Sangh is now telling us such imaginary stories. But even then, they do not disclose the vested interests of their ruling upper castes in this imaginary unification with lower castes.

Non-Brahmin Priests

Dr. Ambedkar

Dr. Ambedkar in 1936, in *Annihilation of Caste*, had observed:

"Indeed, I am so convinced of the necessity of Religion that I feel I ought to tell you in outline what I regard as necessary items in this religious reform. The following in my opinion should be the cardinal items in this reform :

"(1) There should be one and only one standard book of Hindu religion, acceptable to all Hindus and recognised by all Hindus. This, of course, means that all other books of Hindu religion such as *Vedas, Shastras* and *Puranas,* which are treated as sacred and authoritative, must by law cease to be so and the preaching of any doctrine, religious or social contained in these books should be penalised.

"(2) It should be better if priesthood among Hindus was abolished. But as this seems to be impossible, the priesthood must at least cease to be hereditary. Every person who professes to be a Hindu must be eligible for being a priest. It should be provided by law that no Hindu shall be entitled to be a priest unless he has passed an examination prescribed by the State and holds a sanad from the State permitting him to practise.

"(3) No ceremony performed by a priest who does not hold a *sanad* shall be deemed to be valid in law and it should be made penal for a person who has no *sanad* to officiate as a priest.

"(4) A priest should be the servant of the State and should be subject to the disciplinary action by the State in the matter of his morals, beliefs and worship, in addition to his being subject along with other citizens to the ordinary law of the land.

"(5) The number of priests should be limited by law according to the requirements of the State as is done in the case of the I.C.S.

"To some, this may sound radical. But to my mind there is nothing revolutionary in this. Every profession in India is regulated. Engineers must show proficiency, Doctors must show proficiency, Lawyers must show proficiency, before they are allowed to practise their professions. During the whole of their career, they must not only obey the law of the land, civil as well as criminal, but they must also obey the special code of morals prescribed by their respective professions.

"The priest's is the only profession where proficiency is not required. The profession of a Hindu priest is the only profession which is not subject to any code. Mentally a priest may be an idiot, physically a priest may be suffering from a foul disease, such as syphilis or gonorrhea, morally he may be a wreck. But he is fit to officiate at solemn ceremonies, to enter the sanctum sanctorum of a Hindu temple and worship the Hindu God. All this becomes possible among the Hindus because for a priest it is enough to be born in a priestly caste.

"The whole thing is abominable and is due to the fact that the priestly class among Hindus is subject neither to law nor to morality. It recognises no duties. It knows only of rights and privileges. It is a pest which divinity seems to have let loose on the masses for their mental and moral degradation. The priestly class must be brought under control by some such legislation as I have outlined above. It will prevent it from doing mischief and from misguiding people. It will democratise it by throwing it open to every one. It will certainly help to kill the Brahminism and will also help to kill Caste, which is nothing but Brahminism incarnate." [Annihilation of Caste]

Non-Brahmin Priest is Not Tolerated

Temple Panel Dissolved for Obstructing Non-Brahmin Priest

[http://www.indopia.in/India-usa-uk-news/latest-news/590497/National/1/20/1]

A news item from Thiruvananthapuram, published on June 4, 2009 says that on Jun. 3, the Travancore Deveswom Board (TDB) dissolved a temple advisory committee in Kottayam district after inquiry, for allegedly preventing a non-Brahmin priest from taking over the temple duties in Vayappara Temple.

The trained priest was appointed by the Board to take over the priestly duties of the small temple. However, the temple advisory committee of the local people objected and insisted on a Brahmin priest. Meanwhile, the priest was shifted to another temple.

Hindu Priests Hear Chants of Sacred Change

Rajasthan Sanskrit University

[http://timesofindia.indiatimes.com/NEWS-India-Hindu-priests-hear-chants-of-sacred-change/articleshow/4794207.cms] (Accessed Wednesday, February 08, 2012)

Divya A, reports in an article '*Hindu priests hear chants of sacred change*', TNN 19 July 2009, that the Jagadguru Ramanandacharya Rajasthan Sanskrit University is going to train Dalits as priests as Tirumala Tirupati Devasthanams (TTD) did before in 2009, and wonders, 'Will it really smash their monopoly of Male Brahmins?'

No, says sociologist Shiv Visvanathan, who takes the "social engineering" theory with a pinch of salt. Visvanathan says:

> "Traditionally, priests in India have been male Brahmins, with the profession being handed down the generations through oral lessons. But getting that under the umbrella of academic education may lead to a transition of priesthood from *gurukul* to universities. It looks progressive but how it deals with the sacredness and morality of the priesthood is to be seen."

Tamil Nadu Experiment

In Tamil Nadu last year, a batch of 207 priests, including 76 OBCs and 34 Dalits, graduated from the state-run priesthood training institute. They are now getting inducted in some of the 36,000 temples run by the government under a 69 per cent job quota for backward and Dalit priests. The Tamil experiment in inclusiveness comes as part of the DMK government's 2006 order that all Hindus, whatever their caste, would be allowed to become priests if they were "qualified" to be.

Rajasthan Experiment

A year-long priesthood diploma in Rajasthan, with 'senior higher secondary exams' as eligibility for admission was started with a capacity of at least

50 qualified priests per year as stated by Pundit Yugal Sharma, Vice Chancellor of the Sanskrit University.

Brahmin Monopoly of Priesthood Challenged

In 2007, a 300-year-old temple in a Bihar village got its first Dalit priest. A year later, a Dalit was appointed priest of the famous Maniyari Mutt in Muzaffarpur. Dr Karan Singh, however claims that his father had employed Dalit priests in Kashmir as far back as 1929.

The Supreme Court Ruling

In 2002, the Supreme Court ruled that Dalits could be appointed as priests in temples so long as they were qualified to conduct the ritual.

The Gender Issues

In Pune, a social organisation '*Jnana Prabodhini*' offers a one-year informal course in priesthood also to women, without certificates or diploma, to start practicing as 'independent priests' as standbys when male priests are unavailable, but not at Funeral rites.

Is it a Real Social Change?

Not really! Visvanathan says that, "Even today, there are several backward castes with their own priests, but openness about 'professionally qualified' priests doesn't seem likely, if the person is a Dalit or a woman".

In The Temple of Your Gods

[http://www.tehelka.com/story_main42.asp?filename=Ne220809in_the.asp] From Tehelka Magazine, Vol 6, Issue 33, Dated August 22, 2009
CURRENT AFFAIRS special report

In The Temple of Your Gods

In a pioneering move by the government of Tamil Nadu, a May 2006 government order declared that "suitably trained and qualified Hindus, without discrimination of caste, creed, custom or usage" were to be appointed as *archakas* (priests) to any of the 36,000 temples under government administration across the state.

These temples include the revered Meenakshi temple in Madurai, the Murugan temple in Palani, the Parthasarathy Swamy temple in Chennai and the Ranganathaswamy temple in Srirangam.

This bold order made it possible for Dalits to officiate in these prestigious temples, which for generations 'have been exclusive Brahmin bastions'.

As early as 1970, an amendment to the Tamil Nadu Hindu Religious and Charitable Endowments Act had abolished the hereditary appointment of temple *archaka*-s, stating,

> "No person shall be entitled to appointment to any vacancy… merely on the grounds that he is next in the line of succession to the last holder of office."

The 2006 order extended the order passed 30 years earlier. In May 2007, the Tamil Nadu government set up six archaka training centres across the state, which offered a year-long certificate course in '*agama sastras*' (priesthood studies).

Brahmin priests at the Madurai Meenakshi temple have challenged the order. Chief Minister M Karunanidhi claimed that the order fulfilled Dravidian leader Periyar's desire to remove caste barriers.

Out of a maximum intake of 240, 207 students passed their examinations. Only three of the 207 were Brahmins.

Unfortunately, government's attempt to bring to fruition Periyar's struggle against caste discrimination in temples has met with social and legal obstacles.

Several petitioners have challenged the order in the Supreme Court, claiming that the Govt. order violated Articles 25 and 26 of the Constitution, which grant the right to freedom of religion. A stay on the appointments has been granted and hearings are on.

Even as the government fights the legal battle, it has been forced to disband the centres and suspend the training course. Even the students who have completed the courses have not been given certificates of completion, let alone their appointment orders.

Writer's Emailsanjana@tehelka.com

Pariahs Turn Priests in Temples in Bihar

[http://articles.timesofindia.indiatimes.com/2007-07-08/patna/27981660_1_janardan-manjhi-shiva-temple-ram-janki-temple] (Accessed Feb. 8, 2012)

Arun Kumar reports, July 8, 2007, from Patna:

Bihar, notorious for oppression of the Dalits is now having a silent social revolution, and the "pariahs" are performing "puja" as priests in some famous temples of the state.

Kishore Kunal, who became Bihar State Board of Religious Trusts (BSBRT) Administrator in May, 2006, informs that he appointed Dalit priests at various important temples and more Dalit priests would be appointed soon. He said this social revolution in not something unprecedented. The state had witnessed in the past some kind of social revolt against Brahmanism under the banner of Buddhism.

The movement, however, slowed down in the last decades of 20th century. It was revived again by Kunal, who in his capacity as secretary of the famous Hanuman Temple of Patna, made appointments of Dalit priests.

Land Grants to Brahmins Made Them Landlords

Brahmadeya, Devadana and Agrahara Land Grants

[http://win2vin.wordpress.com/2009/10/27/brahmadeya-devadana-and-agrahara-land-grants/] (Accessed Feb. 10, 2012)

It was a question in IAS Mains in 2009.

Land grants to religious institutions were called Brahmadeya, (i.e. donated to Brahmins) Devadana (donated to Gods) and Agrahara (Settlement – of priests)

These lands donated to the temples and monasteries apart from being used as normal tenancy also carried a right vested with the temple authorities to call for unpaid labour (called *Vishti*) as a religious service to the temple from the tillers on the donated land.

Lands were given as brahmadeya either to a single Brahmana or to several Brahmana families which ranged from a few to several hundreds or even more than a thousand, as seen in the South Indian context. Brahmadeyas were invariably located near major irrigation works such as tanks or lakes. Often new irrigation sources were constructed when brahmadeyas were created, especially in areas dependent on rains and in arid and semi-arid regions. When located in areas of intensive agriculture in the river valleys, they served to integrate other settlements of a subsihena level production. Sometimes, two or more settlements were clubbed together to form a brahmadeya or an agrahara.

The taxes from such villages were assigned to the Brahmana donees, who were also given the right to get the donated land cultivated. Boundaries of the donated land or village were very often carefully demarcated. The various types of land, wet, dry and garden land within the village were specified. Sometimes even specific crops and trees are mentioned.

The land donations implied more than the transfer of land rights. For example, in many cases, along with the revenues and economic resources of the village, human resources such as peasants (cultivators), mesons and others were also transferred to donees. There is also growing evidence of the encroachment of the rights of villagers over community lands such as lakes and ponds. Thus, the Brahmanas became managers of agricultural and artisanal production in these settlements for which they organised themselves into assemblies.

Administration of Brahmadeya Villages, Chola Dynasty

[http://www.indianetzone.com/51/administration_brahmadeya_villages.htm] (Acessed Feb. 10, 2012) Administration of Brahmadeya Villages, Chola Dynasty-Informative and researched article on Administration of Brahmadeya Villages, Chola Dynasty.

Administration of Brahmadeya Villages was carried out by the Brahmins to whom these lands had been given. In the Brahmadeya villages, the Brahmins lived and functioned as landlords.

Administration of Brahmadeya villages was carried out by the organisational structure created by the Brahmins. In the Tamil country under the Chola rule (9th-13th century), there were many villages which were granted to Brahmins and described as Brahmadeya. These villages were dominantly inhabited by Brahmins who formed an assembly called Sabha for the village administration. These Brahmadeya villages played a very important role in the local administration of the country.

The administration of Brahmadeya villages was carried out by certain village assemblies. These were mainly Sabha and Parudai.

Sabha was the assembly formed in Brahmadeya villages. Its members were most likely restricted to Brahmins who possessed a certain area of the land in the village. It functioned as an administrative organisation and often had several committees for the various purposes of the village administration. It represented the village to the world outside.

Parudai was probably an organisation discharging duties connected with the temple administration. It worked perhaps under the control of the Sabha of its village.

A good number of Chola inscriptions which record the various activities of these Sabhas have survived in many villages in Tamil Nadu which were Brahmadeyas under the Cholas. The most famous of such villages is Uttaramerur in Chingleput District.

The Brahmadeya villages played an important role in the local administration of the state, and consequently functioned as an apparatus for social integration. They enjoyed a close relation with the Chola kings even wielding a certain amount of influence at times. Their importance can be gauged from the fact that in the central parts of the Chola country, i.e., Cholamandalam and Jayangondachola-mandalam, roughly comprising the present districts of Chingleput, North Arcot, South Arcot, Tiruchirapalli district, Thanjavur and Pudukkottai district, there is a tendency for more than a few Brahmadeya villages to be located in each Nadu (territorial division).

Thus, it was seen that the Brahmadeyas, despite being comparatively few in number to the non-Brahmadeya villages, formed rather important parts of state administration.

• • •

9

Dalits in Foreign Lands

Caste Problem would become a World Problem

'Castes in India, Their Mechanism, Genesis and Development' - In his first speech nearly a century ago, in Anthropology Seminar of Dr. A.A. Goldenweizer at The Columbia University, New York, U.S.A. on 9th May 1916 [Indian Antiquary, May 1917, Vol. XLI], Dr. Ambedkar had warned the western world:

> "The caste problem is a vast one, both theoretically and practically. Practically, it is an institution that portends tremendous consequences. It is a local problem, but one capable of much wider mischief, for as long as caste in India does exist, Hindus will hardly intermarry or have any social intercourse with outsiders; and if Hindus migrate to other regions on earth, Indian caste would become a world problem."

Now we are seeing these effects.

Equality-Bill in Britain

[http://www.telegraph.co.uk/news/worldnews/asia/india/7541598/India-clashes-with-Britain-over-Equality-Bill-racism-law.html] (Accessed on 2/11/2012)

A news item published as above and titled *"India clashes with Britain over Equality Bill racism law"* mentions that, India is set to clash with Britain over Westminster's new Equality Bill which outlaws caste discrimination as a form of racism. As reported by Dean Nelson, in New Delhi, 31 March 2010, it reads as follows:

> "The bill, which has been passed in the House of Lords, has been welcomed by campaigners for India's "Dalits" or "untouchables", a caste which suffers extreme violence and persecution, but has been rejected by their government."
>
> "There are more than 250 million Dalits in India, many of whom are denied water, access to schools, and in some cases the right to pass through villages by upper caste Hindus who believe their presence, or even their shadow, pollutes them. Some Dalits in India still work as "night soil carriers" – transporting human waste from latrines."

"One prominent Dalit campaigner had his arms and legs amputated because he refused to withdraw a police complaint against higher caste men who had raped his daughter."

"Ministers in London have become increasingly concerned about discrimination and persecution against lower caste Indians in Britain following a report last year which claimed thousands had been ill-treated because of their caste."

"The report, by the Anti-Caste Discrimination Alliance, surveyed 300 British Asians and cited cases of children being bullied at school, bus inspectors refusing to work with lower caste drivers, and employees being sacked after their bosses discovered their caste status."

Further it mentions that:

"Until now victims of caste discrimination in Britain have had no recourse to law. India also has legislation outlawing caste discrimination but is fiercely opposed to any comparison with racism."

"The Indian government has made its views known to British delegations at the UN's Human Rights Council in Geneva and at a European Union-India Human Rights Dialogue last month."

"India's position on this issue has been clear and consistent. Caste and race discrimination are two separate issues and there is no case to equate the two. We are opposed to attempts at international fora to equate the issues," said an official source.

"Until the mid-1990s India had back moves to include all discrimination based on descent as a feature of racism in the International Convention on the Elimination of Racial Discrimination. But it changed its position in 1996 when it is understood to have become concerned at onerous reporting obligations under the convention."

Indian Dalits welcomed the Bill.

UK Close to Banning Caste-based Discrimination

[http://news.rediff.com/interview/2010/mar/31/uk-close-to-banning-caste-based-discrimination.htm] (Accessed December 21, 2012), A news item '*UK close to banning caste-based discrimination*' of March 31, 2010: The Gist:

British Parliament has decided to amend equality law to declare caste discrimination as illegal. The Equality Bill, which unites the various strands of diversity legislation, outlaws age discrimination and requires businesses to report on the gender pay gap, is due for final consideration by the House of Commons prior to receiving royal assent.

The House of Commons considered amendments after House of Lords made amendments to outlaw discrimination on the basis of caste. There has been evidence of practice caste based discrimination among people of Indian origin. The Government has accepted to amend the law after finding the evidence of caste based discrimination.

Keith Porteous Wood, executive director of National Secular Society said that the blight of caste discrimination, under which millions in India are regarded as "Untouchable" has spread to Great Britain.

In 2009 research conducted at University of Manchester, Herefordshire and Manchester Metropolitan University found out about the caste discrimination practice prevalent in Britain.

The study conducted by anti-Caste Discrimination Alliance titled "Voice of the Community- A study into caste and caste discrimination in the UK" found out about caste discrimination widespread in workplace, classroom and even doctor's surgery. The study also found out the caste system imported to UK by Asians and there is danger that if UK government does not effectively accept and deal with the issue of caste discrimination the problem will grow unchecked.

Caste in UK

[http://www.equalitylaw.co.uk/news/1494/66/Tribunal-hears-first-UK-caste-based-discrimination-claim/] (Accessed Feb. 11, 2012)

A news item 'Tribunal hears first UK caste-based discrimination claim', dated Aug 19, 2011 a first case of its kind in the UK, of an Indian couple claiming unfair constructive dismissal from their legal jobs due to caste-based discrimination by their bosses at Coventry-based solicitors firm Heer Manak.

Because of the precedent-setting nature of the lawsuit, Home Secretary Theresa May is believed to be watching the case carefully and considering whether to add a section covering caste to the UK's equality legislation.

According to the *Daily Mail*, Vijay Begraj, a Dalit, the company's former practice manager, was sacked after seven years of service in 2010 and his upper caste Jat Sikh wife Amardeep, a former solicitor there, resigned in January this year.

They are both claiming unfair constructive dismissal, unauthorised deduction of wages, unpaid holiday pay, race discrimination, breach of contract, discrimination on the grounds of religion or belief and failure to provide a statement of the terms and conditions of employment.

Mrs. Begraj told the employment tribunal that, once her bosses found out that the couple was in love, she experienced harassment at work, and persuaded not to get married because of low caste of Vijay.

When in July 2008 she returned to the workplace after she was involved in a major car accident, for a 'back-to-work' meeting, Mrs. Begraj claimed that her bosses were reluctant for her to return in case she was planning a family.

The case continues.

Dalit Intelligentsia Consider Caste Worse Than Race

Durban Conference must discuss Caste Issue

A group of 40 academicians, jurists, and representatives of NGOs and Civil society organisations, mostly from Dalit communities, who met at a one day conference in the Indian Social Institute, New Delhi, on 7th May 2001 have denounced the Indian subcontinent's caste system as 'worse than racism'. The plight of the victims of the pernicious caste system demands an international scrutiny and debate, the experts have said in their statement. It is in this context that the meeting has taken serious exception to the political and diplomatic stratagems employed by the Government of India in trying to scuttle a discussion on Caste in the forthcoming World Conference Against Racism organised by the United Nations scheduled to be held from 31st August to 7th September 2001 in Durban, South Africa.

The Delhi meeting has also taken serious note of media reports that the Indian government may not allow NGO and Independent groups to go to South Africa to participate in the conference.

'Caste Discrimination can be Raised at International Fora' Says Justice Verma

Kota Neelima Writes:

The Chairman of the National Human Rights Commission (NHRC), Justice J. S. Verma has never fought shy of controversies. His ruling on Hindutva was no less controversial with some finding saffron shades in it. His interventions have broadened the definition of human rights. **He holds that caste discrimination and starvation deaths are human rights violations.** Earlier in the week the NHRC had issued notices to the Central and Orissa governments taking cognisance of starvation deaths. Nor does he mince words when he attacks the government's position on amnesty to security officials accused of human rights violations. Excerpts...

The NHRC has taken a View Contrary to the Government's on Caste. Why?

No one can dispute that discrimination based on caste or any form of Casteism is a serious violation of human rights. And in the Indian context, it is a flagrant violation of the Constitutional guarantee of equality. Article 15 expressly mentions both race and caste as grounds of discrimination. So for practical purposes, I don't see any need to go into the question whether Casteism amounts to racism or not. Whether it does or not, it is something that needs to be eradicated and it is the job of every institution of governance to work in that direction.

But should it be taken to an International Fora?

This being a human rights issue, the violation being there in practice and since human rights issues are not confined to national boundaries alone, all human rights issues can be discussed at international fora as well. I personally have no problem with this issue being discussed at Durban. I don't consider the need to go into the semantics. It is a serious human rights violation and we are concerned with human rights issues. What was the reason behind the government's stand? The Government of India may have many other reasons, political considerations, etc. I am only concerned about the human rights issue. And the real solution to that is economic empowerment to people at all levels. Why do you think people hide behind semantics? Actually it is because of the mindset. Therefore, what you have to combat really is the evil within all of us.

When I was the Chief Justice of Rajasthan High Court in 1988, Harijans were not being allowed in Nathdwara temple. In a writ petition, I made an order on these constitutional provisions to hold that it was a case of serious discrimination and asked for the director general of police and made him understand. The Harijans were then permitted without any discrimination.

You have now held that Starvation Deaths are also Violation of Rights?

Godowns are overflowing and rodents are consuming more food than what would have been sufficient for feeding the people who are dying. We (the NHRC) can only monitor, we can only tell them what is happening and what can be done.

Who is to be Blamed? Those who Distribute Food should be held Responsible. And those Responsible should be Pulled up?

Yes, that is accountability. An effective mechanism for enforcing accountability is the best check for ensuring performance. Ultimately, we (the NHRC) end up making recommendations. We are constantly making our presence felt by breathing down their neck and speaking loudly, that is all. Is it easy to enforce accountability, especially when the state governments do not respond to cases of human rights violations? There is a general tendency to evade as long as possible, if I may use that expression.

In the case of the J&K, I have, after practicing great restraint for quite some time, in March visited the state. Then they promised better performance. But the situation has remained the same. A similar case happened in Madhya Pradesh. We ordered an immediate interim relief in a case but the state administration feels that they should wait till the end of the court case. Then what does interim relief stand for? Moreover, it is a case where the state itself felt that the police officials involved in the case were high-handed. So I have written to the CM and we are waiting for a response.

What is the General Attitude of Officials Towards Human Rights Violation?

It is like when you are at the receiving end then you appreciate everything. But when you are on the other side, then you feel talking of human rights is a nuisance.

What is your Opinion on the Proposed move to Provide Amnesty to those in the Armed forces facing Complaints of Human Rights Violations?

Insurgency should be fought but within the Constitutional provisions. Even in a war, the prisoners of war are protected under the Geneva Convention. The position of Indian citizen within their own country cannot be worse than a prisoner of war.

Do you feel that Raising Issues of Human Rights Violations can Demoralize the Security Forces?

No. But it is clear that one man cannot act as the investigator, prosecutor, adjudicator and executor, all rolled into one. Yes, for instance, if a hijacker who is holding up hostages is shot dead to save their lives it is understandable. But the allegations we are talking of are about fake encounters. These excesses are against civilians, who are the masters. But won't raising rights issues abroad show India in a bad light? That is only if there is an irrevocable basis to think that instruments of governance and agencies here are lax. But not when the judiciary and the NHRC are monitoring human rights situation and punishing the guilty.

Is it Possible that the Human Rights Scenario in the Country worsens to the Level where International Human Rights Organisations have to Intervene?

There is no justification for any international intervention in this field. But then we have to be more careful about the efficacy of the machinery of detecting human rights violations, like the NHRC. That is why we proposed amendments to the NHRC act (which gives NHRC powers to investigate human rights violation cases pertaining to armed forces and paramilitary forces). It would facilitate us in monitoring the human rights situation better.

Think of the credibility of the NHRC, which is headed by a former chief justice and two judges of the Supreme Court. When we examine a complaint with full facts then it holds a lot of credibility.

Geneva's 'World Conference on Racism' - 2009

Caste: Racism in all but Name?

In April 2009, another conference was organised. It was considered as 'Durban II', and is described by TOI in [http://timesofindia.indiatimes.com/Deep-Focus/Caste-Racism-in-all-but-name/articleshow/4449716.cms] (Accessed Nov. 16, 2012). Shobhan Saxena writes on 26 Apr 2009, an article '*Caste: Racism in all but name*?' about that. The Gist:

It had a shaky start as US stayed away, the Israelis staged a walkout as Iranian president Mahmoud Ahmadinejad began to mock the Holocaust. The meeting ended without including 'Dalits' in its resolution, which was a shock to the scores of Dalit activists camping outside the conference venue.

A Dalit ideologue journalist observed that, "Caste and race are not the same, but their implications are same–discrimination on the basis of one's birth", blaming "stupid NGOs" for the outcome in Geneva, saying it was a mistake to equate caste with race. "It's a technical point, which the Indian government exploited to its advantage".

Before the UN conference in Geneva, church organisations around the world had expressed solidarity with the Dalits at a Bangkok conclave. Only consolation for the Dalits was that UN High Commissioner for Human Rights Naventhem Pillay suggested creating an "observatory on discrimination". One small step for UNHCR, a giant leap against untouchability?

Durban Conference Fails to Soothe 'Dalits'; WCC Regrets

[http://in.christiantoday.com/articles/durban-conference-fails-to-soothe-dalits-wcc-regrets/3755.htm] (Accessed Nov. 13, 2012) An article by: Dibin Samuel, Friday, 24 April 2009. The Gist:

(AP)The UN anti-racism conference has again ended on a sad note with no mention of 'Dalits' in the outcome document ratified by world representatives in Geneva. Two major church organisations, The World Council of Churches (WCC) and the Lutheran World Federation (LWF), expressed regret that the conference "failed to acknowledge the suffering of the more than 200 million people discriminated against on the basis of work and descent". Representatives of church organisations around the world at the Bangkok event had expressed their solidarity with the Dalit struggle for justice.

The WCC and LWF although regretted the shunning of Dalits in the final declaration, they welcomed the proposal of UN High Commissioner for Human Rights, Pillay Navy, who suggested creating an "observatory on discrimination".

U.N. Human Rights Council, 2008, Geneva

The Mother of all Discriminations

The National Chairman of All India Confederation of SC/ST Organisations, Dr. Udit Raj, attended 9th Session of United Nations Human Rights Council at Geneva from 9th to 17th September, 2008.

Salient points from his Press Release statement dated 20 Sept. 2008.

The Implementation Remains Inadequate

The provisions of Indian Constitution for protection and promotion of human rights of Dalits are not implemented. Therefore, atrocities, untouchability, insufficient wages, bounded labour, child labour, landlessness, illiteracy, inequality of opportunities, manual scavenging are still the order of the day in the life of Dalits.

Degree of Discrimination

The last Indian National Bureau of Crime Report (2006) states that in that year 27070 crimes had been committed against Dalits, though many go unreported. 13 Dalits are murdered every week, 5 Dalits homes are burnt every week, 6 Dalits are abducted every week, 3 Dalits women are raped every day, 11 Dalits are beaten every day and a crime is committed against a Dalit every 18 minutes. Literacy rate for Dalits remains abysmal: 54.69 per cent as per Govt. of India's last census (2001) while we are witnessing a deterioration situation. Even more disappointing is the progress made by Dalits at higher education. The enrolment of Dalits in graduate education is 8.37 per cent as against 91.63 per cent for others. Furthermore, 37.8 per cent children had to sit separately while eating in 37.8 per cent of Government schools.

No Dalits in Higher Echelons

The "reservation" has not been fully implemented, e.g., out of more than 200 Secretaries in the Government of India, there is hardly anyone from this community. Discriminatory pronouncements of higher judiciary - High Courts and Supreme Court - are engaged in further eroding the base of "reservation", he said. Privatisation and globalisation processes are further blowing death to the reservation. Government jobs are shrinking fast and private enterprises mostly owned by upper castes, discriminate in recruitment (no Dalits CEO in any corporate establishment).

The Brutal Attacks on Christians

The right wing Hindu organisations such as RSS, VHP and Bajrang Dal have unleashed brutal violence against Christians in Orissa, once again this year, after the murder of Swami Lakshmanananda Saraswati, on 23rd of August, by unknown assailants.

More than 4,000 Christian homes were burned, 52 Christians killed according to list maintained by Dr. Joseph D'Souza, of the All India Christian Council. About 115 churches from all denominations were destroyed or heavily damaged. Furthermore, dozens of women were sexually assaulted and harassed. Dozens of Christian-owned businesses burned down, and about 50,000 Christians displaced, 31,000 of them took refuge in the forest/jungles and live in constant fear.

Discrimination Against Muslims

Muslims constitute about 15 per cent of Indian population but their participation in administration is quite a dismal. Though the reservation has been extended to them also in recommendation of Mandal Commission, obstacles lie at the bottom of implementation. Muslims and Christians Dalits are striving to get reservation at par with Hindu Dalits. However, this has to be achieved yet. Dr. Ejaz Ali of United Muslim Morcha is fighting for this right. He, therefore, urged the Human Rights Council that it should build the pressure on Indian government that the justice is secured.

(Sanjay Kumar) Media In charge 9818659660

Putting Caste on Notice

[http://www.thenation.com/doc/20091109/crossette] (Accessed Nov. 13, 2012), An article '*Putting Caste on Notice*' by Barbara Crossette, on October 26, 2009 describes Dalit issues. The Gist:

Navi Pillay Takes the Initiative

Barbara Crossette says Navi Pillay, the South African judge, who became the United Nations high commissioner for human rights last year, is moving to the forefront of a campaign to free more than 250 million miserable victims living in India, from the indignities and horrors of caste discrimination, unlike any other previous commissioner. Navi Pillay is the first UN human rights commissioner to take on caste discrimination.

New Convention Needed on Caste

"This is the year 2009, and people have been talking about caste oppression for more than a hundred years," Pillay says. "It's time to move on this issue." For Pillay, who is of Indian descent, the subject of caste has been hidden too long by obfuscation on the part of governments. India have successfully argued in UN conferences that existing international conventions against human rights abuses do not apply. Caste did not figure in the official conclusions of a conference on racism and other forms of intolerance in Durban in 2001, because of intense lobbying by India. Therefore, Pillay said in Geneva, there may well have to be a new international convention written to apply directly to caste.

A draft document on eliminating discrimination based on work or descent – in other words, being born into predestined deprivation, assigned to the most menial of jobs and segregated socially is being campaigned for. Pillay wishes to see this draft endorsed by the member nations of the Human Rights Council and by all governments.

Manual Scavenging going on

She relayed a story about a group of women who came to her in Geneva recently with a brick from a latrine they had torn down in protest against being forced to carry away human excrement in their bare hands. They wanted to make the point that despite India's frequent assertions to the contrary, there were still tens of thousands of such latrines in the country, and the filthy, soul-destroying work by Dalits continues. Pillay lamented that there is no implementation of the laws, though discrimination by caste is unconstitutional in India, and even democracy has not helped most of the Dalits.

Nepal Takes Lead

Nepal a majority Hindu nation having 4.5 million Dalits, broke ranks with India in September and publicly joined the campaign against caste discrimination. Women among the Dalits everywhere are especially vulnerable to victimisation of all kinds, most often sexual abuse. Pillay averred that low caste women are accused of witch-craft and harassed, as recently in India's Jharkhand state, village women, apparently Muslims who were labeled witches by accusers, were beaten, stripped naked and forced to eat excrement, the BBC reported.

The *Times of India* described Nepal's unanticipated decision to align with the campaign against caste discrimination as an 'embarrassment' to India. Sweden then piled on an endorsement from the European Union, 'adding to India's discomfiture.'

The influence of the Hindu caste system has seeped across other borders in South Asia, into Pakistan, Sri Lanka and Bangladesh, sometimes affecting even Muslims based on their birth or ancestry.

Converts to Christianity or Buddhism who flee Hinduism to escape caste often remain branded for life nonetheless. Dalits, regarded widely as unclean or polluted, can, and have, faced death at the hands of upper caste people for infractions such as taking water from a well or entering a Hindu temple. There have been lynchings for intermarriage with higher castes. In some places, particularly in north India, Dalits vote at segregated polling stations. At roadside cafes they often get separate utensils, if they are served at all.

It need not be that way, Pillay, 68, notes from her own experience. Indians in South Africa, a minority in a suppressed black majority under apartheid, soon abandoned caste consciousness, she said. "I know that in the early days they did practice that, because my parents told us," she said. "I think it would be my grandparents' generation. But it broke down by force of social pressures."

As High Commissioner for Human Rights, Pillay takes a broad view of her responsibilities, and that applies to causes she is willing to take up as well as to her definition of human rights. She focuses not only on political or civil rights but also societal shortcomings and abuses. On caste, she said she looks for other forms of similar discrimination globally, anywhere people are held in forms of slavery based on birth, for example, or are relegated to second-class citizenship for other reasons.

Caste and new forms of slavery are not unrelated, Pillay argued that landlessness, debt bondage and labour bondage, involving millions of young children, are the lot of the lowest castes. "As high commissioner I promised to be evenhanded and raise all issues affecting all human beings," Pillay said. "Caste is now on notice: the UN has failed, she said, to educate people and change mindsets to combat the taint of caste." "Slavery and apartheid could be removed, so now [caste] can be removed through an international expression of outrage."

About Barbara Crossette

Barbara Crossette, United Nations correspondent for *The Nation*, is a former *New York Times* correspondent and bureau chief in Asia and at the UN. She is the author of many books including, '*So Close to Heaven: The Vanishing Buddhist Kingdoms of the Himalayas*', '*The Great Hill Stations of Asia*', '*India: Old Civilisation in a New World*', '*India Facing the 21st Century*'.

CPI on Durban Conference

[http://pd.cpim.org/2001/sept16/2001_sept_16_durban.htm] (Accessed Nov. 14, 2012), (Weekly Organ of the Communist Party of India (Marxist), Vol. XXV,

No. 37, September 16, 2001, on Durban Conference, '*US Exposed, Indian Govt. Disgraced*', by Prakash Karat. The salient points about India:

The Issues

The problems of Slavery, Zionism and Caste were the main issues. Delegations from 163 countries, including 16 heads of states, participated in the conference. A notable feature was the withdrawal of the United States from the conference along with its trusted ally, Israel. The other issue which dominated the conference was the Palestinian people's struggle against Zionism and Israel trampling upon the rights of the Palestinians.

The first World Conference against Racism was held in 1978. It had categorically rejected the idea of racial discrimination based on the biological idea of race. It had strongly condemned the institutionalised racism represented by apartheid system in South Africa.

The second World Conference against Racism was held in 1983 where institutionalised racism was again condemned. After the historic victory over apartheid, the Durban conference focused more on the remedy to the prolonged history of racism and slavery. Most of the African and Asian countries demanded a formal apology for slavery as well as appropriate reparations to be put on the agenda of the conference.

Stand by Omar Abdullah

The official Indian delegation led by Omar Abdullah, minister of state for external affairs, played a role unworthy of India at Durban. First of all, the Indian government refused to condemn Israel strongly, nor was it prepared to take cognisance of the reactionary features of Zionism. In a reversal of India's long-standing opposition to Zionism, the official delegation took the position that India is now committed to repealing the UN resolution terming Zionism as racism. The pro-Israeli stand reflects the growing nexus between the BJP regime and the Israeli government under American auspices. Nor was India's voice heard strongly in support of the demand for reparations for slavery and the slave trade.

The worst position taken by the official delegation was to oppose the inclusion of any reference to caste oppression within the framework of the theme of the conference. Omar Abdullah, the newly recruited enthusiast for the BJP policies, termed the campaign by Dalit activists from India at Durban about caste oppression "highly exaggerated and misleading propaganda" which was often based on "anecdotal evidence regarding caste based discrimination in India." This is virtually negating the reality of caste oppression in India and an insult to the aspirations of the Dalits who are struggling for equal rights and social justice.

The Indian delegation also vigorously opposed the formulation in para 73 of the draft, which talked of discrimination "**based on work and descent**." The Indian delegation wanted the deletion of "work" which would imply caste-discrimination based on occupation.

National Human Rights Commission

In contrast to the Indian government's stand, the delegation of the National Human Rights Commission took a principled stand stating that caste oppression should find a place in the deliberations as it falls within the purview of the theme of the conference.

It may be recalled that the CPI (M) was the first national party to voice support for the demand that caste oppression of Dalits be included in the agenda of the conference.

The discussions in the non-official NGOs conference, prior to the official meet, highlighted sufficiently the nature of Dalit oppression in India and the inhuman practices like untouchability. The Indian government has only disgraced itself by its reactionary position on the matter.

• • •

10

Dalits and Communism

Ambedkar had No Love for Communism

Ambedkar and Communism

Raosaheb Kasabe, is a frequent speaker at Ambedkarite institutions who invite him for the lectures. I happened to be the chairman in one of such meetings. He has a habit of putting his own views and declaring them to be those of Dr. Ambedkar. He averred that, that Ambedkar wanted the Constitution of India to be on the Communistic lines, but he could not succeed in that, because of the oposition of the Parliament. And I had the unpleasant duty of contradicting his views, and I criticised this contention that Ambedkar wanted a communist Constitution.

Maximum numbers of SC/STs are labourers. Ambedkar labeled his first political party as Independent Labour Party. The contradictions, Ambedkar had to face in ensuring the welfare of the Labour movement without being a communist, must not be overlooked. Therefore, it sometimes appears that some of his statements have undertones of Marxist - Communistic ideas. It does not mean that he favoured communism. In so many places, he has clearly and strongly opposed the Communist ideas.

Ambedkar has proposed in *"States and Minorities"* the nationalisation of insurance and agricultural collectivisation, giving agriculture the status of an industry and keep the reins of that industry in the hands of the government. This certainly does not mean that he has Communist leanings. *He wanted to create a welfare state, and it could have been called state socialism.* When Indira Gandhi nationalised the banks and insurance, nobody called her to be a Communist.

The hatred towards religion, allowing violence to achieve the ends, and dictatorship at the helm of affairs are some of the main characteristics of Communist ideology, which Dr. Ambedkar did not profess. And what he professed was the welfare state, with state socialism. He was very keen on having a religion that would be very useful for the toiling masses. It was his mission to have such a religion. During All India Radio broadcast on October 3, 1954, Ambedkar declared:

"Positively, my social philosophy may be said to be enshrined three words: liberty, equality and fraternity. Let no one however say that I borrowed my philosophy from the French revolution. I have not. My philosophy has roots in religion, and not in political science. I have derived them from the teachings of my master, the Buddha. My philosophy has a mission. I have to do work of conversion to Buddhism." [Jafferelot: 2005: 133]

Even the sworn enemies of lower castes, the Sangh Parivar, express gratitude towards Ambedkar for keeping the Dalits away from Communism. There is a vast literature by Dr. Ambedkar in favour of Buddhism and against Communism, that it could answer all points raised by the communists. Ambedkar had already contemplated over Communism for years before giving Buddhism to the multitudes of Indian masses.

Ambedkar's views are nearly sixty years old, and they are still valid. They do not mention Mao, as his theories had not then come into prominence, but what he says about communism in general should also apply to Maoism too.

Dr. Ambedkar, the modern Religion Giver of Indian Buddhism, explained the meaning of Religion according to Buddhism in his various writings. It is rather unfortunate, that the modern Dalit authors of Communism either misunderstand Marxism or Religion or both.

If any people in the world needed the liberation from oppression, they were the Dalits of India. According to theories of Marxism, the revolution should have started here by these people. But their leader Dr. Ambedkar thought that Communism is no answer, and adopted Buddhism along with his followers. His followers are now about one-fifth population of this country of more than 1000 million people. Was Dr. Ambedkar wrong in discarding Communism and accepting Buddhism?

Pre-requisites of Communism

Dr. Ambedkar avers that there are certain pre-requisites for the Marxism to succeed. These are the society should be a "Free society", meaning it should give importance to an **Individual** over the society and that it should be based on **equality**, fraternity and liberty. [Ambedkar, W&S 3, 95]

These pre-requisites have been provided to China by Buddhism and to Russia by Christianity. The absence of these factors in caste ridden Indian society could not foster the growth of Marxism in India, and **that is why Marx failed in Hindu India**. Marx could not properly evaluate the importance of caste or its influence on Indian masses. Because, Marx failed here, his upper caste followers in India talk of "Class" and not of "Caste". That is the reason why the movement of Marx in India was and still is in the hands of oppressor class.

Residue of Marxism

Marx expounded his theories about 150 years ago, about the same time as Mahatma Phule was fighting against hegemony of Brahmin Baniya monopoly. Most of Marxism is demolished during these years. But what remains of the Karl

Marx, Dr. Ambedkar feels, is a residue of fire, **small but still very important**. The residue in his opinion, consists of four items:

(i) The function of philosophy is to reconstruct the world and not to waste its time in explaining the origin of the world.

(ii) That there is a conflict of interest between class and class.

(iii) That private ownership of property brings power to one class and sorrow to another through exploitation.

(iv) That it is necessary for the good of society that the sorrow be removed by the abolition of private property.

Comparison between Buddha and Karl Marx

Dr. Ambedkar compares the Buddha and Karl Marx from points survived from Marxian Creed. He feels that, on the first point there is complete agreement between the Buddha and Karl Marx. That language is different but the meaning is the same. If for misery one reads exploitation Buddha is not away from Marx. ("*Buddha or Karl Marx*", (W&S Vol. 3), p. 444)

On the question of private property, Dr. Ambedkar quotes the illuminating extract from a dialogue between Buddha and Ananda, Buddha saying avarice is because of possession, which in turn is because of tenacity. Buddha prohibited private property in Sangha, he put more restrictions and "rules are far more rigorous than are to be found in Communism in Russia" (*Ibid.*, p. 446)

Means to Achieve Goals

Having summarised Buddha's tenets, Dr. Ambedkar feels that, it is clear that the means adopted by the Buddha to achieve the goals were to convert a man by changing his moral disposition to follow the path voluntarily. The means adopted by the Communists are equally clear, short and swift. They are (1) Violence and (2) Dictatorship of the Proletariat.

The Communists say that there are the only two means of establishing Communism. The first is violence. Nothing short of it will suffice to break up the existing system. The other is Dictatorship of the Proletariat. Nothing short of it will suffice to continue the new system. It is now clear what are the similarities and differences between Buddha and Karl Marx. The differences are about the means. The end is common to both. (*Ibid.*, p. 450)

The *Bhikshu Sangha* had the most democratic constitution. The Buddha was only one of the *Bhikku-s*. At the most he was like a Prime Minister among members of the Cabinet. He was never a dictator. Twice before his death he was asked to appoint some one as the head of the Sangha to control it. But each time he refused saying that the *Dhamma* is the Supreme Commander of the Sangha. He refused to be a dictator and refused to appoint a dictator.

What about the value of the means? Whose means are superior and lasting in the long run? Can the Communists say that in achieving their valuable they have not destroyed other valuable ends? They have destroyed private property. Assuming that this is a valuable end, can the Communists say that they have not destroyed other valuable end in the process of achieving it? How many people have they killed for achieving their end? Has human life no value? Could they not have taken property without taking the life of the owner? (*Ibid.*, p. 452)

Dictatorship is often defined as absence of liberty or absence of Parliamentary Government. Both interpretations are not quite clear. There is no liberty even when there is Parliamentary Government. For law means want of liberty. The difference between Dictatorship and Parliamentary Government lies in this. In Parliamentary Government every citizen has a right to criticise the restraint on liberty imposed by the Government. In Parliamentary Government you have a duty and a right; the duty to obey the law and right to criticise it. In Dictatorship you have only duty to obey but no right to criticise it. [*Ibid.*, p. 453]

We must now consider whose means are more lasting. One has to choose between Government by force and Government by moral disposition. As Burke has said, force cannot be a lasting means. In his speech on conciliation with America he uttered this memorable warning:

> "First, Sir, permit me to observe, that the use of force alone is but temporary. It may subdue for a moment: But it does not remove the necessity of subduing again; and a nation is not governed which is perpetually to be conquered."
>
> "My next objection is its uncertainty. Terror is not always the effect of force, and an armament is not a victory. If you do not succeed, you are without resource, for, conciliation failing, force remains; but force failing, no further hope of reconciliation is left. Power and authority are sometimes bought by kindness; but they can never be begged as alms by an impoverished and defeated violence.
>
> "A further objection to force is, that you impair the object by your very endeavours to preserve it. The thing you fought for is the thing which you recover, but depreciated, sunk, wasted and consumed in the contest." (*Ibid.*, p. 453)

Withering away of State

Dr. Ambedkar also discusses the Communist theory of "withering away of the state". He says, the Communists themselves admit that their theory of the State as a permanent dictatorship is a weakness in their political philosophy. They take shelter under the plea that the State will ultimately wither away. There are two questions, which they have to answer. (1) When will it wither away? (2) What will take the place of the State when it withers away? To the first question they can give no definite time. (*Ibid.*, p. 459)

Though the second question is more important than the first, Dr. Ambedkar feels, the Communists have no satisfactory answer to the question what would take the place of the State when it withers away. Will it be succeed by Anarchy? If so, he feels, the building up of the Communist State is a useless effort. If it cannot be sustained except by force and if it results in anarchy when the force holding it together is withdrawn what good is the Communist State. [*Ibid*., p. 460]

He, therefore, avers that, the only thing, which could sustain it after force is withdrawn, is Religion. He observes:

"But to the Communists, Religion is anathema. Their hatred to Religion is so deep seated that they will not even discriminate between religions, which are helpful to Communism and religions, which are not. The Communists have carried their hatred of Christianity to Buddhism without waiting to examine the difference between the two." [*Ibid*., p. 460]

Charges Against Christianity

Dr. Ambedkar discusses two charges against Christianity leveled by the Communists. Ambedkar answers these charges as he observes:

"Their first charge against Christianity was that they made people other worldliness and made them suffer poverty in this world. As can be seen from quotations from Buddhism in the earlier part of this tract such a charge cannot be leveled against Buddhism."

Dr. Ambedkar then answers the second charge as follows:

"The second charge leveled by the Communists against Christianity cannot be leveled against Buddhism. This charge is summed up in the statement that Religion is the opium of the people. This charge is based upon the Sermon on the Mount, which is to be found in the Bible. The Sermon on the Mount sublimates poverty and weakness. It promises heaven to the poor and the weak. There is no Sermon on the Mount to be found in the Buddha's teachings. His teaching is to acquire wealth." [*Ibid*., p. 460]

He then gives the Buddha's Sermon on the subject to Anathapindika one of his disciples, wherein Buddha describes how wealth should be acquired justly and legitimately. [*Ibid*., p. 460]

Dr. Ambedkar concludes the discussion by observing:

"The Russians do not seem to be paying any attention to Buddhism as an ultimate aid to sustain Communism when force is withdrawn.

"The Russians are proud of their communism. But they forget that the wonder of all wonders is that the Buddha established Communism so far as the *Sangha* was concerned without dictatorship. It may be that it was a communism on a very small scale but it was communism without dictatorship, a miracle which Lenin failed to do.

"The Buddha's method was different. His method was to change the mind of man: to alter his disposition: so that whatever man does, he does it voluntarily without the use of force or compulsion. His main means to alter the disposition of men was his Dhamma and the constant preaching of his *Dhamma*. The Buddha's way not to force people to do what they did not like to do although it was good for them. His way was to alter the disposition of men so that they would do voluntarily what they would not otherwise to do.

"It has been claimed that the Communist Dictatorship in Russia has wonderful achievements to its credit. There can be no denial of it. That is why I say that a Russian Dictatorship would be good for all backward countries. But this is no argument for permanent Dictatorships. Humanity does not only want economic values, it also wants spiritual values to be retained. Permanent Dictatorship has paid no attention to spiritual values and does not seem to intend to. Carlyle called Political Economy a Pig Philosophy. Carlyle was of course wrong. For man needs material comforts. But the Communist Philosophy seems to be equally wrong for the aim of their philosophy seems to be fatten pigs as though men are no better than pigs. **Man must grow materially as well as spiritually**. Society has been aiming to lay a new foundation was summarised by the French Revolution in three words - Fraternity, Liberty and Equality. The French Revolution was welcomed because of this slogan. It failed to produce equality. We welcome the Russian Revolution because it aims to produce equality. But it cannot be too much emphasised that in producing equality society cannot afford to sacrifice fraternity or liberty. Equality will be of no value without fraternity or liberty. It seems that the three can coexist only if one follows the way of the Buddha. Communism can give one but not all." [*Ibid.*, p. 462]

Tests of Religion

In his memorable treatise, "Buddha and future of His Religion", after comparing Buddhism with Hinduism, while comparing Buddhism with other non-Hindu religions, Dr. Ambedkar concludes by enumerating the tests a religion must pass:

"(i) That society must have either the sanction of law or the sanction of morality to hold it together. Without either society is sure to go pieces. In all societies law plays a very small part. It is intended to keep the minority within the range of social discipline. The majority is left and has to be left to sustain its social life by the postulates and sanction of morality. Religion in the sense of morality, must therefore, remain the governing principle in every society.

(ii) That religion as defined in the first proposition must be in accord with science. Religion is bound to lose it respect and therefore become the subject of ridicule and thereby not merely lose its force as a governing principle of life but might in course of time disintegrated and lapse if it is not in accord with science. In other words, religion if it is to function, must be in accord with reason which is merely another name for science.

(iii) That religion as a code of social morality, must recognise the fundamental tenets of liberty, equality and fraternity. Unless a religion recognises these three fundamental principles of social life religion will be doomed.

(iv) That religion must not sanctify or ennoble poverty. Renunciation of riches by those who have it may be a blessed state. But poverty can never be. To declare poverty to be a blessed state is to pervert religion, to perpetuate vice crime, to consent to make earth a living hell."

Dr. Ambedkar asks, which religion fulfills these requirements today, reminding that the days of the Mahatmas are gone and the world cannot have a new Religion. It will have to make its choice from existing religions. Some of the religions might satisfy one or two tests but Buddhism is the only religion satisfying all tests. He observes:

"So far as I know the only religion which satisfies all these tests is Buddhism. In other words Buddhism is the only religion, which the world can have. If the new world-which be it realised is very different from the old - must have a religion-and the new world needs religion for more than the old world did-then it can only be religion of the Buddha." ["*Buddha and future of his religion",* p. 9]

"Could the Buddha answer Karl Marx?"

Admitting that all this may sound very strange, because most of writers on Buddha have propagated the idea that the only thing Buddha taught was Ahimsa. It is true Buddha taught Ahimsa, he says, he does not want to minimise its importance, because it is a great doctrine and the world cannot be saved without it. He further observes:

"What I wish to emphasise it is that Buddha taught many other things besides Ahimsa. He taught as a part of religion, social freedom, intellectual freedom, economic freedom and political freedom. He taught equality, equality not between man and man only but between man and woman. It would be difficult to find a religious teacher to compare with Buddha whose teachings embrace so many aspects of the social life of a people whose doctrines are so modern and whose main concern was to give salvation to man in his life on earth and not to promise it to him in heaven after he is dead." [*Buddha and future of his religion*", p. 10]

Dr. Ambedkar says many divergent views expressed about Buddha's teachings, including *Samadhi*, *Vippasana*, Esoterism, etc., are because the authors are not students of Buddhism, but of history or anthropology. He asks, "Did the Buddha have no social message?" If pressed for an answer, the Buddhist scholars admit that Buddha taught 1. *Ahimsa* and 2. Peace. But the real questions are seldom asked and replied. These are: Did the Buddha teach 1. Justice, 2. Love, 3. Liberty, 4. Equality, 5. Fraternity, and 6. "Could the Buddha answer Karl Marx?" He further avers, "My answer is that the Buddha has a social message. He answers all these questions. But they have been buried by modern authors." [*Buddha and His Dhamma*, book III, part II, sec. 1. (p. 159)]

The Proof of Buddhism Superseding Marxism

In National Catholic Reporter, of Feb. 26, 1999, the Vatican suggested that Buddhism would replace Marxism as the church's biggest foe by 2000. As per Laws of Contradictions by Mao himself, it shows a great future for Buddhism in World affairs, as Christian world is about to replace Marxism, as its foe, with Buddhism. And Ambedkar's prophecy will come true sooner than later.

Lastly, we would conclude with the famous statement of the renowned scientist and thinker Einstein who observed:

> "The religion of the future will be a cosmic religion. It should transcend a personal god and avoid dogmas and theology. Covering both the natural and the spiritual, it should be based on a religious sense of arising from the experience of all things, a natural and spiritual and a meaningful unity. Buddhism answers this description. **If there is any religion that would cope with modern scientific needs, it would be Buddhism.** [Albert Einstein: '*The Human side*']

Marichjhapi and the Revenge of Bengali Bhadralok

Chandalas of Bengal

Chandalas are very ancient society, denigrated in all Hindu *Shastras*. They were elevated during Buddhist period, and during Pala reign, they became crop-producing society with construction of their own houses and boats. During four hundred years of Pala rule, the Buddhist Siddhas flourished and quite a large number of them were Shudras, and Jogipa was a Chandala. It was a strong community in Bengal being second largest in 1871 census. [Biswas: 2008: 7]

They were the most neglected community in Bengal till advent of Harichand Thakur (1812–1878) founder of Matua religion and his son Guruchand Thakur. Under their leadership they became strong enough to get their name changed to Namashudra by a struggle from 1881 to 1911. They disowned the mainstream national movement for independence, and dissociated with caste Hindus and opposed swadeshi movement. They were opposed to the 'movement opposing divided Bengal'.

They adopted anti-vedic Matua religion, considered separate from Hinduism and is also called '*Lokayat Dharma*'. They diversified in crafts and professions, starting leaving villages and became a political force to recon with. After death of Guruchand Thakur in 1935, various leaders emerged and in 1937, Jogendra Nath Mandal got elected as MLA defeating Congress candidate. When Dr. Ambedkar formed Scheduled Castes Federation, Jogendra Nath Mandal supported and became President of Bengal State Branch. In 1946 general election he was the lone candidate of SCF winning from Reserved seat. [Biswas: 2008: 11 ff.]

Story of woes of Dalits of Bengal under Communist Regime

[http://blog.insightyv.com/?p=864] (Accessed Feb. 18, 2012), in an article '*Marichjhapi and the Revenge of Bengali Bhadralok*', Authors Nilesh Kumar,

Ajay Hela, Anoop Kumar say that the story of a Dalit Genocide that remains untold, based on Mallick, Ross: 1999 and Jalais, Annu: 2005. [Nilesh and Ajay are pursuing their Masters in Social Work, TISS, Mumbai]. The Gist:

In pre-partition Bengal, the Namashudra-s with Muslims, managed to keep Congress away from power. In 1946, the Congress government in Bombay province, headed by B.G. Kher and under instructions from Sardar Patel, ensured that Dr. Ambedkar was not elected. Under the leadership of Jogendra Nath Mandal, they could send Dr. Ambedkar to Constituent Assembly in 1946. For this act of theirs, they were punished by putting **these predominantly Hindu districts** in East Pakistan, and Ambedkar had to resign. And the thousands of Dalits were forced to come to India as refugees, causing a great problem.

B.C. Roy, the then Congress Chief Minister, settled Upper Caste refugees in West Bengal, but about Dalit refugees, wrote to Prime Minister Nehru that 'we have no place for them, send them to other states', and they were dispatched to various places as refugees, 'packed in government vehicles as cattle, under strict police supervision'.

Second exodus occurred during Indira Gandhi's time, when Bangladesh was created of East Pakistan in 1971. In these inhospitable places, even the reservations of these Dalits were not recognised.

While in opposition in late 1960s and till mid-70s, Communists demanded the government to settle them within their native Bengal only. One leader welcomed Refugees from other states saying, "The five crore Bengalis by raising their ten crore hands are welcoming you back."

About 1.5 lakh refugees came back from various settlements, believing Communist Government's appeal to return. They were prevented and various atrocities committed against them. However, about thirty thousand Dalit Refugees, successfully rehabilitated themselves, without government help, in island of Marichjhapi. The Left Government started telling a blatant lie saying 'Marichjhapi is a part of the Sundarbans government reserve forest', and evicted them. There were economic blockade, police firing, starvation, disease and death all over.

The authors describe the loss:

> "After destroying all the huts, markets, schools and all other visible markers of Namashudra settlement, West Bengal government declared, in May 1979, Marichjhapi 'finally free from all refugees'.
>
> "Regarding the total lives lost during the West Bengal government's assault on Marichjhapi we will quote from one of the earliest writings on this incident by A. Biswas who wrote, in 1982, that '...out of the 14,388 families who deserted (for West Bengal), 10,260 families returned to their previous places...and the remaining 4,128 families perished in transit, died of starvation, exhaustion, and many were killed in Kashipur, Kumirmari, and Marichjhapi by police firings". [A. Biswas, 1982, "Why Dandakaranya a Failure, Why Mass Exodus, Where Solution?" *The Oppressed Indian* 4(4):18-20.]"

The authors comment that this was 'the apt revenge' of the Bhadralok, against Namashudras for once successfully challenging upper caste hegemony in undivided Bengal. Because of this successful revenge, the Namashudras now live in complete oblivion and scattered, and no one knows what actually happened in Marichjhapi in 1979.

Views of Raja CPI Leader on OBC Reservation in Higher Education

Storming Bastions of Privilege

Usually the Communists in India refrain from talking of caste, as they only talk of class. It is, therefore, noteworthy that a senior leader of CPI supported reservation on caste lines; may be because he is the only Dalit in Communist High Command.

The national secretary of CPI D. Raja, expressed his opinion about Reservations in higher centres of education, in *TOI* 14th April, 2006:

[http://timesofindia.indiatimes.com/articleshow/1489345.cms] (Accessed Thursday, February 23, 2012), Raja remembers incidences of violent confrontation when in 1915, on refusing a Dalit Girl admission to school in Kerala, Upper Castes burnt down the school to prevent the Dalit (Pulaya) child from entering its premises, like in Maharashtra and Gujarat. Raja comments: 'The attitude today is no different', the upper castes would burn down IITs and IIMs and other central universities to prevent SC, ST, OBC from entering such elite institutions, they built where no reservation would be applicable, after independence.

For upper castes, the decision to implement 27 per cent reservations for OBCs in these institutions is like a bombshell. He predicted that an action replay of the Mandal agitation would be seen. The caste elite will devise new ways and methods to combat reservation – probably debunk IITs, IIMs etc. to prevent SC, ST, OBCs. Raja comments:

> "It is unimaginable for the country's elite in cities that sons and daughters of blacksmiths, potters, shepherds, small farmers, toddy tappers, gardeners, weavers, washermen and barbers with their traditional knowledge and skills can enter the gates of IITs and IIMs."

Knowledge Commission too

D. Raja laments that the members of Knowledge Commission, like laws of Manu, have circulated internal notes, which are far more venomous than anti-reservation pamphlets like in Mandal protests, and prevent equality in society.

The upper caste elite enjoy 77.5 per cent reservations in general quota since 1951. Now the breach of 77.5 per cent reservation for upper castes in IITs and IIMs is causing much consternation among them. The caste elite believes that IITs and IIMs and institutes of excellence are their fiefdom.

D. Raja recommended that, the government should not increase the number of seats just to stave off criticism of reservation for OBCs. He hoped that

Self-immolations, media campaigns and merit mantras will not deter the nation from achieving those ideals enshrined in the Preamble to our Constitution.

(Unfortunately, his hopes did not come true and the government increased the number of seats to keep upper caste numbers intact.)

Caste and Communists

Com. Sharad Patil, a great indological scholar was a senior member of Communist fraternity. He resigned from the party CPM on ideological grounds in 1978 and started his '*Satyashodhak Communist Party*' based on the ideology of 'Marxism–Phule–Ambedkarism' and is working among the Adivasis of Maharashtra for a long time. He explains how a low caste Upali could become a highly respected dignitary in the Buddhist sangha, but it does not happen in Communism because of caste feelings, as he observes:

> " ... This never happened in the Indian Communist movement. Candidates for the Communist Party, the party of the **economic proletarian** class and not of the **social proletariat**, are asked to shed their non-proletarian class, which they automatically shed after becoming fulltimers. But their non-proletarian castes remain. This has perpetuated brahmanical leadership, which has brahminised the communist movement and reinforced the unilinear class methodology of Marxism." [Sharad Patil: 2010: 74, emphasis added]

Land Reforms and Abolition of Castes in Communist Regimes

Sharad Patil narrates an incidence, when a senior communist leader Dipankar Gupta declared that land reforms have been completed so thoroughly that no surplus land is left for redistribution.

Mr. Gupta once asserted that Left Front Governments had abolished the Caste system. On being asked by Sharad Patil, whether the Dalits and Adivasis stayed in the villages or outside in West Bengal, he 'paled and fidgeting for some time', replied 'outside'. "Then how do you say that the LF ruled states have abolished the caste system", asked Sharad Patil. [Sharad Patil: 2010: 86]

• • •

11

Dalits in British Army

Ambedkar's Arguments at RTC

THE UNTOUCHABLES AND THE PAX BRITANNICA

[*The Manuscript consisting of 123 typed pages is a presentation of the case of Ambedkar during his stay for the Round Table Conferences in London according to his Marathi biographer Mr. C.B. Khairmode.*]

While elaborating how the British deceived the Dalits, though the British owe their victory to Dalits to a large extent, Ambedkar argued:

"India was conquered by the British with the help of an Army composed of Indians. Who were these people who joined the army of the East India Company and helped the British to conquer India? The answer that I can give – and it is based on a good deal of study–is that the people who joined the Army of the East India Company were the Untouchables of India. The men who fought with Clive in the battle of Plassey were the Dusads, and the Dusads are Untouchables. The men who fought in the battle of Koregaon were the Mahars, and the Mahars are Untouchables."

"Thus in the first battle and the last battle it was the Untouchables who fought on the side of the British and helped them to conquer India."

"There are many who look upon this conduct of the Untouchables in joining the British as an act of gross treason. Treason or no treason, this act of the Untouchables was quite natural. History abounds with illustrations showing *how one section of people in a Country have shown sympathy with an invader,* in the hope that the new comer will release them from the oppressions of their countrymen."

"Not only did the Untouchables enabled the British to conquer India, they enabled the British to retain. The Mutiny of 1857 was an attempt to destroy British Rule in India. It was an attempt to drive out the English and reconquer India. So far as the Army was concerned the Mutiny was headed by the Bengal Army."

"The Bombay Army and the Madras Army remained loyal and it was with their help that the Mutiny was suppressed. What was the composition of the Bombay Army and the Madras Army? They were mostly drawn from the Untouchables, the Mahars in Bombay and the Pariahs in Madras. It is, therefore, true to say that *the Untouchables not only helped the British to conquer India they helped them to retain India."* [The Untouchables and the Pax Britannica]

Dalit Battles

[http://timesofindia.indiatimes.com/OPINION/Dalit-Battles/articleshow/41879867.cms] Dalit Battles, 31 March 2003.

'The Invaders'

Raja Sekhar Vundru, editor of '*Dalit Millennium*' and the moving force behind the 'Bhopal Declaration', apprised Rajesh Ramachandran of TOI that the Hollywood movie 'The Invaders', proposed to depict the battle of Wadagaon, would inadvertently distort another facet of the war – the martial role of Dalits in pre-independent India. It was not that the White men fought the local Marathas, but the British conquered India with an army composed mainly of Indians, mostly untouchable Mahars fighting against Peshava rulers. It is the lone battle the Marathas won against the British.

Mr. Vundru explains:

'Wadagaon was just one of a series of battles which involved Indians on both sides, and which was subsumed by the defeat of Koregaon. The Battle of Wadagaon pales into insignificance if you consider that it was a 50,000 strong Maratha army that defeated 2,600 men of the British army. Because it was the Mahars in the British army who defeated the Marathas in the battle of Koregaon in 1818. This last Anglo-Maratha battle conclusively established British rule in western India and completed the Company's territorial conquest of the country.'

Why Mahars were not Part of the Peshava Army

Mr. Vundru explains why were the Mahars not part of the Peshava army while they were a vital component in Chhatrapati Shivaji's Army. Shivaji deployed 'low caste' *Ramoshis, Mahars* and *Mangs* in his infantry and naval forces and protection on forts, and they helped him establish his empire.

During the Peshava rule, the rulers oppressed the Mahars, making them hang a pot around their neck to spit and tie a broom around their waist to sweep away their 'impure' footsteps. The social oppression and extreme untouchability led the Mahars to serve the British army to fight against the Peshwa rule.

The British recognised the valour and loyalty of the Mahars and recruited them in such large numbers that they became the biggest caste group in the colonial army and marine forces. During World War I, a separate regiment, 111 Mahar, was raised by the British to fight overseas. The military training and contact helped the Dalits in acquiring English education and modern outlook and motivated them to break free from social shackles.

But the British ditched the untouchables when the 1858 Peel Commission on army reorganisation refused to recognise them as a martial race. However, Dr. Ambedkar could get recruited another Mahar regiment in 1940.

Robert Clive Won the Battle of Plassey with Dushads Army

Mr. Vundru explained:

> "The Bengal army under Robert Clive, which won the battle of Plassey, was largely composed of Dushads. According to Ambedkar it was the Bombay army of Mahars and the Madras army of Pariahs that saved the British during the Mutiny. But the British soon succumbed to the prejudice against lower castes. As a result, when the native sahibs entered the officers' mess for the first time, the descendents of Dalit heroes of Koregaon and Plassey were relegated to the NCO mess."

The British erected a monument in 1821 as a tribute to the valour and loyalty of the Mahars after the battle of Koregaon.

Battle of Koregaon

Details of Battle

A lot of information is available in Dalit literature. We will give only salient points. Koregaon Cenotaph, erected at the site of the battle, has the names of 22 Mahar soldiers who fell in action. Koregaon pillar featured on the Mahar Regiment crest during British rule. Dr. Ambedkar, and later Kanshiram used to visit the site whenever possible to pay tributes to Mahar valour. And now a lot of Ambedkarites visit the place on New Years Day every year.

In the month of November 1817 Peshavas devastated the Regency of Pune giving no scope for the British army to retaliate successfully. The British commanding officer in Pune called the Chief of the second Battalion-first Regiment Native Infantry for help which was encamped in the Shirur Taluka of Pune district.

The Battle of Koregaon took place on January 1, 1818, at the bank of river Bhima in Koregaon near Pune in Maharashtra. A small force of 500 infantry men of the 2nd Battalion 1st Regiment of the Bombay Native Light Infantry mostly Mahars under the command of Capt. F. F. Staunton walked down 25 miles whole night and fought all day non-stop without rest or respite, food or water continuously for twelve hours and defeated a large force of 20,000 horse and 8,000 infantry of Peshava Baji Rao II.

The English Officers were thinking of retreat as odds were high, but Mahar *jawans* refused and declared they would fight till last man last bullet. Peshava commander Bapu Gokhale lost his elder son Govind Baba and started lamenting in the battle field taking son's head on lap. Peshava army lost courage and ran away and were slaughtered.

Its Significance

This battle had great significance for many reasons. First, British army fought this battle with a minuscule army expecting the worst, especially after their experience of the Pune Regency. Secondly, the battle of Koregaon was one of the most important events which helped tear down the Peshava Empire and subsequently the Peshava had to abdicate. Thirdly and most importantly, **it was an attempt by the untouchables of Maharashtra to break the shackles of the age-old caste order**.

'The Great Maratha'—Mahadji Shinde

Maharashtra Government Established Memorial

The Maharashtra Government have lately built a memorial with *Vijay Stambha* and life size bronze statue, at Wadgaon 45 km. from Pune, on Pune Bombay Highway in memory of that 'Great Maratha' – Mahadji Shinde, the great hero of "First Maratha War".

Unfortunately, we are not taught in schools about this "Great Maratha" – popularised by T.V. serial of that name by Sanjay Khan. They teach in schools only fables of Nana Phadnavis.

It was Mahadji (1727 – 1794), survivor with only leg injuries, of Panipat, which "decided the fate of India" – who resuscitated Maratha power after disaster of 1761 Panipat and brought back the power of Maratha Empire to original glory. It was Mahadji who established Maratha control over Imperial Government of Delhi and thus wiped out the disgrace of disastrous Panipat, caused mainly by the attitude of the Peshavas – "narrow conservatism and racial arrogance in the traditional system of caste".

Mahadji had to face the oppositions not only from foes but also from so called friends. He gained "in the teeth of pinpricks and covert opposition by the Court of Poona" – meaning Nana Phadnavis – the "Supreme glory of the Regency of the Empire of Delhi", and many titles practically single-handed. But the Government at Pune denied him "money and armed help in his sorest need" and openly insulted him in public.

It was the public humiliation by his master to the "greatest and the most successful Maratha General then living". He was even called by Poona, a cheat, a disloyal servant, a selfish upstart selfishly robbing his "holy Brahmin Shrimant" of Delhi's fabulous wealth.

He tolerated all this in the greater interest of the nation, and so it is said of him that, "He towers over Maratha History in solitary grandeur, a ruler of India without an ally, without a party."

He was observing no caste or communal barriers. His best friend, philosopher and guide was a Muslim – Rana Khan, his chief adviser – who saved him in Panipat and nursed his leg wounds to recovery. His many sardars were untouchables and his "religious guide" was Mansur Shah.

Mahajan, from whom most of information is drawn, observes:

"... He was free from caste and religious bias. He was equally respected by the Muslims and the Hindus. He employed Brahmins, Prabhus, Marathas, and the Mahars. Saraswat Brahmins attained special distinction in his service as soldiers and diplomats. Mahadji was always careful and faithful to Peshava family. He never tried to assert his independence. (though he could have easily done that) (But) It was unfortunate that Nana Phadnavis was jealous of Mahadji and always tried to keep him away from Poona." [Mahajan: 2001: 121]

It is said, if Nana Phadnavis had co-operated with Mahadji, "the course of Maratha History would have been different" – **not only Maratha history but history of India would have changed**. But that had not to be. Nana – no doubt a genius, the last genius of Maratha kingdom – who lacked military leadership and had excessive love for power and money, "did not like open methods of Mahadji and always worked in secret".

Captain Browning said after his death, "Nana is gone and with him the Brahmin Raj". Nana had gradually and systematically eliminated the "*Baara Bhai*" (twelve sardars) warriors in Confederacy, one by one, and had become the virtual dictator in reign of Sawai Madhavrao. Nana was not only jealous of Mahadji but also always opposed him. As per the depiction of Sanjay Khan's serial "Great Maratha", Nana poisoned Mahadji, who died in February 1794, and the whole course of history changed.

It is said of Mahadji, if he had survived a little longer, he would have united and "brought under one standard the horsemen and the French contingent of Tipu, the powerful artillery of the Nizam, the whole force of the Rajput and every spear which Maratha influence could have collected from Poona (Peshava), from Indore (Holkars), from Baroda (Gaekwads) and from Nagpur (Bhosales)".

But that was not to be. With Mahadji gone, gone were the hopes of pan-Indian unity and even the components of the Maratha power – Poona, Indore, Baroda and Nagpur – could not unite. The important confederating units of Maratha Confederacy – the Holkars, the Gaekwads, the Bhosles and the Shindes – intrigued against one another and helped other powers against each other.

Two years after death of Mahadji, Nana brought in worthless Bajirao II on throne. Nana died in 1800. Bajirao submitted to control of Shindes but ran away to Bassein to seek help from the English Company against Holkars, who defeated Shindes. He entered into disgraceful "Treaty of Bassein" (31st December 1802) with the English, who took him to Pune and put him in throne in 1803.

They also established the English Residency there. Maratha sardars – Bhosles and Shindes first and later Holkars – individually, fought this "Second Maratha war" (1802-04), but lost one by one.

Bajirao disliked his status and decided to revolt. But "tortured by fear and indecision, urged by hatred to attack the English but confused by the fumes of indolence and debauchery and bewildered by conflicting counsel of soothsayers and astrologers", Bajirao was late by a week, and British reinforcements had arrived. When he finally attacked the Residency, it was already abandoned and Elphinstone watched the blaze saying "We went to observe the enemy. The sight was magnificent". Then Elphinstone attacked and at the end "found themselves alone in field and Sun set" and thus won the battle of Kirkee. That was part of the "Third Maratha War" (1817-18).

The battles of Ashti and Koregaon also formed part of that war. British victory of Mahar Battalion in the battle of Bhima Koregaon – where the pillar in memory martyrs of battle erected by the British in 1882 stands today and which Dr. Ambedkar and later Kanshiram used to visit to pay respects to bravery of Mahar warriors every year, whenever they could – led to Bajirao being deposed in 1818.

Thus ended the tyrannical Brahmin rule of debauch Peshava Bajirao II. Not a single soul, apart from a few *'aashrits'*, shed any tears for the end of Peshava rule. The men in Peshava army joined the service of the East India Company within 36 hours. Untouchables – Mahars Mangs – were happy. In Peshava rule, they had to have earthen pot in neck as a spittoon and a broom to waist. It was rejoiced by women, who said, "good happened, he was destroyed" (*bare zale, melya che talpat zale*). Many women of Wai had earlier committed mass suicide by jumping in a well on hearing the news of arrival of Bajirao to the town. In a civic reception to the British Resident people expressed gratitude.

One wonders what would have been the history of Marathas and the history of India if Nana had not poisoned Mahadji Shinde – the "Great Maratha"!

Matadin Valmiki, a Forgotten Hero of 1857 Sepoy Mutiny

A Movie 'Mangal Pande'

A movie by Amir Khan, 'Mangal Pande' was released on 12th of August 2005, with great hype in media. He was a Brahmin soldier in British Army of Bengal, who is said to have had fired the first shot and started the 'Sepoy Mutiny' of 1857.

This mutiny was aptly described by Mahatma Phule as, "*Bhat Pandya che band*", meaning the 'Mutiny of the Brahmins'. He had expressed pleasure that the mutiny failed and the Bahujans of India were saved the tyranny of Brahmanism. [Keer: *Mahatma Phule*, p. 90]

In the whole episode, the name of a Dalit soldier, Matadin Valmiki, is completely forgotten. Matadin had said to Mangal Pande, "Look here, your Hindu religion is very delicate and weak. I picked up your '*lota*' (a mug) to answer the call of nature, and that spoiled your '*dharma*'. Your mug gets polluted if I touch it and your *Hindutva* is corrupted. But when you peel the cartridges by your mouth to load your guns, the cartridges, which are smeared with fat of the cow, your religion is not spoiled."

Matadin Valmiki showed them the factory where the tallow of the animals was being brought in. That enraged the already aggrieved soldiers, and led Mangal

Pande to fire the first shot and kill a British Army officer. Mangal Pande did NOT fight for country; he fought for preserving his Caste.

It was Matadin Valmiki, as reported, who organised the revolt in the camp. Subsequently, both Mangal Pande, and Matadin Valmiki were tried in the court martial and sentenced to be hanged to death. It was Matadin Valmiki who was hanged first, and after him Mangal Pande was hanged.

But the Indian psyche is such that name of Matadin Valmiki is forgotten, and only Mangal Pande remembered. That is the mystery of the caste ridden India.

It is pity that the new film too did not do any justice to Matadin Valmiki.

A few Dalit authors seem to take pride in maintaining that the Dalits participated in 'Sepoy Mutiny' 1857, and ignore the Ambedkar's statement that it were the Dalits who not only won India for the British, but also maintained it in 1857. Only because Arun Shorey found faults with Ambedkar's above statement, no one underestimates Dalit role in the British conquest of India, rather *Dalits are proud of it.* Out of three British Armies, only Bengal Army had more Brahmins, but not in Bombay or Madras Army, which preponderated with Dalits. These two armies did not participate in mutiny.

Sawarkar called it 'First War of Independence'. We need to evaluate it from the Dalit angle. A Dalit scholar Dr. Vaibhav Wasnik from USA agreed with my views. And Ms. Gail Omvedt remarked it was crazy making this fellow Pande a hero out of those who object to being polluted in this way.

Dalits welcomed the Turks as '*Bodhisatta*' and adopted Islam. They won India for the British. This should be an eye opener to the Brahmanism and a warning for the future, that Dalits will find the ways of their emancipation with utter disregard for Brahmanism.

Dr. Ambedkar and Second World War

There was only one Indian leader who was worried about the situation, if Hitler wins the war, what kind of calamity will fall on the whole world; it was Ambedkar. 'All Indians should remain united and bring victory to democracy', he was telling the whole world, 'then nobody can dare to deny the independence to India'.

Sawarkar could not think beyond Hinduisation of politics and militarization of Hindus, with the sole aim of opposing the Muslims, which today we find resulting into partition of the country. He considered Muslims as greater enemy of India than the British. His biographer Dhananjay Keer observes that he was not concerned whether Hitler or Churchill wins.

Nehru supported war efforts, but was isolated as Gandhi was full of confusion and opposed the war efforts. Gandhi tried to create anarchy and chaos in the middle of war by 1942 unplanned 'Quit India' movement, which proved ineffective and disastrous.

Muslim leaders did not have any pan-India vision. They concentrated only on creation of Pakistan.

No leader worth the name understood the seriousness of Nazi danger.

Second world war started just after Ambedkar declared conversion. The British acted treacherously against the Dalits; even then Ambedkar remained steadfast supporter of the British from start to end.

Communists labeled it 'war of imperialists' before 1942, and started calling it 'peoples war' after Russia entered it.

Subhash Chandra Bose preferred to align with the forces of Germany, Italy and Japan hoping that if they would give India independence on platter and make him Indian Hitler, after the British lose.

He, no doubt, loved India, but was a very ambitious person. When side-tracked by Gandhi, he tried to achieve India's independence bypassing Congress and Gandhi. For that he sought the help from fascist Hitler, dictator Stalin and imperial Japan, without realising its implications.

The soldiers of *Aazad Hind Sena* in Germany were shot down when they refused to fight against Russia. Indians do not stop to think what would have been the result if after India got freedom with German help, and if Indians would have refused to help Germany. [Chimankar: 1993: 118]

If the axis forces had won the Second World War, what would have been the condition of India and Indian masses, nobody seems to have discussed. Only Ambedkar thought in the context of the world. His thoughts were more mature than not only Indian leaders like Gandhi, Sawarkar and Bose but also Churchill, Stalin and Hitler, who were fighting for their own countries, whereas Ambedkar fought for democracy versus dictatorship. Those who blame Ambedkar for joining the viceroy's council, during World War II, need to think on these lines.

• • •

12

Dalits and Reservations

History of Reservations

In this country, only cows and Brahmins had special human rights before arrival of the British. SCs, STs and OBCs, were not treated as human beings until then. After the British came, they decided that everybody in the country should get education, and accordingly the SCs, the STs, and the OBCs received some attention of the state.

Out of these education facilities, there was the rise of Mahatma Phule. Phule found that most of the posts of the government were occupied by the Brahmins leading to the exploitation of the farmers and the lower castes.

He demanded of the British government that all the government posts should be reserved for the lower castes, and there should be proportionate quota for all different castes in the country. This was the beginning of the concept of reservations in this country.

It was Rajarshi Chatrapati Shahu, who for the first time in this country introduced the system of reservations in the government services. He allotted 50 per cent of all the posts to the lower castes, by which he meant all the castes except the Brahmins, the Parasis, the Shenavis and the Prabhus. This was done in a small state of Kolhapur.

It was Dr. Babasaheb Ambedkar, who introduced the system of reservations in the whole country through the Indian Constitution.

Different Types of Reservations

There is a lot of confusion about the reservations in this country. There are different types of reservations, given according to the different articles of the Constitution like in politics, admissions to the institutions of the knowledge, the services of the government and the semi-government bodies.

Then there is a demand of reservations in unreserved fields like the army and navy and air force and the demand for reservations in the judiciary, and a demand of reservations in the upper houses of the Parliament and assemblies.

Only the political reservations had a time limit of ten years, and for last 60 years they have been extended every time for ten years each, even though opposed by organisations of SC, STs. All other reservations have no time limit and never had any, such time limit. But the media wrongly project that the reservations of the colleges and services end in ten years.

Poona Pact

Background

It seems the people of my generation knew the ill-effects of Poona Pact in a better way, as at the age of 12, we used to participate in processions denouncing it. It seems, now the Dalits do not seems to be aware of that.

On 20th September at 12 noon, Gandhi started 'fast unto death'. He fasted about 21 times in his life time of 79 years, for Hindu Muslim unity, in Noakhali, in Bengal, in Delhi etc., up to 21 days some times. But in this one at Poona, his health deteriorted within two days. Had Devdas Gandhi and Kasturba Gandhi not approached Ambedkar with moist eyes with a request to save Gandhi's life, perhaps there would have been no Poona Pact.

Early in twentieth century, in 1901, the Dalits in Bengal and Maharashtra started demanding of the British government, certain facilities, as their condition is worst and they are separate from the Hindus, on parity with Muslims.

In 1909, the Muslims were the first to get any sort of special constitutional safeguards in the history of India. They were given the separate electorates.

Shahu Maharaj put forward a demand of similar nature for the Dalits and backward classes. Dr. Ambedkar also put forward demand for separate electorate and reserved seats to Southborough Committee in 1919, but there were no constitutional recognition or safeguards of any kind till 1919 for Dalits or OBCs.

Montague Chelmsford Act of 1919 recognised the depressed classes and promised to **nominate** members in assemblies. Accordingly, M.C. Rajah from Madras was the first Member of Parliament in 1923-24 from Depressed Classes.

Ambedkar founded '*Bahishkrut Hitkarni Sabha*' in 1924, and started Mahad Satyagraha in 1927.

British parliament decided to send a 'statutory commission', later called Simon Commission, to decide the nature of future constitution of India. Dr. Ambedkar was a nominated member of Bombay Legislative Council during that time. He was nominated to work with the Simon Commission by the Legislative Council. Ambedkar put forward some important points on behalf of *Bahishkrut Hitkarni Sabha*.

Motilal Nehru Committee, formed with Congress and Muslim members, also put forward its view before the Simon Commission. Thus, there were two views in front of Commission.

Important Points put Forward by Ambedkar

1. Adult Franchise: Ambedkar asked for franchise for all including woman.
2. Voting Rights for Adivasis: Though Adivasis were illiterate, Ambedkar thought they understood where lies their welfare and deserved voting rights.

3. Constitutional protection and safeguards for Adivasis.
4. Ambedkar advised OBC leaders to demand special protection and reservations.
5. Ambedkar demanded for Depressed Classes, a separate electorate if no adult franchise, but general electorate would do, if adult franchise were given.

The Report of Simon Commission came out in February 1930, and on 3rd March 1930 *Satyagraha* of Kalaram Temple was started by Ambedkar about same time, Ambedkar was invited to attend Round Table Conference (RTC).

In first RTC Ambedkar demanded:

1. free enjoyment of equal citizenship
2. civic rights and fundamental rights for all
3. infringement of these to be punishable offence
4. social boycott due to untouchability to be made punishable offence
5. adequate representation of depressed classes in legislature
6. adequate representation of depressed classes services
7. adequate representation of depressed classes cabinet
8. and Dr. Ambedkar declared that depressed classes (SC, ST, OBCs) are not Hindus and the British started recognising this fact on ethnographical, sociological and anthropological ground.

The Reservations in Public Services, though demanded by Ambedkar in Simon Commission and in Round Table Conference, were not given in Prime Minister Macdonald's Communal Award, and were not part of Poona Pact, which concerned only with Political Safeguards. When Ambedkar was Labour Minister in Governor General's Cabinet, he got these sanctioned by Lord Linlithgo. First 8.5 per cent was given on 11th August 1943 and later extended to 12.5 per cent on 15th June 1946.

Reservations and Objections

Great Turmoil in Country

Today, we find tremendous objections to reservations, specially after Mandal Commission. Objections are more for OBCs rather than SC/ST. Why? Because the elites know that SC/ST cannot hurt them, whatever they get, but the OBCs could.

Objections and Replies

- *It increases hostility among the castes.*

Was there no hostility before reservations started? Is it more or less now? It has become less. And in any case why the have-nots should suffer the deprivations only because the haves have objected to part with their privileges? Why should they forgo their legitimate share in the assets and duties of the nation and lead life in penury?

- *Reservation should be only for limited period.*

This is wrong assumption. Reservation is birth right and should continue till the castes last. That is why Ambedkar included the reservations, i.e. the representation in the fundamental civil rights.

- *Those in power today are there because of their merit.*

This is wrong assumption. Before 1950, were all our forefathers without merit? Merit does not depend on birth. A person is good at farming, but if has no land how can he show his merit. At the time of transfer of power in 1947, the slogan was 'Land to the tiller'. So the Dalit Bahujans raised the voice – 'What about those who have no land to till'. Some half hazard methods were taken and land ceiling act was put in and distribution of surplus land to landless was contemplated but not properly implemented.

- *Caste based reservations have always been present in Indian society.*

System of *Chaturvarnya* is neither reservation nor division of labour. It is division of labourers and only the *dwija-s* enjoyed all the privileges of education, state and bureaucracy and 85 per cent population of *Shudra-s* and *Ati-shudra-s* had only servility to suffer due to prohibition to get educated, to bear arms and to acquire property. To tell a scavenger that he has got 100 per cent reservation to clean the latrines by bare hands, is the greatest cruelty. Tilak had said why the *Kunbis* and *Teli Tambolis* want education, they should not go to legislature. And Gandhi had advised a sweeper graduate to perform scavenging in a better way.

- *Reservation should be given on economic basis as only rich are now being benefited and the poor are deprived.*

This is a wrong assumption. This goes against the very concept of reservations. Reservation is not poverty alliviation programme. It is not a famin relief. It is for giving human rights equality and participation in national affairs. It is given on that criterion, on which the **discrimination** in the society is observed. In the west, it is based on black and white, in India it is on **caste**, that the discrimination is made. So reservation must be on caste.

- *All Brahmins are not bad.*

A Brahmin may be good to you at times. But when it comes to preserving hegemony of Brahmins, they are all the same. We do not have to bother about Brahmins. We have to awaken those Bahujans who talk language of Brahmins.

- *Backward communities have made good progress and do not need reservations any more.*

If a few people from any community become rich, it does not mean whole community has become rich. The majority of about 90 per cent living in villages and urban slums are still away from all progress and are rotting in penury. Reservation means every community must be represented in state institutions and take part in running the affairs of the society.

- *Reservation is anti-social.*

Reservation is not anti-social. It is an arrangement for creating social justice. It is meant for deprived subaltern communities and not for deprived individuals. The opposition to reservations is anti-national, as it prevents reducing the gaps among various elements of the society.

- *The age of reservation is over. It is now age of competition. There should be healthy competition based on merit.*

Because of caste discrimination, there is no equality of opportunity. So caste reservation is necessary. For healthy competition there must be equality of opportunity. Otherwise, it would be race between a mule and a racing stallion.

- *There should be no reservations to creamy layers among* SC/ST/OBC

  Restricting benefits to 'creamy layers' among SC/ST/OBC is not justifiable. As it is not poverty releaving programmes. It at all creamy layer restrictions are to be applied, they should be applied to general category quota, which is a fifty per cent.

Reservations in 'Private' Sector

Remedies Taken by Elites to Negate Reservations

The elites and the privileged castes are quite aware of the dangers the Reservation can cause to their hegemony, and they have taken preventive measures to protect their privileged position, and new methods are always discovered, and this will go on till they amend the Constitution. How?

First, by Judicial decisions
Second, by privatising Educational Institutions
Third, by excluding key positions
Fourth, by excluding fields like armed forces, judiciary
Fifth, by excluding and upper houses in Assemblies and Parliament
Sixth, by limiting to fifty per cent ceiling
Seventh, by heavy propaganda against reservation
Eighth, by militant means
Ninth, by handing over all development to private sector

Demand for Reservation in Private Sector

Guru Gobind Singh had rightly said, nobody hands you power without struggle. And Reservations are Power. If Bahujans acquire political power, they will become Givers of Reservations instead of Beneficiaries, and there will be no need for it. Till that happens, they have to struggle for Reservations.

And they did struggle. So Prime Minister had to initiate talks. This was in UPA-1, probably because of presence of Left Parties, in govt. UPA-2 is totally silent on the subject. Only future will tell what happens after next elections after 2014. So all the writings on this subjects are of period of UPA-1.

Land of Reservations

India always had reservations since the days of "*Purush Sukta*", perhaps the first declaration of Reservations on Caste basis. And these were always based on caste. If admission to army in ancient India were not based on caste, and not limited to Kshatriyas, India would not have been slave of aliens for centuries.

Givers of reservations and takers of reservations were always opposed to each other's interests. As of today, the takers of reservations should try to become givers of reservations. They are trying for that.

Never on Economic Status

Reservations should never be based on economic status for various reasons:

1. The problem of poverty is not the main problem of the "excluded humanity". Poverty is not the CAUSE of Social exclusion. On the contrary poverty and deprivation and even destitution is the RESULT of Social exclusion. And as far as India is concerned, CASTE is the main form of social exclusion. And the reason for that is the religion of four fold graded inequality.
2. An individual's Economic status can change. Low income may be taken to mean poverty. But the purchasing value of money, in India, depends upon caste. For example, a Dalit cannot buy a cup of tea even in some places, or rent a house in area wanted by him.
3. Practical difficulties in proving economic status of individual to the state machinery are many. The weak may suffer.
4. In caste ridden India infested with rampant corruption, even for an unchangeable status like caste, the false "Caste Certificate" can be purchased. How much easier will it be to purchase a false "Income Certificate"? So income based reservation is impractical. It is no use arguing when both certificates can be bought, why caste only should form basis of reservation. It is certainly more difficult to buy a false caste certificate than a false income certificate.
5. Reservation is not an end in itself. It is a means to an end. The main aim is to achieve the active participation and sharing by the "socially excluded" humanity in all the fields of the affairs of the society. It is not panacea for all ills, neither it is permanent. It would be a temporary measure till such time the matrimonial advertisements in newspaper columns continue to contain the mention of caste.
6. The fields of reservations should be ALL fields of life. This includes education, jobs, judiciary, armed forces, industry, corporate life trade and commerce. It should include 'quota within quota' in Women's Reservation and it would also include affirmative action to all including Muslims and Christians. Various methods would have to be devised to fulfill these objectives. What they call "private" sector is not at all private it is fully Public.
7. If this generation avoids the responsibility of dealing with social exclusion, their future generations would suffer. It must never be forgotten that whenever India became slave country, it was always because the givers of powers avoided granting reservations to excluded multitudes and sharing power with them. There is no reason why history would not repeat itself. The slogan, therefore, should be "Share or Suffer". One

needs to understand the speech Dr. Ambedkar delivered while presenting the Indian Constitution to the Country on 26th November 1949 – 'the Constitution Day'. (See *infra*).

Wrong Propaganda

In June 2004, the Maharashtra Government thought of implementing the legislation for 52 per cent reservation in 'Private Sector' companies, i.e. "Public Limited" companies. The 52 per cent include the SC, ST, OBC and VJ NT. But the media, both print as well as electronic, were falsely talking as if the reservations were only for SCs. This was similar to misunderstanding created during 'Mandal Agitation', that beneficiaries were only SCs. Another misunderstanding created by the media was that the reservations were meant only for ten years and it is being extended only for gaining political mileage. Nobody brought forward the point that the reservation for Legislatures alone, was for ten years but the reservation for educational institutions and government, semi-government jobs were not limited by time. Nobody also pointed out how even that reservation also is not filled up. Nobody brought out the fact that reservation in promotions was stopped and many other restrictions were put in, some by legislature, some by executives and some by judiciary. Nobody mentioned about 50 per cent limit put by Supreme Court on total seats that could be considered 'reserved'. Nobody talked about various 'rosters' put forward by authorities to scuttle the reservations. Nobody put forward why there should be no reservation in Armed Forces and Higher Judiciary and Rajya Sabha and *Vidhan Parishads*. Nobody even mentioned that the reserved seats reduced in the name of 'conversion to Buddhism' have not been restored even after the Buddhists have been later brought under the ambit of reservation.

Reservations in Judiciary

An IAS or IPS or IFS can reach to the level of Secretary in State or Central Ministry; nobody explained why one could not reach a stage of judge in High Court or Supreme Court. Nobody discussed why the age limit was raised by two years so that no recruitment becomes necessary. Nobody talked of the number of vacant posts of Officers in Armed Forces or Judiciary. When everybody is crying hoarse about the number of cases pending in various courts all over the country, nobody even talked about increasing the seats in Law Colleges and posts of junior Officers in Judiciary. When everybody is talking of scarcity doctors, they are not increasing the seats of Medical students. They have purposefully increased the fees in Medical, Engineering and Dental Colleges so that, students coming from lower strata of society could be kept out. Why there should be private Medical Colleges at all? Why all the Government District Hospitals could not be elevated to the level of so called 'Teaching Hospitals'? With just a nominal increase in expenditure, all these district hospitals could be functioning as Teaching Hospitals. All these policies are used to create and maintain the hegemony of upper castes over the society. All the Governmental agencies, kind of, work in tandem to keep the students from marginalised societies out of the mainstream vocations. They talk of facilities in countries like USA, but do not give the same numbers of lawyers, judges, dentists, doctors and other service men in proportion to total population. If we try to analyse the figures, our requirement of such human resources would be about ten times higher than at the present.

Where there is a will there is a way

It is useless to say that there is no money to create more manpower. It does not require money. What is required is political will power.

It must be remembered that Shahu Maharaj had given Lawyer's *sanad-s* to many non-graduates during his times. Gandhi was only matriculate, when he joined Inn to become a barrister-at-law. Even today many of the Chinese Judges are not Law Graduates in China, we are told. If it is decided to reduce the number of pending cases in court, it can be done within a period of three to five years. But in that case, the judges would not all be from upper castes alone. Former High Court Justice Kolse Patil has mentioned how a vacancy in High Court was not filled for three years to facilitate a relative of the ruling judge.

They sold the family silver to pay the butler

In spite of all these hurdles, the SC, ST and OBC youth are progressing. This has become intolerable to the upper caste rulers and they decided to stop the participation of these people in the governance of the society. For this purpose they decided to sell off Government assets at throw away prices to their near and dear ones. They created a new ministry to dispose these assets off. They created a hue and cry that government industries were making huge losses. But when it came to disposing of these Government units, they did not dispose off the loss making concerns; they sold the most profit making concerns even trying to dispose of the '*Nava-Ratnas*'. Even Shiv Sena Chief Bal Thakre did not approve of some of the sales. This was because of absence of transparency. Some concerns had utilised the '*Adivasi*' lands, which by law could not be transferred. Even such units were sold out at throwaway prices. A lot of talk was heard to utilise the sale proceeds for development of education and health care. No such corpus is seen to have been formed.

When such Government concerns, which employed people from Reserved Categories, were sold out, the question of reservation in Private Industries became more acute and urgent.

But it must be clearly understood that privatisation and so-called 'disinvestment' is not limited to job reservations alone. It is a conspiracy to keep the Bahujans away from avenues of powers, property and prestige generally.

Who robbed the seats of OBCs?

They were telling the OBCs that their share of jobs was being taken away by the SC and STs, thus creating rift among the OBCs and SC/STs. With the increase in understanding and awakening following the 'Mandal Agitation', the OBCs-Bahujans got awakened and understood that it was not the SC/STs who usurped their share of jobs. They now understand that the SC/ST quota is still not fulfilled, so it is the 15 per cent higher castes that have monopolised the 80 per cent jobs. The participation of OBCs in agitations for Reservation got a boost, which is a must.

How are they Private Industries?

It is now well settled principle that the under-privileged castes are entitled to reservations in the state owned offices, factories and establishments–that is government and semi-government enterprises. It remains to be seen how the so-called 'private sector' is immune to the same rules.

Let us remember when we say 'private' sector we mean the corporate sector, and **not** a shop owner in the shop round the corner, not private businessmen, not private partnership firms, or not even so-called 'Private Limited' companies. We are talking **only** of public limited companies. What are 'limited' are their liabilities, not their exploitation. The company is not 'private' in any sense of the word. It is public by name, by definition, by concept, by convention and even by law. It is not even a group of persons and cannot use M/s behind its name. Even legally it is not private, it is a Public Limited Company. I just fail to understand why it should ever be called a 'Private Sector'.

Fistfuls of people cull a small amount from each of them and label themselves as 'promoters'. On the basis of this they collect huge amounts as share capital from the Public. On the basis of this they collect huge amounts of loans from the Public financial institutions, including Government Institutions. The present ambit of Law only includes such companies, which have taken advantage of Government resources. What is 'private' about all this money? It is all Public money they are using. Thus their capital and all resources are public and they thrive as parasites on Public funds.

They get the public lands from the Government, many times acquiring from the poor peasants and even Adivasis – against law. They get public water, and even do not build their own approach roads and culverts but want the public agencies to foot the bill for the roads meant entirely for their exclusive use.

Mostly they depend for electricity on already impoverished State Electricity Boards. There is no reason why they should not generate their own captive power when they invest so much on other machinery. Just putting a small power plant for their own use would not be a great burden for them. But they wish to deprive the people of whatever little power becomes available to them. If you see the list of those involved in theft of power from State Electricity Boards, periodically published, the big fish are these companies and not individuals. Let us remember, they are not running the industries for the sake of nation, they are doing it for their own benefit at the public expense.

They never pay attention to local environmental laws and cause so much pollution that after a few years the judiciary has to intervene. A slight attention by local authorities in the starting phases and their intervention from the very beginning would have prevented many hazards.

They enjoy the tax holidays for a number of years from all kinds of taxes. And when the time comes, after enjoying the free moratorium period, for paying taxes, they close the unit, make it 'sick' and start a new unit where the pastures are greener. **The industries get sick, but the industrialists never get sick**. They, their relatives, their friends and their caste men continue reaping the benefits in salaries, commissions, allowances, advances, stay in guest houses, perks, and other emoluments. Sometimes, it is so obvious that the unit was opened just to get government facilities and dupe the financial institutions. Some years back thousands of such companies just 'vanished' after collecting huge amounts from public.

They want to Shift, so why not?

Times of India reported on 11th June 2004 that many companies might shift their factories out of Maharashtra if the Government implemented 52 per cent reservation for SC, ST, OBCs. It was no surprise, as the business community has always been reactionary and casteist and against the common man. They say it would 'handicap the domestic firms' and 'cripple the private sector'. But they never elaborate to say how.

Merit my foot, said VTR

These meritorious competent industrial people should explain why the 'Club of hundred' asked for protection. They may also clarify why the foreign law firms, foreign newspapers and also foreign Insurance companies were not allowed? Before nationalisation of Banks, the officers were mostly Brahmins as the Marathas were included in Open category and hence were less in numbers. It is mentioned that their caliber was definitely low in comparison to Dalit candidates and they were much less competent than SC/STs. As a matter of fact, **a backward student getting same marks should be treated as having more merit** because he secured these marks against great odds.

Indian industry remained not only conservative but casteist, as rightly observed by Kancha Ilaiah, who has asked in 2004, why is it that Dalits, Tribals and OBCs could not, on their own, make it to executive positions in Indian industry in any significant number, even after 56 years of Independence. Actually, he should have said after 156 years (2004-1848) since Mahatma Phule opened the gates of education to all. Since independence, the Brahminical governments always wished that the educational facilities be restricted to only the upper castes, and mention of so-called 'Independence' for Dalit Bahujan cause is irrelevant.

They say if reservations are introduced, competitiveness will suffer, as if they are very efficient and competitive now. This is a great insult to Dalit Bahujans, to question their merit, which has been amply proved for generations. It is proved in battlefields, in factories, in Railways, in Banks and everywhere, wherever they are given opportunities. The workers in factories are doing good jobs. They are mostly SC/ST/OBCs. But these are not elevated to lower, middle or upper top management cadres. There only the upper castes are employed. As a matter of strategy, it should be made mandatory for the List of Employees published along with 'Annual Report' to contain the **category** also.

To such people who want to question our merit, one may politely ask, what is their own merit. A 'Club of hundred' had asked for protective measures from foreign companies. Even now in business parlance, the merit and efficiency means how skilful you are in avoiding taxes, finding loop holes in laws, bribing the law enforcing machinery, 'managing' the banks, financial institutions and government officers and finding ways of exploiting the labour. It is a open secret that every company worth the name has a team of 'persuaders' with all resources, legal and not so legal, at their disposal, in the capitals of the provinces and capital of country for only getting their jobs done from the Government and Semi-Government offices, by hook or crook.

Change the Company Law

The real changes are needed to be made in Company Law to stop exploitation. The experts among us should talk openly and let the 'Planning Commission' hear our arguments. Company Law has not seen many changes since the days of C.D. Deshmukh. Even the family law of *Mitakshara* needs to be replaced by *Dayabhag* as Dr. Ambedkar wanted but could not get through the Hindu Code.

Who Abolished Gift Tax and Estate Duty, and Why?

They are fighting for the 'credit' of abolishing the Gift Tax. Was it Chidambaram or Yashvant Sinha? Whoever it was, they did a great disservice to the nation. More disservice was the abolition of Estate Duty. That one Tax had the potential of bringing in some sort of equality, if properly implemented and rates kept high. The reduction of Corporate tax was also a move not in the best interests of the common man.

Training is Just Eyewash

Some talk is going on about First providing educational facilities and Then giving jobs to these SC/ST/OBCs. This is just eyewash. If there were a will, there would be a way. Why education, training and job cannot go hand in hand? Ramvilas Paswan has reportedly asked for 33 per cent allocation for the SC/ST/(OBC) training for industry from the 'profits' (he said 'Capital' on TV but perhaps meant profit. The net profit – after tax and depreciation – is usually very meager compared to turn over) It seems CII has approved of the idea. I understand the Birlas allocated five per cent of their profit for the Brahmin temples. So why not for Training? But Education, Training, Apprenticeship and Jobs all can go on simultaneously.

NPA – Non Performing Assets

A few years back, *Indian Express* had run a series of articles showing how the industrialists have duped the country by Non Performing Assets of Banks, an euphemistic term for bad debts, to the tune of 115,000 crores of rupees. The figure now seems to have gone to 150,000 crores. When Global Trust Bank got into trouble, some how the government managed to bail it out. But the culprit, same old notorious businessman was not seen to be punished. In any case, these people cannot be sentenced to death. It is only the farmers who owe a few lakh of rupees who commit suicide. The industrialists, brokers and financial criminals, who borrow thousands of crores from banks, do not ever die, only the farmers do. Let us remember the NPA funds are Public property of poor citizens, embezzled by Private Industrialists.

Their Religion

The 'business class' of India is mostly restricted to a group of a few castes, and all industries are monopolised by less than about 200 families. The reactionary and casteist forces among the generally **endogamous** business community do not want to employ meritorious and competent people from the 85 per cent of the community comprising of the SC/ST/OBC and RM. They either want their own caste men or people from 15 per cent of population. They think the merit lies alone in their caste.

But these business community people traditionally called the '*Vaishyas*' and assigned the 3rd grade in the Brahminic order of society and listed among the '*paap-yoni*' by the *Bhagwat Gita*, need not be blamed. They behave like this not because they are cruel or inhuman or enemies of Bahujans. It is because they are pious and religious people and believe in their religion and their religion teaches them to behave with caste discrimination. They are very religious people and in refusing the status of equality to the Bahujans they are following the tenets taught to them by their masters, the Brahmins.

Many feed sugar to the ants, open the '*paan-poyees*' (water kiosks), build temples for the benefit of Brahmins, feed and shelter them and spend on their comforts. Some even reportedly allow the deities in temples as their regular partners in profit. Some run TV channels glorifying Brahmins and spreading 'blind faiths' as all these are supposed to be virtuous acts as per the preaching of their religion.

This is the Land of Reservations

Those who oppose the reservations on 'principle' do not seem to understand that there has always been reservations in India on the caste / *varna* basis. Even now the religious books, the so-called '*dharma-grantha*-s' are full of such laws reserving different jobs to different castes. No *Shankaracharya*-s or '*mathadhipati*-s' or other responsible persons have as yet declared these books unauthentic or out of date. On the contrary, many dignitaries have declared that they wish to rule the country on the basis of these books. These things are well known to the Indian masses and need not be repeated here.

Will they Shift Industries to Other States?

But the main question remains, if it comes to that, where would they take their industries? Is there any state or Union Territory free of SC, ST or OBCs? It is not properly realised that the Maharashtra Government, if they want to implement the law, it is not an act of charity or benevolence or a sudden found love for Bahujans. It is because of the pressure of Bahujan awakening. And suppose after shifting their factories to new places, how are they going to ensure that in their respective new locations, the respective government would not bring the same or similar laws, sooner or later? This is just an attempt to play one state against the other and should not allowed to be successful, if Government is really serious about the move. As far as Bahujans of Maharashtra are concerned, it makes no difference, if the other state gets benefits of a shifted factory. That state also is a part of India, and has got full right to get such benefits. In any case, if the new site is found lucrative, and if you do not go there, your competitor will go in this open market economy.

Governments have come down

Industry does have the ability to bring in power, the government that suits it. But this is true only to a certain extent. If the masses are awakened, not only that the new government coming in power could be unpleasant to the Industry, but also as a consumer the masses could play a great role in uplifting the selected industries from the country. If the masses, who are also the consumers, are enlightened enough to change the well-entrenched governments, as we saw happening before, they could as well ruin a particular firm or a concern if they set their mind to it. It is time that the industry should realise this and join in the efforts of the Government in a positive spirit. As Kancha Ilaiah has rightly observed the Indian industrialists have always been leading caste-feudal lives of pomp and luxury and that is good neither for themselves nor for the nation. Sooner they realise this better for all concerned.

The verdict of 14th Lok Sabha, did not teach them any lesson. The 15th Lok Sabha seems to have bent before them. The 16th Lok Sabha is on the way of seeing Foreign Direct Investment (FDI) in 'multi-brand' retail trade, and the business community seems to be happy to welcome the foreign capital in selling *bhindi*, *aaloo* and *tamatar*.

If the exorbitant reliance on the 'foreign' capital investment does not bother the Industrialists that the control is likely to pass, slowly, gradually but definitely, to the aliens, then let us be clear that Bahujan employee will definitely prefer a really foreign employer to a caste ridden Indian one.

American Example

Many people are appealing to the conscience of these Industrialists by quoting the example of American Industry. I doubt whether America could be a Role Model for India, but Japan could. So somebody could also remind them how Japanese *Samurai-s* surrendered their powers in the national interests, which led to overall growth of the Japanese nation. Such rhetoric makes absolutely no sense to the caste conscious Indian businessmen. They only know two things. One is their caste and other is money. They would be willing to implement the reservations only if there is more money in that. A spokes-person of Industrialists, in the TV interview, when asked whether they would consider reservation if any 'incentives' are given, promptly said, it could be considered if such a proposal is made.

So there lies the hitch, if the Government wishes to put into practice, they would first consider the incentives. Even then the idea put forward by Dr. Satinath Chaudhari to calculate the index of implementation of Reservations in Private industries, is a proper strategy for all.

Get Ready for a Fight

The strategy has got to be multi pronged. It should comprise of (1) Negotiation (2) Boycott (3) Pressure on Governments (4) Incentives to Industries and (5) OBC participation. It is rather difficult to say what course the agitation takes. There are already hostile reactions from all the conceivable Brahminical quarters. But if all Dalit Bahujan forces transgressing their party loyalties support, it is bound to succeed. After all, this is nothing but a second Mandal Agitation.

Reservations in Higher Education-Kancha

[http://www.dnaindia.com/india/report_institutes-like-iits-and-iims-should-be-closed-down_1023204] (Accessed Dec. 1, 2012)

Article by Daipayan Halder, titled 'Institutes like IITs and IIMs should be closed down', Published: Sunday, April 9, 2006 in DNA discusses the desperate words uttered by OBC Professor Kancha Ilaiah at his disillusion finding that these institutions are getting blocked for backward students. The Gist:

News appeared of payments up to a crore per year for passing out students from IITs and IIMs. Same time news appeared of a proposal to reserve 27 per cent seats there for OBC students is under active consideration of the Government. There has been an instant uproar in the corporate sector and the student community.

Daipayan Halder reports an interview of author of '*Why I am not a Hindu?*' and one of the country's foremost OBC intellectuals, Kancha Ilaiah, wrongly described as 'Dalit'

The learned Professor, reportedly said:

"The opposition to the proposal only exposes the casteist and racist mindset of those who are opposing it. Even the Election Commission is not free from the malaise. Today or tomorrow, the government had to introduce reservation because that is what the Constitution says."

On the question of 'merit', Dr. Kancha observed:

"We should close down the IITs and the IIMs as they pander to the upper-caste economy of the country. Those who pass out from these institutes use their technical and managerial skills to earn dollars abroad. Are they using their skill sets to the benefit of the agro-based economy of the country? Tell me, with rising incomes of our B-school graduates are farmer suicide rates coming down? So what is the use of such education if it cannot be put to any use within the country or for the uplift of the majority of the population who live in villages?"

On the question that quota is often perceived as an unfair advantage over upper caste students, Prof. Kancha said:

"In the book, The Shape of the River, William (G) Bowen and Derek (Curtis) Bok argue for more racial diversity in the US' student population. Today, because of affirmative action in the US, the entry of coloured people in the education, employment and political systems are being increasingly ensured and has benefited their society. There is no reverse discrimination there. In India, on the other hand, there is no democratic space for the SC, ST and OBCs. This move was long overdue."

On the question of other form of affirmative action instead of caste-based, Prof. said:

"Reservation is absolutely essential. But there should also be other forms of affirmative action. Successive governments have failed to implement the constitutional promise of introducing free and compulsory education after independence. There should be mass English language primary schools for Dalits. There should also be reservation in the private sector. We will soon take to the streets to ensure that."

On suggestion that OBC students cannot cope up with the pressure of the course and drop out, Prof. said:

"This is incorrect. When you say backward caste students are not good enough, you display a casteist bias. When I was the head of the political science department of Osmania University, a Dalit student had secured the highest marks."

"Backward caste students are generally discriminated against in these premier institutes. Instead of providing them a leg-up, they are made to feel unwanted. Given a favourable condition and a fair chance, they can do as well as the others."

Other Writings

PUCL Bulletin August 2005

Mahi Pal Singh

CMP of UPA (1) on May 27, 2004. promised SCs and STs, that all reservation quotas, including those relating to promotions, will be fulfilled in a time-bound manner.

It was reported that during the previous government of the NDA, the public sector had lost as many as 45 lakh jobs, as the government recruitment was frozen both at the Centre and in States.

Author laments about indiscriminate use of natural resources like land, forests, water and air by Industries 'causing great exploitation of masses'. He blames them for accumulation of wealth 'through dubious means, even verging on criminality'.

The author laments that these capitalists spend no money on employment of BCs, but have extravagant lifestyle and vulgar, or 'should I say criminal' display of wealth, and quotes some examples including that of Subroto Roy spending 140 crores for weddings.

Author appeals to Govt. to enforce by law Reservations in 'Private' Industries, and failing that advises the SC/ST/OBCs, to throw out such governments coming to power on their strength and working for a few hundred capitalists and industrialists.

PM Appeals for Reservation in Private Industry

[http://news.oneindia.in/2006/04/18/pm-urges-industry-to-give-employment-to-weaker-sections-1145354891.html] Accessed 5:22 AM 1/26/2012

Prime Minister Manmohan Singh on April 18, 2006, addressing the annual conference of the CII at New Delhi urged industry to voluntarily enhance educational and employment opportunities for weaker sections, to make 'it more broad-based and representative of our nation, at large' by 'seriously investing in their skill enhancement and promoting their employment in an affirmative manner', and hoped to build 'the inclusive society'.

Reservations in Private Industries by Mayavati

Early in August 2007, it was a great news to know that Bahen Mayavati, who has been a strong votary of reservations in the private sector, has declared the reservation of 30 per cent in the industries in the private sector in Uttar Pradesh. The private entrepreneurs seeking special concessions for setting up new industrial or business units in the state would have to reserve 30 per cent positions divided equally between SCs, OBCs including those belonging to the minority community and the economically weak among upper castes. It was also declared:

> "The new policy would not only apply to industrial units but also to trading houses, business ventures, divested units as well as educational institutions that have sought concessions like subsidised land, tax holidays or any other grant or special rebate either directly from the state or from any agency of the state."

Reservation in Private Industry Kamal Nath

[http://ibnlive.in.com/news/devils-advocate-kamal-nath/10443-4.html] (Accessed on Jan. 12, 2012) Karan Thapar, under the title, '*Devil's Advocate: Kamal Nath*' interviewed the Industries Minister. The Gist:

Interview of Kamal Nath was more important. While trying to evade question 'Reservation or Affirmative action', he said 'It is a commitment to affirmative action, which does not preclude reservation'.

Kamal Nath was displeased of dragging name of Nehru, who 'disliked all kinds of Reservations', but admitted inclusive growth has not occurred and hence reservations are necessary.

He confirmed along with SC/STs, 'it did include OBCs'.

To the question, 'Is it voluntary or legislative?', the Minister replied:

'First we want to try the voluntary process. If it does not work then the government will have to look at it. We will then have to look at other options.'

On question of Sunil Mittal appealing to government to give industry two years to prove itself before legislative measures, Kamal Nath promised to consider formal positive proposals from industry.

Kamal Nath said it could be possible to give incentives – in the form of tax concessions, excise holidays, land subsidies etc. – to industry, if they go to ST/SC and OBC districts and invest and create employment opportunities in adequate numbers.

Six years passed; UPA (1) has gone; UPA (2) has finished three years; nothing materialised till today.

Mere Appeal Won't do, Enact Law: Left Parties

[http://news.oneindia.in/2006/04/19/mere-appeal-wont-do-enact-law-left-to-pm-1145441966.html] (Accessed Thursday, January 26, 2012)

A news item of Wednesday, April 19, 2006, from New Delhi, says that Left parties, i.e. the CPI (M), CPI and Forward Bloc also supported the Prime Minister in job reservations for the underprivileged in the private sector. But they demanded legislation to this effect, saying "Mere appeal to the industry will not serve the purpose as they continue to harp on merit and efficiency."

But CII former president Rahul Bajaj along with other captains of industry threatened to go to court if the government legislated it.

CPI General Secretary A B Bardhan said the Cabinet should discuss the crucial issue without further delay and get the new law passed in the Parliament.

'We Want Affirmative Action in the Private Sector': Moily

[http://www.outlookindia.com/article.aspx?240678] (Acessed Jan. 7, 2012)

On May 28, 2009, Verrappa Moily was inducted into new government. Chandrani Banerjee reports On Jun 15, 2009 that, he was asked about plans of Reservation in the corporate sector. His reply was:

> "There is a concept called corporate social responsibility. Corporates must identify the importance of equal opportunity. They should recognise talent by rewarding it and also encourage others to come forward. They must talk of oneness. Good business means equal opportunity to everyone. Keeping a class away is not good even for the private sector."

Well, nothing seems to have come out as yet.

He was also asked: What about the higher levels of judiciary? Is there need to introduce reservation there as well? His reply was:

> "We have not applied our mind to this issue. Reservation in the judiciary is initiated at the lower level. As of now, there is no such plan for the higher judiciary."

• • •

13

Dalits and Saints

Osho on Gorakhnath

[http://www.messagefrommasters.com/Osho/oshomystics/Osho-on-GorakhNath.html] (Accessed April 27, 2012)

Osho on Gorakhnath

Osho - The great Hindi poet, Sumitranandan Pant, once asked me: who in the vast sky of Indian religion are the twelve people, who in my opinion are the brightest shining stars? I gave him this list:

List of Twelve

Krishna, Patanjali, Buddha, Mahavira, Nagarjuna, Shankara, Gorakh, Kabir, Nanak, Meera, Ramakrishna and Krishnamurti.

Sumitranandan Pant closed his eyes and slipped into thought. Making a list is not easy, because the Indian sky is filled with so many stars! Whom to cut, whom to include?

He opened his eyes and said to me: "You have excluded Rama!"

I said: "If I am allowed to choose only twelve; many names will have to be cut. So I have chosen those twelve people who have made some original contribution. Rama has made no original contribution, Krishna has. This is why Hindus call Krishna a complete incarnation, but not Rama."

List of Seven

He asked me further, "Next, could you give me seven names?" Now the question had become more difficult!

I gave him seven names:

Krishna, Patanjali, Buddha, Mahavira, Shankara, Gorakh and Kabir.

He said: "The five you have deleted, on what basis did you drop them?"

I said: "Nagarjuna is contained in Buddha. That which was a seed in Buddha, manifested itself in Nagarjuna. Nagarjuna can be dropped when it is a question of saving, trees can be dropped, but not seeds, because seeds will again become trees. They will become new trees. When Buddha is born, hundreds of Nagarjunas will soon be born, but no Nagarjuna can give birth to Buddha. Buddha is the headwater of the Ganges. Nagarjuna is just a place of pilgrimage that appears along the course of the Ganges. Lovely, but if cutting is needed, then the place of pilgrimage can be dropped, not the source of the Ganges.

"Similarly Krishnamurti is included in Buddha. Krishnamurti is Buddha's newest edition – the freshest; in today's language. But the difference is only of language. Krishnamurti is just an elaboration of Buddha's final sutra '*appa dipo bhau*' – be a light unto yourself.' A commentary on one *sutra*–deep, profound, tremendously vast, immensely significant! But he's just a commentary on 'Be a light unto yourself: *appa dipo bhau*'. These were Buddha's last words on this earth. Before leaving his body, he had given this essential sutra... As if the treasure of his whole life, his whole life's experience was concentrated into this small sutra.

"Ramakrishna can easily be included in Krishna.

"Meera and Nanak can be dissolved into Kabir. They are like branches of Kabir. As if half of what came together in Kabir has manifested in Nanak and half has manifested in Meera. In Nanak the male aspect of Kabir has manifested, so it is not surprising that Sikhism became a warrior's religion, a religion of the soldier. In Meera, Kabir's feminine aspect is manifested – hence his entire sweetness, his entire fragrance, his entire music resound from the bells on Meera's ankles. The woman in Kabir has sung on the one string of Meera's *ektara*. In Nanak the man in Kabir has spoken. Both are contained in Kabir.

"This is how" I said, "I made the list seven."

List of five

Now his curiosity had become tremendously aroused. He said, "And if you had to make a list of five?"

I said, "Then it will be even more difficult for me."

I gave him this list:

Krishna, Patanjali, Buddha, Mahavira, Gorakh.

... because Kabir is merged into Gorakh. Gorakh is the root. Gorakh cannot be left out. And Shankara easily merges into Krishna. He is the exposition of one part of Krishna, the philosophic interpretation of just one aspect of Krishna.

List of four

Then he said: "One more time... if only four are to be kept?"

Then I listed for him:

Krishna, Patanjali, Buddha, Gorakh...

...because Mahavira is not very different from Buddha. Just a tiny difference and that too only a difference in expression. Mahavira's greatness can be encompassed in the greatness of Buddha.

He started, saying: "Just one more time... please choose three persons."

I said: "Now it is impossible. I can not drop any of these four." Then I told him: "**These four individualities are like the four directions**. These four dimensions are like the four dimensions of time and space. These four arms are like the four armed conception of god. In fact there is only one, but that one has four arms. To leave out any one would be like cutting off an arm. I cannot do that. Until now I've been going along with you. I was continuing to decrease the number, because until now the one's that had to be put aside were clothes. Now limbs would have to be broken, I cannot fracture limbs. Please don't insist on such violence."

Gorakh cannot be Dropped

He said: "Some questions have arisen, one is: you can drop Mahavira, but not Gorakh?"

Gorakh cannot be dropped, because **Gorakh became a new beginning for this country**. No new beginning came from Mahavira. He was a rare man; but for centuries the first twenty-three Jaina *tirthankaras* had already said what he was saying. He was just their repetition. He is not the beginning of a new journey. He is not the first link in a new chain, rather the last link.

Gorakh is the first link of a chain. Through him a new type of religion was born. Without Gorakh, there could be no Kabir, no Nanak, no Dadu, no Vajid, no Farid, no Meera – without Gorakh none of these are possible. The basic root of all of them is in Gorakh. Since then the temple has been built high. On this temple many golden spires have been raised... but the foundation stone is the foundation stone. Though the golden spires may be seen from afar, they cannot be more important than the foundation stone. And the foundation is not visible to anyone, but on this very stone stands the whole structure, all the walls, all the high peaks... The peaks are worshipped. People simply forget about the foundation. Gorakh has been similarly forgotten.

But India's whole *'sant'* tradition – those innumerable devotees of love – is indebted to Gorakh. Just as without Patanjali there would be no possibility of yoga in India; as without Buddha the foundation stone of meditation would be uprooted; just as without Krishna the path of love would not find expression – similarly, without Gorakh the search that began for methods and techniques of *sadhana*, of spiritual practice to attain the ultimate truth would not have been possible.

Gorakh made many discoveries within man for the inner search, more perhaps than anyone else has made. He has given so many methods, that in terms of methods Gorakh is the greatest inventor. He pushed open so many doors for going into man's inner being, he created so many doors that people got caught in them. Hence we have one word that remains with us – people have forgotten Gorakh – but not the word *Gorakhdhandha*, this word for maze remains. He gave so many methods, that people were confused, which method is right, which is wrong, which to do, which to drop? He gave so many methods that people became absolutely dumbfounded, hence the word Gorakhdhandha, maze. Now if somebody is entangled in something, we say, "What Gorakhdhandha have you gotten into?"

Gorakh had a rare individuality, similar to Einstein. Einstein gave such penetrating methods for investigating the truth of the universe, as no one before him had given. Yes, now they can be further developed, now a finer edge can be put on them. But Einstein has done the primary work. Those who follow will be secondary. Now they cannot be first. The road was first broken by Einstein. Many will come who improve this road: ones who build it up, ones who place the milestones, ones who beautify it and make it comfortable. Many people will come, but no one can take Einstein's place. In the inner world the same situation exists with Gorakh.

But why have people forgotten Gorakh? The milestones are remembered, the path breaker is forgotten. The ones who have decorated the path are remembered, the one who has first broken the path is forgotten. Forgotten because, those who come after have the leisure to dress it up. One who comes first, will be unpolished, unfinished. Gorakh is like a diamond just out of the mine. If Gorakh and Kabir are sitting together, you will be impressed by Kabir, not by Gorakh. Because Gorakh is a freshly mined diamond, but on Kabir the jewellers have worked hard, on him the chisel has worked hard, much polishing has been done.

Do you know that when the Kohinoor diamond was first discovered, the man who found it didn't know it was a Kohinoor? He had given it to his children to play with, thinking it was a pretty coloured stone. He was a poor man. He had found the Kohinoor in the waters of a small river flowing through his fields. For months it remained in his house, the children kept on playing with it, they kept throwing it from one corner to another, it remained in the courtyard... You wouldn't have been able to recognise the Kohinoor. The Kohinoor's original weight was three times as much as it is today. The edges were set, it was polished, cut, its facets were brought out. Today only one third of the weight remains, but the value has become millions of times greater. The weight became less, the value increased, because it kept being refined — more and more polished.

If Kabir and Gorakh are sitting together, perhaps you won't even recognise Gorakh; because Gorakh is a diamond just removed from the Golconda mines. On Kabir much cutting has been done, the jewellers have worked hard... you will be able to recognise Kabir. Hence Gorakh has been forgotten. The foundation stones are forgotten.

You will be very surprised when you hear Gorakh's words. A little finishing is needed; they are uncut. This sharpening of the edges is what I am doing here. You will be amazed as you begin to know him a little. Gorakh has said the most essential. He has said the most valuable.

List Cannot be below Four

So I told Sumitranandan Pant, "I cannot drop Gorakh – therefore the number cannot go below four." Naturally he must have thought that I will leave out Gorakh and keep Mahavira. Mahavira is a Kohinoor, he's no rough diamond just out of the mines. There is the whole tradition of twenty three tirthankaras, thousands of years, in which the finishing has been done, has been sharpened—has become shiny. Do you see? Mahavira is the twenty fourth tirthankara. People have forgotten the names of the remaining twenty three! Those who are not Jainas do not even know those twenty three names. And those who are Jainas cannot count out the twenty three in correct order, they will forget or omit someone. Mahavira is the last, the pinnacle of the temple. The spire of the temple is remembered. We still discuss him. Who discusses the foundation stone?

Today we begin the discussion of one such foundation stone. The whole palace of India's *sant* literature stands on him. All is based on this one individual. He has said all that slowly slowly becomes very beautiful, a many coloured splendor. Upon this base people will do *sadhana* and meditate for centuries. Who knows how many enlightened beings shall be born through him! [*Source* - Osho Book "Death is Divine"]

Our Opinion

Above is the remarkable analysis of Indian Religious scene from beginning. There is a remarkable absence of Vedic dignitary, like Yajnavalkya. May be Osho includes that religion in Krishna.

We concur with this list of last names – Krishna, Buddha, Patanjali and Gorakh, but from slightly different aspect. Ills of old Indian religion were corrected by the Buddha. Patanjali caused counter-revolution by performing *Ashwamedha yajnyas*, hardening *Chaturvarnya*; *Gita* and *Manusmriti* are creations of his age. Brahmanical hegemony flourished till Gorakh came, who corrected the scene and his religion prevails today. We have discussed this subject in '*Materialism in Ancient India*': 2012.

Nathas and Siddhas were Precursors of Bhakti

Confusion and Ignorance

There is tremendous ignorance and confusion in society about Siddhas and Nathas, vilified by modern scholars like Vivekananda and P.V. Kane, ostensibly because of their '*Sandhya-Bhasha*', '*pancha-makkara*' and '*mudra*' etc. We discussed the subject in detail elsewhere. [*Devadasis Ancient and Modern*': 2007, and '*Materialism in Ancient India*': 2012] Here we like to stress only one point that they were Buddhist and are precursors of Bhakti, the modern form of Brahmanism.

Real Reason of Vilification

We feel that the real cause of irritation to these Brahminist scholars is not 'five-Ms' but the attitude of Siddhas against the *Chaturvarnya*, against caste system, and against slavery of women.

L.M. Joshi has ably refuted all charges and observed that the so called 'hideous practices' and 'obscene books' that were associated with 'degraded Buddhism' were also produced by Hinduism or Neo-Brahmanism during its best and golden days (500-1500 A.D.). [Joshi L.M.: 1977: 120]

Time of Siddhas and Nathas

The approximate time limits, considered more feasible for these Siddhas are from c.800 to 875 CE for Sarahappa – the Adi Siddha, Shabarappa, Lueepa etc.; c.875 - 925 CE for Matsyendra, Meenapa etc.; c. 925 - 1000 CE for Gorakh, Jalandhari, Kannahpa etc. and c.1000 - 1100 CE for Tilopa, Naaropa, Maitripa etc. [Bharati: 1968: 45]

Revolt of Siddhas and helplessness of Bhaktas

It is an accepted fact that the origin of Bhakti has roots in *Tantras*. The roots are Tantras and the pinnacle we see is the Bhakti, avers Dr. Bharati. But the '*Nirgun*' poetry of the '*Sant-s*' (Saint poets), who denied the incarnations, is entirely different from that of the '*Bhakta-s*', who propagated '*saguna*' Bhakti with the theory of '*avatars*'.

The revolt of eighth century by the Buddhist Siddhas against the Caste system and puritanical practices, which manifested in form of Tantras, was due to the awakening of lower castes. It ended in Brahminic arrogance leading to injustice over these same lower castes in spite of the Saints. Thus, the conditions of saints became pitiable; Dr. Bharati explains why. He says it was because of four reasons:

First, the Saints were representatives of defeated and sufferers of social injustice,

Second, they got realisation of the hollowness of the revolt by Tantric practices,

Third, they could not welcome the religious dogmatism of the Muslim invaders, and

Fourth, though attracted towards the practices of Vaishnavism, could not accept the logic of the theory of the '*Avatars*'. [Bharati: 1968: 478]

Nathas and Siddhas

The Siddhas were mostly lower caste nonconformist Shramanic ascetics belonged to the anti-Brahminic heterodox traditions like Buddhists, Jains, Sahajiya Buddhists, Tantrika and Natha sects and preached in *Bhasha* and not in Sanskrit, and were very popular in Eastern India. Anyone irrespective of caste or gender and even untouchable women did become their *gurus* and were well accepted. Theirs was the open revolt against Brahminic injunctions of food and drinks. Brahmins and feudal lords hated and persecuted them, so they had to use secretive manners and language. **Under charismatic leadership of Gorakh Nath,** they adopted a high moral tone and escaped Brahminical atrocities to some extent, and succeeded in establishing their centres in East, West and even South. [Mani: 2005: 141]

Nathas were Buddhist

Though Brahminic scholarship labels the Nathas as '*Shaiva Yogis*', to project them in Brahminic fold, they were actually Buddhist wanderers and were following, preaching and propagating Buddhist tenets. [Bharati: 1968: 19]

Siddhas were Favouring Social Equality

Siddhas reformed, according to

L.M. Joshi explains how Siddhas and Nathas reformed a number of ugly features of Indian society, and concludes:

> "...Siddhas and their pupils seem to have helped in lessening caste-distinctions, bonds of Varna in matters of marriage, food, education, and religious avocation." [Joshi L.M.: 1977: 295]

Philosophy and Practice of Siddhas

With the advent of Esoteric Buddhism, some fundamental changes took place in Buddhist society. But the central philosophical idea remains the same old idealistic absolute called differently as 'Vajra', 'Shunya', 'Bodhichitta', 'Vajrasattva', and 'Prajnopaaya'. But its nature is now described as 'mahasukha' or great delight, which was to be achieved here and now in this very life by practicing both 'Prajnyaa' and 'Upaaya' with good intentions. [Joshi L.M.: 1977: 119]

Ambedkar on Role of Saints

After Mahad in January 1928 when the Dalits of Maharashtra were looking for 'spiritual and historic inspiration', they wished to build a temple for Chokhamela, a medieval Dalit saint. After Ambedkar's advice, meeting decided NOT to erect the temple, as untiring efforts to remove untouchability was more important.

Keer describes the views of Ambedkar about saints:

> "It was Ambedkar's view that the Saint poets of Maharashtra (1300 -1600) belonging to Bhagwat dharma did not preach directly against the caste system which stood for the domination of one caste over others, for social inequality and social injustice. The efforts of these Saint poets were directed to establishing equality, not between a Brahmin as an individual and a Shudra as an individual, but between a Brahmin and a Shudra devotee of God. In this struggle the saints succeeded, and the Brahmins had to accept the superiority of the devotee irrespective of caste."
>
> "Yet from the view of point of annihilation of caste', Ambedkar stated, "the struggle for the saints did not have any effect on society. The value of man is axiomatic, self-evident; it does not come to him as the result of gilding of *bhakti*. The saints did not struggle to establish this point. On the contrary, their struggle had a very unhealthy effect on the depressed classes. It provided the Brahmins with an excuse to silence them by telling that they would be respected, if they also attained the status of Chokhamela." As the followers of different cults of *bhakti* were themselves filled with caste prejudices, Ambedkar proceeded, they not only turned a blind eye to their message of equality, justice and humanitarianism, but also described their incredible miracles with utmost exaggeration."

"As regards, the cult of Ramdas, he said that his followers were notorious for their caste prejudices since its inception, and their founder himself was obsessed with the idea as Brahmin superiority. According to Ramdas, even a fallen Brahmin was superior to men of other castes in heaven, and on earth; nay, a Brahmin was one to whom even the gods made an obeisance." [Keer: 2005: 109 ff.]

Annihilation of Caste and Saints

Those who are today trying to liberate Dalits though teaching of saints must understand their ways are wrong. In a rejoinder to Gandhi's comments on 'Annihilation of Caste', that saints are the people who interpreted shastras, Ambedkar explains the futility of the work of saints.

"With regard to the saints, one must admit that howsoever different and elevating their teachings may have been as compared to those of the merely learned they have been lamentably ineffective. They have been ineffective for two reasons. Firstly, none of the saints ever attacked the Caste System. On the contrary, they were staunch believers in the System of Castes. Most of them lived and died as members of the castes which they respectively belonged. So passionately attached was Jnyandeo to his status as a Brahmin that when the Brahmins of Paithan would not admit him to their fold he moved heaven and earth to get his status as a Brahmin recognised by the Brahmin fraternity. And even the saint Eknath who now figures in the film "*Dharmatma*" as a hero for having shown courage to touch the untouchables and dine with them, did so not because he was opposed to Caste and Untouchability but because he felt that the pollution caused thereby could be washed away by a bath in the sacred waters of the river Ganges. [*antajya cha vital jyasi ganga snane pavitra tyasi-* eknathi bhagwat] The saints have never according to my study carried on a campaign against Caste and Untouchability. They were not concerned with the struggle between men. They were concerned with the relation between man and God. They did not preach that all men were equal. They preached that all men were equal, in the eyes of God a very different and a very innocuous proposition which nobody can find difficult to preach or dangerous to believe in. The second reason why the teachings of the saints proved ineffective was because the masses have been taught that a saint might break Caste but the common man must not. A saint, therefore, never became an example to follow. He always remained a pious man to be honoured. That the masses have remained staunch believers in Caste and Untouchability shows that the pious lives and noble sermons of the saints have had no effect on their life and conduct as against the teachings of the Shastras. Thus, it can be a matter of no consolation that there were saints or that there is a Mahatma who understands the Shastras differently from the learned few or ignorant many. That the masses hold different view of the Shastras is fact which should and must be reckoned with. How is that to be dealt with except by denouncing the authority of the Shastras, which continue to govern their conduct, is a question which the Mahatma has not considered. "But whatever the plan the Mahatma puts forth as an effective means to free the masses from the teachings of the Shastras, he must accept that the pious life led by one good Samaritan may be very elevating to himself but in India, with the attitude the common man has to saints and to Mahatmas—to honour but not to follow—one cannot make much out of it. [W&S 1:87]

• • •

14

Dalits and Sikhism

Dera-s, Caste Conflicts and Recent Violence in Punjab

[http://www.mainstreamweekly.net/article1425.html] (Accessed November 30, 2012)

Surinder Singh, a Research Fellow, Department of Political Science, Punjab University, Chandigarh has written a well researched article in *Mainstream*, Vol. XLVII, No. 26, June 13, 2009, titled '*Dera-s*, Caste Conflicts and Recent Violence in Punjab'. The Gist:

The Shootings in a Ravidass Temple in Vienna

The recent violence in Punjab has taken place as a repercussion of the shootings in a Ravidass temple in Vienna in which the Dera Sachkhand head, Saint Niranjan Dass, was injured and his second-in-command, Saint Ramanand, was killed. This hurt the feelings of the followers of the Dera all over world. The Doaba region in particular was in flames for almost two days before the situation came under control following the appeal by the sants of the Dera.

The Article is divided into Three Parts

His article has three parts: (1) history of emergence of the Deras in Punjab; (2) role of these Dera-s in creating a consciousness among the lower-caste people in the region; and (3) conflicts between the dominant Jat Sikh landed peasantry and the followers of *Dera-s* at different periods of times.

Emergence of Deras

Surinder explains causes of the emergence of a large number of Dera-s due to "the continued social exclusion and pervading inequality in the social and economic order", in spite of rise of Sikhism, is opposed to caste discrimination. Another factor is the concentration of land in the hands of a minority. Deras are increasing in the Doaba, Majha and Malwa regions of Punjab is due to the denial of a respectable place to the Dalits and Backward Caste people in religious places and the Sikh Panth. [Manak, 2007]

Number of Dera-s

In Punjab, the number of Deras are not in hundreds but in thousands. A study conducted by the *Desh Sewak*, a Punjabi newspaper published from Chandigarh, gives figures that there are more than 9000 Sikh as well as non-Sikh Deras in the 12,000 villages of Punjab. [Ram, 2007, 4067; see also Tehna et al., 2007]

There are about 300 major Deras across Punjab and the neighbouring State of Haryana, and these are popular in both States. Out of these a dozen have over one lakh devotees each. [Pubby et al., 2009]

There are some prominent *Dera-s* like Radha Soami (Beas), Sacha Sauda (Sirsa), Nirankaris, Namdharis, Divya Jyoti Jagran Sansthan (Nurmahal), Dera Sant Bhaniarawalla, Dera Sachkhand (Ballan), Dera Sant Phuriwala, Dera Baba Budha Dal, Dera Begowal, Nanaksarwale.

Almost all of them have branches in every district of the State and even outside Punjab in the neighbouring States. Some of them have popularity among the Punjabi Diaspora. Though all these *Dera-s* have following among every caste, however, most of the followers of these *Dera-s* are Dalits and Backward Caste people who are often economically marginal also.

The history of the Deras in Punjab is older than the Sikh Panth. The Deras in Punjab before the Sikh Panth belong to the Muslim Peer and Yog Nath's Dera. With the emergence of the Sikh Panth, some prominent Sikh and non-Sikh Deras came into existence as like Udasi Deras, Dera Baba Ram Thaman, Namdhari, Nanaksar. In the twentieth century most Deras came into existence, which are popular today, as Radha Soami, Sacha Sauda, Nirankari, Dera Sachkhand Ballan and Dera Bhaniarawalla.

Deras and Dalit Consciousness

These Deras have their egalitarian ideology, and no place for caste or religion based discrimination, and present simple but sharp elements of social protest. [Ram, 2008, 1341]

Some *Dera-s* have established their schools and health care centres. They encourage the lower-caste poor children to study and help them financially. Dera Sachkhand Ballan, has played an important role in raising Dalit consciousness.

Ad Dharm Movement of 1920

The Ad Dharm movement of 1920 and Ravidass Deras played a historical role in the formation of Dalit consciousness in Punjab, and has carved a separate religious identity for the lower-caste people. The movement projects Ravidass as their spiritual Guru, a sacred book **Ad Parkash**, their own separate ritual traditions; their salutation as 'Jai Guru Dev' and response as 'Dhan Guru Dev', thus creating a separate religious identity. [Ram, 2004, 335-36] The schools of *Dera-s* are not only providing quality of education in a Dalit friendly environment but also act as an agency for generating Dalit consciousness. [Ram, 2008, 1342]

Education provides them both social consciousness and makes them financially well off. Today the Ad Dharmis and followers of this Dera have been far more educated, more conscious and are also financially better off than other Dalit communities in Punjab especially in the Doaba region.

Causes of Caste Conflicts in Punjab

Surinder Singh, explaining the causes observes:

"The recent violence that has taken place in Punjab has its genesis in the lopsided polity of Punjab and its closed nature of land-property relationship. The Dalits and backward classes in Punjab feel excluded from making the political and economic choices for the State as Jat Sikhs, constituting 20 per cent of the population, own 60 per cent of the land and control the politics and economy of Punjab. The recently awakened and economically empowered marginal classes have been moving out of the villages and even when they live in the villages they are increasingly taking on non-agricultural activities. One also finds separate Gurudwaras and community centres for the Dalits in the villages of Punjab."

Shamlat Land Disputes

He further observes:

"There has also been struggle over the common property resources (*Shamlat* Land) in rural Punjab where land is scarce. The newfound assertion of their identity and demand for political and economic space along with social respectability have often met with the violence by the dominant Jat Sikh peasantry. [Thakural, 2009]

"Significantly the Dalits constitute almost one-third of the population of Punjab which is the highest in the country as a whole."

The Recent Dera Conflict

Surinder explains cause of recent Vienna episode as:

"It is also due to the fundamentalist Sikh organisations' objection to treating the Dera Gurus at par with the ten Sikh Gurus and for keeping the Guru Granth Sahib along with the idols of Sant Ravidass."

Recent Dera conflict is not a new phenomenon, Surinder informs us, as many such conflicts between fundamentalist Sikhs and Dera followers have taken place in Punjab and mentions Sikh-Nirankari conflict (1978), Sikh-Bhaniarawalla follower's conflict (2001), Sikh-Sacha Sauda followers conflict (2007).

Author Sums Up

Surinder acknowledges help of Dr. Ronki Ram and Dr. Ashutosh Kumar and gives detail references, and sums up:

"The emergence of Deras all over Punjab is indicative of the assertion of the Dalits in the State trying to discover and consolidate their distinct identity to attain self-respect and also asking for their autonomous space in the social, economic and political life of the State. The recent conflict is yet another illustration, though an unfortunate one, of the community's anguish over their historic denial in the land of the Sikh Gurus who vehemently opposed caste based discrimination, nay, rejected the caste system outright."

Dalits Assertion in Punjab

[http://www.countercurrents.org/rawat280509.htm] (Accessed 1/11/2012)

An article by Vidya Bhushan Rawat, on Countercurrents.org dated in 28 May, 2009, titled 'Fire at Vienna exposes Ugly realities of caste discrimination in Punjab' describes contradictions in present day Punjab. The Gist:

Why Deras Face Attack?

The attack on Sant Niranjan Dass, head of Dera Guru Ravidas Sachkhand Baḷan and death of Sant Ramanand sparked violent protest by Dalits in Punjab. First point is that the Deras face attack by the fundamentalist Sikh groups because they have provided a glimpse of hope and identity to a massive Dalit population in Punjab. These Deras are also giving the upper caste Sikhs a run for their money and power, Rawat observes.

Punjab as a Casteless Society?

Guru Granth Saheb advocated casteless society, but the leadership that emerged in Punjab is upper caste dominated feudal Sikhs. And they have used the Gurudwaras for their political purposes. The Dalits were just not wanted in these Gurudwars. After the Ravidasis and Majahabis also started creating their own temples. The slogan of 'Guru Ravidas Mahraj ki Jai' reverberating in Gurudwaras is considered a challenge to mainstream Sikhism.

Green Revolution Strengthened Feudal Values

Punjab is supposed to be the state of green revolution. The author stresses that Punjab's green revolution actually strengthened the feudal values. Feudalism is not just enemy of egalitarian values but thoroughly against nature and environment. Today, water level in Punjab is getting depleted and the mustard fields are being replaced for cash crops and shopping malls are showing the 'growth' of Punjab.

Failure of World Conference

Vienna has happened at a time when we were still analysing our poll results, and we were looking forward for a 'progressive' government, free from 'regionalism', and Casteism. Also the review committee meeting of World Conference Against Racism and Xenophobia, had taken place to review Durban conference, wherein, unfortunately, the government of India ensured that nothing happens on this front.

Caste goes to Foreign Lands

But then old habits die hard. Those, whose lives have been based on purity of castes, do not really change even when they go abroad.

Those who believe in superiority of a particular race do not change even staying in countries where they enjoy freedom and civil liberties.

Two most important and visible communities of India abroad are from Gujarat and Punjab. Both these states are supposed to be growing with a growth rate more than our central figures. Both these states are fantastic for 'investors' and are providing 'stable' governments yet they are far behind the national figure of male female ratio. While the Muslims in Gujarat are still far boycotted and Dalits completely on the margins in the absence of a popular Dalit movement there, in Punjab the situation is different.

Jats Hijacked the Social Justice Agenda

Sikhism actually revolted against the caste hierarchies. Guru Granth Saheb, Rawat says, is perhaps the only holy book where you have '*sabad'* and *kirtans* of different Sufi Saints including Kabir, Ravidas, Dadu, Nanak and Jaisi. Yet, the Jats hijacked the social justice agenda of Sikhism. The agenda then turned to Sikh identity ignoring the demands and assertions of the Dalits, mostly the Majhabis and Ravidasis.

Discrimination and Atrocities

Punjab has the highest percentage of Dalit population (27 per cent) and yet despite good economic changes, Dalits are discriminated by the Jats and atrocities committed. For example, case of Baant Singh, a Majahabi Sikh cannot be ignored. His hands and legs were chopped off by the powerful Jats because he objected to molestation of his daughter. Rawat laments that Punjab did not burn then.

The Land Grab by Jat Sikhs

Author quotes a case, wherein he is involved himself, in fight for the Dalit rights in the Uttarakhand state's Tarai where over 150 landless Dalit families are fighting against the land grab by this powerful Jat Sikhs in the Tarai belt, the victims being predominantly the Dalits and tribal, who are still tilling their own land as bonded labour.

The Dirty side of Indian Social System

The massacre in Vienna, as some Austrian papers wrote, is the sign of dirty side of Indian social system. Despite our government and intellectual hiding their misdeeds, caste is a reality in this country and Dalits at the receiving end.

It is not therefore strange that the reports coming from Vienna blame the Ravidasis for 'denigrating' the Guru Granth Saheb.

To justify a murder we make statement. Every fundamentalist create a situation to ensure that his viewpoint look rational.

A dynamic way of life like Sikhism could easily become victim of the caste hierarchies reflect that the Indians as a society become a follower of a person not because of his or her ideals but because of the birth based identity.

Therefore, we end up respecting the person for being one among us and 'preaching' certain gospel and doing miracles in their names.

A revolutionary, therefore, is brahmanised and converted into a money-minting machine for the greedy leaders who make big business in the name of religion. This is true about every one.

Religion the Biggest Threat to World Peace

When a revolutionary like Bhagat Singh, who wrote against religion and caste becomes a symbol of '*Jaat*' 'pride or simply '*Chhora Jaat da*', the Dalits would automatically opt for Udham Singh, a martyr who died for the cause of the country. It creates such divide based on caste, which unfortunately happened in Vienna.

The Power Politics

Sikhism in Punjab is closely associated with power politics particularly as *Akali*-s have used the SGPC for their own purposes, and the Gurudwaras help them to control the sentiments of Sikh community. It is rare, the Author avers, that this SGPC could ever come out against the caste based violence and caste system.

The Honour Killing

The 'shameless killing' by the Indian Diaspora, labeled as 'honour killing' in inter-caste love marriages, practiced predominantly by the Sikhs from Punjab, the author opines, reflects the ugly side of our growth pattern, and observes:

> "Growth in term of economy cannot really make a country great. Punjab's caste discrimination actually reflects its ugly side that despite all this hoopla about *Punjabiat*, there is a darker side often hidden by our media and intellectuals."

The Mixing of Sikhism with Political Agenda

Sikhism was initially meant to demolish the caste system and idol worship. Guru Nanak's message was universal and Gurudwaras played important role in social mobilisation. Also Punjab had less violence against the Dalits than many other states in India, and there was no brahmanical hegemony. But Punjab's problems started with mixing of political agenda with Sikhism, when SGPC became a part to control minds of people.

The Influence of Sufism

The powerful movements like that of Nanak's would have demolished the caste structure in Punjab. But the caste discrimination grew because of feudal values. Punjab's prosperity is because of the harder Dalit labour. The influence of Sufism in Punjab was tremendous. *Majahabi-s* and *Ravidasi-s* started their *Dera-s* and sects when caste discrimination got rampant. And today the number of these *Dera-s* are over 300 in entire state.

Revolutionary Sufi Saint Ravidas

Punjab's Dalits mostly wanted to fight a battle through religiosity. Revolutionary Sufi saint Ravidas wrote:

"Paradhinata paap hai, jaan lehu re meet, ravidas das pradhin se kaun karre hai preet"

It means: please understand that enslavement is sin, Saint Ravidas says, who loves an enslaved person. Now such a person who talks of freedom, says that those who studied Vedas were called *Pandits* (Knowledgeable) and those who make your shoes were called *Chamars*. How can you divide one human race into so many caste and Varnas?

No Help to Dalits to Escape Hindu Varna Fold

Ravidas attacked the brahmanical system and the Dalits in Punjab got liberation in his spiritual values. Many of the *Ravidasi-s* shifted to Europe and America and have actually followed the same pattern as the SGPC and other upper caste Sikhs in Punjab.

Free float of money and lot of leisure only led to empty institutions. Punjab's religious sects are more spiritual in nature and have rarely helped the Dalits to get out of the Hindu *Varna* fold. As a result, the Dalits got agitated on the social discrimination issues.

Ambedkar's Methods

Author always wondered why the poor Dalits, mostly *Chamar-s*, could get political wisdom in Uttar Pradesh yet remain on the margin in Punjab despite better economic status, and comes to the conclusion that in Uttar Pradesh, despite poverty, they embraced Ambedkar's methods of fighting a battle politically.

Whereas, in Punjab, it is still a spiritual battle for getting recognition and the concentration of one sect and one cult and without much social change, with focus more on temples and charity, just like Sikhism. In Punjab, Dalits concentrated more on Gurudwaras and neglected more enlightened political battle.

A Broader Political Front Required

Economic changes have made the Dalits of Punjab powerful enough to fight against the powerful people, but they will have to understand that they will only be helping the *status quoist-s* if they do not raise their issues on a broader political front. They have to understand that just using the spiritual battle will take them nowhere.

Author stresses the point that as long as the Jaat Sikhs will have their leadership from the powerful SGPC, the Deras will continue to provide alternative to Dalits, and believes the incidents in Vienna are not isolated. It is basically to control the Sikh mind.

Dalits Do Not Disrespect Guru Granth Saheb

The upper caste Sikhs seem to be deeply concerned of the growing power of the *Ravidasi-s* and *Majahabi-s*, particularly those living abroad. To control NRI Dalits, false charges are leveled against *Ravidasi-s* that they disrespect the Guru Granth Saheb. These charges are false, according to his personal knowledge, says Mr. Rawat. He avers that the real fear of the upper caste Sikhs is the matching power of Dalits with them.

The Statues of Ravidas

Similarly, the presence of statues of Ravidas in the Gurudwaras is a matter of heartburn for many of the upper caste Sikhs. Punjabi Dalit writer Balbir Madhopuri's autobiography clearly mentions how the Upper Caste Gurudwaras discriminated against the Dalits. As long as this continues, these Deras would always provide strength to Dalits.

The Gap between the Sikhs and the Dalit Sikhs

The author advises the upper caste Sikh leadership to start a process of reconciliation and concludes:

> "Punjab's problem is the increasing gap between the Sikhs and the Dalit Sikhs. The Sikh leadership has failed to realise this issue and became equally brahmanical in nature therefore ignoring the vast interests of the Dalits in Punjab. Punjab's Dalit need sharing in power and respect at every forum. Such threat as emerged from Vienna which tried to eliminate the spiritual leadership of Dalit will only anger them and create a further wage between the two communities which will end in clashes and fragile peace in Punjab, perhaps more dangerous than what we saw in the height of violence in Punjab in 1980s." [Vidya Bhushan Rawat]

Sikhism is Facing an Urgent and Violent Sectarian Crisis. Why?

[http://www.tehelka.com/story_main42.asp?filename=Op060609holier_than.asp] (Accessed November 30, 2012)

A Senior Journalist Kanwar Sandhu, in an article '*Holier Than Thou*', Sikhism is facing an urgent and violent sectarian crisis. Why? From Tehelka Magazine, Vol. 6, Issue 22, Dated June 06, 2009 explains Punjab situation. The Gist:

It is for the second time within two years, that Punjab and areas of Haryana are engulfed in the explosive nature of the caste divide, bringing back horrendous memories of the late 1970s of sectarian violence concerning Nirankari sect.

Affiliated to Different Gurudwaras

Two years ago, the Sirsa-based Dera Sacha Sauda was at the centre of the controversy. This time, two leaders, Sant Niranjan Dass and his deputy, Sant Ramanand of 109-year old Dera Sachkhand Ballan, who were in Vienna – Austria, to conduct a special service, were attacked on Sunday May 24, 2009, by people reportedly affiliated to another Sikh Gurudwara in Austria, killing Ramanand and injuring Niranjan Dass. This was the provocation for the violence.

The Failure of the Indian Diplomatic Mission in Austria

Sandhu attributes the violence in Punjab to the failure of the Indian diplomatic mission in Austria, which should have sounded an alarm back home, to take preventive measures, as soon as the incident took place.

The Sectarian Divide

Although Guru Gobind Singh had included all sections of society, including Dalits, into the Sikh fold, sectarian divide is most pronounced in Sikhism today, with more than two dozen sects and nearly a hundred *Dera-s*. Many of them have living Gurus, which is anathema to mainstream Sikhs, who consider the holy book, *Guru Granth Sahib* as the Guru ordained.

Dera Sachkhand

One such sect is Dera Sachkhand. Its followers, Ravidasi Sikhs, adhere to the teachings of Sant Ravidas, whose *Bani*, among those of other saints, form a part of the Guru Granth Sahib. Sandhu says, 'it was when discrimination against the Dalits continued in Gurudwaras, separate Ravidas Gurudwaras started surfacing in the middle of the 20th century', estimated to be 75 abroad, where portraits of Guru Ravidas are also displayed.

Why Differences?

Mainstream Sikhs, especially the radical elements among them, are piqued with the Dera Sachkhand on a number of counts.

For instance, most *Ravidasia-s*, who do not sport a turban, insist on referring to their places of worship as 'Gurudwaras', where the Guru Granth Sahib is worshipped.

Soon, ideological differences too cropped up when Dera followers started believing in a living Guru—Sant Niranjan Dass enjoys that status now—an issue on which Sikhs are extremely touchy.

Earlier, differences with Dera Sacha Sauda came to the fore when its head, Ram Rahim Singh was accused by Sikh groups of trying to copy Guru Gobind Singh in dress and form.

Many of the two dozen sects and hundreds of deras have living Gurus, anathema to mainstream Sikhs.

Incidentally, the mainstay of most other Sikh deras and sects are either the Dalits or the poor. Among the reasons for their mass appeal are the Dera-run charitable institutions like hospitals and schools.

Since these Dera-s also emphasise education and condemn child marriage and drug abuse, they are seen by the poor as a panacea for their misfortunes. Properties of these sects dot not just Punjab but almost all states in north India. Moreover, they are liberal in the form of Sikhism they practice.

Sandhu observes:

"Political observers in Punjab feel that the recent incident should act as a wake-up call to the government and religious organisations like the SGPC to start the process of social reconstruction in the state. Late Prof Teja Singh, in his treatise *Essays on Sikhism*, argued for the need to take all sects into the wider fold of Sikhism. However, this advice had few takers. In the late 1970s, when the Nirankari sect clashed with the Sikh groups, reconciliation efforts were initiated. But they did not fructify."

A Case Pending in High Court

SGPC has been cagey on initiating reforms for fear of criticism from orthodox elements and weakening of the Khalsa identity and "would result in more people opting out of the form of Sikhism as ordained by the tenth Guru."

Sandhu mentions that a decision on the issue of the *Shahajdhari* Sikhs being given the same rights as the *Keshadhari* Sikhs (baptized Sikhs) is pending in the Punjab and Haryana High Court. A girl student, who was denied admission in an SGPC-run medical college for having trimmed her hair, had moved the court.

The Separatist Tendencies

About widening the schism, Sandhu observes:

"Another underlying reason for the SGPC's reluctance to introduce reforms and provide acceptability to other sects is the fear that it could drastically alter the power equation within the SGPC, which acts as a handmaiden of the Shiromani Akali Dal (Badal) in Punjab. They worry that power would slip out of their grip. SGPC is already out of reckoning in Delhi's gurdwara politics and the demand to have a separate gurdwara body in Haryana too is growing. As Sikhs move to different parts of the world, independent streaks are becoming more pronounced. For example, a gurdwara in Europe has decided to modify the *ardas* (daily Sikh prayer), which the SGPC leaders resent."

The separatist tendency among powerful sections of the Sikh Diaspora abroad, where Gurudwaras are controlled by radical Sikhs is widening the schism, Sandhu observes.

He hopes the things would now improve because, he thinks, Punjab has come a long way since its earlier violent phase when politics, both at the Centre and in the State.

New 'Ravidassia Religion' formed

Following turmoil in Punjab following the killing of Dera dignitary, the leaders of Dera, decided to form a new 'Ravidassia Religion' and brought in practice that decision. They also published their '*granth*', called 'AMRITBANI'. English translator their '*granth*' observes:

"The enlightened people of the world, immediately rose to the occasion, and they launched powerful protest against this inhuman and ghastly killing of the holy sant. The Intellectuals started thinking, seriously about this hideous heinous crime. They reached the conclusion that a separate identity, for the followers of Guru Ravidass is the need of the hour. The whole world was looking towards *Dera* Ballan, whose great spiritual visionary had acquired martyrdom in the gruesome tragedy."

"When *Gaddi Nashin* of *Dera*, Sant Niranjan Dass recovered from the wounds of bullets and regained sound health, under his guidance, Saint Surinder Dass Bawa and other learned dignitaries of the world, specially linked with Dera began brainstorming sessions about the situation in order to provide separate identity to the disciples of Guru Ravidass and other peace loving people. It took almost seven months to reach the conclusion."

"A unique congregation to celebrate 633rd anniversary of Guru Ravidass was organised at Birth Place Temple, Seer Govardhanpur, Varanasi, India, on the 30th of January 2010. Lakhs of devotees from India and abroad were present on the auspicious occasion. In the presence of *Sant Samaj*, an historic decision was taken unanimously to form the Ravidassia Religion. This decision was welcomed by all. The mammoth gathering adopted the new religion immediately. The principles of newly formed Ravidassia Religion were accepted."

"*Amritbani*, containing the hymns of Guru Ravidass was declared the religious Granth of newly formed Ravidassia religion. This holy *Ganth* contains 140 *Shabads*, 40 *Pade*, *Paintee Akhari*, *Bani Haftawaar*, *Bani Mass Updesh*, *Saand Bani*, *Shadi Updesh*, *Manglachar* and 231 *shaloks* of Satguru Ravidass. This *Granth* is available at present in two languages, i.e. Devnagri and Gurmukhi scripts." [Siri Ram Arsh: 2012: 24]

Whether they achieve their desired goal, only future will tell. We wish them all good luck for their new religion. From our point of view, their efforts are not in the lines advocated by Ambedkar.

• • •

15

Dalits and Periyar

Charges Against Periyar

It seems the BSO, as always, does not stop denigrating Periyar Ramasami Naikkar. Nowadays it has been successful in threading in a few Dalits to do this dirty job, and we find even the misguided Dalits raise points against Periyar. They raise the points like national flag, his views about women leading to promiscuity, his '*Ravan Leelas'* etc.

But the real reason seems to be that they are frustrated because they can neither refute the points raised by him in '*True Reading of Ramayana*', nor they can afford an open discussion on this also. They just want to somehow malign him. I wish the Dalits should refrain from such activities.

They complain that Periyar burned the national flag thrice. I have no knowledge of that; he must be having some good reasons to do so. Let us not discuss that. I remember, in Maharashtra, long time back, the then Dalit Panther leader, Mr. Raja Dhale, who is now a prominent leader of RPI, had uttered some words considered to be denigrating to national flag, when some Dalit woman was molested. There was hue and cry in Brahminical press. But every Dalit activist and common man considered the action of Raja Dhale to be appropriate as the respect to the womanhood of Dalit woman was equally important as the respect for national flag.

The other complaint was that Periyar asked that women could have immoral sex. This is utterly wrong. He respected women and was for their equality. What he said was:

> "If the man has the right to claim a woman, then a woman also should have right to claim a man. If conditions are imposed for the worship of man by woman, let there be conditions imposed for the worship of woman by man." [See below]

Vaicom Struggle

They even deny his role in Vaikom by saying, "Vaikom struggle was achieved by Maharaja of Travancore and not by Periyar". This also is not true. Periyar's interest in Temple entry programmes was to assert Human Rights and not for Puja. He believed in no God and no Puja. The facts about Temple Entry in Travancore are thus:

The Maharaja of Travancore issued a Proclamation on the 12th November 1936 opening the Temples in the State to the Untouchables, claiming a lot of spirituality. A great lot has been made by the Congressmen and by Gandhi about this Proclamation.

But there was nothing great about it. Though the proclamation was issued in name of Maharaja, the real active force behind the scene was the Prime Minister, Sir C.P. Ramaswami lyer. In 1932, he was against the entry of the Untouchables into the Guruvayur Temple. His statement in *Times of India* dated November 10, 1932, shows that in 1933 there were no spiritual considerations. But he took a different view in 1936. What compelled this change of opinion was the 'Yevala Declaration' of Dr. Ambedkar for '*Dharmantar*' (conversion) in 1935. This was followed in 1936, by a Travancore Conference of the Yezawa Community, held to consider whether the Yezawas should not abandon the Hindu Religion in pursuance of the Ambedkar's Yeola Declaration of *Dharmantar*. Maharaja's Proclamation was issued to forestall this danger.

Even then the later events bear the fact that this Proclamation bore no fruit as mentioned by Sir T. Pannirselvam, that the people who used to worship previously before Dalits were allowed to enter the temples, had stopped worshipping in temples. Also the private temples of the Senior Maharani were excluded from the Proclamation. Also during the marriage of the daughter of Senior Maharani a purificatory ceremony of the temple was performed.

Explaining all these events in detail, Dr. Ambedkar observed, "Less said about the Malabar Temple Entry Proclamation as a spiritual testament, the better."

Mahad and Nasik Vs. Vaikom

Gandhi was in favour of the *Satyagraha* at Vaikom because it was carried on by the Untouchables under the auspices of the Congress but he was against similar *Satyagraha* at Mahad and Nasik. Ambedkar remarks, "Perhaps Mr. Gandhi was not prepared to protect the lambs who would not accept him as their shepherd."

Mayavati and Periyar Statue

Some Dalit activists are worried that Mayavati could not install Periyar statue in UP. Also during her last regime earlier, Mayavati had to divert the image of Periyar to south, and now again she could not install it. This is because of her compulsions of politics. There appear, in politics, several contradictions at the same time, and under such circumstances, the primary contradiction has to be resolved first. Therefore, in my humble opinion, it is rather premature to say that Mayavati is neglecting socio-cultural revolution. Let us forget about her for the time being and concentrate on Periyar.

Poverty in South

Some claimed that there is more percentage of landless Dalit labourers in South than in North and that poverty among Dalits in South is due to Periyar's movement. This has no basis. If there was poor progress of "land reforms" in South, how is Periyar movement responsible for it? It is just like saying Phule's and Ambedkar's thoughts are responsible for present day wretched condition of RPIs.

Atrocities against Dalits

One could not blame Periyar's movement for atrocities against Dalits in present day South India. It only means his followers could not carry on his task after him. About atrocities against Dalits, there is no region that can boast to be more liberal or more ugly. All are more or less same, even the so-called "forward" Maharashtra is no exception.

Was Periyar a Conman?

There are constant efforts by Manuvadis to cause rift among OBCs and Dalits. At one time a Dalit journalist, called Periyar as a "social conman" and observed:

> "Periyar was a great social scamster, who plundered Dalit consciousness. He made a fix deposit of it for growth of what I call social fascism. Old Dalits bore the Periyar burden. New Dalits must dump that mind robber."

This is very unfortunate, uncharitable and ungrateful charge, to be made by a Dalit. His estimate of Periyar is utterly wrong. Periyar's work for Dalits – Adi Dravidas – as they are referred to in his writings, was not eyewash unlike that of Gandhi. It was real work and the then Dalits responded with equal responsibility. Their sentiments were reciprocal. Neither the Dalits of old bore Periyar's burden, nor the present day Dalits have to discard him. He was, he is and he will remain the ideal and idol of the multitudes of Dalits, the world over. Only the 'harijans' – followers of Gandhi – have discarded him, as they did Phule, Shahu and Ambedkar.

Ideals of Periyar

He founded Self-Respect Movement in 1925. Through it, he carried out a vigorous and ceaseless propaganda against ridiculous and harmful superstitions, traditions, customs and habits. He wanted to dispel the blind faith and ignorance of the people and make them enlightened. He exhorted them to change the institutions and values that led to meaningless divisions and unjust discrimination of caste and gender. He criticised the religious books, legends and stories rampant among the people, which supported such discriminations. He made them keep pace with the modern conditions, and change according to the requirements of the changing times.

Self-respecters did not believe in existence of God, ridiculed superstitions and performed marriages without Brahmin priests, without Brahminic rites and *mantras*. They insisted on equality between men and women in all walks of life. They encouraged inter-caste and widow marriages. He supported abolition of Devadasi system by Law and opposed the child marriages. He was one of firsts, who propagated the need for family planning as early as late 1920s.

Acts of Self-Respecters for Dalit Upliftment

One could write a thesis on Periyar's work about Dalits. He struggled all his life for abolition of caste, which according to him will be achieved, by "abolition of God, Religion (Hinduism), the *Shastras* and the Brahmins". He and his Self Respecters never got tired of repeating that Untouchability and caste differentiations were root cause of Indian slavery and always declared that it was not enough that OBCs rebelled against Brahmins but they had to abandon Untouchability and treat them as equals. They always struggled for OBC-Dalit unity.

One incident is worth mentioning. At some place he was addressing OBCs and advocating unity with Dalits.

One of his listeners complained that people had come there to hear about Brahmin tyranny and not to hear about love for Adi-Dravidas. Periyar's curt reply was that, to show love towards a *Pariah* is the real method of opposing the Brahmin tyranny.

They believed in proportional representation of all castes in positions of power, services, legislature and education. In a caste bound society they worked for socialism and gave in 'Samadharma' a non-brahmin alternative on cultural basis. Periyar denounced the 'separate' facilities like wells for Dalits. They had adi-dravida concerns in mind while opposing Gandhi, or "Poona Pact" or Harijan Sewak Sangha or Christian clergy observing Untouchability against Christian Dalits. They gave more importance to schooling and drinking water for Dalits than 'salt satyagraha' of Gandhi.

Should the Oppressed Suffer Forever?

God, if exists and is merciful and just must punish the wicked. As this is not seen to happen, he disbelieved in his existence. He observed:

> "Men should not touch each other, see each other; and cannot enter temples, fetch water from the village pond: in a land where such inhuman practices are ripe, it is a wonder that the earthquakes have not destroyed us, volcanoes not burnt us; it is a wonder that the earth has not split at its heart and plunge this land into an abyss, that a typhoon has not shattered us. I leave it to you to decide if you still like to trust to a divinity that has not punished us thus; if you still consider that God a just God, a Merciful Being. How long do you desire a vast section of the oppressed, the depressed classes to remain patient, peaceful and quiet? Would you consider it wrong if these oppressed were to choose death rather than lead such a life as they do now?"

Liberation of Shudras and Panchamas

Periyar's dictum was "liberation of Shudras depended on liberation of Panchamas". They fought for common eating, inter-caste marriages, temple entry to exert the right, and opposed Congressmen, who only talked and did nothing. When Dr. Subbarayan became Chief Minister, he nominated two Adi-Dravidas to Devasthanam committee. Guruswami declared, if he becomes Viceroy he would appoint Dr. Ambedkar as Law Minister of India.

Political Power

They forced bus operators to accept Dalits in buses and resolved for unrestricted passage to Dalits to ponds, wells, schools and roads, which is a good example to show how political power can help solve social issues, contrary to some people's understanding. They performed many inter-caste marriages with Dalits in 'Self-Respect' method, which was given due publicity.

Political Struggle of Dalits supported

There were three major incidents in political life of Dalits during those days – 'Simon Commission', 'Second Round Table Conference' and 'the Poona Pact'. In all those, the Self-Respecters and Periyar stood firmly with Dr. Ambedkar and against Gandhi and his Congress. The important work done by '*Kudi Arasu*' by organising protests, editorials and articles cannot be forgotten. They even opposed 'Raja-Moonje Pact' and declared that Nationalists' fight against the British was only for maintaining Brahminic hegemony and benefits.

Gandhi as Sanatanist

Periyar had joined Congress, attracted towards the party by Vinoba Bhave, C Rajagopalachari, and Gandhi. He liked Gandhian way of using khadi. However, he soon became disappointed with the Congress because of their caste discrimination.

The Self-Respecters opposed Gandhian ideology and condemned Gandhi to be with those who burnt Dalits huts and butchered Dalit men and women. They remarked Gandhi's fast 'unto death' was because of 'over seven crores corpses had dared to seek a separate representation for themselves'.

Gandhi's Ramrajya idea was selfish. He wanted everybody to maintain ones own status by birth and wished Dalits to have 'peaceful co-existence' with upper castes. The Self-Respecters declared Gandhi as '*sanatanist*' believing in Smritis and Gita and condemned his ideals of Ramrajya.

Buddhism

We know Dr. Ambedkar wanted the oppressed communities to leave the Brahmanism based on caste, and ultimately millions of Dalits converted to Buddhism with Dr. Ambedkar.

Dr. Ambedkar challenged the concept of "tolerance of Hinduism", he mocked at their so called holy scriptures and so called holy gods in his wonderful analysis in "Riddles of Hinduism" and other writings.

The same work had been done in South under the able leadership of EVR, whose rationalist viewpoint removed to a great extent the blind faiths among the masses.

Caste system with graded inequality, created by Brahminic cunningness with the object of cheating the Indian masses, through the so-called scriptures, ensured Brahmincal domination because every caste hated the lower ones and hence the Brahmin enjoyed the supremacy over the vast Indian ignorant masses.

Ambedkar and Periyar, both were clear that the solution to the caste problem was not to be found within the boundaries of Hinduism but whereas Dr. Ambedkar found his answers in Buddhism, Periyar felt the answer lay in humanism and going down that route, he became progressively an atheist and a rationalist.

Working on ideas of Iyothee Thass, who was first person to think of revival of Buddhism in India, the Self-Respecters even organised seminars on Buddhism in early thirties.

Burning of Manusmriti

For Self-Respecters, temple entry was a problem of human rights – not of religion, they castigated existence of gods and temples as centres of caste oppression, proclaimed the uselessness of worship and exhorted Adi-dravidas to renounce Hinduism.

Self-Respecters burned the copies of 'Manusmriti' in public meetings, and several such instances were reported in 'Kudi Arasu' of 4.12. 1927. This means that these were earlier instances to the burning of '*Manusmriti'* by Dr. Ambedkar on 25th December 1927 at Mahad, the day the Dalits all the world over celebrate as 'Manusmriti Dahan Deen'. [Geetha : 1998 : 359]

Nandanar Charithram

'*Kudi Arasu'* carried an article titled '*Nandanar Charithram'* condemning the traditional fable of Adi-Dravida saint Nandanar depicted as a derogatory figure by birth, living in a foul smelling 'cheri' where bones were strewn everywhere and where men and women were always drunk, and Nandanar had to get burnt himself to meet god. The Self-Respecters considered this as a wily trick to build consent system among Dalits and make them accept slavery. So they condemned the play based on this fable, and asked for a ban on it.

Supported Ambedkar

Periyar and Self-Respecters always supported Ambedkar. Dalit Conference in 1929 in Jalgaon in Maharashtra by Dr. Ambedkar got a message of good wishes and support from Periyar, and the news appeared in '*Kudi Arasu'*, describing this as a "First Self-Respect Conference of Maharashtra". [Geetha : 1998 : 366]

Ambedkar's views on Gandhi, Poona Pact, Harijan Sewak Sangha, caste and separate electorates were always highlighted. Ambedkar's "Annihilation of Caste" was translated and serialised in '*Kudi Arasu'* and later printed as a book in 1937.

Criticised Non-Brahmins Also

Periyar and Self-Respecters did not spare non-brahmins also. In 1930, in an attempt at 'sanskritisation', an OBC caste put restrictions on Adi-Dravidas in dress etc. They were highly criticised, comparing their cruelty with that of notorious General Dyre. Later, in violent atrocities against Dalits, the Dalit side was upheld by Self-Respecters, various resolutions passed and various attempts made towards awakening the Shudras, stressing that Brahmin-non-Brahmin division was fundamental.

Periyar always warned against upgrading of castes, e.g. he denounced the practice by Palas – an untouchable caste – to call themselves Devendra kula Vellalas, Vanniyars wishing to call themselves Kshatriyas and Chettiars referring themselves as Vaishyas, and declared these acts are the acts of degrading rather than upgrading. [Geetha : 1998 : 369]

The rich community of Nattukotti Chettis thought of spending their riches on study of Vedas for Brahmin students. Periyar advised them to spend that money on Education of Dalits. [Geetha : 1998 : 371]

On many instances, Periyar expressed disgust at non-Brahmins orthodoxy towards Adi-dravidas and remarked that non-Brahmins are more orthodox than the Brahmins.

Liberation of Women

Periyar considered the position of women degraded by the Brahminic *Shastras* to a mere '*dasi*', a term which to a Self-Respecter was akin to 'slave' having no freedom in sexual matters, and resembled Tamil word '*vesi*' meaning prostitute.

This idea of non-Brahmin woman as a sexual slave is fixed in Shudras' minds by the dharma-Shastras, argued Self-Respecters.

They were also strong opponents of Devadasi system, where non-Brahmin women were made the prostitutes in the name of god, religion and rituals. They supported the Devadasi Abolition Bill with great vehemence. Self-Respecters saw the collective dishonour of non-Brahmin women in Devadasi exploitation of low caste women.

Periyar and Self-Respecters supported 'Sarada Act', denounced the concept of chastity of women, run a sort of home for women facing atrocities, supported Miss Catherine Mayo's book *Mother India* depicting woes of Devadasis, Hindu wives, Hindu widows and holding responsible Shastras, Brahmins and Brahmanism for them. In degrading women, Brahmanism had the motive of controlling knowledge, they averred. They considered the degradation of women and Dalits were inter-related. They advocated "self-respect marriages" without Brahmins, without Sanskrit mantras and without consideration of caste. [V. Geetha : 1998 : 388]

Dalits be Careful

One might say that the lieutenants of Periyar were not that capable to complete the revolution started by him, but no Dalit, in his senses, will show disrespect for Periyar's work or doubt his motives. (but a 'harijan' may)

From time to time, Manuvadis start propaganda against Phule and Periyar and try to create rift among Dalits and OBCs. The various contradictions apart, let us remember Shudras and Dalits are the natural friends and will have to accommodate each other, no matter what the Manuvadis say and do. There is no other alternative, whether you like it or not. There are efforts by the vested interests to sabotage the Dalit OBC unity. We better be careful not to fall a prey to Brahminic propaganda, they undertake from time to time to denigrate Phule and Periyar, and they utilise people in Dalit movement for this purpose.

• • •

16

Dalits and Buddhism

Buddhism: Is it A Caste, A Sect or A Religion?

Ambedkar's Advice

Dr. Ambedkar has given a beautiful example of how if one severs the links harshly with old traditions, one can progress. A well to do family had to see bad days of penury and was somehow surviving by selling lentils from an old tree of lentils (*shevagya chya shenga*) in their courtyard, without doing any other work as they thought it below dignity to work. A guest coming to their house realised this and early next morning cut down the tree, and quietly left. The family had no option but to work. Gradually their condition improved. Thus, the fellow who cut down the source of income of the family was a blessing, which the family realised later.

Remember that well-known instance, when Dr. Ambedkar had admonished the representative of "Kesari" in a public meeting. The journalist blamed Ambedkar for depriving the Dalits of the income they could derive from lifting the dead cattle, which was stopped by Ambedkar. Ambedkar had said he would give him five hundred rupees extra if the journalist and his family undertook the work and obtain all the monetary benefits of lifting dead cattle, and processing them, the hide, bones and flesh and all the rest.

Ambedkar motivated the Dalits to give up their *vatan-s*, i.e. old "rights" to work for the village as a menial servant for which they were given a small piece of land, on which the whole family worked to etch out its meagerly livelihood. In return they got the "right" to beg for some grain at the harvest.

So Dr. Ambedkar gave more importance to self-respect. Those who followed Ambedkar and gave up their old professions, today, we find comparatively more prosperous. They are called "Dalits", the rest, who followed Gandhi and did not give up their old vocations, remained "Harijans".

This is why we find dichotomy among the SCs. This is the reason of differential rate of progress and this is also the reason why these different castes could not come together to fight the common enemy. This ultimately led to internal rivalry, schism and fighting and ultimate division of various castes into unfortunate categories in some provinces.

Though some of our friends have welcomed this categorisation as being conducive to more equitable distribution of positive discrimination by the state, it is not a good sign. The unutilised reservation quota resources will not go to other categories but will be treated as "general". This is our experience for last many years. Therefore, who fought for categorisation did a disservice to the society.

Have we given up our Caste

To this feeling of dualism, another factor is added. Those who got converted to Buddhism, did abolish the subcastes, but could not go beyond that. They could not transgress the caste, a Mahar does not marry a Matang and *vice-versa* for example. Herlekar has given example of some Matang families, who were supporters and followers of Ambedkar and had adopted Buddhism along with him in 1956, could not find match for their daughters in new religion. Even their old caste fellows alienated from them as they had embraced Buddhism and were discarded from both sides.

In spite of a lot of talk, we still like to get married within our own old caste. This is the ground reality. If this continues, after some time, it may come to the fact that Buddhist would become a new caste in the old structure of caste frame of Hindus.

Depicting Buddha as Hindu

For a last few years, RSS activists are trying to depict to the international community, that they respect the Buddha. While doing that they use terminology depicting him as a Hindu, and Buddhism as a "sect" or "*panth*" of Hinduism. What they want is "*samasata*" and not "*samata*". *Samasata* means all should accept the *status quo* and be happy with their lot without struggling for transformation. Live and let live as it is.

Books are written to show the work of Hegdewar and Ambedkar was same, and Shankaracharya-s garland the photo of Dr. Ambedkar, Brahmanic dignitaries pay a visit to Nagpur *Diksha-bhoomi* to pay tributes. And even RSS supremo Sudarshan garlands the statue of Ambedkar - the maker of the Indian Constitution- on Deekshabhoomi at Nagpur, (and the Ambedkarites have washed and "purified" the statue "polluted" by touch of someone who condemns the Constitution.)

They had achieved their goal of maintaining supremacy by declaring the Buddha as an *avatara* of god, some times around eighth century, as a verse to this effect from *Matsya Purana* is engraved in a monument at Mahabalipuram. The process was complete by the time of Jaydeo writing "*Git-Govind*" and including Buddha's name in it as an "*Avatara*", in 12th century. All this caused confusion in the minds of people with the result that Buddhism came to be treated as a "heretical" and "aesthetic" branch of Brahmanism.

But we are also aware that an average Brahmin takes a great pride that Buddhism was driven away from this land by Adi-Sankara. If Buddhism was a sect of "Hinduism", then one may well ask the proud supporters of Shankaracharya, what was that religion which was "driven out by Adi Sankara", as they claim? Was it also Hinduism?

Buddhism is not a sect of Hinduism

Swami Dharmatirtha has rightly observed, in an answer to those, who treat Buddhism as a sect of Hinduism, that we do not know of any Hinduism having existed before the Buddha and if Hinduism did not exist, Buddhism could not have been a sect of it. He observed that, Buddhism was a revolt against both the prevailing systems, Brahmanic as well as tribal religion of sorts. In fact it was the first organised religion in the modern sense of the term "religion". [Swami Dharmatirtha: "*Menace of Hindu Imperialism*, 1946: p. 109]

Buddhism was the National Religion of India

But the decline of Buddhism is a historical fact, and is the cause of all ills, India had to face in the past, and is facing at the present. That the ills of common people of India today are due to the decline and fall of Buddhism in historical times, is not well understood by the masses, and how it affected the life of common people and what kind of miseries the subsequent generations had to suffer, is a subject which not many scholars have given much thought to.

The fact that at one time Buddhism was the national religion of India and was followed by the majority of population, must not be forgotten. That India is and was a Hindu country having always had a majority of Hindus is a misconception. In historical times the population of India never had majority of Hindus. Swami Vivekananda, estimated Buddhists to be two-thirds of population [L.M. Joshi: 1977: 358] and Dr. Ambedkar says Buddhist were in majority. [W&S, Vol.7, p. 345] Then there were Jains and Veerashaivas and Tribal religions in addition to Muslims, Sikhs and Christians coming in the later times. The word "Hindu" itself has no relevance in pre-Islamic times. It is by trickery, as Gail Omvedt has observed, that they claim it as Hindu nation.

Buddhism: National Religion

The fact is, Buddhism was not only the faith practiced by majority of people but had eclipsed Brahmanism to a great extent and the Brahmins had lost all the respect of masses as well as rulers. They were smarting under this defeat. [W&S, Vol.7, p. 346] They did everything in their power to finish off Buddhism and after Muslim invasion, succeeded in it.

Buddhism was the national religion of India, not only because the Buddha was an Indian, descended from an Indian king of the Sakya clan, but, observed Swami Dharma Teertha, because Buddhism was the source and inspiration of the national awakening witnessed in the Indian empires and kingdoms which controlled the destinies of the country for over a thousand years, and because it, for the first time, united India in a common cultural synthesis and organisation, and because unlike Brahmanism, which was the religion of the privileged classes,

Buddhism was the first religion of the common people, not forced on them, but accepted by their free will and pleasure, because Buddhism brought out in the fullest measure the immense potentialities of the nation in all its manifold aspects - science and art, literature and religion, commerce and industry, internal progress and international reputation, and also, because no other religion has till this day been able to make India a great nation as Buddhism did. [Dharmateertha, p. 76]

Brahmins usurped Buddhism

Brahmans became the leaders of Buddhism because they kept education to themselves, and first disfigured it thoroughly with mythology and ritualism, and destroyed its separate organisation of monasteries and monks with the help of the foreign masters who came into power. But the Buddhism of Harsha and Nagarjuna did not disappear, it formed the nucleus of the later Hinduism, superadded with horrors of caste.

To become the sole leaders of the country and to enforce their system of castes, has always been the prime motive of Brahmanism, and if Buddhist order of monks and monasteries had survived, the Brahmins could not have achieved this goal. So they completely destroyed the external institution of Buddhism, the monks and monasteries. Brahmins became the undisputed leaders, and a new popular religion, Hinduism, emerged with important aspect of caste.

Dharmateertha observed that Caste is an entirely independent social order which was neither in the ancient Aryan religion nor in primitive Indian religion nor in Buddhism. It is the unique contribution of the priestly class, and none else ever wanted it, until the country lost its national religion and political freedom, and they succeeded in imposing the system upon the people almost at the point of the bayonet with of alien masters. [p.110]

What do the Present Ambedkarites Want?

Do they want that, the religion given to them by their saviour, should become a Caste. If they isolate themselves, this is sure to happen. Or do they want Buddhism to become a "*panth*" (sect) of Brahmanism as the RSS and their supporters want? Or do they want it to progress as a religion? The difference being conversion of new people. If you wish to make it a religion, you must undertake conversion of others to Buddhism. If not, it becomes a caste or at the most a "*panth*". If you wish to spread by conversion, who is your target group? In my humble opinion, it is the OBCs group, which are also sailing in the same boat. Forget about the top creamy layer among OBCs, who have same interests as BBK group. The rest of OBCs, specially the MBCs are also smarting under the tyranny of BSO. They could be your allies. At the same time, let us take care that our 'creamy layer' does not acquire tendencies of BSO.

Stages of Progress

The first stage would be political. That is the easiest. Then comes the Religious and finally the Social stage, when the whole society becomes one, a casteless society as dreamt by our great saviours. The ball lies in the court of Ambedkarites. Would they accept the challenge? Or will they like to shun the OBCs, to great peril of us all?

How India will become Once Again Buddhist?

Various different Sects of Buddhism in Present Day India

A friend asks whether there is anything wrong in having different sects of Buddhism in India. The frank reply to that is there is absolutely nothing wrong in having various sects of Buddhism.

At the moment, we have got various kinds of Buddhists. Firstly, there are the original Buddhists, who are there for centuries, mostly concentrated in Laddhak, Sikkim and North East. Secondly, the successors of missionaries from foreign lands like Anagarik Dharmapal, who not only resurrected Buddhism in India, but also motivated Swami Vivekananda to attend Chicago Conference along with him. Let it be remembered that Sanatanists opposed Vivekanand attending the World Conference as he was a non-brahmin. Thirdly, there are those who became Buddhists under influence of Dharmapala, like Kosambi, Rahul, Kashyap etc. from whom very few may now be alive. Fourthly, there is a vast mass who became Buddhists after Dr. Ambedkar's appeal and mass conversion. In addition, there are two kinds of Refugee Buddhists, one group is followers of H.H. the Dalai Lama, and others are the neglected Chakma Refugees, who, I believe, have been mostly driven out, very much in contrast to Kashmiri Pundits Refugees.

Here we like to talk about those who became Buddhists because of Teachings of Dr. Ambedkar. They are said to be 68 lakhs, as per census of 1991, in a population of about hundred crores, which comes to less than one per cent. If we have to fulfill the dream of Dr. Ambedkar, to make India Buddhist, at least there should be 30 to 40 crores of Buddhists.

Within these 68 lakh Buddhists, there appeared various sects also, though I feel that various castes among the people who embraced Buddhism have mostly disappeared. There are Manuvadis who do not like that the Buddhists should consolidate. They are projecting the Buddha as Hindu. Enough has been written about this tendency.

There are some who follow Goenka, who runs Vippasana Centres. His followers, in most parts, are lost to Ambedkarism. This is because most of them have dissociated themselves from the Ambedkarite movement. (If there are exceptions, salutes to them.) There is nothing wrong, *per se*, in Vippasana. But they think, Vippasana is the only teaching that the Buddha taught. There are followers of Osho, who run *Dhyana* Centres. Their activities are such that the majority of population disapproves. There are some Ambedkarites praising Osho also. These two groups, the Goenka and Osho followers are condemned by authors like Yashvant Manohar as "pollutions" among the Ambedkarite movements.

If these two groups could concentrate on the Social aspects and Egalitarian teachings of the Buddha, and advise their followers to denounce the caste as the

Buddha did, and later his followers of all the sects, including highly maligned Vajrayanis, did, and as the followers of Ambedkar are trying to do, perhaps the days for Buddhism in India would be bright. Unfortunately, their activities are either not very clear, or are in consonance with the Manuvadis. These are two groups, who are well supported by the Buddhist community outside India. It is here we have to warn our friends outside India to take care that they are not playing in the hands of Manuvadis.

There are '*Trilokya Boudha Maha Sangha*' people, trying to propagate the Dhamma. Whatever may be their activities outside India, they are doing reasonably good job. Though some may say, their type of religion is not the same as Dr. Ambedkar taught.

The Creed of Buddha

Dr. Ambedkar, the greatest Indian of modern times, gave Buddhism to India after it had disappeared about thousand years ago. Millions accepted this "new" religion. It was new in the sense, it was almost forgotten and the tenets advocated at one time by the Buddha, got mixed up with the so called "Hinduism". During his last days, he was asked about the rituals, principles and other peculiarities of this religion. To all such questions, he said, he would reply in next meeting at Bombay, in the middle of December 1956. That day never arose.

The followers started following the religion as per what they perceived was proper in their own thoughts. So it got more and more corrupted. Therefore, some people decided to chart out a "Code of Conduct" for the followers of Buddhism.

Spread of Buddhism

Dr. Ambedkar had said, he would make India Buddhist again - (*mee bhatat buddha maya karen*). Who were these people, Ambedkar had in mind? Whom was he to teach his religion? Obviously, all the poor depressed and deprived people of this land divided by tradition into thousands of castes, the SCs, STs, OBCs, and other smaller deprived under-privileged groups. But his dream was not fulfilled. Not only the OBCs and others did not join his religion, but not even all the SCs joined it. So there are two aims facing the today's Ambedkarites. First is to spread the religion to the masses, and second is to teach what is "proper" Buddhism of Ambedkar's mind, which needs to be followed. Faced with this dual task, we have to analyse how we are behaving. We have also to decide our priorities.

Ambedkar's Religion not same as Traditional Buddhism

During conversion days, Dr. Ambedkar was interviewed by "*Tarun Bharat*" of Nagpur, asking him which '*yana*' he professes. Dr. Ambedkar said his propagation of Buddhism depends upon the original teachings of the Buddha. The traditional teachings have been corrupted during the course of time by the views of various Teachers of different sects. I am putting forward the teachings in proper perspective. I happened to be present during a part of this interview, which was well documented and well published. '*Tarun Bharat*' correspondent said "then we can call this a '*Bhim yaan*'. Ambedkar said 'No'! If you want to give it a new name, you may call it "Nava yaan", but what I propagate is according to original teachings of Buddha, and are based on rational thinking."

Buddha and His Dhamma

Later, he put all his teachings in "Buddha and His Dhamma". Unfortunately, the world leaders of Buddhism do not accept the book as "Standard". Therefore, it is necessary to discuss this point with the world authorities and try to come to some understanding. It must be understood, for followers of Ambedkar, the book is like a gospel. In the light of this fact, if there is proper understanding, the things will improve and Buddhism would spread.

I have no objection to have various sects being present simultaneously and they coexist, provided that they do not form the part of Hinduism.

India can not become Buddhist without Political Power

There are many who quote Ambedkar advocating social awakening first can only give political power. That is very true, but I feel, that stage is now over. Now is the stage to Unite all "Dalitbahujans" and capture the political power. India can only become Buddhist through political power. Let us remember the examples of Ashoka, Kanishka, Harsha and Pala-s.

Buddhist Ahimsa

Sanyasta Khadga

The tendency to blame the Buddha for all the ills of Hindu society is not new. Some years back, a physician from Nagpur had blamed the decline of surgical skills in ancient India on the Buddha's *ahimsa*, claiming that surgery is based violence '*hinsa*'. The learned doctor could not understand the skill of surgery was never considered as violence by any society in the world. The first ever known surgeon in history of India was Buddhist Jivaka. Not only that but all the medical men from Buddha's times to about seventh century CE, including Nagarjuna, Charak, Vagbhatta-junior and senior-were all Buddhists, unlike an imaginary Brahminic god physician '*Dhanvantari*'.

More serious objections on the Buddha's *ahimsa* was taken by Brahmin leader Veer Vinayak Damodar Savarkar. About seventy years ago, he wrote a play titled '*Sanyasta Khadga*'. It is a type parody, ridiculing the Buddha for his non-violence and blaming him for decline of military prowess of India and thereby falling it a prey to foreign invasions.

Ahimsa of the Buddha

It is worth understanding that Buddhism has spread all over the world and no force was ever used by the Buddhists for its spread.

Ambedkar believed that Buddha's *Ahimsa* was not as absolute as the *Ahimsa* preached by Mahavira. About Buddha's Ahimsa Ambedkar observed:

"The Buddha was against violence. But he was also in favour of justice and where justice required he permitted the use of force."

He quotes the Buddha's dialogue with Sinha Senapati the Commander-in-Chief of Vaishali.

Sinha having come to know that the Buddha preached Ahimsa went to him and asked:

> "The Bhagvan preaches *Ahimsa*. Does the Bhagvan preach an offender to be given freedom from punishment? Does the Bhagvan preach that we should not go to war to save our wives, our children and our wealth? Should we suffer at the hands of criminals in the name of Ahimsa?"
>
> "Does the Tathagata prohibit all war even when it is in the interest of Truth and Justice?"
>
> Buddha replied.
>
> "You have wrongly understood what I have been preaching. An offender must be punished and an innocent man must be freed. It is not a fault of the Magistrate if he punishes an offender. The cause of punishment is the fault of the offender. The Magistrate who inflicts the punishment is only carrying out the law. He does not become stained with Ahimsa. A man who fights for justice and safety cannot be accused of Ahimsa. If all the means of maintaining peace have failed then the responsibility for *Himsa* falls on him who starts war. One must never surrender to evil powers. War there may be. But it must not be for selfish ends...." [Buddha and Karl Marx]

The strife between Buddhists and Brahmins is the Crucial Point

It is well known that the glorious epoch of Indian history was Buddhist and not Brahminic. During the Buddhist period the special privileges of the Brahmins were eroded. So the Buddhists became their enemies. The strife between Buddhists and Brahmins is the crucial point in the Indian history. Ultimately, the Buddhists lost. But the Hindu society got the slavery of women and curse of the caste. That caused the downgrading of India. But the elites blame the *ahimsa* of Buddhists as the root cause of defeat in all foreign invasions. Sawarkar, Golwalkar etc. mention this throughout their literature.

Hindus have History of Defeats

When Ambedkar pointed out that the history of India is the history of defeats, Sawarkar wrote a book, as a rejoinder, '*saha soneri pane*' (six golden pages) describing six 'golden' episodes in 2500 years of Indian History.

Sawarkar was in favour of advocated militarisation of Hindus. He criticised the Buddha in very bitter words. He wrote drama '*Sanyasta Khadga*' about sixty - seventy years ago ridiculing the Buddha for his *ahimsa*. The funny part is that drama is being staged even now by them. There was a news item about its being staged a few months ago. This drama is also taught in Graduate courses in Universities in Maharashtra.

Therefore, it becomes necessary to examine whether the *ahimsa* of the Buddha was responsible for the defeat of Indians at the hands of foreign invaders. It was the caste system and not the *ahimsa* of Buddha that caused the defeat of Hindus.

Buddhists Never Practiced Ahimsa in War

Two centuries after the Buddha **Chandragupta Maurya** established an empire. He was reportedly a Jain. Jains are famous for absolute *ahimsa.* But his Jain religion did neither come in his way in driving out the Greeks, nor it was a hindrance in marrying the daughter of Greek Ambassador Selucus.

It is noteworthy that Alexander the great had come a little earlier and defeated many Hindu kings and returned back. His victory was because of the fact that the Hindu kings and tribes fought dividedly and Hindu kings like Ambhi helped the invaders. It was not that Indians were less brave or because they were practicing *Ahimsa* as preached by Mahavira or the Buddha.

Ashoka (273 – 236 BCE) was a staunch Buddhist. He extended his empire to the extreme end of India with the aid of the sword. Even after the Kalinga war, he was maintaining a strong army.

Ashoka's grandson **Bahidratha** was treacherously murdered by his Brahmin commander Pushyamitra during the military parade, which means, he was also maintaining an army. His only fault was he appointed a Brahmin in his army as commander. *Purohita* of Pushyamitra was Patanjali. This Pushyamitra Shunga, a great persecutor of Buddhism, is highly praised by Sawarkar and constitutes the first of the 'six pages'.

Satvahanas used to be considered Brahminic because of Nanaghat inscription of Nayanika describes *Ashwamedha.* But they were Buddhists and Buddhism flourished in their rule. They were the 'Lords of three oceans'. They were brave and ruled by strong hand.

King **Milind**, noted for his religious discourses with Buddhist Bhikku Nagsena, was from Kabul. He settled in India at Sialkot in Punjab and became a Buddhist. He was a brave soldier and had a vast army. He had decided to invade the empire of Magadha, and caught hold of the horse of Ashwamedha of the then ruler Agnimitra Shunga. But had to return back to Punjab, as Shakas had invaded his kingdom.

Kanishka of Kushana Kula was also an important Buddhist Emperor. His empire was vast and militarily so strong that he had even threatened to invade king of China.

Naga kings flourished at Vidisha, Kantipuri, Mathura and Padmavati. They were patrons of Buddhism. It was because of their matrimonial support that the Imperial Guptas emerged.

Harshavardhana was very important Buddhist Emperor. He was a great warrior and conqueror. His army was increased to 60,000 elephants, 100,000 cavalry and several lakhs infantry, as is described by Huen Tsang.

History of defeats during Hindu Period

After death of Harsha in 647 CE, Rajputs were created by the Brahmins from Tribals and remnants of foreign hordes to fight Buddhism militantly. In north India, it was from '*Havan at Mount Abu*' and in South India it was through '*Hiranya Garbha*' ceremonies. Rajputs were staunch supporters of Brahmanism and enemies of Buddhism. Except for a Buddhist Pala dynasty, which ruled Eastern India right up to Mathura for about four hundred years, the Rajputs ruled rest of India till the Muslims came.

Rajputs were trained to fight right from childhood after their '*khadgabandh*'. They were motivated to fight by preaching them stories of Ramayana, Mahabharata and Gita.

In certain parts of Rajasthan, Mahajan [Mahajan: 1972: 550 ff.] tells us that, the word 'Rajput' is used to denote the illegitimate sons of a Kshatriya chiefs or *Jagirdar*. But by and large they are considered as higher castes. They fought the Buddhists and when no Buddhists remained they fought among themselves. The Rajputs were not followers of *Ahimsa* of Buddha. Why then, were they defeated by Muslims? By the time Muslims under Bakhtyar Khilji invaded Bengal, the Buddhist Pala-s were replaced by Brahminic Sena-s – the originator of *Kulin* system – who, perhaps purposefully, neglected to protect Nalanda and other Buddhist Universities.

When Md. Bin Kasim invaded Sindh in 712 CE, Buddhism had disappeared from Western India and Brahmin kings were ruling. Even then this juvenile lad of Khalifa conquered Sindh and killed the Hindu king there and sent his daughters as presents to Khalifa.

One hundred years after the Muslims captured Sindh and part of Punjab, Adi Shankara arose, flourished and taught *Vedanta*. Shudras must not read or hear the Vedas, if they hear Vedas molten lead should be poured in their ears, if they utter Vedas their tongues should be cut, and if they learned Vedas, they should be killed. This was his *Vedanta* in practice.

Rajputs were strong supporters of violence. They were shattered under horses' feet by Md. of Gazani. In '*Thoughts on Pakistan*', Ambedkar described the pitiable way that Rajput suffered. How did it happen? Was it because of *Ahimsa* of Buddha?

The last Buddhist king of India Jaichandra

Jaichandra is wrongly blamed as a traitor and maligned without any reason by elites for inviting Md. Ghori to invade Prithwiraj Chauhan. It is propagated right from the school textbooks. This is based on account in '*Prithwiraj Raso*', creation of a bard, worthless as history. This is ostensibly, because Jaichandra was Buddhist – the last Buddhist King of India, as proved by inscriptions and Tibetan text '*Chandraraj Lekh*'. *M.M.* Dr. Gaurishankar Hirachand Ojha has conclusively proved that *Raso* is not created before 16th century. Scholars like D.C. Ganguli aver that *Raso* is created 300 years after Prithwiraj and the stories of Sanyogita etc. in it are highly unreliable, romantic and improbable. [Ganguli: 1989: 105]

There was no friendship or enmity between Jaichandra and Prithwiraj. [Dharmarakshit: 1956: 63]

Why eulogize Prithviraj?

The question nobody likes to deal with is why in the sixteenth century, Brahmins needed to eulogize the three centuries old Prithviraj Chauhan as a hero? And why malign Jaichandra, the last great Buddhist Monarch of India, who was dead 300 years ago? As Jaichandra was known to be a Buddhist, **was it anti-Muslim propaganda or an anti-Buddhist one?**

We have discussed this in detail elsewhere. ['*Decline and Fall of Buddhism*', p. 52 ff.]

Peshava rule

Peshava rule was purely Brahminic. Last Bajirao was famous for his orthodoxy. Violence was on its zenith during Peshava rule. They were the great devotees of violence and should have spread all over India. But they had to surrender to the British – hundred times less violent than Peshavas. Why? Were the Peshavas following *Ahimsa* of the Buddha?

Buddhist Countries Fought Wars

Japan is Buddhist for last more than thousand years. When in 1853, Commander Perry directed canons against them, they all united. Why the religion of Buddha did not make them cowards.

Vietnam is Buddhist. How did they defeat mighty enemy like Americans? How did the Vietnamese people fought for social economic cause? Why did the Buddhist Ahimsa not prevent them from fighting?

Cause of defeats of Hindus is system of castes

It is very clear that the cause of defeat of Hindus for centuries is something different from the teachings of Buddha or Mahavira. Then why are the *Hindutvawadi*-s annoyed and angry with the Buddhists? It is not because India lost freedom. It is because Buddhism was successful in fighting against the Brahmin supremacy, bringing in atmosphere of equality and stop the Brahminic exploitation of the masses.

Macauley, Marxists and Muslims blamed

The three main enemies of elites are Muslims, Communists and Christians. The common factor is all these three do not accept the supremacy of Brahmins.

Hindutvawadi-s like Golwalkar and others are prompt in blaming the British for creating divisive tendencies among Indians. But they forget that seeds of these tendencies were sown by them only in their Brahminic culture.

One example should suffice. During the famine of Pune in 1803 – 1804, the Peshava Bajirao II, only helped the Brahmin population and refused to accept the responsibility of non-Brahmins even on humanitarian grounds. It was the British and Parsees of Bombay who helped them. Decision of Bajirao II to ignore non-Brahmins was according to Brahminic *Shastras*, as the Brahmins must be fed first, say the *Shastras*.

When today RSS talks of revival *Chaturvarnya* and glory of Hindu culture, this history comes forward. There we find no reference to the social or economic justice for the Non-Brahmins. On the contrary, the picture appears to confirm that **the 'Hindu' culture means the preservation of supremacy of Brahmins.**

Even then the likes of Sawarkar blame Ambedkar for praising and paying tributes to the Mahar (SC) soldiers in the British army and for visiting Koregaon Pillar, erected in honour of them, who fought bravely with strength of five hundred against thirty thousand Peshava soldiers, and lost their lives while defeating the Peshava army in Koregaon Battle (1818), which brought down Peshava rule in 1820.

Legacy of Buddhism

Dr. Ambedkar has mentioned that the Buddha's teachings were rational that he differentiated the killing into '**will** to kill' and '**need** to kill'. This explains the rational thinking of the Buddha.

The spread and development into Japanese and Chinese of the martial arts have their origin in martial arts in Buddhist South India.

Those Eventful Days of the Great Mass Conversions

Dr. Ambedkar's Conversion

Most of the events are well known and well documented. I mention only those facts, which I personally experienced and are not well outside.

"It was not within my capacity to be born in a particular religion. But though I was born as Hindu, I will not die as a Hindu." This was the declaration of Dr. Ambedkar made by him as early as 1935, at Yeola in Nashik district in Maharashtra. He made this declaration after his disillusion of Hindu reforms due to experiences with the *Satyagraha* at Mahad to drink water from the public lake, burning of *Manusmruti*, Kalaram Temple *Satyagraha* for temple entry and treacherous behaviour of Gandhi at Round Table Conference and subsequent coercive Poona Pact. There is already a vast literature available on these subjects. After this declaration, he convened a conference in Bombay, wherein he delivered a speech, which goes by the name of '*Mukti kon pathe*?' 'what way emancipation?' which is available verbatim in his volumes [W&S Vol. 17, Part 3, p. 113], describing the need for religious conversion for the lowered castes. His inclination was towards Buddhism from the beginning, but from 1950 or so, it became clear that he would adopt Buddhism and finally he decided to adopt Buddhism in 1956.

Background Preparations

After global celebration of 2500 years of Buddha Jayanti, it had become clear, early in 1956, that conversion to Buddhism will take place that year, either at Sarnath, Kanpur or Bombay. But about three months in advance, Babasaheb decided Nagpur as the venue, and 14th October – Dasera day – as date. When the news reached Nagpur, the whole atmosphere got charged with enthusiasm and every leader and worker, big and small, started earnestly for the preparation. There were public meetings at all *moholla-s* (wards) in Nagpur. S.M. Meshram, Babu Hardas Awale and Bar. Rajabhau Khobaragade were the main political leaders of Nagpur, who started organising public opinion for conversion. The whole atmosphere was charged with a feeling of enthusiasm, vigor, excitement, and zeal about the coming event. Dadasaheb Gaikwad made two or three trips to Chandrapur to supervise preparations of Conversion here. I also visited Chandrapur more frequently.

I was hectically preparing for my final year MBBS exam in Nagpur in Nov./ Dec. We as students decided to hold the Students' Convention on this occasion, in the Dhanwate Chambers, which was near Hotel Shyam, where Babasaheb was scheduled to stay.

Ambedkar's Conception of Buddhism

When asked about which vehicle of Buddhism he is propagating, he remarked that he would preach the original teachings of the Buddha. What are the differences from traditional Buddhism? One is about Siddhartha's renouncement. Ambedkar believes traditional story of 'diseased, old man, dead man, hermit' etc. could not be the real cause. Second he doubted 'suffering' to be the main of 'four noble truths'. Third was his conception of *karma* and rebirth not conforming to traditional views and lastly he believed the Buddha created '*Bhikku*' not as a priest or a superman but as a friend, philosopher and guide for the laymen, and hence he liked the standing Buddha rather than one in meditation.

The Great Mass Conversion at Nagpur

All the events about the Grand Conversion ceremony are well recorded. The crowd was more than the present "*Diksha Bhoomi*" could accommodate. The area beyond the road, where today there are big buildings was a vacant plot of land. The Deputy Mayor being an Ambedkarite the whole labour gangs of Corporation along with volunteers of "Samta Sainik Dal" (SSD - Volunteer Corps for Equality) were busy in uprooting small shrubs and clearing and cleaning the wasteland into a vast ground for the function. The stage was huge, and protected from all sides. By the side, there was a road built right from the main street to the stage for Babasaheb's car and protected by bamboo matting from both sides. Excellent arrangement was for sound projection. Stage of shape of Sanchi stupa was erected and covered with white cloth. All the stalls of eatables and free meals were arranged beyond the streets by various organisations.

It was ordained that those who wish to get converted, must come in white apparel, but in the markets all white cloth was exhausted, and then it had to be announced that, any clean clothes of any colour would do. Similarly, it was declared that all those wishing to be converted should enroll themselves in Godbole's office. The rush was so much that in spite of hundreds of volunteers for record keeping, the arrangement broke down. That was the magnitude of the numbers. A conservative estimate was half a million people, who poured down from all directions with whatever conveyances they could get. Many walked down with meals packed for three days, dried pieces of homemade *jaur* bread and an onion or two.

The ceremony of conversion and Babasaheb's historical speech are well documented. I mention only salient points. It was Maha Thera Bhikku Chandramani, the most senior Buddhist monk in the country, who gave *Diksha* to Dr. Ambedkar. He was of Burmese origin but was resident in India for forty odd years. After his own conversion, Babasaheb converted all the rest of half a million people by *trisaran*, *panchasila*, and '22 vows'. This was a historical event in more ways than one. Never in history half a million were converted to any religion at one time, and never had conversion been effected by a lay Buddhist, and never ever the Hindu gods and goddesses were denounced by '22 vows' which became the inseparable part of 'rite' of conversion to Buddhism in India, and never before it was declared that all and every Buddhist lay person was authorised to convert other willing person. There used to be rite of '*upasampada'* for conversion as a Bhikku, but for Lay Buddhist there was traditionally no rite. Ambedkar started this, as he believed one of reasons of disappearance of Buddhism from India was absence of such a rite.

Speech of Dharmantar

It is well documented. He explained Nagpur was selected, as this was the land of Nagas, the great patrons of Buddhism, and we are the progeny of a single Naga warrior Takshak, who was saved from Brahminic genocide of Nagas in '*naga satra'*. He refuted all Brahminic criticism against his conversion. A clear reference to Marx, he said that man cannot live on bread alone and stressed the importance of self-respect more than mundane pleasures. If the Hindu religion had allowed lowered castes to bear arms, India would never have suffered political slavery, he averred. He explained how Buddhism gives hope of progress, which is absent in Hinduism. He asked his followers to be ready to sacrifice for Buddhism; at the same time he declared that he did not want blind followers. He declared that he was feeling relieved from the "Hell of Hinduism".

Students Convention

As the President of Students' organisation, I led a deputation to Dr. Babasaheb to ask for his blessings for Students' Convention and congratulate him on the occasion. SSD volunteers led us to a small hall on the second floor of Hotel Shyam after a strong security check.

As we stood in the corner, Dadasaheb Gaikwad told Babasaheb that some students have come to see him. Babasaheb thundered as to what we wanted. Everybody kept mum. Nobody dared to utter a word. After a long pause, I dared to stammer out that we came to congratulate him, and we wanted his blessings. He said something soothing and Adv. S.M. Meshram said, "Do you students wish to ask Babasaheb, anything?" I gathered courage to say, "Babasaheb! We are worried about our scholarships". No sooner, I uttered these words, Babasaheb started talking loudly, everybody around, and there would be about hundred people around, all sat down at once on the floor, as Babasaheb kept on talking. He said how, we students have gone lazy, are reluctant to study and avoid hard work. In spite of facilities we don't do exams. well, and the lot. Lastly, he consoled us, the facilities, he got for us was his effort and he will snatch it again for us, and that the scholarships are in his pocket. After about ten minutes' speech, it was time for us to leave. Students' Convention was well attended, there were more people than the hall could accommodate. Main speakers were Adv. S.M. Meshram and Dadasaheb Gaikwad. Many resolutions were passed and all that, but later, the police had come to our hostels repeatedly and wanted to know more and more details, which we had none.

Civic Reception

More important was Babasaheb's speech at the Civic Reception given by the Nagpur Municipal Corporation. After explaining the working of democracy in Parliament, he told the stunned gathering that there are many lady members of Parliament, who talk of Prime Minister Nehru as "*aamche he*, *aamche te*", the mode of addressing used, in Maharashtra, by women only while talking about their husbands. He said that he was ashamed that there were some Maharashtrian lady members among them. He said, he tried to apprise Prime Minister Nehru about this, but Nehru couldn't care less. All this obviously was a severe criticism about Nehru, but the organisations of upper castes women came down heavily on Ambedkar the next day in Newspapers, curiously enough not for criticising Nehru, but for defaming womanhood of Maharashtra. Such was the mentality of Press and Media in twisting the facts to suit their purpose, those days not really much different from today, was it?

Tea Party at Shyam Hotel

I was then 24 years old student and perhaps the youngest in the tea-party and perhaps the only person living, who were present in the tea-party. In the night there was a "Tea Party", only meant for senior workers of the Party from all over India, and entry was by passes. I was given three passes for students. I, along with our secretary Nagdeote, and a senior Ph.D. student from Hindi speaking area, attended. Babu Hardas Awale gave an introductory speech as usual in Hindi, and requested Babasaheb to address the gathering of, may be fifty or sixty people sitting around tables with the snacks served. I had heard Babasaheb on many occasions before, but that was the first time, I was hearing him talk in fluent Hindi. The speech though brief had many new points, and very scanty reports of this speech are available. He said, that we all cared more for politics than social and religious change. He had achieved everything in his life for himself. There was nothing more to be achieved for himself, "except perhaps the post of Prime Minister", among cheers, he declared. But he was worried for all of us, as we keep on fighting amongst ourselves. He said, we were not used to work with people of other castes. Though the "Scheduled Castes Federation" (SCF) would be in existence for some more time and though Buddhists, we could still be members of it, as he had already made provisions in Constitution of SCF for "sympathizers", it was time we change our ways and start learning to work together with other castes. He was already in touch with other leaders like R.M. Lohia, N.G. Gore, Madhu Limaye, P.K. Atre, S.M. Joshi and others and he had prepared the Constitution of new party, which would be launched soon. He gave a lot of stress on mixing with the people of democratic thoughts, belonging to other castes. It is rather unfortunate, that this aspect of his speech, is totally neglected by the next generation of leaders, our predecessors. When next year in 1957, Republican Party of India was formed, there was not one single member of other castes.

Dattopant Thengadi in this Private Meeting

What kills me most, about this tea party, is that Dattopant Thengadi, one of the top most leaders of RSS, says in his book, '*samrasate shivay samata ashakya'*, p. 9, published by '*bhartiya vichar sadhana prakshan*' of Pune, (year not mentioned), that he was present in this meeting as a "boy serving snacks dishes". The meeting was so select and admission was by passes and everybody had to be scrutinised on entry, how could a strong activist of RSS be allowed entry to such a meeting? Was there a slip in security by SSD? Was Dattopant a regular employee of Hotel Shyam and just happened to be there around Dr. Ambedkar, or was he planted there to spy on Ambedkar, is a question I cannot find any answer to. I honestly do not think he was a regular employee of the Hotel. Thengadi himself has not clarified, nor anybody else did, to the best of my knowledge. Anyway, it throws ample light on the working of RSS and its long time planning.

Chandrapur Mass Conversion

A *sramner* Sumedh wrote a book, wherein he raised three allegations against this mass conversion at Chandrapur that (*i*) it was not prearranged, (*ii*) Babasaheb was brought by wrong road and hence had to suffer and (*iii*) Conversion was carried out not by Babasaheb but by someone else. All these are wrong allegations, which I refuted many times from public platform and in writings, including functions on *Diksha-Bhumi*. The Conversion ceremony was arranged well in advance, there was no other road then and Babasaheb himself conducted ceremony of *Diksha*. It is pity the *sramner* could not even understand that a function of such a magnitude of 300,000 people cannot be arranged at the eleventh hour without preplanning. Reception Committee was formed in meeting of all leaders from all over the district in town hall, funds were collected and all arrangements were made, and enthusiasm was so great that there was no shortage of funds.

On 16th October, 1956, we left by morning passenger train from Nagpur for Chandrapur, in an uncontrollable crowd. Babasaheb was to come by Car via Umerd, Nagbhid and Mul. The present road direct from Nagpur to Chandrapur via Jam was not ready then. It opened for traffic in 1962.

When I reached the stage around 3 p.m., there were hardly any leaders on the stage, and huge ground was over-flooding with people. Myself, another student Raipure and Adv. Umre managed the stage for three hours, with local leaders speaking. The news came that Babasaheb has reached Mul (about 35 km. from Chandrapur) and is having rest because of tiredness of journey, thanks to the worst roads of that time, and all the leaders on the stage left for Mul, leaving three of us students to manage and pacify the crowds, and I must say, we did manage it rather magnificently, come to think of it now.

It was sunset, the stage was well lit, and some one was speaking on the mike. There was commotion on the road, I took charge of mike and started slogan shouting, Babasaheb was approaching after a long wait. He climbed the stage and sat on the sofa there, with Mrs. Ambedkar. Some leader started welcome speech. Babasaheb was too tired and now he got irritated due to green small insects, which appear around lights in that season. He ordered the light to be switched off. I was right behind the sofa. I shouted at the electrician to switch off the light shining on face of Babasaheb. The electrician did switch off. But the wiring was such, not only one tube light but nearly half of the stage where Babasaheb was sitting, went into darkness, though the other half was well lit. In that partial darkness, Babasaheb asked the speaker to stop, took to mike and asked everybody to rise who wish to get converted and started "*namo tassa bhagvato*", *trisaran, panchsheela* and administered "*22 vows*". Somebody held a lighted bulb in front of him to read the vows. Then he said that all he wanted to talk was talked at Nagpur, advised all to read that from newspapers, and climbed down the stage and started walking back to car waiting on the road. All was over within five minutes, and the leaders who were gradually coming to stage rushed back behind him to the Circuit House, just nearby. Again the stage was vacant and I found myself shouting slogans over the dispersing crowds.

Well, everybody was very unhappy, that he could not hear the words of Babasaheb, after hours or days of waiting. With heavy heart, everyone dispersed, only to gather around the Circuit House, which was surrounded by heavy security of SSD volunteers there were no police either at Nagpur or at Chandrapur just to get a glimpse or a hear a word of Babasaheb.

We requested Bar. Rajabhau, and Dadasaheb to arrange to bring Babasaheb out for a few minutes in Verandah. But Mrs. Ambedkar would not agree, neither she would let any body approach Babasaheb. Only Dadasaheb Gaikwad could enter his suite, for all those 36 hours he stayed there. Dadasaheb Gaikwad decided that Babasaheb needed a day's rest before his journey, so morning journey was off.

The Day after Conversion

The next day started with great expectation. There was constant flow of people coming and going, but Mrs. Ambedkar allowed no entry to Babasaheb's suite except for Dadasaheb Gaikwad. A plan was conceived to send Mrs. Ambedkar out for "shopping" and for giving her presents and ultimately she departed from the scene at about 5 p.m. After she left, Dadasaheb brought Babasaheb to verandah. It was just getting dusky. There were lights in veranda, but none outside, but a pleasant moonlight around. There was no loud speaker. As soon as the word spread that Babasaheb is sitting outside, gradually within minutes and in pin drop silence a crowd of thousands gathered and squatted in the road in front of verandah and a garden outside. Then there was a session of about two hours, when Babasaheb was talking and all of us listening, with an intermittent question being asked by Dadasaheb for motivating him to talk.

He talked of his childhood. How he was moving around in a "langoti" (loin cloth) and saluting a padre always going by the locality, how they were sleeping on the ground within an island made of earth around and filling it with water so that the bed bugs could not enter. He talked how he stole some money and ran away from home, when his father once expressed concern what would happen to him as his father married again. He never returned back till last moment of his father.

Many questions about Buddhism, and its practices and new party were put to him. For all those questions, he said he would make everything clear in a meeting scheduled in mid-December in Bombay. Unfortunately that day never arose. There were only two mass conversions effected by him at Nagpur and Chandrapur.

Around 8 p.m., Mrs. Savita Ambedkar came back, started scolding everybody, and took Babasaheb inside, that was the last time I saw him, so did many like me. But the people were happy that they could hear their Messiah and departed home happily. Next morning Babasaheb left Chandrapur by Grand Trunk Express at about 5 a.m.

I went back to Nagpur, got busy in studies, and gave my last paper of final MBBS examination, and came out of the hall at 1 p.m., only to be told the tragedy of demise of our Messiah on 6th of December 1956.

Conversion and afterwards

The immediate effects of conversion were dramatic. The whole community seemed united. Even a few days before conversion ceremony, when Babu Hardas Awale announced in a public meeting that "*mangal sutra*" (black beaded wedding necklace considered sacred by married Hindu women) is a symbol of slavery of women a tenet opposed to Buddhism about 500 women removed their *mangal sutras* then and there.

There was an impression among Buddhist converts, that eating of meat is not permitted and many who reared hens, left them to go anywhere they liked and sold off their goats for Rs. ten or so, and stopped eating meat. But it has again started, as it became known that Buddhism never prevented meat eating and even Bhikkus were allowed to eat certain types of meat.

There were images of Hindu gods of all descriptions in the houses of Buddhists, they were all thrown away in wells, lakes, and rivers, some times in processions all over the villages. People stopped going to Hindu pilgrimages like "Mahadeva".

As Babasaheb had said, the marriages should be performed without expenses, on simple white clothes. So all the bands, *barat-s* (processions), and "*bashing-s*" (headgear for marriage) were discarded. A bridegroom in a marriage procession could not be pointed out from others. Unfortunately gusto could not be maintained, again the expensive marriages by taking loans and all that started later. The band has disappeared but loudspeaker has taken its place. All things have now come back, as it was in Hinduism, including expensive marriages, dinners and wasteful ceremonies. Even system of dowry in some form or other is making appearance a system never existed even before conversion.

Many mass conversion ceremonies took place later all over the place, but only the "*Mahars*" got converted in Maharashtra. There were some followers of Ambedkar from other SC communities, who got converted at different places. It was reported by people like Herlekar, that those people faced troubles in getting their daughters married among the erstwhile "Mahars". The process of conversion went on for half century and recent conversions by other castes have raised the hopes that Buddhism in India would not become just another caste of Hinduism. It was the dream of Ambedkar that he will convert whole of India to Buddhism. Recently, after 50 years, people like Laxman Mane, who belong to caste other than Mahars, conducted some mass conversions to Buddhism. This has raised the hope that some day India will definitely become Buddhist again.

The Famous 22 Vows

1. I shall have no faith in Brahma, Vishnu and Mahesh nor shall I worship them.
2. I shall have no faith in Rama and Krishna who are believed to be incarnation of God nor shall I worship them.
3. I shall have no faith in 'Gauri', Ganapati and other gods and goddesses of Hindus nor shall I worship them.
4. I do not believe in the incarnation of God.
5. I do not and shall not believe that Lord Buddha was the incarnation of Vishnu. I believe this to be sheer madness and false propaganda.
6. I shall not perform 'Shraddha' (Brahminic funeral rites) nor shall I give 'pind-dan' (funeral oblations of food to the dead).
7. I shall not act in a manner violating the principles and teachings of the Buddha.
8. I shall not allow any ceremonies to be performed by Brahmins.
9. I shall believe in the equality of man.
10. I shall endeavour to establish equality.
11. I shall follow the 'noble eightfold path' of the Buddha.
12. I shall follow the 'paramitas' prescribed by the Buddha.
13. I shall have compassion and loving kindness for all living beings and protect them.
14. I shall not steal.
15. I shall not tell lies.

16. I shall not commit carnal sins.
17. I shall not take intoxicants like liquor, drugs etc.
18. I shall endeavour to follow the noble eightfold path and practise compassion and loving kindness in every day life.
19. I renounce Hinduism, which is harmful for humanity and impedes the advancement and development of humanity because it is based on inequality, and adopt Buddhism as my religion.
20. I firmly believe the Dhamma of the Buddha is the only true religion.
21. I believe that I am having a re-birth.
22. I solemnly declare and affirm that I shall hereafter lead my life according to the principles and teachings of the Buddha and his Dhamma.

Clarification

These 22 vows, especially prepared by him for conversion and which are used now in all conversions, now form the main principles of guidance for the Indian Buddhists. Ambedkar achieved three things thereby.

(*i*) It clarified that adopting Buddhism means denouncing Hinduism

(*ii*) It clarified that even Lay Buddhists were elements of Buddhist society and

(*iii*) It clarified that even Lay Buddhist have to follow the tenets of Buddhism. They struck a blow at the roots of Hindu beliefs and practices, and protect Indian Buddhism from confusion and contradictions caused by Brahmanism and wasteful expenditure.

Sawarkar on Babasaheb's Conversion

Mass Conversion of Dalits by Dr. Ambedkar in 1956

Savarkar's reaction to the Mass Conversion of Dalits by Dr. Ambedkar in 1956 is not widely known outside Marathi speaking people. He wrote in the "*Kesari*" of 30 October 1956, (pp.17-18), an article, bitterly criticising Ambedkar in venomous language. [Khairmode: Vol.12, p. 81 ff.] Ignoring the polemics of *Hindutva*, the main points of his article are worth remembering by the followers of Ambedkar.

He mentions the number of people embracing Buddhism was hardly one lakh, for which he was not surprised, because of the propaganda in "*Maharwadas*" of Maharashtra for last eight years and the direct indirect financial help from rulers like Nehru, and help from foreign Buddhists, and as this help would continue in future, Savarkar was afraid that the number within ten years could reach a million.

Worry not - but think

When Buddha himself and Asoka could not make any dent in "*Sanatan-dharma*", what is an Ambedkar? But such movements, being disruptive and anti-national, we must prevent them from the beginning.

No Obligations

That Ambedkar did not become Christian or Muslim, is no obligation on us. Ambedkar had threatened to embrace Islam, Christianity or Sikhism for many years. Now that he hankers after saying that Buddhism is the greatest religion in the world, did he not know this, that time? It was a sign of immature intellect or misguiding declarations. Ambedkar knew the untouchability practiced in Islam, Christianity and Sikhism. And also because of some other internal reasons, the bargain could not be struck that time. Therefore, he could not embrace these religions and not because of his soft feelings about Hindus, as some Hindu leaders seem to think.

It is Shameless for the Hindus to Admire the "Batage"

(*Batge* is a derogatory word for Converts from Hinduism, having connotations of 'polluted')

For last many years Ambedkar and his followers are showering such abuses in dirty language against Hindu religious books, practices, gods and customs. No other people than the tolerant Hindus would have tolerated such words. They have no guts to criticise the other religions for similar practices. Excepting a few sayings of the Buddha, which were probably borrowed from Hindu sages, the rest of Buddhist books are full of same rubbish like any other religion.

Ambedkar's Vow is Broken

He said he would not die as a Hindu. His vow is already broken, as he will have to die within Hinduism. His jump outside the sphere of Hinduism has fallen within the boundary of Hinduism. As a Hindu is one whose father-land and holy-land (*pitru-bhu* and *punya-bhu*) is Bharat, Ambedkar will live and die as a Hindu, irrespective of his repeatedly denying it, and irrespective of his saying that he is denouncing Hinduism, and irrespective of including vows in conversion ceremony condemning Hindu religion, like an arrogant child denying his own parentage. It is not possible for him to break the bondage of Hindutva and also the fetters of Untouchability will not break just by embracing Buddhism.

Untouchability is dying out in Indian cities, and would gradually disappear in villages. Just by embracing Buddhism, their Untouchability has not been reduced a bit, and they would not be accepted as 'touchable' by the 'touchable' Hindus in villages. On the other hand, they would be treated as outsiders. Therefore, the leaders like Jagjivanram, Tapase, Kajrolkar, Rajbhoj etc. do not wish to be entrapped in this net and fall in the pit of Conversion.

A Warning! - Boudhasthan and Naga Kingdoms

Ambedkar embraced Buddhism, not because of any love for it, but, in a dark corner of his mind, there is one more treacherous, anti-national, political ambition. And that is, to establish an Independent "Boudha Sthan", an Independent "Naga Sthan", by uniting all the divisive split forces, like Zarkhand, if he could raise enough strength of Buddhists under his religious dominance. This is evident from the speeches of his followers and his own writings. So let not Hindus admire this conversion. Now that, they are bringing back the digged out bones of Buddha from foreign lands and carry these reverently on their head, we must analyse the increasing influence of Buddhism from religious and political situation angle, and read again the ancient history from Yavana, Shaka, Kushana, Pallava and Huna invasions to Muslim conquest, and how Indian Buddhists have joined hands with these invaders. It is better to be safe than sorry and not test the poison by drinking it.

Depicting the Buddha as Hindu God

A news item in *Vrutratna Samrat*, 12.6.2008, reports that an animation film, '*Dashavatar*', produced in Pune depicted the Buddha as *avatar* of Vishnu, a Brahminic god. When some Dalit activists protested, the management apologised in writing and arranged to remove that part from the film.

The moot point is what made the *Manuvadi* producers to depict such a scene in the first place. It could not be just ignorance. Everybody knows that the Buddha was a historic figure and not imaginary Puranic one. The depiction must be purposeful to depict the Buddha as a Hindu god.

The tendency is not new. Ever since, Dr. Ambedkar converted his followers to Buddhism in 1956, it is seen that, somehow the *Manuvadi-s* try to denigrate the Buddha. About fifteen years back VHP had organised many conferences, wherein Buddha was depicted as an *avatar* of Hindu god. The unfortunate part of it was that even Dalai Lama and *Vippasana Guru* Goenka also attended these conferences, a fact highly condemned by Ambedkarite Buddhists. Dalai Lama and Goenka could not be the representatives of the Indian Buddhists. However, a three-point agreement was arrived at between Goenka and Shankaracharya. One of the conditions was not to indulge in activities denigrating each other's gods. It seems nobody cares for the word of Shankaracharya and such acts of depicting the Buddha as an *avatar* and also in other derogatory ways goes on.

• • •

17

Dalits and Planning Commission

A Letter to Member of Planning Commission

We reproduce a letter, with slight modification, written by us to Dr. John Dayal. He replied that he would place it, as it is, in front of the Planning Commission. Letter is self-explanatory.

Ideas in what we want in 12th Five Year Plan

Thursday, June 30, 2011

Dr. John Dayal,

John.dayal@gmail.com

finicy@gmail.com

Dear sir,

This refers to your letter published in '*Dalit Voice*', dated 1-15 July 2011, received just today. As you have put the deadline as 1st July, I have to write this letter extempore. But I could elaborate any point in detail later, if necessary.

A Country of Castes and Corruption

This is an illiterate country of castes and corruption with leaders looking backward towards Middle Ages. Some progress was brought in by the British, but they came in too late and left too early. Even then as luck would prevail, we got Dr. Ambedkar, the '*Bharat Bhagya Vidhata*', who tried to set the things right against a mountain of opposition. His mission is still left unfinished. Let us hope the people like you could bring in some changes.

Illiteracy and Work of Christian Missions

Whole country is illiterate. Only two states, Kerala and Northeast states are progressed. That is due to the efforts of Christian Missionaries; Kudos for them. But these days, they are neglecting children of SC/ST/OBCs and even of the poor Christians. How many doctors, lawyers, engineers and professors are found among Christians?

Even the Christian hospitals and colleges are manned by others. Why? It is because they are only educating the children of Brahminists, who after growing, one day, will bite them back as a serpent, and try to whisk them away out of the country. This was warned by V.T. Rajshekhar of DV, about twenty years back, in '*Unchristian side of Christian church*'. Does not seem to have much effect. The leaders of church are looking after themselves, selling mission property left by the British for self-gain and neglecting even evangelical work. Sorry to point this out, a real Ambedkarite is pained at this state of affairs.

Even today there are good mission hospitals all over the country, (I worked for some time in one of them) but they are languishing for want of good leadership. Many hospitals are there, but only two Medical Colleges, Ludhiana and Vellore, to the best of my knowledge. Why? Religious bias of political authorities, caste discrimination or just plain simple lethargy of the dioceses? You know better.

How to Resolve Oil Crisis?

We are fighting for it but doing not much fundamentally. I suggest:

(a) Stop all spending on domestic Air traffic and Highway roads and concentrate more on Railways. May be it takes longer gestation and heavy investment, but is profitable in long run. Only roads to be newly built should be the ones connecting villages to nearby small towns. All villages should be connected with all weather twelve months motorable trafficking tar roads.

(b) They built new highway from Pune to Mumbai a few years back. It would have been more prudent to put new railway line instead.

(c) China is starting bullet trains at the speed of three hundred kilometers per hour; why can't we? That would reduce dependence on oil to a great extent and will also boost employment. There is nothing like railway for employment generation–the main problem of India. That would also reduce the demand for more air traffic.

(d) At least four metros Mumbai, Delhi, Kolkata and Chennai be connected peripherally and centrally Delhi-Chennai and Kolkata-Mumbai via Nagpur. These minimum lines should be considered for Bullet trains. Six short distance Bullet Trains are being contemplated for daily commuters near metros. No sir. We require bullet trains for long distances as first priority, to reduce dependence on air traffic.

(e) One more railway line (not bullet) should be considered. This is rather urgent to alleviate Naxal problem. Railway from Macherial in Telangana passing through the Naxal areas of Maharashtra to Dantewada in Chhattisgarh through Angul in Orissa to connect to Ranchi, is necessary. This would solve a lot many problems.

(f) Funding for railway lines could be from internal accruals by increasing the Rail fares and freights by hundred per cent, from central and state budgets and supplemented, if necessary, by issuing long term bonds with attractive interest rates. Rail fares are not increased for last may be ten years and are only about 20 per cent of road transport tariffs.

(g) The number of trains on existing permanent way can be tripled or even quadrupled just by installing new signalling system like in metro and local trains and increasing the number of blocks, with no more than one and half kilometers distance. So let us think of signals instead of new lines, wherever possible.

(h) All the two tier cities are bursting on seams and an urgent fast local transport would be necessary for them within next fifty years. Why not start making arrangements for metro trains? Why not start planning right now?

(i) It should be remembered that cost of one passenger aircraft could buy about 800 to 1,000 passenger buses. (No Volvo please) So let the air companies buy less aircrafts and add to their fleet more busses for alleviating traffic blues in metros and on highways. It would also reduce the fuel bill, give more employment and would be more useful to masses than the classes.

(j) There seems to be more demand for trained pilots. Let the government start training colleges for commercial pilots at government cost. Arrange for about 300 to 400 students per year. Let there be reservation for candidates as per norms of the Constitution.

Create more Districts

Some districts need to be split into two, three or even four. Their population or dimension demands that for efficient governance and creation of more employment.

Decide about smaller States Urgently

Many problems among the masses are pending for no reasons. If some people want states of their own, let them have it. Only for the benefit of some rich business and vested interests, such problems are lingering, like Telangana, Vidarbha, Gorakhaland etc. A lot of time, money and goodwill is being spent in these problems.

Land Reforms

This is urgent need. Enforce land ceiling and tenancy laws, with due consideration of SC, ST and religious minority rights. Distribute the surplus lands to these people. Stop all grabbing land by mafias, with or without consents of bureaucrats and/or ministers and politicians.

Punish the guilty, recover back the lands from mafia, demolish all illegal constructions and cancel all SEZs and prevent all land grabbing by vested interests.

Bring in new proper laws for acquiring land from farmers, and pay them according to market rates. Define clearly, what constitutes 'public interests' and keep a strict vigil on implementation.

Land of Adivasis

Land of Adivasis should be treated as special category. If they are sitting over metal ore or forest produce, the ore and produce must belong to them. They should get the benefit of that product. But our business community is not willing even to give them 26 per cent share in the profit. It must be realised that it is the property of Adivasis and they are entitled for hundred per cent profit, why only 26 per cent? If they cannot utilise the ore themselves, government should form their co-operative societies and fund them in initial stages or arrange finance for tapping these resources and bring it to the market and export by financing by state agencies or by long-term bonds at government guarantee.

The iron ore is exported and Indian companies buy and run steel mills in foreign lands. Why can they not open steel mills in India and make use of Indian iron ore?

As a matter of policy, no raw products should be exported. Only finished products should be exported.

Regulate Export of Food Products

There should be no export of tea, coffee, cotton and sugar and cause scarcity and price rise within country. Even fruits and vegetables need not be exported. Enough land should be brought under cultivation for oil seeds so that there remains no need for import of edible oil.

Let us use Coal not Oil

There should be no need to import coal. Our own coal mines should be perfected, environment issues be tackled and coal mafia dealt with. If the quality of coal is inferior more 'washeries' be started and our own coal should be used.

Atomic energy for power generation should not be insisted where people do not want it. The Solar power should be considered even though it may be more expensive.

Gow-rakshan

There should be no ban on cow-slaughter. Complete cleanliness and hygiene and modern technology should be used in Abattoirs. Those who wish not to eat beef let them not eat. But those who wish to have it, for them, clean meat should be made available in hygienic conditions. Even Veer Sawarkar had said cow is a useful animal and so it must be killed for beef. The cows and bullocks rendered useless must be allowed to be sold to abattoirs. The animals dying in gorakshan camps, must be used at least for hide, instead of burying.

Destroy the Villages

Villages proliferate because there is no mechanised farming. If that is brought in, people could manage their farms from a distance of about twenty kilometers or so. You cannot modernise the villages, you have to let them die a natural death and promote people to leave the villages, as Dr. Ambedkar wanted. For that, you have to provide housing and other facilities in cities. Start right now.

Urban Housing

There should be no internal refugees, settling under the bridges or along river paths or gutters, or along railway lines in the cities. They should be provided with affordable houses. It is not all that impossible, if housing and infrastructure activities are brought under a Regulator.

It is essential to scrap the old rent control laws, if you want to increase urban housing.

FSI norms and other building regulations must be strictly followed. Illegal construction should be demolished. The watch should be kept on the constructions, right from the beginning. This should be given to a newly created agency under central government and removed from the local authority or state government.

The housing loans should be provided to the end users and not to the builders, at lower interest rates, and only for smaller tenements, say under 15 lakhs.

Most of the mafia wars in cities, and under-world activities are for land grabbing. Proper implementation of urban land ceiling act must be ensured.

Temple Assets

Plenty of lands are in the name of deities. These should be regulated and *pattas* should be given to actual tillers of these lands, and actual physical tilling by them should be ensured removing all encroachments.

The temple income is more than the revenue of the exchequer of India. All this must be brought under central control and utilised for providing health and educational facilities. Temple income should be properly utilised for the use of masses.

All lands of *babas*, *ammas* etc. should also be brought under same category. All these people should be brought under Income Tax Act and Wealth Tax Act etc.

Appointment of TemplePujari

Appointment of temple *pujari-s* must be by training imparted in a school, where admission is open to all castes and proper reservations provided as per the Constitution. Proper syllabi must be prepared for them and minimum qualification for entry should be a graduate with related subjects. After training they should be given a license to practice as a *pujari*. Even a rickshaw puller needs a license, why not a *pujari*?

Black Money in Foreign Countries

This is not as big a problem, as made out to be. If there is political will, it can be solved with minimal hurt to every one concerned.

Amend Hindu Personal Laws

A lot of Laws need to be amended. Hindu Code by Ambedkar is said to be implemented into new Hindu Laws. This is not true. Main and first point of Hindu Code Bill of Dr. Ambedkar was bringing in **Daybhag** law all over the country instead of Mitakshara. That is not done yet.

Military Services

A lot of posts of officers are vacant in armed forces. Proper admissions to military schools and defense academies should be ensured with proper reservation.

Education

The system of education needs a lot of basic changes. The thrust of government spending should be on higher education and not on elementary education, which could be managed by the society itself. The government spending should be on higher education. It should be made free. The students of even poorer families should able to study in IIMs, IITs, and such other institutions of high repute. They should not be required to take loans; there should be absolutely no fees.

Medical Education

We need about ten times more doctors. The requirement could not be fulfilled because the higher officers in the Indian Medical Council were corrupt. First thing to do is scrap the Indian Medical Council, and let the Central Ministry of Health in Union Government take hold of affairs, let the Ministry submit annual report to the Parliament and let the affairs of the medical education be discussed in Parliament.

It must be realised that crucial requirement in Medical education, in these days of global knowledge, internet access and distant education, is not the money, not the building, not the teachers, not the equipment, not the library, but the Patients. And we have a lot of patients, no dearth of them. Number of MBBS graduates and post graduates admissions to the presently existing colleges can be increased to ten times, **without** lowering the standards of education, if there is political will, at just a **nominal** expenditure. How?

First, nationalise all private medical colleges. Let medical education be the ole responsibility of central government. This will stop all illegal capitation fees n millions of rupees. If not possible to do it, cancel all management quotas for dmission of students and strictly regulate the admissions and fix a moderate uition fees.

Second, increase the admissions for MBBS gradually about twenty per cent very year till it reaches the desired number.

Third, just declare all the Government District Hospitals to be Teaching Hospitals, and attach them to the nearest Medical Colleges. Arrange for Residents, which cost much less than regular doctors.

Fourth, How to get Residents? Allow the Residents to appear for post-graduate xaminations. All the rush of exodus to foreign countries would stop and the esident posts would be filled. The existing medical officers in district hospitals would be enough as teachers. No need to recruit new teachers. No gestation period s required. It can be done immediately without much expense.

Fifth, Change the syllabi and system of education. The two years 11th and 2th classes are wasted because they are common to all disciplines. Let the students ecide at level of tenth whether to go for Mathematics or Biology. There could be admission after tenth to medical colleges and first two years 11th and 12th be taught in Medical Colleges, with strong bias on medicine.

This will allow the next five or four and half years directly in Clinical subjects.

Lastly, After MBBS, give 'Temporary Registration'. And provide them - not Internship but – Residency, which must be mandatory for two years, including one year in Primary Health Centers. 'Full Registration' should be given only after this.

Postgraduate Medical Education

More value should be given to practical degrees of the DNB of National Board, than the regular academic MS, MD etc., stopping their quarrel. DNB standards and disciplines should be drastically revised. All hospitals, government, semi-government, corporate or private and all postgraduate doctors, all over the country, should be declared as recognised venues and recognised teachers, to accept students as residents for appearing for DNB examinations. This one measure would give the country, required number of post-graduate trained and qualified doctors within shortest times, without much expense.

No Degree below MBBS

The plans were announced for starting separate lower grade graduates courses less than MBBS for rural areas. This is not a good idea. Let MBBS be the minimum qualification. Stop all degrees less than this. All allied branches like Homeopathy, Ayurveda etc. must be learned after MBBS. (I was also a Principal in a Homeopathy College for a year)

Malpractices can be Stopped

Malpractices by examiners in examinations in practical and theory can be stopped by creating **honourary** examiners from the **local** senior specialists from the city. Now the examiners are sitting in ivory towers. Let each answer for each question be written in separate answer sheet and sent to two examiners for spot valuation and sending the marks for tabulation directly. Thus, if there are five questions in a paper, each paper would be thus, valued by ten different examiners and chances of undue favour or harassment would be reduced. Similarly, let there be multiple sets of examiners for oral and practical examination. Let each student face about six examiners from among say sixty or so. Let the results be declared on the evening of last day of examination.

Let our Doctors be World Class

There was a time, during early sixties, when I was in England, that Indian doctors (and nurses) were recognised by British Medical Council for immediate registration. Thanks to the authorities in Indian Medical Council, now our doctors have to pass their examination before being allowed to practice there. They even want to test our language ability of English. Situation is same in Australia, Canada and USA.

English is Our National Language

We need to introspect our own teaching methods, linguistic problems and strengthen ourselves so that, any English speaking country could recognise our degrees and our English language abilities. After all what is our national language? It is not Hindi, though declared as such by majority of **one** vote. It is English. All our commerce, law, cinema, TV, athletics, sports and games, literature, poetry, novels, dramas etc. all are thought of in English first. In spite of Brahminist efforts, we are able to retain English at least till now as a national language. Let us preserve that.

Law and Engineering Education

Similar regulations must be enforced in all disciplines of higher education. All subjects must be taught in English medium. All admissions regulated and all private colleges nationalised or brought under strict surveillance of the state. Proper reservations must be maintained as per the norms in the Constitution.

Judiciary Commission

With plethora of cases pending in various courts, we need at least ten times the number of judges. But they do not want to increase the number. They do not want to even fill up the vacant posts. Why? They are afraid that their control over the society, that they are exploitatively enjoying now, would be reduced. It is possible to increase the number of law students ten times within two or three years, if there is political will. Evening classes, night classes, and free admission to open universities, declaring every university as 'open university' etc. are the measures necessary.

China is said to have judges who are not lawyers. We also had, during British regime, the jury system, which our caste-ridden society could not sustain. Let us remember M. K. Gandhi was just a matriculate, when he was called to the bar after Bar-at-Law. But we need not employ non-graduates now, we could now have educated, trained law graduate lawyers in plenty to work as judges, if there is a political will.

Appointments must be made to junior judiciary only through Public Service Commission just like all other UPSC posts like IAS, IPS etc. There should full reservation as per Constitution. Higher judiciary of High Courts ad Supreme Court must be recruited **only** through this cadre, and nor from the bar. Let it be recruited by the college of judges or whatever, but it must be from the regular cadre and not from the bar. Those who want to become judges must come from UPSC or any other new commission created for this purpose, like Railway Service Commission etc. All appointments to the bench from the bar must be stopped.

English Primary and Middle Education

The vernacular regional languages are the medium of instructions in primary schools run by local self-government bodies. As the parents want their children to study in English medium, there are no students. Therefore, the municipal authorities are closing down the schools and using the building for commercial purposes, causing harassment to poor parents. Instead, all these schools must be converted into English medium schools with the **same** teachers, with extra training. May be some additional teachers would be required in some schools. Unwilling teachers could be compulsorily retired or voluntary retired with compensation.

Similar is the situation in middle schools teaching up to 10th class. They also need to be converted to English medium schools gradually. Otherwise there is danger of situation being created where a second grade education to the poor and high grade to the rich would be imparted.

There are three or four boards conducting the examinations of Tenth class. And question of admissions to the Eleventh class is caught in controversy of comparing the standards of each board. Let there be only one board. And that should be CBSE. One and only one board for whole of India under central control with branches in states. Remove all state control over exams.

The subjects of English, elementary computer course and typewriting by touch, without looking at keyboard must be started and made compulsory since beginning.

The 'Junior Colleges' of 11th and 12th Class

Great changes are required in teaching of these classes. The syllabi of these are more difficult than those of graduate classes in many subjects. Most of unnecessary subjects are cramped. Let there be division of medical, engineering and science and arts, commerce and business, civil administration etc. right at the level of tenth class. Now those going to engineering are also taught biology and those going to medical are also taught mathematics. There is urgent need to stop wastage of two years. A candidate passing twelfth class is no better than one passing tenth class for any further studies. Proper lines could be selected after tenth class and these two years be added to the graduate teaching.

Higher Education in Colleges for Graduation and Post Graduation

In subjects of humanities, change of medium to English needs to be brought in gradually. The present teachers are not going to like it. They have paid donations in lakhs to the management for getting the job. Gradually they could be asked to prepare themselves for English medium.

Subjects of mathematics and science are already being taught in English medium. And commerce needs to be changed to English medium. More subjects of business management and similar subjects need to be added.

I am writing all this in detail because the likes of Ramdev Baba are instigating for all higher education to be in regional languages. If that were done, country would drop down to middle ages. Medium of instruction all over the country in all disciplines must be brought under English as soon as possible.

The same applies to postgraduate education. But it might be easier to bring in total English medium in MA classes.

Ph.D. Level Education

There is a lot of confusion about appointment of College Lecturers, Readers, Professors and Principals. Let the rules be declared and let us stick to them. In my opinion, the examinations of NET and SET must be considered more important than M. Phil. and Ph.D. for college teachers. Even in SET English medium should be made compulsory.

There are a lot of malpractices in Ph.D. education. The students are harassed, their labour is exploited and they are turned into sycophants. We see a crowd of Ph.D. students hovering around senior guides in University campuses. The worst part is unless s/he agrees with guide's views, the student is not awarded Ph.D. It was only the creed of the British scholars that they awarded Doctorate to Dr. Ambedkar, even though he criticised the British. Such rare dignified guides are rare in caste India. The students submit thesis according to wishes of guide, get the Ph.D. and then change their thesis and print in changed form. This is a dishonest method of doing research.

But really, **do we need guides?** Students could receive guidance from where ever they can get, in these days of liberalisation, globalisation and privatisation and bestowed with facilities at a touch of button from any corner of the globe with Internet and distant teaching, on-line interviews and on-line examinations and video conferencing.

Ph.D. is made compulsory for post of Principal. Is it necessary? How does a Ph.D. candidate manage college affairs better than a just M.A. or M.Sc. etc.?

Let there be less number of Ph.Ds. But whatever are there, let them be of world class. For this, the theses should only be accepted in English and English alone, by all universities without exception. Let one copy of thesis be sent to universities in Europe, UK, USA, Japan or China or any other country. Other two copies should be sent to scholars of other universities in India, one in south and one in north. And two copies should be sent to guides of same university, but not to the same guide under whom he wrote the thesis. If any one of these external guides wants to interview the student, let **his regular guide also be interviewed**.

Electoral Reforms

Just a few points. How to stop criminal elements entering Assemblies, Councils, and Parliament? If a charge sheet is filed one year before and case is still pending, he should not be allowed to contest. A minor offence, or a politically motivated charge, one year should be considered enough time for him to clear it out.

How to stop corruption? How to recall back? Simple solution. Let there be general elections every **two** or at the most **three** years. Let the elected members face the electorate early before they get time for corrupt practices. No candidate will spend much on such frequent elections, if he has to face electorate and obtain fresh mandate every alternate year. There should be no problem of expenses, by government. Amount of corruption involved is hundred times more than legitimate expenses involved by the state, in election. Other measures to make elections cheaper can be worked out. Out of all the expenses by candidate, expenses of petrol are waste; let us reduce that. All other expenses benefit the poor masses.

Suggestions are made by Brahminist forces to bring in direct election of Prime Minister. It is a venomous idea of Hindutva forces to destroy the Constitution and bring in a **dictator** and fix his term for five years. What they could not do while in power, they want to do it through the means of so-called 'Civil Society', which is neither civil nor society.

Language Policy

There seems to be three-language formula. Exclude regional languages. Only English and **Hindustani** are required. And only two scripts are necessary Roman and Deva-Nagari. These can fulfill all our needs. India, during Ashokan times, was much bigger and still had only two languages, Sanskrit for Brahmins and Prakrit for the masses. And had only one script – *Brahmi* – for centuries, with *Kharshti* on Gandhar region.

Around eleventh century, after the fall of Buddhism, the Brahmins decided to divide the country on linguistic lines and started writing in regional languages, thus converting the dialects among the *Prakrit* into full fledged languages and started adding newer scripts modifying *Brahmi*. They took care that their own language, throughout country, remains same – Sanskrit. This led to present chaos. Some order has been brought by the British but again, when they left, we brought in linguistic provinces. And against the warning by Dr. Ambedkar, the regional languages are made the languages of the Government. This needs to be **reversed**.

The Brahmins are clever. Their conferences are multilingual, but we still indulge in Marathi, Kanada, Telugu etc. conferences; even the Ambedkarites are no exception.

Reservation in Private Industry

Whether you like it or not, the fact remains that the business Corporates are running the country with US guidance. And the things are going to remain same or rather deteriorate further. All said and done, you cannot ensure CSR (Corporate Civil Responsibility). You cannot make reservations in industry, by making it mandatory. They are calling it 'private'. What is private about them? How are they private? They thrive on public capital, funds, banks, land, water, electric power, manpower all from the public resources, and still like to call it 'private' industry, and you can do nothing about it.

So what is the solution? You have to give them incentives and tax relieves to ensure that they give reservations as per constitution. My suggestion is as follows The Corporate Tax was once 55 per cent; now it is around 30 per cent. Raise it back to 55 per cent and give concession of 20 per cent to those who have implemented effective reservation for SC, ST, OBC and minorities.

Wealth Tax and Estate Duty

The person, who removed Estate Duty and made Wealth Tax ineffective in India, has done a great disservice to the masses. Bring them back. It would go a long way in bringing back an egalitarian society by reducing the gap between the poor and the rich.

These are some ideas coming to my mind. May be there should be debates over all such issues.

Thanks!

• • •

18

Dalits Tomorrow

Let us bring in Dayabhag

Hindu Code Bill Sought to Weaken the Caste

Some learned workers in Ambedkarite movement were seen inquiring what was so great in Hindu Code Bill that Babasaheb resigned for it in despair. There was hardly anything of benefit to the Dalits as such in the Hindu Code Bill, they thought.

Why the Brahminical dignitaries opposed it then? This was the question I next asked. Obviously that "they thought it an insult that an untouchable was meddling with their Law", was a very superficial answer. And real reason is that it sought to lessen the grip of Caste System and Brahminic hegemony.

Six Signs of Caste System

M.M. P.V. Kane has described six cardinal signs of caste. They are :

1. Heredity
2. Occupations based on birth
3. Ban on matrimony outside the caste
4. Ban on dining with other castes
5. Hierarchy of the caste and caste colonies, and
6. The Caste Panchayats.

But all these six signs did not appear simultaneously. Sharad Patil tells us that, the first sign of heredity was the only sign seen till second century CE, the other signs being stopped by the caste-less institutions of '*pug*' and '*shreni-s*'. [Sharad Patil : 2003 15- marathi, Vol. 3, p. 15]. Though the Brahminic counter-revolution started around second century, it could not succeed fully over the non-Brahminic camp till the caste system did not stop developing. Kumaril Bhatta, the strongest opponent of Buddhism, in eighth century CE, tells us that most of the Shudras were the worshipers of the Buddha. Thus the caste system hardened gradually for twelve centuries from sixth century BCE to eighth century CE. After the death of Harsha (640 CE), during Rajput age, it got hardened more and more. By the seventh or eighth century CE, the caste system reached its full blown up form, by the time of the rise of the Rajputs. Till the arrival of Turks, Brahmanism pushed all the castes engaged in production into category of 'untouchables'.

The Arrival of Muslims

After the arrival of Muslims around 1000 CE, though the Buddhist cults like '*Dharma-Mangal*' were available, these could not give relief to the masses against the Brahminic caste atrocities, and hence the masses welcomed the Arab and Turk invaders as '*Bodhisattva-s*' and accepted Islam. The invaders went into written agreement with the Hindu feudal lords – *Jamindar-s*, who appeared for the first time after death of Harsha – for collection of revenue and their struggle against the invaders stopped, thus leading to a compromise. The Sufi saints developed rapport with the masses and led a life of cooperation keeping away from Islamic rulers, but they did not lead an agitation against the Caste system, unlike Kabir did. [Sharad Patil : 2003: 87] During the Muslim period, Muslim *Amir-s* above and the Hindu *Jamindar-s* below ruled the masses. Egalitarian Islam could not prevent caste system entering the new Muslim society. Story of Anarkali, real or imaginary, shows discrimination.

The Royal Romance of Prince Salim and Anarkali

We might as well have a peep into story of Anarkali – Urdu "*Pomegranate Blossom*". There is one of the oldest markets in Lahore in Pakistan, dating back to at least 200 years in her name. Some consider the story of the love between Prince Salim, who was later to became Emperor Jahangir (c. 1605-26) and a commoner Anarkali, to be imaginary and has its roots in folklore. They point out that there is not the slightest evidence that Prince Salim ever fell in love with a courtesan and she is nowhere mentioned in Salim's autobiography.

Salim, a spoilt teenager sent away for military training, later proves himself to be a worthy warrior and invited back to the palace. The original name of Anarkali, a dancer at the court of Emperor Akbar, it is said, was Nadira or Sharfunnisa and that Anarkali was her title (*literally meaning pomegranate bud*) given by Akbar for her beauty. The Emperor's eldest son and heir apparent, Salim, fell in love with her. Akbar did not approve of the relation as the dancer was of lowly birth and hence considered not fit to be the queen of the future Emperor of India.

Emperor Akbar deems the romance against the royal dignity. The prince rebels and is sentenced to death. Anarkali steps forward and offers that she be sentenced instead but wished to spend one night with her lover. They have that one night. In the morning, the palace guards take her away and she is sandwiched alive in a brick wall. Some feel that Anarkali was not killed by Akbar but he allowed mother and daughter to leave the empire never to return.

This tale was told in the 1922 Urdu play, Anarkali, written by Syed Imitiaz Ali Taj of Lahore, and was later captured in various plays and films, most important being the most famous Indian epic *Mughal-e Azam* (1960). Some put the twist to the age-old tale, that Anarkali was actually Noor Jehan.

Some admirers of Anarkali, who believe it to be a true story, lament that her tomb situated inside the Lahore Civil Secretariat at the Lower Mall Rd, is not given much importance as a monument of love, unlike Taj Mahal in India or the city of Verona in Italy as a tourist spot, where Romeo and Juliet lived.

Some feel that Anarkali is a story of love of a coward, a lousy person, who could not stand up for his love and married Noor Jehan, the wife of Sher Afghan, murdered on his orders.

Three Pillars of Caste System

It was Rajwade who had observed that the history of '*Chaturvarnya'* is the history of Shudras and women. It must be realised that the caste system perpetuated all these years because it rests on three pillars. These are:

1. Village structure of the country
2. Slavery of the women, and
3. Joint family among the Indians.

Village Structure of the Country

That India is divided into numerous small villages very near to each other is well known. What is not properly understood is that the reason is that the agriculture is based on the bullock cart economy. A farmer cannot till the land at a distance greater than three or four kilometers from his residence and so has to stay within that distance.

If the mechanised farming is used, this need can be obviated and a farmer could easily till the land from a distance of say ten to fifteen kilometers. In that case, the villages could be located at a distance of, say, thirty or forty kilometers from one another and be bigger in size and population and have better amenities. **But then that would be a danger to caste system and to Brahmin supremacy**. The Brahmins know this and therefore propagate the cow culture to the detriment of the Bahujans, who are too gullible to understand the Brahminic designs.

Ambedkar was a strong antagonist of the village culture. He strongly opposed the idea of '*gram swaraj'* of Gandhi. He did not accept the village as the 'autonomous administrative unit' of the Indian society. He denounced villages in strong words calling them the 'greatest calamity'. All villages, he said, are made up of two villages, inside and outside village boundaries, both opposing each other as enemy nations. [W&S 5, pp. 19, 62]

Knowing all the ill effects of village Panchayats and caste councils, Dr. Ambedkar wanted to abolish the village structure. But after independence, the misguided leaders under the Brahminic advice brought in the '*Panchayat Raj'* during Rajiv Gandhi's rule, and strengthened the caste, as most of the times the village *panchayats* are in the hands of leaders of 'caste panchayats' of the dominant caste. Everybody knows the menace of caste panchayats. We have seen the ills of panchayats in recent judgments of, even death sentences awarded and executed by the caste panchayats – *Khap-s* – to the newly wedded couples of mixed marriages.

Emancipation of Women

Woman is the main factor, which sustains the perpetuation of caste system. That was the reason, why the Brahminic Law Books thrust severe restrictions and conditions on women. Dr. Ambedkar has discussed the problem in '*Rise and Fall of Hindu Woman*', and needs no more discussion, as enough has been said by Ambedkarites in later times.

Unless the women are freed from the clutches of financial slavery, their real emancipation cannot be achieved and they cannot stand on their own feet to face the challenges of the Brahminic oppression. Dr. Ambedkar, therefore, provided the women with relief from family atrocities by giving monogamous marriages, easier divorces, and financial relief by provided equal rights in properties of families of father as well as husband. Most of his thoughts are already implemented.

Joint Family Destruction

It is not properly realised that staying away from the parental house for service or otherwise of the couple does not constitute a break up of 'joint family'. Such so-called 'nuclear families' are still part of joint family and are governed by the *Mitakshara* Law, which is in force in practically whole of India. **Dr. Ambedkar wanted that the *Dayabhag* Law should replace it**. This is not achieved as yet. Unfortunately, the Ambedkarites are not fighting for the demand of introduction of Dayabhag Law all over the country. They have not yet realised that this one single measure would give a strong blow to the caste system.

Differences between Mitakshara and Dayabhag Laws

While stating that the main difference after Hindu Code would be 'the abolition of the right by birth and the principle of survivorship and the substitution of the *Dayabhag* for *Mitakshara* in the Mitakshara Provinces, Dr. Ambedkar, in his speech on Hindu code, explained the fundamental differences between two systems of inheritance in *Mitakshara* and *Dayabhag* Law. According to *Mitakshara*, the property of a Hindu is not his individual property. It is property, which belongs to what is called a coparcenary, which consists of father, son, grandson and great grandson (the '*sapinda-s*'). All these people have a birthright in that property and the property on the death of any member of this coparcenary passes by survivorship to the members who remain behind, and does not pass to the heirs of the deceased.

'The Bill, while it does away with coparcenary', Dr. Ambedkar said, 'maintains the joint family'. He further clarified that, 'The only distinction will be that the members of the joints family instead of holding their rights as **joint tenants**, will hold them as **tenants in common**'.

Smt. G. Durgabai, strongly expressing her approval of the Dayabhag law, observed that 'the Dayabhag system has in actual experience proved very satisfactory' and believed that 'the greater prosperity of the people in Bengal and their increasing commercial enterprise is due to a large extent to the Dayabhag system'. Also the Nattukottai Chettiyars in Madras, she believed, progressed mostly because they considered their family members, unlike Brahmin joint families, as partners.

The Hindu Code Bill wanted the *Dayabhag* rule, under which the property was to be held by the heir as his personal property with an absolute right to dispose it of either by gift or by will or any other manner that he chooses. Babasaheb wanted this fundamental change to universalise the law of inheritance by extending the *Dayabhag* rule to whole of India.

The order of succession among the heirs also differs. Under the Mitakshara rule the *agnates* of a deceased are preferred to his *cognates*; under the Dayabhag the basis of heirship is blood relationship to the deceased and not the relationship based on cognatic or agnatic relationship.

Let us remember Babasaheb, in '22 vows', put in restriction on '*pind-daan*', thus killing the concept of '*sapinda*'.

Let us fight to bring in Dayabhag

It is time that the Ambedkarites should stop lamenting about the killing of Hindu Code Bill and devote their attention to the unfinished work of Ambedkar about the Hindu Code Bill. They must demand the implementation of such clauses of Hindu Code Bill, which are not converted into Law yet. One important aspect Babasaheb wanted to introduce in Hindu Law was only *Dayabhag* system instead of *Mitakshara* - all over India. This is his unfulfilled desire.

Let us kill Village Republics

Kings could not Interfere with Caste Panchayats

All the court cases were tried by the caste *panchayats,* only a few appeals were heard by the monarch. And **Even the king could not interfere in their affairs.** Even Ch. Shivaji was asked by *panchayat* of Bhandari Koli caste not to interfare in their caste affairs. The decision of Panchayats was binding and if not obeyed the punishment was excommunication. [Sharad Patil: 2004: 81]

Karl Marks on Villages in India

Rajiv Rawat in an article '*Marx on British Rule in India - Historical and Contemporary perspectives*', quotes Karl Marx showing displeasure about system of Indian villages:
[http://download.tales.com.br/marxismo/Marxismo/rawat,%20rajiv.%20marx%20on%20british%20rule%20in%20india.pdf] (Accessed Saturday, February 04, 2012)

> "These idyllic village-communities, inoffensive though they may appear, had always been the solid foundation of Oriental despotism, that they restrained the human mind within the smallest possible compass, making it the unresisting tool of superstition, enslaving it beneath traditional rules, depriving it of all grandeur and historical energies." [Marx, K. (1853). "The British Rule in India." *New York Daily Tribune*, 25 June 2005]

Rawat comments:

> "What Marx saw as stagnation, Gandhi claimed stability, especially as Marx himself noted that the turmoil of invasions and wars between kingdoms rarely intruded in the internal affairs of the villages that persisted in spite of the chaos often swirling around them. However, what Gandhi saw as the building block of a genuinely free India, Ambedkar dismissed as 'a sink of localism, a den of ignorance, narrow-mindedness and communalism'." [Rawat, *Ibid*]

It is pity that the Indian followers of Marx did not pay any attention to Marx. As is well known, Gandhi considered village republics for *Gram Swaraj*, as the smallest unit of participatory democracy and advocated village economy. Whereas, Dr. Ambedkar always advocated destruction of villages.

Criticising those who wished the new Constitution should have been built upon village Panchayats and District Panchayats, Dr. Ambedkar, during first reading of the draft constitution, observed that, no doubt the village communities have lasted, but had miserable existence and have played no part in the affairs and the destiny of the country, as described by Metcalfe himself who says:

> "Dynasty after dynasty tumbles down. Revolution succeeds to revolution. Hindu, Pathan, Mogul, Maharatha, Sikh, English, are all masters in turn but the village communities remain the same. In times of trouble they arm and fortify: themselves. A hostile army passes through the country. The village communities collect their little, cattle within their walls and let the enemy pass unprovoked."

Ambedkar proceeds:

> "Such is the part the village communities have played in the history of their country. Knowing this, what pride can one feel in them? That they have survived through all vicissitudes may be a fact. But mere survival has no value. The question is on what plane they have survived; surely on a tow, on a selfish level. I hold that these village republics have been the ruination of India. I am therefore surprised that those who condemn Provincialism and communalism should come forward as champions of the village. ..." [Section Three, November 4, 1948 to November 9, 1948]

Panchayats during Constitution Making

The Dalits always knew that the thoughts of Gandhi are always retrograde. Gandhi means opposition to progress, science, technology and machinery. Gandhi means Casteism. The daily life of villages is infested with Casteism; this '*Gram-Rajya*', Gandhi wanted to bring in as '*Ram-Rajya*'.

Dr. Ambedkar had asked the Dalits to leave the villages. He observed about the villages, during debates in the Constituent Assembly:

> "What is the village but a sink of localism, a den of ignorance, narrow-mindedness and communalism? I am glad that the Draft Constitution has discarded the village and adopted individual as its unit" [Jaffrelot: 2005: 110]

Though the Congressmen accepted that a strong centre is essential, they had a tacit love for maintaining their upper caste hegemony into villages. That was their vested interest. They were opposed to the centralisation of power and wanted decentralisation granting of autonomy to the village panchayats.

They brought in an amendment, which read as:

> "Member states of the union of India shall be organised on the uniform basis of groups of village panchayats cooperatively organised *inter se* and functioning and as democratic units within the union." [Jaffrelot: 2005: 110]

Ambedkar opposed the amendment, which was rejected. However, at a later date, he accepted an amendment to section 31, coming under Directive Principles, as:

> "The State shall take steps to organise village panchayats and endow them with such powers and authority as may be necessary to function as units of self-government." [Jaffrelot: 2005: 110]

Let us Stop Arrogance of Panchayats

Touch of Dalits pollutes a fisherman

Akshaya Kumar Sahoo reports in *Asian Age,* Delhi, Mumbai, Kolkata, London. Thursday, 23 July 2009, Bauribandhu, who belongs to the fisherman community, complained that his caste status was affected as the "untouchable" Pana community man Trilochan touched his body during the scuffle on March 25, 2007. Zilla Parishad member, Mr. Satpathy, a Brahmin by caste, prevented Bauribandhu from lodging police complaint and asked him to go back to village, assuring that the matter would be solved by the village committee. Panchayat meeting held in premises Shiv Temple fined Trilochan of Rs. 2,000 towards the medical expenditure of Bauribandhu and Rs. 20,000 for "harming the caste status of the complainant". Trilochan had to sell all his belongings – utensils, goats stored grains and borrow money from the local moneylenders at hefty interest rates, stop sending his children to schools. He also had to discontinue his share-cultivation activity and from a tiny farmer, Trilochan turned into a daily-wage earner.

Bikram Jena of Orissa Dalit Adhikar Manch observes:

> "Trilochan's is a clear case of atrocity and punishable under the Scheduled Castes and Tribes (Prevention of Atrocities) Act, 1989. The committee members, who subjected him to such inhuman behaviour, need to be punished. But nothing such has happened. Despite our repeated requests, the district administration has not yet cared to bring the culprits into the book."

Direct funds to Panchayats Criticised

After 2004 Budget, Arun Bhatia, a well-known retired IAS officer, in a TV interview lamented that the budget proposals have placed money directly in the hands of panchayats ostensibly to avoid misappropriation by middlemen. These panchayats are the symbol of old feudal mentality and are controlled by feudal lords. These are the very same people who are against the progress of the people for whom the money is meant, Bhatia rightly opined.

What Bhatia did not, however, say is that these holders of posts in rural areas are what Khedekar calls '*Bahudhan-s*' among the Bahujans and M.M. Deshmukh puts them under the 'latjee' - the rural kulaks. They are a group against any upliftment of Kunbi-Marathas, for which MSS started Shiva Dharma.

Let us Declare Panchayats Illegal

[http://timesofindia.indiatimes.com/NEWS/City/Jaipur/Police-intervene-to-save-Dalit-woman-from-firman/articleshow/4952971.cms] (Accessed on Monday, January 09, 2012)

Police Intervene to Save Dalit Woman from 'Firman'

Rao Jaswant Singh, TNN 31 August 2009, reports a case from Jaipur: A prompt intervention by the administration and police on Sunday saved a Dalit woman from humiliation and losing her home, following the village panchayat's '*firman*' to blacken her face and throw her out of the village, following a petty dispute. However, they could not save, a couple Subhash and Babita earlier on August 22 from similar humiliation, from the wrath of the villagers when they returned to the village after eloping a few months back.

73rd Amendment

Some ill-informed misguided politicians got this amendment passed to the Constitution and have given legal status to these Panchayats. Some people are pressing for more powers and more funds and some people are asking for more strict implementation. Whereas some saner elements are showing ill-effects and wish to curb the Panchayat Raj. As we know there is likely to be spread of more Casteism, likelihood of Khap and Caste Panchayats getting hold of Panchayat Raj at ground level, the Dalits should try to curb the Panchayat Raj.

Let us Stop Bonded Labour

Everybody is aware that the feudal tendency among the village upper castes has not disappeared as yet. In case any Dalit labours try to flee the village to migrate to a city where they could be industrial workers, the local landlords always prevent them forcibly. They are caught, and brought back to the village to rot in their old lot. Let us try to prevent these landlords.

Let us become Governing Class

Political Power is Master Key

Varied reactions are expressed to Mayavati's political achievements. Some had frivolous views and others – the sworn enemies of BSP – always find faults; all these views should be ignored. But even some true Ambedkarites have expressed doubts, which need healthy discussion. Though not very euphoric about her victory, I am definitely happy about it and I believe the steps taken by her are in right direction. Though not a Social Revolution, it is a Social Transformation, and political power, though not the main aim, must be in the Dalit Agenda.

Did Mayavati Get Power by Bowing Down?

I think not. Mayavati did not use any short cuts. Those who know the working of BSP cadres would know that the BSP workers use the most grass root level and reach all voters. Is Mayavati likely to work under pressure of Brahmins? This is very unlikely, if we remember her past actions. In 2003, she resigned instead of submitting to pressure of giving 80 per cent seats to BJP.

Mayavati not against Buddhism

Let us not forget that Mayavati is not a religious leader, she is a political leader. Those who wish to propagate religion are most welcome to do so. Mayavati has never objected to workers who wish to propagate Buddhism. She had in past helped such workers and would do in future whatever is possible for her to do.

Maharashtra Ignored Kanshiram

Dr. Ambedkar, during the days of conversion in Nagpur had advised his workers to develop mindset to work with other castes in tandem. Unfortunately, that advice was not followed during and after the formation of RPI. When there was the rise of Kanshiram in Northern India with multi-caste party, people in Maharashtra ignored his rise.

Mixing Politics and Religion Defeats both Causes

It is our experience that, if the religious movement and political movement are not kept separate, neither grows and both suffer. Those who want to mix religion and politics do justice neither to religion nor to politics. In spite of this, time and again, some people keep on saying that RPI and Buddha Mahasabha are both the wheels of the same chariot of Ambedkar's movement and they should work in tandem.

I have time and again stressed the danger in keeping both the organisations dependent on each other. I think, they must be both independent of each other and work independently for their own aims. Chariot of Ambedkar has multiple wheels, not only religious and political, others being cultural, educational, economic, co-operative and many more. All must work in cooperation, no doubt, but still be entirely independent.

Hathi nahi Ganesh hai

In 22 vows, Babasaheb asked converts to Buddhism, not to worship *Gauri, Ganpati* etc. Mayavati has asked **her Hindu followers – not Buddhists –** to see their '*ishta devata'* Ganesh in the BSP election symbol elephant. What is wrong in that?

She did not denigrate Buddhism in saying that in any way. **She did not ask her followers, who do not worship Ganesh - like Muslims and Buddhists - to**

worship Ganesh. Otherwise, the Muslims would have been the first to protest. Did any Muslim follower of BSP complain? Then why should the Buddhists?

Those Buddhists who criticise Mayavati on this ground have forgotten that these vows given by Babasaheb are meant for the **Buddhist converts, and not for Hindus**. These were the religious injunctions for the Buddhists. At the same time, he gave orders to the Political leaders of Scheduled Caste Federation, the very next day in Tea Party at Shyam Hotel, to work in cooperation with other caste leaders, and named some leaders, most of whom were Brahmins. That is what Mayavati is doing; so why outcry?

Babasaheb formed his Parties of all castes

Did Babasaheb, anytime, say that Hindus should be kept away from the Ambedkarite political party? As a matter of fact, he always wanted people from all religions to join his political parties, he formed from time to time. His Independent Labour Party was for all castes and religions. Dr. Panjabrao Deshmukh was its president of the province. He had to start Scheduled Castes Federation only under some restrictions put by the British, the history of which is well known to Ambedkarites. But even in that party, there was admission of non-scheduled caste sympathisers. This I know because I heard Babasaheb saying so in Shyam Hotel Tea Party.

When Republican Party of India was envisaged, he told in the speech that, he had already contacted leaders from other political parties like Dr. Ram Manohar Lohia, Pralhad Keshav Atre, S.M. Joshi, Nanasaheb Gore, Madhu Limaye etc. If RPI was formed during his life time, all these dignitaries would have been among the leaders of the party of Dr. Ambedkar, and all the old leaders of SCF, now converted to Buddhist faith, were ordered by him to work along with them. That was the main item in Babasaheb's speech in the Tea Party of Shyam Hotel.

If he were alive for some more time, and if the party of his vision had come in effect during his lifetime, all these Hindu leaders would have been the members of the Babasaheb's Party. Those who object to Mayavati's admitting Brahmins to her Party should try and understand, what the Babasaheb's vision of his Political Party was. Does this mean Babasaheb's views about Buddhism were clouded by political thoughts?

Had Babasaheb shunned Brahmins?

Babasaheb never shunned away the Brahmins. Right from the days of *Manu Smruti Dahan Day* in 1927, till the formation of People's Education Society, Brahmins were associated with him.

One may remember that he had fought a case for Dinkarrao Jawalkar and got him acquitted from charges of defamation of B.G. Tilak. Jawalkar put a condition that, if Babasaheb kept away the Brahmins from his movement, he would join Ambedkar's movement. Babasaheb refused to accept this saying he was against the *Barhmanya* and not against Brahmins.

One would also remember Babasaheb was friendly with the son of B.G. Tilak, and had common interests and organisations.

Even during the earlier days of RPI, I remember entertaining and honouring Brahmin leaders like Sriram Lagu and Anant Kanekar, who were invited for a functions like Ambedkar Jayanti and even in political meetings.

So why object to Mayavati admitting Brahmins to her Party? Let us remember that BSP, right from the times of BAMCEF and DS4 was **never a Dalit Party, it has always been a Bahujan Party**. Now only change is that Brahmins are also admitted, making it a *Sarvajana* Party. Right from the beginning, there were members of all castes and religions in BSP. There were Hindus of all castes - Dalit and non-dalits, Buddhists, Sikhs, Muslims and Christians. If one comprehends 'the concept of Bahujan' expounded by Kanshiram, it is not very difficult to understand the concept of '*sarvajana*' now expanded by Mayavati in the changed environment.

Mayavati and Reservations

Mayavati and Reservations is a subject not understood by many. Those who heard Kanshiram would remember that he never wanted to be beneficiary of Reservations. He always said that we must become the givers of reservations and not the Receivers. That status, of 'giver of reservations', Mayavati has now achieved. For those who have a mindset of becoming the '*picchlaggu*' (in Kanshiram's words), it would be difficult to understand this sentiment. Still she seems to have done a lot in this field.

Social Engineering

The Brahminic authors and journalists have termed this change of political power as "Social Engineering", thereby implying that there is some element of trickery, dishonesty, deception, or deceit and a feeling of impermanence in her victory. This is because they are not digesting her victory. Unfortunately, our own people are also using that term. It is not "Social Engineering" but is "Social Transformation", which has always been the aim of BSP and which was always elucidated by Kanshiram.

Kanshiram, referring to Andhra, had said that giving rice for two rupees a kilo may be social justice, but enabling people to buy rice at market price of Rs. Seven is the Social Transformation, and that BSP always stood for Social Transformation and Economic emancipation of all.

Mayavati is Trying no Different Experiment

Those not acquainted with BSP rhetoric may think what Mayavati is trying to do is a new thing. But there is nothing new in what she is doing, may be just a little more expansion of old strategy. What was taught by Babasaheb was perfected for practical purposes by Kanshiram. And that is only being implemented by Mayavati. Therefore, I have always said that '**Teach Ambedkar to the Hindus and Teach Kanshiram to the Buddhists**'. Let our intelligentsia be not misguided.

A Casteless Society

Mayavati has set new goals for herself - to rule India some day as the Prime Minister and build a "casteless society". This is reported in Brahminic press with some sense of implied ridicule. This is not a new goal. It has **always** been the goal of BSP to capture political power for purposes of effecting **Social Change**, and always declared in public meetings, private sittings and cadre camps. As the Brahminic press never does proper reporting of BSP, the general public may not know this, but those attending Kanshiram's public meetings know it well. Will she succeed in this? It is difficult to say, but surely she is on the right path.

Dr. Ambedkar envisaged the ideal society in the Constitution, to make it a socialistic, democratic, secular republic with equal rights to all varied castes and creeds, religions and regions, varied cultures and taboos, thus forming a casteless society. Mayavati is trying to fulfill that aim. Let us remember that "casteless society" cannot be created by annihilating people of any particular caste. It certainly does not mean society devoid of Brahmins. Let us all try and strengthen her hands instead of expressing any doubts.

Prime Minister of India

Will Mayavati become the Prime Minister of India? Why not? I see no reason why this cannot be accomplished. Not failure but low aim is crime. We must aspire to become the supreme in each and every field. If Devegauda, Gujral, Chandrashekhar (and may be Devilal) could aspire even when their scope was limited, why not Mayavati, who is the leader of an All Indian National Party of **Number Three** stature? Let us not forget that BSP is the National party and not a Dalit party, and not a party of Buddhists alone, it equally a party of Hindus, Sikhs, Muslims and all others, who like to follow Phule, Shahu, Ambedkar, Periyar and ideals and idols of BSP.

Let Us Protect Our Constitution

Warning by Dr. Ambedkar

While presenting the Constitution to the nation, Dr. Ambedkar had said the Constitution is as good or as bad as the people implementing it are serious about it.

A few years ago, when the NPA government had been in power, they had planned to have what they called 'Review' of Constitution. They were very careful NOT to elaborate the changes they want.

Our Constitution is very flexible and can be amended easily, at the same time, the basic structure is rather hard to amend. These people, it seems, wanted to change the basic structure and, make it suitable to Brahminical forces, by bringing in dictatorship in disguise. They wanted to have fixed term of five years, when Government would not change. The wanted Presidential form of Government with all powers concentrated in hands of one person–a virtual Dictator.

Anyway, the calamity has passed away, at least temporarily; thanks to the Supreme Court. It must be realised that for the benefits of the political freedom to reach the common Dalit Bahujan, not only the Constitution needs to be preserved but needs to be implemented in letter and spirit.

The India of the vision of Dr. Ambedkar can only be achieved if the grip of Brahmanism was loosened on the social, economical and political life of the masses. For this accurate implementation of the Constitution is necessary. Political organisations would have to be got ready for this purpose, and those organisations, which like to go against the tenets of the Constitution need to be discouraged.

Followers of Ambedkar had to be careful about this. The people whose forefathers insulted Chatrapati Shivaji, opposed his coronation and ultimately murdered him, are the very same people today who are praising him and projecting him as '*go brahmin pratipalak*' and as Muslim hater. It must be realised that that such anti-national propaganda must be stopped.

Country is being run on the lines of *Manuvadi-s* propagating inequality. Justice to poor and rich is different. Even those who suffer from this kind of slavery are enjoying their slavery.

It is necessary to curb the feeling of regionalism, provincialism and linguistic differences. Those poor people who cannot speak Marathi are being targeted in Mumbai and beaten up and tormented. But the rich builders, businessmen and millionaires are taken on head and ornate. Conditions are created such that the farmers have to commit suicide. Corruption is flourishing and the politics is criminalised.

The preamble of the Constitution is praiseworthy but nobody tries to implement it. About sixty years after the rule of the Constitution, the Rule of Law is yet to be established. All the problems have arisen because it is not implemented.

Since How Long the Problem Existed

We calculate the timing from the transfer of power by the British to the Indian rulers. That means from the white masters to Black Masters. But that was not real time measure.

Unfortunately India is a calendar-less country. Some measure their slavery since the advent of the British. Some measure their slavery since the formation of Islamic empire at Delhi in 1206 CE. Whereas there are some who consider that liberation of Indian masses started from the advent of the British rule.

There are some who consider Muslim rule as a period of Slavery and a Dark period of India. Whereas, there are some like us, who consider Rajput Age as the Dark Age of India.

Some consider the Brahminic Gupta Age, as the '*Golden Age of the Indian History*' however most would agree that Mauryan Period was the '*Golden Age*'.

Unity in Diversity

All agree that this country is divided into numerous castes, languages, mode of life, dress, customs, manners of worship, religions, physical features, climate, topography, etc.

Some people think in spite of all this diversity, there is underlined unity. We think that there is no unity. But it is possible to create unity and this nation can be one. This was the idea of the founding fathers of Constitution and so made the Constitution for "We – the People" of India. Sooner we realise that at present there is no unity, but unity can be created, better it is. We want real unity.

The Pointing Finger of Dr. Ambedkar

Our founding fathers were worried whether the democracy that we are adopting for ourselves would remain or the land would pass again into slavery of others or would pass into dictatorship. While presenting the Constitution to the nation, on 25th November 1949, after explaining various provisions in the constitution, Dr. Ambedkar observed that he was anxious about future of our democracy and explained the dangers and remedies. That day is being celebrated by some Dalit organisations as "Constitution Day". His guidance and warning to the nation is worth remembering for all times. All over India, there are statues of Ambedkar with a pointing finger and Constitution in other hand. That pointing finger is the Warning.

Dictatorship or Democracy

In addition to 'our old enemies in the form of castes and creeds', Ambedkar said, we are going to have many political parties with diverse and opposing political creeds. If the parties place their own creed above country, our independence will be put in jeopardy. This eventuality we must all resolutely guard against. Among cheers, he said, "We must be determined to defend our independence with the last drop of our blood".

He said, India had democratic system in old republics and Buddhist Sanghas. India lost those. He pointed out the danger that, "It is quite possible for this new born democracy to **retain its form but give place to dictatorship** in fact." To prevent such calamity he suggested remedies.

First, we must hold fast to constitutional methods of achieving our social and economic objectives and must abandon the bloody methods of revolution like civil disobedience, non-cooperation and *Satyagraha*. As constitutional methods are now open, there is no justification for these unconstitutional methods, which are "nothing but the Grammar of Anarchy".

Second, we must have no hero-worship, or devotion or *bhakti*. As John Stuart Mill cautioned, we must not lay our liberties at the feet of even a great man, or to trust him with powers, which enable him to subvert our institutions. We could be grateful to great men, but there are limits to gratefulness. We must always remember Irish patriot Daniel O'Connel, who had said: 'no man can be grateful at the cost of his honour, no woman can be grateful at the cost of her chastity and no nation can be grateful at the-cost of its liberty.' Ambedkar averred that Bhakti or hero-worship in Politics is a sure road to degradation and to eventual dictatorship.

Third, we must achieve Social democracy, because Political democracy cannot last unless there lies at the base of it social democracy. The social democracy means, a way of life which recognises liberty, equality and fraternity as the principles of life, all taken together, because to divorce one from the other is to defeat the very purpose of democracy. He averred:

> "Without equality, liberty would produce the supremacy of the few over the many. Equality without liberty would kill individual initiative. Without fraternity, liberty and equality could not become a natural course of things. It would require a constable to enforce them."

We must acknowledge there is complete absence of social and economic equality in Indian society, and therefore there would be "a life of contradictions" between social and political life, he said. He warned that if this contradiction is not removed early, "those who suffer from inequality will blow up the structure of political democracy which this Assembly has so laboriously built up".

There is no substitute to brotherhood

Fraternity, meaning a sense of common brotherhood of all Indians, is a difficult thing to achieve, but it must be achieved to make us a 'Nation', because without fraternity, equality and liberty will be no deeper than coats of paint, he warned saying:

> "The sooner we realise that we are not as yet a nation in the social and psychological sense of the word, the better for us. For then only we shall realise the necessity of becoming a nation and seriously think of ways and means of realising the goal. The realisation of this goal is going to be very difficult—far more difficult than it has been in the United States. The United States has no caste problem. In India there are castes. The castes are anti-national."

He lamented that a vast majority in this country are deprived of political power and are made "not only beasts of burden, but also beasts of prey", and warned:

> "These downtrodden classes are tired of being governed; they are impatient to govern themselves. This urge for self-realisation in the downtrodden classes must not be allowed to develop into a class struggle or class war. It would lead to a division of the House. That would indeed be a day of disaster."

He stressed that room must be made for the realisation of the aspiration of downtrodden and averred that, sooner it is done, "the better for the few, the better for the country, the better for the maintenance for its independence and the better for the continuance of its democratic structure."

Lastly, he averred that, we have opted for the principle of "Government of the people, for the people and by the people" in our Constitution. We must preserve that.

Non-implementation of Constitution

Indian Constitution is not even ten per cent implemented properly. That is the reason Human Development Index in 192 countries is on the 134th number. 53.7 per cent Indians are victims of 'Multi-dimensional poverty'. 75.6 per cent Indians earn less than $2.00, i.e. approximately Rs. 100 per day. 46 per cent of our children are malnourished.

Planning Commission published a report on Human Development Index for the year 2011. SC/ST/OBC Muslims etc. on Education, Health, Shelter, Employment etc. Inequalities in social and economic inequalities are mentioned. However, discriminations created by social exclusion and social inequalities various indices are not shown. For example, income inequalities are mentioned but Inequalities in Assets like land, house, gold, diamonds, jewellery, shares etc.

Let Us Enforce the Atrocity Act

Maya's Right is for Everyone to use

[http://timesofindia.indiatimes.com/NEWS-Sunday-TOI-View-From-Venus-Mayas-right-is-for-everyone/articleshow/ 4794369.cms] (Accessed Monday, January 09, 2012

Meenakshi Kumar, TNN 19 July 2009 writes how the 'Atrocity Act', though powerful, remains ineffectual. The Gist:

When UP Congress chief Ms. Rita Bahuguna Joshi made derogatory remarks about her, Mayavati used the 'Scheduled Caste and Scheduled Tribe (Prevention of Atrocities) Act 1989' to send Joshi to prison. **This has to count as one of the very few instances of a Dalit woman using the Act in the 10 years it has existed in its present form.** Public insult, or intimidation or assault or outrage of modesty or sexual exploitation of a Dalit woman–all these offenses are non-bailable; but few Dalit women are recorded as having used the Act.

Martin Macwan, Dalit rights activist and founder of Navsarjan Trust in Gujarat explains why:

> "The poor uneducated women can't be blamed. It's the implementation officers who should be taken to task. In most cases, the police will refuse to register an FIR. Unless that is done, the Act cannot be implemented."

He cites the example of two Dalit women who were gang-raped by uppercaste men in a UP village – Mayavati's home turf – two years ago. They received no medical aid; no FIR was filed. And this is the scenario across India.

Last year, however, the Act notched up a relatively rare, positive result when six professors at an institute in Patan in Gujarat were booked for gang-raping an 18-year-old Dalit student. The professors were later convicted. But that was a rarity, says Macwan. The Act was used in the case because it had become high-profile due to involvement of an NGO.

Kancha Ilaiah, Dalit rights activist and chairman of political science at Osmania University, Hyderabad, also expressed same opinion blaming illiteracy and unawareness of the rights, of Dalit women.

Dalit writer Chandra Bhan observes that, though it is a very powerful Act, an ordinary Dalit woman doesn't get the same justice and at the same speed as an upper-caste woman, unless the male member of the family decides to do something.

Let Us Remove Manual Scavenging

[http://www.hindu.com/thehindu/holnus/002200907191878.htm] (Accessed on Monday, January 09, 2012)

A news item from *The Hindu* of 19th July 2009, depicts the attitude of leaders of the country towards Dalit Problems.

BJP's SC front meet ends, lukewarm response from top brass BJP

New Delhi (PTI) The two-day BJP Schedule Caste Front national executive meet, which ended here on Sunday, saw a lukewarm response from the organisation's top brass with President Rajnath Singh keeping away and others choosing to speak on general issues instead of focusing on Dalits.

Mr. Singh, who was to deliver the concluding address, preferred to attend programmes in his constituency Ghaziabad.

Senior party leader L.K. Advani, who gave the inaugural address on Saturday, preferred to speak primarily on the BJP's dismal performance in the recent Lok Sabha polls and had nothing significant to say about Dalits.

Leader of Opposition in the Rajya Sabha, Arun Jaitley too did not speak much on Dalit issues in his address on Saturday.

SC Leader Speaks

It was left to other leaders to discuss the issues.

"The practice of human scavenging has still not been removed. Even when we were in power for six years we could not do anything," BJP leader Kailash Meghwal said in his address.

RSS Representatives were not Present

He also lamented that RSS representatives were not present in the two-day meet. Mr. Meghwal felt that apprising RSS functionaries of Dalit issues would have helped their cause.

Secretary (Organisation) Ramlal, however, made some practical suggestions in the meet. Using the Right to Information Act to ask state governments about four steps taken by them for Dalit welfare was one of them. He said the BJP does not believe in using Dalits as mere vote banks.

Let Us Stop Discrimination of Dalits in Calamities

[http://timesofindia.indiatimes.com/city/hubli/Raw-deal-for-dalits/articleshow/5107250.cms] (Accessed on Jan. 09, 2012)

Rishikesh Bahadur Desai, TNN 9 October 2009, reports a case, Raw deal for dalits, from BIJAPUR: Don Budihal in Sindagi taluk, out of around 200 houses half of them collapsed. The government officials enumerated all the houses, except six houses belonging to Dalits.

> " 'Officials did not go house to house, assessing damage. They held a meeting of villagers in the temple and asked them about the damage each had suffered. Since we are not allowed inside the temple, we could not speak to officials. Neither did they ask us about the damage after the meeting,' said Anasubai Yamanappa Walikar. Similar is the case with the other five Dalit families in Don Budihal."

Let Us Stop Caste Discrimination in Higher Centres of Learning

[http://tehelka.com/story_main39.asp?filename=Ne050708outsiders.asp] (Accessed Jan. 09, 2012)

A new case of caste discrimination in IIT Delhi highlights the miserable plight of Dalit students in India's premier technical institute, reports Shobhita Naithani in the article describes various methods how Dalit students are harassed, humiliated and atrocities showered on them even in IIT Delhi, and describes some cases.

Author also informs about anti-reservation protests and the attitude of privileged castes students towards Dalits:

> "Along with AIIMS, IIT-D was at the vanguard of anti-reservation protests in 2006, when the human resources development ministry sought to expand reservations for Other Backward Classes (OBCs) in State-funded institutions of higher learning. The anti-quota campaign reached a nadir of vulgarity when IIT-D students took to articulating their protest by pretending in public places to mend shoes and sweep roads, implying that these "low" professions (to which Dalits have traditionally been confined) would be the upper-caste IIT aspirant's only career options were the quota law to be enforced."
>
> "Propaganda through SMS and e-mail was a highlight of the campaign – these and other inspired ideas were, it was later found, the brainchild of a Gurgaon-based public relations firm, which had offered to help out."
>
> [From *Tehelka Magazine*, Vol. 5, Issue 26, Dated July 5, 2008]

Let Us Create Human Capital

It must be realised that unemployment is the main cause of poverty. It is realised that the divide between the poor and rich is being increased and the only cause for prevalence of poverty is lack of jobs and that poverty can be removed if jobs are created in the country. So jobs for one person in each rural family for 100 days a year is envisaged. These measures are like Famine measures in olden days, such 'foods for work programmes' are useless. There are better ways and it is to enrich Human Capital by improving skills by training and education, even of the unskilled labours.

The solution to the problem of poverty lies in making the people more skilled with greater investment in primary and secondary education with a slant to a vocational training raising the standard of those schools that poor children enter and improve the quality of the teachers with provision of Positive discrimination for students and teachers.

A discriminatory fee structure, discriminatory curriculum and different Boards should be done away with and uniform education for all should be ensured.

Let Us Bring in Rule of Lower Castes

Rahul Gandhi blames Mayavati and Mulayam for last 22 years of rule. Meghnad Desai calls it 'a strange case of amnesia', and reminds it was upper caste rule Congress in these words:

> "Yet the roots of UP's decline go right back to the 42 years of Congress rule where upper caste chief ministers treated the lower castes and Dalits like dirt. Indeed, the history of North India is remarkable in this regard. UP, Bihar and to some extent, West Bengal, saw Congress failure to cater to OBCs and Dalits, which is why Mandal became necessary." [*Indian Express*, 12th Feb. 2012]

For country like India, it is the lower caste welfare rule, like that of Lalu, Mulayam, Nitish and Mayavati, is more important, avers Desai. "15 years of Lalu rule", Desai considers, "had as its agenda the sole aim of restoring respect for the downtrodden", and he says Nitish Kumar brought development to Bihar. UP has had the Lalu phase thanks to Mulayam Singh, though it has been muddled by intermittent BJP rule, which was as bad as the Congress in favouring upper castes. Desai praises Mayavati in these terms:

> "Mayavati has brought development despite the statues and may yet garner the fruits for that. UP's growth rate has now caught up with the Indian average for the first time in decades."

Let Us Catch them Young

Lastly, We close this tract with a suggestion:

Indian scene is so polluted with regionalism, provincialism, linguistic arrogance, casteism, feeling of low and high and lately by all the ill effects of Liberalization, Privatization and Globalisation, that a great overhaul is required in the society. The problem is where to start and who should do it.

We have to make an humble suggestion. That you catch them young. At least we should do two things:

One. Let every student in every school or college in the country, recite the 'Preamble' of the Constitution of India, along with usual morning prayers.

Two. Let the 'Annihilation of Caste', a document as important as 'Communist Manifesto' be taught in all schools from Class VIII to Class XII.

With these two suggestions, we present this tract for the consideration of all.

• • •

Bibliography

Ambedkar B.R. Dr., Writings and Speeches, published by Government of Maharashtra, All references are marked as [W&S Vol. #, page #]

Ambedkar B.R., 'Buddha and future of his religion', a booklet from Taiwan.

Anavrat Vinod: 2011: Vinod Anavrat, Dr., 'Shivaji che udatti karan-padadya aad che vastava', Sugava Prakashan, Pune, (Marathi) ISBN 987-93-80166-34-6.

Bali: 1988: L.R. Bali, 'Hinduism: Dharma ya kalank', (Hindi), Bhim Patrika Press, Jalundhar.

Basu Nagendranath, bhakti margi baudha dharma, (hindi), Allahabad.

Bhalekar: 1994: Sandesh Bhalekar, 'Dr. Ambedkar aur Osho', Vision Publication, Nagpur.

Bharati: 1968: Dharmveer Bharati Dr., 'Siddha Sahitya', (Hindi), Kitab Mahal Allahabad, Second ed.

Biswas: 2008: Biswas Manohar Mouli: 'Dalit Mirror', March-June 2008, Bimonthly from Calcutta, editor-self.

Biswas: 1982: Biswas A., 'Why Dandakaranya a Failure, Why Mass Exodus, Where Solution?' 'The Oppressed Indian' 4 (4):18-20

Chimankar: 1993: Vimalsurya Chimankar, 'dwitiya maha yuddha aani dr. ambedkar', pub. Samata sangar, Nagpur, 1993, (Marathi).

Dahat: 1997: Dhanraj Dahat, 'Dr. Ambedkar aani Kashmir Samashya', (Marathi), Sanket Prakashan, Nagpur.

Desai: 1985: Desai I. P., 'Caste, Caste Conflict and Reservation', Surat, 1985.

Deshmukh M.M.: Deshmukh M.M., 'rashtra nirmate', (Marathi), Shiva Bharati Prakashan, Nagpur-Rashtra Jagruti Lekhmala - Vol. 3.

Dharmarakshit: 1956: Dharmarakhit Bhikku, 'Sarnath - Varanasi', (Hindi), Mahabodhi Sabha, Sarnath.

Dharma Teertha: 1946: Swami Dharma Teertha, 'The Menace of Hindu Imperialism', Second edition, Happy Home Publication, Krishnanagar, Lahore.

Dinkar: 2006: Ramdhari Singh Dinkar, 'Sanskruti ke char adhyay', Lokbharati Prakashan, Allahabad, (Hindi), First edition 1956, Reprint 2006, ISBN 81-86341-05-2.

Ganguli: 1989: Ganguli D.C., 'Struggle for Empire', HCIP, Vol. V, Bharatiya Vidya Bhavan, 4th ed. 1989.

Ganjare Vol. III: Ganjare M.F. Prof., 'Dr. Babasaheb Ambedkar yanchi Bhashane', Nagpur, (Marathi).

Gawai: 1990: Gawai P.A., 'peshave kalin gulamgiri va asprushta', (Marathi), Aurangabad.

Holger Kersten: 1997: 'Jesus lived in India', Elements Books Ltd., 1994, Reprint 1997, USA.

Jaffrelot: 2005: Christopher Jaffrelot: 'Dr Ambedkar and untouchability', published by PERMANENT BLACK, Delhi, 2005.

Jalais, Annu, 'Dwelling on Morichjhanpi: When Tigers Became 'Citizens', Refugees 'Tiger-Food', *Economic and Political Weekly,* April 23, 2005.

Jamanadas: 2002: Jamanadas K. Dr., an article 'Untouchables in Twenty first century', in anthology 'Everything you know is wrong', published by Disinformation Co. Ltd. 163, Third Avenue, Suit 108, New York, Editor Russ Kick.

Jamanadas: 2004: Jamanadas K. Dr., 'Decline and Fall of Buddhism - A Tragedy in Ancient India', Bluemoon Books, Delhi.

Jamanadas: 2007: Jamanadas K. Dr., 'Devadasis Ancient to Modern', Kalpaz Publications, 2007.

Jamanadas: 2009: Jamanadas K. Dr., 'Tirupati Balaji was a Buddhist Shrine', second English edition, (first ed. 1991), Sanjivan Publication, Chandrapur.

Jamanadas: 2012: Jamanadas K. Dr., 'Materialism in Ancient India', published by AIMBSCS - Blue World Series, Nagpur.

Joshi L.M.: 1977: 'Studies in Buddhistic Culture of India', Motilal Banarasidas.

Kancha Ilaiah: 1998: "Why I am not a Hindu", Samaya, Calcutta.

Keer: 2005: Keer Dhananjay, 'Dr. Ambedkar Life and Mission': Popular Prakashan, Reprint 2005, first published 1954.

Keer: 2005: Dhananjay Keer, 'Mahatma Jotirao Phule: Father of the Indian Social Revolution', Publisher-Popular Prakashan.

Keer: Keer Dhananjay, 'Mahatma Phule, (Marathi), Popular Prakashan.

Mahajan: 1972: Mahajan Vidya Dhar, 'Ancient India', 5th Edition, Reprint 1972, S. Chand & Co. New Delhi.

Mahajan: 2001: Mahajan Vidya Dhar, 'India Since 1526', S. Chand & Co. New Delhi, 14th Edition, Reprint 2001.

Majumdar: 1989: Majumdar R.C., 'Struggle for Empire', HCIP, Vol. V, Bharatiya Vidya Bhavan, 4th ed. 1989.

Mallick, Ross, 'Refugee Resettlement in Forest Reserves: West Bengal Policy Reversal and the Marichjhapi Massacre', The Journal of Asian Studies, Vol. 58, No. 1. (Feb., 1999), pp. 104-125.

Mani: 2005: Braj Ranjan Mani, 'Debrahmanising History, Manohar, 2005.

Mankar: 2011: Mankar Vijay, 'aadivasi-mulnivasi yo ko gair-aadivasi banakar unhe jal-jamin-jangal-sanskruti evam sanvidhan se bedakhal karne ki brahaman vadi sajish: ambedkarism hee ekmatra samadhan', second edition, published by Blue World Series, Nagpur.

Nadgonde: 1986: Nadgonde Gurunath D. Dr., 'Bhartiya Adivasi', (Marathi), Continental Prakashan, Pune, 1979, Reprint 1986.

Nair: 1959: 29, Nair Balkrishna N., 'The Dynamic Brahmin', Popular Book Depot, Lamington Road, Bombay -7.

Pardeshi: 1996: Ranjit Pardeshi, 'phule - ambedkara che brahmanikaran-sangh bhajapa che davpech', (Marathi), Krantisimha Nana Patil Academy, published on 6th December, 1996 from Yeole, Dist. Nasik.

Rattu: 1997: Nanak Chand Rattu, 'Last few years of Dr. Ambedkar', Amrit Publishing House, New Delhi.

Rhys Davids: Rhys Davids T. W., 'Buddhist India', Motilal Banarasidass Delhi, 1903, Indian Reprint 1993, Original edition England, 1903.

Santram: 'Sarita Mukta Reprints' Vol. 8, (Hindi), Delhi Press, New Delhi.

Sharad Patil: 2003: 'Jatyantak bhandwaldari lokshahi kranti va tichi samajwadi purti, Vol. 3, (Marathi), Sugawa Prakashan, Pune, ISBN 81-86182-96-9.

Sharad Patil: 2004: 'Shivaji chya hindavi swarajya che khare shatru kon-mahmadi ki brahmani?', Mavalai Prakashan, Shirur, 2nd ed. (first ed. 1992) - Marathi.

Sharad Patil: 2010: 'Primitive Communism, Matriarchy-Gynocracy and Modern Socialism, Vol. IV; Mavalai Prakashan, Shirur.

Siri Ram Arsh: 2012: 'Amritbani', publ. Shri Guru Ravidass Janam Asthan Public Charitable Trust, Seer Goverdhanpur, Varanasi (U.P.).

Swami Dharma Teertha: 1946: 'Menace of Hindu Imperialism', Lahore (supra).

Tehran: 2003: Prof. H.M.Z. Shams Tehran, 'Dalit Agony and Islam', an anthology published (2003) by Board of Islamic Publications.

Thakre: 1928: Thakre Keshav Sitaram Prabodhankar, 'Devala cha dharma aani dharma chi devale, 1928, reprint Gawali Prakashan.

VTR: 1989: V.T. Rajsheker: Gandhi and Ambedkar, Dalit Sahitya Academy, Banglore.

VTR: 1986: V.T. Rajsheker, 'Why Godse killed Gandhi' (1986) Dalit Sahitya Academy, Banglore.

V. Geetha: 1998: V. Geetha and S.V. Rajadurai, 'Towards a Non-brahmin Millennium', Samaya, ISBN 81-85604-37-1.

W&S Vol. 1, Ambedkar B.R., 'Annihilation of Caste' undelivered speech for Lahore, (1936).

W&S Vol. 1: Ambedkar B.R., 'Castes in India'.

W&S Vol. 2: (p. 471): Ambedkar B.R.: 'Evidence before Simon Commission'.

W&S Vol. 3: Ambedkar B.R., 'India and the Pre-requisites of Communism'.

W&S Vol. 3: Ambedkar B.R., 'Buddha or Karl Marx'.

W&S Vol. 4: Ambedkar B.R., 'Riddles in Hinduism'.

W&S Vol. 7: Ambedkar B.R., 'Who were the Shudras?'.

W&S Vol. 7: Ambedkar B.R., 'The Untouchables'.

W&S Vol. 8: (p. 347 ff.): Ambedkar B.R.: 'Pakistan or the Partition of India'.

W&S Vol.12: (p.741ff.): Ambedkar B.R.: 'Which is worse Slavery or Untouchabilty?'.

W&S Vol. 14 part 2, p. 886-7: Ambedkar B.R.: "Dr. Ambedkar and the Hindu Code Bill".

W&S Vol.12: (p.71ff.): Ambedkar B.R.: 'The Untouchables and the Pax Britannica'.

W&S Vol. 13: (p.1213ff.): Ambedkar B.R.: 'Constitution Presented - speech'

W&S Vol. 17: Part 3: Ambedkar B.R.: 'Mukti kon pathe?'.

W&S Vol. 17: Part 3: Ambedkar B.R.: 'Dharmantar speech'.

Yashwant Manohar 1999: 'Ambedkar wadi marathi sahitya', Bhimratna Prakashan, Nagpur.

Index

D

E

F

G

H

M

P

T

W

Y